HISTORICAL ESSAYS ON THE PRAIRIE PROVINCES

HISTORICAL ESSAYS
ON THE
PRAIRIE
PROVINCES

DONALD SWAINSON

The Carleton Library No. 53

McClelland and Stewart Limited
Toronto/Montreal

THE CARLETON LIBRARY

A series of Canadian reprints and new collections of source material relating to Canada, issued under the editorial supervision of the Institute of Canadian Studies of Carleton University, Ottawa.

The Canadian Publishers
McClelland and Stewart Limited
25 Hollinger Road, Toronto 374

Printed and bound in Canada by
T. H. Best Printing Company Limited

CONTENTS

Introduction

Exploitation and control by outside metropolitan centres is a main theme in prairie history. In 1670, the Hudson's Bay Company obtained its famous charter. Over the years it built up a trading empire dependent upon North American furs, but centred in London. For generations, much of the economic life of the present prairie provinces was controlled from London and based on a communications network radiating from Hudson Bay. The North-West Company, using knowledge accumulated by French Canadian explorers, was the Hudson's Bay Company's most potent challenger. It, too, represented a metropolitan thrust, but this time from the St. Lawrence Valley. The Nor'Westers constructed a resilient and brilliant organization, but ultimately they failed in their bid to compete with the Hudson's Bay Company and were absorbed by that great English firm.

In the middle of the nineteenth century, St. Paul-Minneapolis emerged as a contender for the trade of the British North-West. American transportation routes were, in fact, so much more economical than others that even Hudson's Bay Company goods were shipped via American railroads. Prior to the completion of the Canadian Pacific Railway, some Canadians feared that, in economic terms, Minnesota would annex the North-West.

London, St. Paul-Minneapolis, and the St. Lawrence Valley were crucial influences in the development of the prairie region. Over the years they quarrelled and fought for supremacy. Their spheres of influence altered in scope and nature. But for most of the known history of the prairies, they held the region in thrall. In the late nineteenth century the St. Lawrence Valley emerged triumphant, although its victory was never complete. The traditional power centres retained influence, and the new city of Vancouver became a not inconsiderable force.

The contemporary West has been heavily influenced by the power centres of the St. Lawrence Valley. Settlement was supervised by eastern-controlled governments. Land policy was formulated by Ottawa and extensively influenced by the Montreal-based Canadian Pacific Railway. Freight rates and transportation policies were established by eastern politicians and businessmen in Toronto and Montreal. The all-important tariff was administered by easterners, and designed to further a concept of nationhood evolved from the traditions and assumptions of Central Canadians. Culture is not outside the range of metropolitan ambition. Eastern Canadian interests have influenced the development of western Canadian policies on language and education.

Western Canadians have not been passive tools of outside interests. They have not been content simply to observe the play of metropolitan forces. Instead, they have fought back, and their discontent constitutes another major theme of western development.

Used by the North-West Company to harass Hudson's Bay Company servants and Selkirk settlers, the Métis developed a self-conscious and distinctly western sense of identity. They called themselves the "New Nation" and, from Seven Oaks to Batoche, were a force on the prairies. They provided the muscle behind the opposition to the Hudson's Bay Company's fur monopoly and, through the Sayer Case of 1849, were able to free the trade. Under Louis Riel they spearheaded the resistance to Canadian annexation of Rupert's Land in 1869-70. The North-West Rebellion of 1885 represented much general discontent (Métis, Indian, and white) with Sir John A. Macdonald's second government.

In the nineteenth century the Métis were not isolated agitators. During the 1869-70 Resistance, they had the approval of many white settlers who resented the attitudes and activities of the Canadian government. The arrival of the C.P.R. provoked an almost immediate assault on both its monopoly and its freight-rate structure. The federal government's clear right to disallow provincial legislation was challenged by Manitoba during the 1880s, and, during the 1890s, the province's majority revoked the federal guarantees given to the French Canadian minority in the Manitoba Act. In the North-West Territories, a campaign was waged for greater autonomy through responsible government. All the while farmers were organizing to fight for lower freight rates, higher prices, and better grain handling facilities. At the same time, nineteenth-century westerners displayed little real desire to opt for control by an alternate metropolitan centre. As R. C. Brown comments in the article reprinted below, "the Canadian West much preferred dependence on Ottawa to dependence on Washington."

During the twentieth century, the prairies became a veritable laboratory of protest. The Non-Partisan League moved onto the prairies from the United States, and, after the First World War, the Progressive Party challenged both the National Policy and the two-party system. The One Big Union movement indicated that labour resented eastern control of unions; the Winnipeg General Strike helped to mould Winnipeg's tradition of labour activism. The forces of agrarian unrest captured the governments of Manitoba and Alberta. Part of their appeal was a deep suspicion of "old-line" parties which were regarded as agents of eastern interests.

The Depression constituted a major crisis for the prairies, and again protest movements were launched. Social Credit put much of the blame on federal policies, eastern business, and international finance. The Co-operative Commonwealth Federation, by no means a narrow agrarian movement, capitalized on traditional and regional forms of discontent. Social Credit captured Alberta in 1935 and is still comfortably ensconced in power. The C.C.F. took Saskatchewan in 1944 and held it for two decades. The present New Democratic Party government in Manitoba is certainly in part a product of a reaction against federal policies and leadership. Premier Ed Schreyer represented this tradition when in February, 1970, he commented:

In fact, the problems of the West are economic, not racial or linguistic. The culprit, if there is one, is not French Canada, but the constant catering to the vested industrial interests of Central Canada, concentrated in the St. Lawrence Valley, and centred around the industrial "Golden Horseshoe" in Southern Ontario.[1]

Scholars as well as political leaders protest. Hence W. L. Morton's acid comment: "For Confederation was brought about to increase the wealth of Central Canada, and until that original purpose is altered, and the concentration of wealth and population by national policy in Central Canada ceases, Confederation must remain an instrument of injustice."[2] It is in fact not possible to understand the prairies without coming to terms

---

[1] Quoted in the Ottawa *Citizen*, February 18, 1970.
[2] W. L. Morton, "Clio in Canada: The Interpretation of Canadian History," in Carl Berger, ed., Approaches to Canadian History, (*Canadian Historical Readings*, I, Toronto, 1967), p. 47.

with this tension between the outside metropolis and the internal opposition which struggles for a more autonomous West, or a reformed national order in which westerners feel that they can fully participate. This aspect of prairie history is brilliantly illuminated in W. L. Morton's "The Bias of Prairie Politics," reprinted in this volume.

Metropolitan domination and regional protest are central themes, but all western history cannot be seen in terms of the fur trade, schools crises, freight rates problems, and third parties. Some aspects of prairie history are more domestic and, while often crucial to westerners, have not captured the interest of other Canadians. Cities have developed and grown. Traditional parties have been transformed by western conditions, and all prairie governments have had to learn how to accommodate unique situations. Various ethnic groups have adapted to the prairies. The 1969 general election in Manitoba indicates that social change is occurring at a tremendous pace. In the oldest prairie province the political balance has swung dramatically away from agro-Manitoba, and Canada has its first provincial government with an overwhelming majority of ethnics. Such developments merit attention and prompt curiosity about these often neglected areas of prairie history. The western provinces, in fact, constitute an area of tremendous research potential.

Prairie historiography mirrors these developments. Scholars from other provinces and countries tend to concentrate on the themes of metropolitanism and protest. The result has been a great deal of concentrated attention and some brilliant work. Exploration and the fur trade have received extensive treatment. Some of the finest work on the latter topic is by Britishers like E. E. Rich and Central Canadians like Harold Innis. Transportation and the tariff have hardly been neglected, while settlement problems prompted the excellent *Canadian Frontiers of Settlement* series.

Various forms of protest have received massive treatment. Louis Riel and the movements he led have been studied by westerners, easterners, and Americans. The Progressive Party has received extensive treatment, while Social Credit has been honoured with a series of its own. The best book on the Saskatchewan C.C.F. is by an American sociologist. Western Canadian third parties are the most intensively studied of all Canadian political movements.

More local problems have simply not received the same quantity or quality of attention. W. L. Morton's *Manitoba: A*

History is the only first-class survey of a prairie province, and many aspects of prairie history remain obscure. No premier of Manitoba, for example, has received a major biography. Urban history is still in an undeveloped state. Indian history has been ignored and social conditions neglected. The Liberal and Conservative parties have received insufficient attention. Regional industries like fishing and ranching are often forgotten. What attention these themes receive is often from amateur historians who live in the West. Their work is indispensable to the student of prairie history.

Manitoba, by far the oldest prairie community, has the longest and most mature historiographical tradition. The second selection in this volume, Alexander Ross's "Hudson's Bay Company *versus* Sayer," was originally published in 1856 as part of his *Red River Settlement*. This pioneering book is well written, sensitive, and necessary to an understanding of the social development of old Red River. Ross was joined by other men who lived in Red River and combined the writing of history with other vocations – of whom J. J. Hargrave and Alexander Begg are notable examples. Alexander Begg's work was broadly conceived, for he concerned himself not only with Manitoba but also with the North-West Territories. The Historical and Scientific Society of Manitoba was founded in 1878 and incorporated in 1879. It sponsored and encouraged a great deal of local research. Thus, by the end of the nineteenth century, Manitoba possessed a mature and distinguished tradition of historical study. Upon this solid base was built a not-inconsiderable twentieth-century edifice by men like Chester Martin, R. O. MacFarlane, Kenneth McNaught, Ramsay Cook, and W. L. Morton. The latter particularly has produced an enormous amount of fine work on his native province.

The Historical and Scientific Society of Manitoba has for some years sponsored a series of ethnic studies, the best titles of which are listed in the Select Bibliography. The importance of these volumes cannot be underestimated for they have injected ethnic Canadians into the historiographical mainstream. This development is leading to a more realistic understanding of both Manitoban and prairie history in general. Ethnic Canadians have had a major share in creating western societies which are unique, not merely transplants from eastern Canada, the United States, or Great Britain.

Manitoba's history as an agricultural settlement dates from the second decade of the nineteenth century. Saskatchewan and Alberta lagged two generations behind. They are not only younger provinces but also far younger societies. Their historiographical traditions are less well developed, and they have had much more assistance from the outside. Saskatchewan's most famous historian was doubtless A. S. Morton, whose major interest was the Hudson's Bay Company period. The best-known literature on Saskatchewan is concerned with the C.C.F. and the wheat economy. While the wheat economy is not exclusive to Saskatchewan, it is centred in that province and was of overriding interest to such scholars as G. E. Britnell and V. C. Fowke. Alberta studies have been dominated by the United Farmers of Alberta and Social Credit. *The Social Credit Series* includes a large amount of material on Alberta, most of it by scholars from other provinces. Henry Wise Wood has received a scholarly biography and various students have studied the Alberta Progressives. Alberta's indigenous historiographical tradition, however, is easily the most poorly developed on the prairies.

Each province has its Historical Society, and each society publishes a journal – *Manitoba Scientific and Historical Society Transactions*, *Saskatchewan History*, and *The Alberta Historical Review*. Their articles vary from the unfortunate to the brilliant. For the most part these publications are concerned with material of local interest. They make available an enormous amount of scholarship germane to social history. The prairie provinces also have a surprising number of printing and publishing firms willing to publish local history. It is now almost impossible to enter a good western bookshop without seeing a dozen or more local histories written by amateur historians, and published locally. And of course, prairie universities offer graduate programs in western history, which produce numerous research papers and theses. Many of these find their way into the provincial journals. A couple are reprinted below.

A notable point concerning prairie scholarship is its interdisciplinary character. The great themes of metropolitanism and protest have attracted the attention of political scientists, political theorists, economists, philosophers, and sociologists. The more domestic areas of concern attract scholars from a variety of vocations. Several first-class professional historians have focused their attention on the prairie region. The result is a body of regional historical literature unmatched elsewhere in Canada for either quality or interest.

This selection of essays is concerned with the prairies during the era of settled and permanent communities. In order to permit a fuller treatment of nineteenth- and twentieth-century problems, exploration and the fur trade have not been considered. Many of the essays selected are more concerned with local problems than with the great themes of metropolitanism and protest, because much of the key literature on the latter problems is easily accessible and well known while many essentially local items are known only to the keenest students. An attempt has been made to illustrate the quality of western historical writing, and some of the selections will be easily recognized as major contributions to our understanding of the prairie provinces. Most of the essays are tightly organized and well written. They span the period from the Selkirk Settlement to the Second World War. Each province is represented, although Manitoba receives a preponderant amount of attention because it has a much longer history than Saskatchewan or Alberta. It was not possible to include maps, but atlases illustrating prairie geography are plentiful. As a centennial project the Manitoba Historical Society is publishing in 1970 a massive *Historical Atlas of Manitoba* (edited by John Warkentin and Richard I. Ruggles). It will include the location of the Canadian place-names mentioned in William Friesen's "A Mennonite Community in the East Reserve: Its Origin and Growth" and John Friesen's "Expansion of Settlement in Manitoba, 1870-1900."

The first three selections are not, strictly speaking, essays. They are excerpts from books. It was felt that examples of the work of nineteenth-century historians should be included, and this seemed the most expeditious method of doing so. There has been the occasional silent modification of spelling and punctuation, for obvious reasons of clarity and consistency, more in the older selections from books than in the newer articles from the journals. Otherwise the works are printed as they originally appeared.

Finally, I would like to dedicate this book to my parents, present-day pioneers.

DONALD SWAINSON
February, 1970
Ottawa, Canada

Early History of the Selkirk Settlement

Alexander Begg

The youths employed by the North-West Company, chiefly
Scotch, were articled as apprentice clerks, for seven years, receiving their subsistence and one hundred pounds. The prospective reward of their toil and fidelity was to become partners,
and this [as was previously shown] induced them to work with
a will, while the life of adventure which they led and the
excitement and novel scenes incident to the fur trade resulted
in attaching them firmly to it. Indian maidens cast in their lot
with those clerks and with the wintering partners of the company, and it was the offspring of these and others, principally
Canadians (French fathers and Indian mothers), that there
came to be such a numerous progeny of half-breeds. When the
Hudson's Bay Company entered the country, their officers and
servants followed the course pursued by their predecessors of
the North-West Company in having wives from among the
natives, and the population of mixed blood increased in proportion. The half-breeds, of French parentage, far outnumbered
those of the English and Scotch – the *coureurs de bois* and
voyageurs, who were chiefly of Canadian origin, being largely
in excess of other nationalities – and from their mixed, inherited, and transmitted qualities, their abandon, vivacity, reck-
lessness, and ready affiliation with Indian ways, these French
half-breeds were held to be superior for the service required by
the fur trade. At one time, the North-West Company, and later
on the Hudson's Bay Company, had over two thousand of this
unique class of employees, going and coming, toiling after a
rollicking fashion, paddling and rowing the canoe or the boat,
threading the reedy marshes, running the cascades, crossing
the portage with their burdens, trailing along the cataracts,
bearing all the stern severities of winter in the woods, driving
dog-sleds, camping in snowdrifts, ready on their return for wild
carousals and dances, parting with the year's gains for finery

SOURCE: Alexander Begg, *History of the North-West*, vol. I (Toronto,
1894), pp. 161-184.

or frolic, wild and improvident in their nature, but faithful to their employers.

In the rivalry and strife between the two great fur companies these half-breeds played a prominent part, and were often the tools of their superiors in the many lawless deeds committed about that time. It was not, however, until Lord Selkirk appeared upon the scene that any serious outrages were perpetrated by the companies upon each other, and it is about that period in the history of the North-West that we are now about to speak.

When the Earl of Selkirk came to the conclusion that the Hudson's Bay Company were masters of the situation in the fur trade, he set to work to purchase a controlling interest in its stock and ultimately succeeded in obtaining about £40,000 in shares, the capital of the company at that time being less than £100,000. This, combined with the fact that near relatives and friends of his were placed on the Board of Directors, practically gave him unlimited control, and he hastened to take advantage of it in favour of a scheme of colonization which he had in view.

At a general court of the company, convened in May, 1811, the proprietors were informed that the governor and committee recommended a grant, in fee simple, of 116,000 square miles of territory to the Earl of Selkirk, on condition that he should establish a colony thereon, and furnish, on certain terms, such laborers as were required by the company in their trade. This was opposed by a number of the proprietors, but, notwithstanding their protest, Lord Selkirk succeeded in obtaining the grant which is described as follows:

Beginning at the western shores of Lake Winnipeg, at a point on 52° 30′ north latitude, and thence running due west to Lake Winnipegoosis, otherwise called Lake Winnipeg; thence in a southerly direction through said lake, so as to strike its western shore in latitude 52°; thence due west to the place where the parallel 52° intersects the western branch of the Red River, otherwise called the Assiniboine River; thence due south from that point of intersection to the heights of land which separate the waters running into the Hudson's Bay from those of the Missouri and the Mississippi Rivers; thence in an easterly direction along the height of land to the sources of the River Winnipeg, meaning by such last named river the principal branch of the waters which unite in the Lake Saginagas; thence along the main stream of those waters, and the middle of the several lakes through which they flow, to the mouth of the Winnipeg River, and thence in a northerly direction through the middle of Lake Winnipeg to the place of beginning, which territory is called Assiniboia.

The grant of land having been obtained, Lord Selkirk issued a prospectus, which, being well calculated to quicken the spirit of emigration prevailing at that time, was circulated in Ireland and in the highlands of Scotland. The scheme was to induce a number of the people in those parts to join the colony which it was proposed to establish in the North-West, and the man appointed to carry it out was Captain Miles Macdonell. Stornoway was the place selected for the assembling of the colonists, and there, in May, 1811, a number of Irish and Scotch congregated to await the coming of the ships in which they were to embark for Hudson's Bay. The vessels did not arrive until June, and by that time a number of the emigrants had become dissatisfied with the prospect before them, and were prepared to desert. When, therefore, the day came for them to embark, a number refused to go, and others, after going on board, demanded to be put on shore.

In a letter addressed by Captain Miles Macdonell to Lord Selkirk, on July 4, 1811, he complains of the high wages promised to some of the colonists by the captain of the ship, and on the twenty-fifth, writing again to his Lordship, he gives some account of the dissatisfaction existing among them, and the causes that gave rise to it. He blames an article in the Inverness *Journal*, which was circulated in the Orkneys and Highlands, and which he describes in the following words:

If that piece originated in London, I should expect to find in it more candor, knowledge of the country, and regard to truth than it contains; but some part is not unlike the language that was held out there to discourage and dissuade people from embarking in the enterprise.

An attempt had evidently been made by interested parties on shore to sow discontent in the minds of the emigrants, the result being that a number refused to go, and a certain Captain McKenzie, whom Macdonell describes as a mean fellow, visited the ships, and endeavoured to induce others to return to shore. But he was not allowed on board, and, as his boat lay alongside one of the vessels, a sailor, it is said, dropped a nine-pound round shot through the bottom, causing the gallant captain to return to land to avoid sinking. The irritated McKenzie sent a challenge to Captain Roderick, the commander of the ship, who paid no attention to it, and a fair wind springing up in the night, he set sail. Miles Macdonell, in his letter to Lord Selkirk, blames the customs authorities for the trouble that took place, but there is very little doubt that those opposed to the colonization scheme were at the bottom of it. Macdonell writes:

This, my Lord, is a most unfortunate business. I cannot now state what number we may be able to take along, the delay for these last two days by the customs house has occasioned all this, and the manifest part taken by the collector, his friends and adherents, against this business.

In another letter, he says:

Mrs. Reid, wife of the collector at Stornoway, is aunt to Sir Alexander McKenzie, and he called Captain McKenzie, is married to a daughter of the collector; these, with all their adherents, are in a united opposition to Mr. Robertson, and perhaps influenced, in some degree, from London to act as they did.

It would seem, then, from this that the North-West Company had even thus early in the day endeavoured to put obstacles in the way of Lord Selkirk's enterprise.

The expedition, however, sailed from Stornoway on July 26, 1811, and arrived at York Factory on September 24 after a passage of sixty-one days, at that time the longest and latest ever known to Hudson Bay. In a letter to Lord Selkirk, dated October 1, Miles Macdonell writes:

I forward a general return of the number of men, effective and non-effective, according to the lists which have reached me; by this your Lordship will see our strength at one view, and deficiency from non-appearance and desertion; our total numbers on board all the ships amount only to 90 laborers and 15 writers, including Mr. Bourke; making a grand total of 105, exclusive of us who embarked at Gravesend.

This band was composed of people from Ireland, Orkney and Glasgow, the latter, it appears, being the most turbulent and dissatisfied.

In November, Miles Macdonell, with a number of the emigrants, moved to a point on the Nelson River, about fifty miles from its mouth, and wintered there, and from all accounts they suffered from many hardships, through insufficiency of provisions, disease, and other causes. Insubordination and discontent among the colonists appeared, and the leaders of the expedition had much difficulty in quieting them. It is evident also from letters written at the time that Macdonell looked forward to troublesome times ahead, and he does not conceal his opinion that the North-West Company would do all in their power to destroy the proposed settlement on the Red River. He thus writes on December 25 to Mr. William Auld, the Hudson's Bay Superintendent at York Factory:

Were we to form a judgment of all Indians by the present in-offensive and docile state of the natives in the vicinity of the shores of Hudson's Bay, a full security might be reposed in their friendship; but the Ossineboine nation, into whose country we are going, are represented as among the most warlike Indians of North America. We have already been threatened in London with those people by a person that knows them well [Sir Alexander McKenzie], and who has pledged himself in the most unequivocal and decisive manner to oppose the establishment of this colony by all means in his power. The London merchants connected with the North-West Company are inimical to it, and I have reason to expect that every means the North-West Company can attempt to thwart it will be resorted to – to what extent their influence may direct the conduct of the nations is to me uncertain, and justifies being on our guard at all points.

The Glasgow colonists seem to have given Macdonell the most trouble during the winter and following spring, and he was obliged to resort to harsh measures with them, but on June 19, 1812, he writes to Lord Selkirk as follows:

I am happy to inform your Lordship that the insurgents have at length come to terms, acknowledged their guilt, and have thrown themselves entirely at the mercy of the committee, so that none of them shall now be sent home for the affair of the 12th February. They crossed from here to the Factory on 24th May, and thought the ice too unsafe to return. Mr. Auld turned them out of the factory, and refused them provisions until they surrendered their arms. By this decisive conduct towards them, having no leader, the Glasgow writers, Carswell, Fisher and Brown, being on this side of the river, as likewise

Mr. Finlay, who had remained behind, find[ing] themselves destitute and unsupported, they immediately came to a proper sense of their situation and submitted. This is so far well; they are, however, lost to us, as I cannot think of taking any of them to Red River settlement.

Thus ended the insubordination for the time being, and before leaving their quarters on the Nelson River, Macdonell sent to Lord Selkirk samples of stone and sand which he found there and which he thus describes:

Mr. Bourke, who may justly claim the merit of the discovery, supposes them to be of the most valuable kinds. Diamonds, rubies, etc., etc., and gold dust. Should they be found valuable on their analysis, immediate advantage ought to be taken of it. Your Lordship might obtain a grant of the Nelson with a mile on each side of it, from the Hudson's Bay Company. I have enjoined the closest secrecy on Mr. Bourke, and no person here has the least idea of the matter. We may make further important discoveries in going up.

Nothing, however, came of this, as the diamonds and rubies did not prove to be genuine.

For several months the colonists remained at York Factory, having returned there from their winter-quarters, and early in July, the party, now much diminished in numbers from one cause or another, made a start for the Red River country, arriving there early in August. The men who composed this band of pioneers were picked from the party of emigrants who left Stornoway, in July, 1811, on account of their good behaviour and faithful discharge of their duties. They were chiefly men from the island of Lewis, who, although not in any way exempted from the trials and privations undergone by their companions, yet, throughout all these trying times, exhibited an unconquerable spirit of patient endurance and were ever ready to obey their superiors. Mr. Auld, the superintendent, did not overlook this exemplary conduct, for on the first opportunity that offered, he represented these men's good behaviour to the committee, and that honorable body presented, through their agents in Stornoway, each of their parents with the sum of five pounds sterling, as a substantial token of their approbation of the young men's merits.

On the arrival of the first batch of Lord Selkirk's colonists at Red River, in August, 1812, they were met by a party of employees of the North-West Company, disguised in the dress of Indians, who warned them that they were unwelcome visitors. The appearance and manner of the Nor'Westers seemed to be so hostile and menacing that the settlers became frightened and ready to adopt any proposition made to them for their safety. It was then resolved to move on to Pembina, to which place the disguised Indians offered to conduct them. Accordingly, the Scotch colonists, already nearly worn out with fatigue, were obliged to undertake another journey, almost immediately on their arrival at the Red River, and after much suffering through having to walk the entire distance, they arrived at Pembina, where they passed the winter in tents and huts, and lived on the products of the chase. In May, 1813, they returned to their colony on the Red River, and being undisturbed, commenced the labors of agriculture. For some time the North-West Company did not molest them, and they succeeded in erecting buildings and establishing a post, which was named Fort Douglas, but, the difficulty in procuring sufficient food, dread of the winter, and a desire to husband their seed for another year, caused them to return voluntarily to Pembina, in the Autumn of 1813.

Early in 1813, Lord Selkirk visited Ireland for the purpose of recruiting colonists for his settlement on the Red River, and in June, a party of Irish emigrants for the Hudson's Bay Company's service, with several newly married couples and young men from the western islands of Scotland, left Sligo. No desertions took place this season, but a mutiny occurred during the voyage, which came near being successful. The mutineers intended seizing the captain and crew and taking the ship and cargo to some port for the purpose of disposing of them, but their conspiracy being discovered, its accomplishment was prevented, the conspirators overpowered, and the ship reached York Factory in safety, during the month of August. A Mr. Owen Keveny[1] had been placed in charge of this party by Lord Selkirk, and he, it is said, was somewhat of a martinet in dealing with the colonists, but, judging from the conduct of a few of them during the voyage, it would appear as if the strictest discipline was necessary.

We must now refer to Mr. or, rather, Father Bourke, whom we have already mentioned as the individual who found the

---

[1] Mr. Keveney returned to the North-West from Ireland, in the fall of 1815, and the following year, was killed by an Indian, his brutal conduct to the men under his charge, being the cause which led to the murder.

supposed diamonds and rubies at the Nelson encampment, in 1812. It seems that he did not accompany the first party to Red River, but returned to Ireland, when Miles Macdonell wrote of him as follows:

To Mr. Bourke, I have granted leave to go home at his own desire and enclose his letter. He was only an encumbrance to me, irregular and eccentric in his conduct as a clergyman. He has no sway over his flock, and religion is turned to ridicule among strangers. If he can do any good to the colony in Ireland, it is well; as a priest, he can be of no service here, particularly in the infancy of the settlement; and I hope Your Lordship will not be in haste to send him out to us.

But it would seem as if Father Bourke accompanied the second party of emigrants in 1813, and it is said married a couple on that occasion at York Factory. He however returned in the ship that brought him out, and never went further inland than the encampment on Nelson River, yet he had the credit of being the first minister of religion from the British Isles who ever set foot on the shores of Hudson Bay.

In October, 1813, Mr. Keveney arrived at Red River with his party and consigned his charge to Miles Macdonell. It is a singular coincidence that the second batch of emigrants had to make their way to Pembina like the first, almost immediately after their arrival at Fort Douglas. Provisions had been scarce previous to their coming, but their presence made matters worse, and so the whole colony proceeded south to their winter-quarters. The winter proved a hard one, and although, in justice to the officers of the North-West Company, it must be said that they assisted the settlers with food, and in other ways, the sufferings of the new comers were very great. So much so that they resolved never to return to Pembina again.

In the meantime, Lord Selkirk was busy at home securing fresh emigrants for his colony, and about that time the Duchess of Sutherland commenced the cruel policy of driving many of her tenants from their once happy homes to make room for extensive sheep-tracts. A number of these unhappy people were induced to join the Selkirk colony, and in the Summer of 1813, sailed from Stromness for Hudson Bay. During the voyage, fever broke out among the passengers, and when they arrived at their destination, the party of Scotch emigrants were in a dreadful condition, and utterly unfit to undergo the overland journey to Red River, many of them dying before and after landing, and the remainder, being so worn out with sickness, were obliged to remain at the bay the whole of the following winter. From all accounts it would appear that these poor people were not properly cared for by the agents of Lord Selkirk, and that the food and shelter provided were totally inadequate for their comfort or protection from the severities of the weather. After spending a most miserable winter at Churchill and York Factory, the survivors of this third batch of emigrants started in the summer of 1814, for Red River, arriving there early in autumn. A few days after their arrival, each head of a family was put in possession of 100 acres of land, but there were neither implements to till the soil, nor a sufficiency of food to be had.

Added to this, the settlement was on the eve of a series of disturbances which shortly afterwards resulted in the destruction of the colony by the servants of the North-West Company.

It seems that a few months before the arrival of this last batch of emigrants, Mr. Miles Macdonell, who had been appointed Governor by Lord Selkirk, issued the following proclamation:

Whereas the Right Honorable Thomas Earl of Selkirk, is anxious to provide for the families at present forming settlements on his lands at Red River with those on the way to it, passing the winter at York and Churchill Forts, in Hudson's Bay, as also those who are expected to arrive next autumn, renders it a necessary and indispensable part of my duty to provide for their support. In the yet uncultivated state of the country, the ordinary resources derived from the buffalo and other wild animals hunted within the territory, are not deemed more than adequate for the requisite supply.

Whereas it is hereby ordered, that no person trading furs or provisions within the territory for the Honorable Hudson's Bay Company or the North-West Company, or any individual, or unconnected traders, or persons whatever, shall take any provisions, either of flesh, fish, grain, or vegetable, procured or raised within the said territory, by water or land carriage, for one twelvemonth from the date hereof; save and except what may be judged necessary for the trading parties at this present time within the territory, to carry them to their respective destinations; and who may, on due application to me, obtain a license for the same.

The provisions procured and raised as above shall be taken for the use of the colony; and that no loss may accrue to the parties concerned, they will be paid for by British bills at the customary rates. And be it hereby further made known, that whosoever shall be detected in attempting to convey out, or shall aid and assist in carrying out, or attempting to carry out, any provisions prohibited as above, either by water or land, shall be taken into custody, and prosecuted as the laws in such cases direct, and the provisions so taken, as well as any goods and chattels, of what nature soever, which may be taken along with them, and also the craft, carriages and cattle, instrumental in conveying away the same to any part but to the settlement on Red River, shall be forfeited.

Given under my hand at Fort Daer [Pembina] the 8th day of January, 1814

(Signed) MILES MACDONELL, *Governor.*

By order of the Governor.

(Signed) JOHN SPENCER, *Secretary.*

When we take into consideration the fact that Red River was likely at any time to become the only base of supplies for the people of the North-West Company in the prosecution of their fur trade, it is not surprising to hear that the foregoing proclamation excited the bitterest feelings on their part against the Scotch settlers, added to which, Mr. Macdonell had placed arms in the hands of the colonists, and was drilling them regularly as soldiers. For a time after this one disturbance followed another as the governor endeavoured to enforce the provisions of his proclamation, and although bloodshed was happily averted, the condition of the colony grew worse day by day.

Several seizures of provisions from the North-West Company were made by orders of Macdonell, and at last, when their traders from the interior, on their way to Fort William, arrived at Red River, there were no provisions to carry them on their journey to their destination. It would not have been surprising if they had endeavoured to take by force the supplies which were stored in the Hudson's Bay Company's fort, and which properly belonged to them, as Macdonell had seized them without, as they considered, any authority, but instead of this, they made an arrangement with him by which they secured sufficient to take the brigades to Fort William. Here the council of the North-West Company discussed the whole situation, and it was learned that not only had Macdonell seized their provisions, but he had sent out directions to the different Hudson's Bay Company's posts to eject the Nor'Westers and destroy their buildings.

Here is a copy of one of the notices said to have been sent out by Macdonell:

You must give them [the North-West Company] solemn warning that the land belongs to the Hudson's Bay Company, and that they must remove from it; after this warning they should not be allowed to cut any timber either for building or fuel. What they have cut ought to be openly and forcibly seized, and their buildings destroyed. In like manner they should be warned not to fish in your waters, and if they put down nets, seize them, as you would in England those of a poacher. We are so fully advised by the unimpeachable validity of the rights of property that there can be no scruple in enforcing them, wherever you have the physical means. If they make forcible resistance, they are acting illegally, and are responsible for the consequences of what they do, while you are safe, so long as you take only the reasonable and necessary means of enforcing that which is right.

No stronger declaration of war could have been framed than the above, and the council of the North-West Company decided to resist, to the utmost of their power, any violence or encroachments on the part of their opponents. It was further agreed to cause the arrest under the Act 43, George III., of Miles Macdonell, and his secretary, Spencer, for what they had already done, and Mr. Duncan Cameron was entrusted with the warrant for their apprehension.

Some idea of the feelings and intentions of the North-West Company about this time may be judged from a letter written by Mr. Alexander McDonell, who was associated with Mr. Cameron at the time, and who afterwards sent down the party of half-breeds, whose action at Fort Douglas caused the death of Governor Semple. The letter is dated August 5, 1814, and is addressed to his brother-in-law, Mr. William McGillivray.

You see myself and our mutual friend Mr. Cameron, so far on our way to commence open hostilities against the enemy. Much is expected from us. One thing certain is that we will do our best to defend what we consider our rights in the interior. Nothing but the complete downfall of the colony will satisfy some, by fair or foul means – a most desirable object if it can be effected. So here is at them, with all my heart and energy.

In the meantime the settlers became much dissatisfied with their lot, but bravely bore up against their difficulties, and in the spring of 1815 had resumed their agricultural labors and were cherishing the hope of future peace and a prosperous summer. But in the midst of this calm, which certainly preceded a storm, Mr. Cameron arrived from Fort William and endeavoured to put his warrant for the arrest of Macdonell into force. A fight ensued, in which several were injured and a Mr. Warren killed, when Governor Macdonell, to avoid further bloodshed, surrendered himself as a prisoner.

After his arrest, Mr. James Sutherland was left in charge, and when that gentleman saw that the colony was utterly at the mercy of the Nor'Westers, he and Surgeon James White, who was afterwards killed in the Semple tragedy, signed the following agreement on June 25, 1815:

Articles of Agreement entered into between the Half-Breed Indians of the Indian Territory, on one part, and the Honorable Hudson's Bay Company on the other, viz.:

1. *All settlers to retire immediately from this river, and no appearance of a colony to remain.*

2. *Peace and amity to subsist between all parties, traders, Indians, and freemen in future throughout these two rivers, and on no account is any person to be molested in his lawful pursuits.*

3. *The Honorable Hudson's Bay Company will, as customary, enter this river with, if they think proper, three to four of the former trading boats, and from four to five men per boat, as usual.*

4. *Whatever former disturbance has taken place between both parties, that is to say, the Honorable Hudson's Bay Company and the Half-Breeds of the Indian Territory, to be totally forgot, and not to be recalled by either party.*

5. *Every person retiring peaceably from the river immediately, shall not be molested in their passage out.*

6. *The people passing the summer for the Honorable Hudson's Bay Company, shall not remain in the buildings of the colony, but shall retire to some other spot where they will establish for the purpose of trade.*

Chiefs of the Half-Breeds . . . . . {
CUTHBERT GRANT,
BASTONNOIS PANGMAN,
WM. SHAW,
BONHOMME MONTOUR.

and

For Hudson's Bay Company . . . {
JAMES SUTHERLAND,
Chief Factor,
JAMES WHITE,
Surgeon.

The result of Cameron's attack on Fort Douglas was the destruction of the settlers' houses, and the breaking up of the colony. Some of the colonists entered the service of the Hudson's Bay Company; others repaired to Jack River, on Lake Winnipeg, one or two returned to York Factory, a few remained, and about fifty families were, at their own solicitation, conveyed to Canada by the North-West Company, and landed at York, now the city of Toronto, and it seemed for the time being as if Lord Selkirk's colony was at an end. Governor Macdonell and his secretary, Spencer, were never brought to trial, as there appeared to be no hope of obtaining a conviction against them under the peculiar circumstances of the case, and the prosecution was dropped.

The Hudson's Bay Company now interposed, and, under their protection, the Scotch settlers were brought back from Jack River to Fort Douglas, but their trials and vicissitudes were not at an end. On November 5, 1815, a fresh batch of emigrants arrived, having left Stromness on the previous June 15, and, like their predecessors, the colonists found that no preparation had been made for their reception. Instead of a thriving settlement, they found houses in ruins, and a scene of desolation, where they expected to see a prosperous community, but worse than all, there was no food to feed them, and in consequence, they had to continue their journey in company with those who had returned from Jack River, in the cold and snow, to Pembina. Here they set to work to erect rude huts to shelter themselves, but in a month or so they had to leave these temporary houses, and journey to the plains in the hope of procuring food, there being a scarcity of provisions at Pembina and no means of procuring any near that place. These unfortunate people had to journey a distance of about one hundred and fifty miles, and as they were ill-provided with suitable clothes to protect their persons from the cold, they suffered dreadfully. Meeting with a party of hunters, they remained with them during the winter, performing such work as they were capable of doing, in return for which they were fed and sheltered until the spring, when they returned to Pembina, and from thence descended the Red River by water in April to Fort Douglas. They then began to cultivate the soil, and everything appeared propitious to their becoming comfortably settled in their new home, when, on June 19, 1816, an event happened which once more brought desolation to the colony.

The high-handed proceedings of Miles Macdonell, and the subsequent aggressive policy of the Earl of Selkirk, created very bitter feelings between the officers of the Hudson's Bay and North-West companies, and several collisions took place, resulting in loss of life and property on both sides. Lord Selkirk's policy was to extend the trade of the Hudson's Bay Company into distant parts hitherto monopolized by the rival Canadian association, and for this purpose he, in 1814, despatched a Mr. James Sutherland to Montreal to engage agents there for the prosecution of this new departure in trading. Mr. Colin Robertson was induced to enter the service, and to him Lord Selkirk entrusted the chief management of the undertaking. French Canadians, who had been employees of the North-West Company, were engaged instead of Orkney men, and in May, 1815, a brigade of twenty-two canoes, manned by these veteran *voyageurs*, left Lachine, bound for the north. At Jack River they took on the supplies which had been brought from York Factory and stored there, and then forming into different bands, they proceeded, some to Athabasca district, others to the Lesser and Greater Slave Lakes, and a third party, under command of Mr. Clarke, who was one of Mr. Astor's partners in the Pacific Fur Company, went up the Peace River. This first attempt to penetrate the northern districts was, however, only partly successful, owing to the lateness of the season when the brigades reached their destination, and the lack of provisions, which, owing to the opposition of the North-West Company, the newcomers had difficulty in obtaining from the Indians.

In the meantime, Mr. Robert Semple was appointed Governor-in-Chief of the northern department, and was entrusted with powers far exceeding those conferred on any of his predecessors in office, as will be seen from the following extracts, taken from resolutions passed by the stockholders of the Hudson's Bay Company on May 19, 1815.

These are the extracts:

First — That there shall be appointed a Governor-in-chief and Council, who shall have paramount authority over the whole of the territories in Hudson's Bay.

Secondly — That the Governor, with any two of his Council, shall be competent to form a Council for the administration of justice, and the exercise of the power vested in them by charter.

Thirdly — That the Governor of Assiniboia, and the Governor of Moose, within their respective districts, and with any two of their respective Councils, shall have the same power; but their power shall be suspended, while the Governor-in-chief is actually present for judicial purposes.

Fourthly — That a sheriff be appointed for each of the districts of Assiniboia and Moose, and one for the remainder of the company's territory, for the execution of all such processes as shall be directed to them according to law.

Fifthly — That in the case of death, or absence of any Councillor or Sheriff, the Governor-in-chief shall appoint a person to do the duty of the office till the pleasure of the company be known.

In the spring of 1816, Governor Semple, while on a tour of inspection visiting the different posts of the company, placed Mr. Colin Robertson in charge at Fort Douglas, and that gentleman, being a thorough fur trader, at once determined to declare open war against the servants of the North-West Company in his vicinity. His efforts were particularly directed against Mr. Duncan Cameron, who had caused the arrest of Miles Macdonell, and on March 17 an attack was made on Fort Gibraltar, the headquarters of the Nor'Westers, where Mr. Cameron was stationed. That gentleman and all his clerks were taken prisoners and placed in confinement, much to their surprise, as the assault made on them was entirely unexpected. The North-West Company's express bearing the mail from Fort William was captured, the letters confiscated, and all the arms, goods, and furs in Fort Gibraltar taken possession of. Mr. Cameron protested strongly against these high-handed proceedings, and demanded restoration of the fort and other property, but he was told by Mr. Robertson that as Gibraltar was the key of the Red River, the Hudson's Bay Company was resolved to keep it at all hazards. A force of Mr. Robertson's men fully armed was stationed at the spot to guard the prisoners and prevent the place from being re-taken, and attacks were then made on other stations belonging to the North-West Company, and their servants driven from their homes. Property belonging to the Canadians was confiscated right and left, and for a time the power of the Nor'Westers seemed to be broken in that part of the country. An attempt was even made to capture the [North-West Company's] post at Qu'Appelle, but without success, and Mr. Alexander McDonell, who was in charge, determined to resent the insult and repair the losses inflicted upon his company, as he realized the importance of the step taken by Mr. Robertson, and the disastrous effect it would have on the whole inland trade of his company unless it was thwarted. Fort Douglas being armed with artillery, and situated close to the river bank, commanded a position which would enable the Hudson's Bay Company to intercept all intercourse by water between Fort William and the interior posts. It was therefore of the utmost importance to regain possession of Fort Gibraltar, and, in order to accomplish this, he sent messengers to the North-West [Company's] agents on the Saskatchewan and Swan Rivers to send him a force of men for the purpose. His appeal for assistance met with a favourable response, and a number of men, chiefly French half-breeds, were sent to him. But Mr. Robertson, hearing of this force collected to attack him, at once tore down Fort Gibraltar, and then left the Red River for York Factory, taking Mr. Cameron with him as prisoner, and Governor Semple, returning from his trip, took command at Fort Douglas. Mr. McDonell had learned that a brigade of North-West [Company] boats was expected to arrive in the Red River about June 20, and as he knew that the Hudson's Bay Company were in a position to intercept and probably capture the supplies, he undertook to send a party to open communication by land between Lake Winnipeg and the stations on the Assiniboine. For this purpose a band of about sixty half-breeds and Indians on horseback was sent with instructions to pass at a distance behind Fort Douglas, which no doubt was the programme intended by Mr. McDonell, and was the wisest course to pursue, because any attempt to take the stronghold of the Hudson's Bay Company, strongly fortified as it was, would have been a useless sacrifice of life. One section of McDonell's men succeeded in passing Fort Douglas unperceived, and at once made an assault on the settlers' houses along the river. The second section, however, when passing the fort on June 19, 1816, was discovered by Governor Semple and his men, who, supposing that it was either an attack on the settlement or a party going to join the expected brigade from Fort William, left the fort with about twenty-seven of his followers to meet the Nor'Westers, and on coming up to them, angry words passed, followed immediately by the discharge of firearms and a general fight between the two parties. Governor Semple was wounded, and several of his men killed at the very commencement, and afterwards a slaughter of nearly the whole of the Hudson's Bay Company people took place, twenty-one of them being either slain outright or wounded. Different versions of who fired the first shot have been given, but the exact truth of the matter will never be known. Governor Semple's party was composed of raw and inexperienced men, mostly youths utterly unable to cope with the fierce half-breeds and Indians opposed to them, and this no doubt accounts for the large number killed on the side of the Hudson's Bay Company people, while the Nor'Westers only lost one man killed and another wounded. Governor Semple, although not mortally injured in the fight, was afterwards shot dead by an Indian, and many of the killed were barbarously treated by the half-breeds and savages, although Mr. Cuthbert Grant, who commanded the party, did all in his power to prevent any undue cruelty on the part of his men. After the death of Semple there was a disposition on the part of the settlers, most of whom had crowded into the fort, to resist any further attack on the part of the Nor'Westers, but having heard of a movement of armed men to reinforce Grant, and fearing that they could not hold out against large numbers, they finally agreed to capitulate, and Mr. Alexander McDonell, who took charge on the death of Semple, gave up Fort Douglas to the North-West Company, taking, however, an inventory of all it contained, for which he received a receipt from Mr. Grant.

The settlers now looked upon their prospect of success in the colony as almost hopeless, and embarking on boats furnished by the Nor'Westers, they bade adieu to the settlement and proceeded to Jack River, where most of them remained until the following year, when they returned to Red River under the protection of Lord Selkirk and his company of de Meurons.

Hudson's Bay Company *versus* Sayer

Alexander Ross

In the spring of 1849, William Sayer, a French half-breed, who had been implicated and imprisoned but afterwards liberated on bail, and McGillis, Laronde, and Goullé, three others of the same class, held to bail but not imprisoned, were to stand their trial at the first criminal court, for illicitly trafficking in furs with the natives. This was the charge against them, namely, their accepting of furs from the Indians in exchange for goods, which was construed to be contrary to the rules and regulations of the Company's charter, wherein it is stated, "That the Hudson's Bay Company shall have the sole and exclusive trade and commerce of all the territories within Rupert's Land."

Notwithstanding the hue and cry that had been raised against the Company's misrule of late years, no half-breed or other, we may here observe, had been deprived of his liberty, or molested for meddling in the fur trade, with the exception . . . of one solitary instance, during the whole quarter of a century in which the Company's officer presided over the affairs of the colony. It was reserved for Major Caldwell, a Government man, to exhibit this new feature of severity. Had His Excellency, however, issued an official notice, giving the people timely warning beforehand that they were to be so dealt with, the Major, as well as Recorder Thom, might have escaped that odium cast upon them in the present instance, nor would they have been taught this severe lesson of humility, nor the public peace have been disturbed as it was.

The seventeenth of May was the day appointed for the Criminal Court to sit and decide this celebrated case, "Hudson's Bay Company *verses* Sayer." For some days previous it was rumoured about that a hostile party would be prepared to watch the motions of the authorities during the trial. About 9 o'clock in the morning of that day, the French Canadians, as well as

SOURCE: Alexander Ross, *The Red River Settlement: Its Rise, Progress, and Present State* (London, 1856), pp. 372-86.

half-breeds, began to move from all quarters, so that the banks of the river, above and below the fort, were literally crowded with armed men, moving to and fro in wild agitation, having all the marks of a seditious meeting or, rather, a revolutionary movement. As the hostile demonstration proceeded, boats and canoes were laid hold of wherever found, for the purpose of conveying over the crowd, who no sooner reached the west bank of the river, than they drew together about Fort Garry and the court-house. This movement took place about half-past 10 o'clock; and the whole affair was watched by the writer from his own door. At this moment a deputation of the ring-leaders called on me (for I must here speak in the first person, as I am sometimes compelled to do) to announce the fact, that they intended resisting the proceedings of the court. "My friends," observed I to them, "you are acting under false impressions. Beware of disturbing the peace! The 6th are gone, but the 7th may come" – alluding to the military – "and those who may now sow the wind may live to reap the whirlwind for their pains." With this deputation, however, I walked up to the fort, as the hour of the court approached. The object of the mob was to resist the infliction of any punishment, whether of fine or imprisonment, on the offenders; and their anger was provoked by a report that the Major was to have his pensioners under arms on the day of the trial to repel force by force. The pensioners themselves had imprudently boasted what they could do, and what they would do, if the half-breeds dared to show themselves.

At 11 o'clock, the authorities, not intimidated by the storm which threatened them, entered the court, and proceeded to business – but what business could be done under the menace of an armed rabble? At this time 377 guns were counted; besides, here and there, groups armed with other missiles of every description. Imminent as the danger appeared to us – for an accidental shot or a fist raised in anger might have set these inflammable elements in a blaze – many incidents occurred to cause a reluctant smile. Some running one way, some another; one party taking up a position here, another there; whilst many present knew not for what they had come, kept running amongst the crowd, yelling and whooping like savages, calling out, "What is it, what is it? Who are you going to shoot? who are you going to shoot?" This was the aspect of things when the court was opened, and the Major, Judge Thom, and magistrates, took their seats on the bench; on this occasion, however, the Major dispensed with his usual guard of honour, and walked to the courthouse like another private gentleman.

As soon as the court was opened, Sayer, the first on the court calendar, was summoned to appear; but he, with the other offenders, was held in close custody by an armed force of their countrymen out-doors, and we were not so imprudent as to direct the application of force, or even to insist on his bail bringing him forward. Other business of minor importance was taken up to pass away the time, which occupied the court till 1 o'clock, when Sayer was again called for, but in vain: at the same time, a Mr. McLaughlan, an Irishman, who was not a settler, being on a visit to a relative, and who considered he possessed some influence over the half-breeds, attempted to interfere, but was suddenly repulsed; and, in fine, peremptorily ordered off. The court then held a consultation, and sent word to the half-breeds, that they might appoint a leader, and send in a deputation to assist Sayer during his trial, and state in open court what they had to urge in his defence. This suggestion was ultimately adopted. A gentleman named Sinclair, well known among the half-breeds, and eleven others of his class, took up a position in the court-room, with Sayer under their protection.

At the moment Sayer entered, about twenty of the half-breeds, all armed, took up their station at the court-house door, as sentinels, and held in their possession the arms of the deputation. At the outer gate of the court-yard about fifty others were placed as a guard, and couriers kept in constant motion going the rounds, and conveying intelligence of the proceedings in court to the main party outside, so that at a moment's warning, had anything gone wrong, a rush was to have been made to rescue Sayer and the deputation from the fangs of the law. While all this manœuvring occupied their attention out-doors, the proceedings within the court were not less interesting; nine out of the twelve jurymen were challenged by Mr. Sinclair, but it was a needless interruption to the trial. Sayer confessed the fact that he did trade furs from an Indian. A verdict of guilty was recorded against him, upon which Sayer proved that a gentleman named Harriott, connected with the fur trade, had given him permission to traffic, and on this pretext he was discharged. The cases of Goullé, McGillis, and Laronde were not proceeded with, and they all left the court together, greeted with loud huzzas.

As the offenders troubled themselves very little with the subtleties of the law, it was their own belief, and that of their people, that they were honourably acquitted, and that trading in

furs was no longer a crime. Not a word was said whether the
half-breeds were or were not to trade furs in future, and so
obscure were their perceptions of the real value of the decision
that one of the jurymen, on reaching the court door, gave three
hearty cheers, and in a stentorian voice bawled out, "Le
commerce est libre! Le commerce est libre! Vive la liberté!" a
cri de joie which was soon repeated by another. These men,
we ought to observe, were Canadians, but the half-breeds soon
followed their example; and in the midst of yelling, whooping,
and firing, kept shouting over and over again, "Le commerce
est libre! Le commerce est libre!" all the way from the court-
house to the water's edge, and that in the midst of the court
officials, Governor, Judge, and Magistrates. As soon as they
were boated across, they gave three cheers, followed by three
volleys in testimony of their victory, and from that day, these
deluded people have been incited and worked upon by disaffected demagogues to entertain the idea that the trade is free.
When this is really the case, we much fear, with such elements
of disaffection, it will be the signal for every honest and peace-
loving man to leave Red River; and the more so, as the
Americans are on the eve of planting their starry banner at
our door.

The trial we have just described suggests for our consideration several leading questions of importance; and first – Why
this perpetual hostility against the authorities on the part of the
French inhabitants?

In answering this query, we must repeat what we have
already stated more than once, namely, that the French
Canadians and half-breeds form the majority of the population,
and, to a man, speak nothing but a jargon of French and Indian.
In all fairness they ought to have been represented in the
Legislative Council, and have had the laws expounded to them
in their own language in the courts of justice. The facts,
however, are as follows:

*1. There are twelve legislative councillors, exclusive of the
Governor, who is president; of these, nine are Protestants, and
three Catholics; that is, three to one in favour of the former.*

*2. Mixed juries have never had the benefit of a competent
French interpreter, nor have the laws bearing on the cases been
otherwise explained to them.*

*3. The laws have always been administered in the English
language, as indeed ought to be the case in an English colony;*

but they have never been professionally interpreted in the French language, which is a real grievance.

4. The laws have all been framed for the benefit of the commercial and agricultural classes; but not one for the half-breeds or hunters.

5. Their being legally disqualified by Mr. Thom's interpretation of the charter, from trafficking in furs with the Indians, is the greatest of all their grievances; as furs are the only circulating medium the country affords, beyond the limits of the colony.

Secondly, we may here inquire for what reason Judge Thom became so obnoxious to all our subjects of French extraction? To answer this candidly, we believe that Judge Thom's unpopularity has grown up, not from any dereliction of duty, or defect in his official character as judge, but simply because he was the professional organ of the court. As the interpreter of the laws, and the Company's legal adviser, he was looked upon by an uninstructed people as the cause of all their grievances; and this unfavourable opinion was grounded on the impression they had formed of him on his first arrival in the settlement [which was stated in a previous chapter]. In short, any other judge without a knowledge of the French language must prove as objectionable here as Mr. Thom has been. To remedy these evils, either reduce the councillors to an equal number on both sides, or grant the people of Red River a constitution similar to that of Vancouver Island. Take care also that the judge of the colony be equally independent in his official capacity of the populace and the Company. Above all, a knowledge of the French tongue is indispensable.

Thirdly, did the court pursue the wisest policy in proceeding to business in Sayer's case? We think not. So long as the court authorities were menaced by the hostile rabble, their wisest proceeding had been to shut up the court and retire without proceeding to business at all.

Fourthly, it may be worth inquiring, Of what use are the pensioners, as a protective force, in Red River? As they are, squatted down as settlers and scattered about, they neither are, nor ever will be, of any manner of use. Any efficient force, either here or elsewhere, must be under strict military discipline. With these suggestive remarks before us, relative to Sayer's case and Judge Thom, we may be permitted to pass a comment on the laws generally.

Under the letters patent of Charles the Second, the Governor and Council of Rupert's Land, in addition, of course, to executive functions and legislative authority, exercise also judicial power. But as the union of these incompatible duties must have been sanctioned through necessity rather than enjoined from choice by the framers of the charter, other tribunals have long been established in the respective districts of the settlement, with the view of more speedily and conveniently adjusting civil causes of inferior importance.

According to the terms of the same document, the laws of England are to be the rule of decision. But in the absence of professional aid, every tribunal becomes, in a greater or less degree, a court of conscience or equity; and the more numerous the bench (particularly if the equal units have been educated in different countries, and under different systems) the more extensively must this be the case. In such a state of things, there remains no room for a jury; and as those who are thus arbiters both of law and of fact cannot be forced to unanimity, the results are little likely to give satisfaction. At the same time, it must not be omitted that the decisions have been satisfactory where the grounds upon which they were formed have been clearly expressed. To these inherent evils must be added the difficulties incident to the primitive condition of our little community: that everybody knows everybody; that people of all classes are closely connected by blood or marriage; and that any story, good or evil, with all its additions and deductions, reaches every ear.

It was for these and other like reasons, therefore, that the Hudson's Bay Company introduced into the settlement in 1839, as already noticed, Mr. Thom as Recorder of Rupert's Land, who, as senior member of the Governor's Council, was virtually to preside in the general court. In order to secure the great object in view, namely, the separate consideration of law and fact, a municipal regulation was immediately passed to the effect that every criminal issue, and every such civil issue as could come before the general court, should be tried by a jury.

The reader must not suppose, however, that we were now enabled to reduce into actual practice the laws of England. For instance, in civil cases, thanks to the "plentiful lack" of practising attorneys, we have no written pleadings, while execution may be stayed by the Company's notes, which, though practically better than Her Majesty's stamped gold, yet neither are, nor can be declared to be, a legal tender. In criminal cases, again, with the exception of a few floggings, and the terror of one execution . . . , we have no resource but imprisonment — no tread-mills, no hulks, no pillory, no penitentiary, no white sheets, no Botany Bay. Fortunately, our only available punishment is generally speaking quite sufficient. The mere confinement is far more severely felt in a state of nature than in civilized life, and as the daily ration of a pound of pemmican, and water at discretion, is adhered to in all cases, it is rendered more irksome. We are neither rich enough nor philanthropic enough to feed our gaol-birds with dainty fare, and the mere support of life must afford to a denison of the wilderness but poor compensation for such misfortunes as loss of liberty, privation of gossip, and prohibition of beer and tobacco.

Nor are our juries more punctiliously modeled after the pattern of the old country than our laws. Without regard to any rules of selection, we desire nothing more than the presence of twelve householders, as little interested as possible in the victory or defeat of either of the parties. So powerful is the obligation of an oath over the unhackneyed consciences of the mass of the population — for, on all administrative points, we are contented with an unsworn declaration — that wilful perverseness, in a jury of Red River, is hardly to be imagined for a moment. On the trial of Sayer, notwithstanding the alarm excited by the popular feeling against the Company and the court, the jury unhesitatingly returned a verdit in conformity with the laws. A still more remarkable fact may be mentioned, as showing that scrupulous regard of our common people for an oath which forms the grand justification of our apparently loose mode of selecting jurymen. In addition to the proof of the defendant's own voluntary confession — a confession not sufficiently circumstantial to have convicted him by itself — the only evidence was that of the defendant's son, who, under the stern injunction of one parent, told the whole truth, without any attempt at delay or equivocation, against the other.

In what court of England or Scotland could the moral beauty of this scene have been surpassed? However, to give an instance of more decisive character and wider application. Our local enactments against the selling of beer to Indians, besides imposing a public fine on the seller, condemn him to make restitution for every article of barter thus received, at first price. Under all the temptations of these enactments, the original buyer of the article is admitted as a witness; this being the only means of preventing an entire failure of justice. Perjury, in such cases, the writer has never known, and if the Indian has hesitated, the reluctance obviously arose from the feeling that speak the truth he must, if he speak at all. What an example does our untutored savage thus show to those who call themselves civilized, in most parts of the world!

The intelligent reader can hardly require to be told, that the position of our Recorder was, from the beginning, rather an invidious one. As the only professional man in a country where printing was unknown, he was exempted from nearly all the checks which might be expected elsewhere to influence a lawyer on the bench. So far as any knowledge of law at all existed in the settlement, it was derived from the systems of Scotland or of Canada, which differed essentially from our chartered rule of right; and even if some few of us could be said to have made a study of the system we were bound to administer, it proved of little advantage to us when the Recorder announced his principle, (doubtless a correct one) that our "Laws of England" were not those of the present day, but those of the date of the Letters Patent, namely, the "Laws of England" of the May 2, 1670. Nor was our legal associate much less independent of control with regard to our local enactments, whether such enactments professed to provide for the indigenous peculiarities of this secluded colony, or to modify and modernize our imported code. It was the Recorder that penned them; it was the Recorder that argued them through the council in a masterly manner; it was the Recorder that interpreted them, so as to make their inevitable generalities fit particular cases. In these respects, he may be said to have always had his own way – less would not satisfy him; and this often raised up difficulties between himself and his colleagues. People said he possessed the gift of twisting and untwisting his interpretations, so as always to fit his own cause.

Accordingly, with his command of language, and his fertility in argument, Mr. Thom was supposed by the many to be able to mould the law to his own wish. To meet a difficulty, which he appeared to foresee from the very beginning of his residence among us, he resolved, (at the hazard, as he seemed to be aware, of being tiresome) to expound the law of each case so fully as to forestal himself, as he expressed it, against any other exposition of the same on his part. He strove, in short, to make the public a present of the *argumentum ad hominem* against himself. But the more diligently he showed that he could split hairs, the more readily did the many believe that he would split them whether they needed splitting or not. On another point, also, Mr. Thom has been less circumspect and less successful than most of his colleagues in uniting public sentiment

in his favour. He has had far less to do with the people, generally speaking, than any of the other officials; nor has he ever
wished to interfere with our more purely ministerial duties;
and yet it was generally thought he had too much in his
power. It was in vain he guarded – by publicly stating the extent
of his intervention, in open court – when circumstances had
connected him, perhaps, with the preliminaries of any measure.
So it was on the bench. As might have been expected, his
charge was almost uniformly echoed by the verdict: and yet
this uniformity of success, which would elsewhere be reckoned
a proof of the truth and reasonableness of a judge's views,
tended here to inspire the multitude with a notion, that Mr.
Thom could turn black into white and white into black.

Again, the Recorder's influence in our little legislature was
sure to be regarded as disproportionably great. Any measure
that he proposed was pretty sure to be carried – not that he
ever attempted beforehand to make a party, for everyone
opposed him in turn; but that, by dint of talking, he always
brought over some majority or other to his side. Nor was Mr.
Thom so careful as he ought to have been under such circumstances, to blend the *suaviter in modo* with the *fortiter in re*,
though his demeanour, to do him justice, savoured rather of a
confidence in his own views than of any disregard of the feelings of others. Some of his measures, too, were by no means
acceptable to a certain section of the people. We allude more
particularly to those enactments which subjected our traffic
with the United States to the differential duties of such Imperial statutes as regulated the foreign commerce of colonies.
Although that law affected the settlers of French origin far
more extensively than their English brethren, Mr. Thom introduced a measure to impose a duty of ten per cent on all
American articles, with some trifling exceptions; while the
English importer paid only four! The measure, however, fell to
the ground; but the odium it created lives to this day; though,
in point of fact, the exemptions in favour of the actual adventurers were so large and liberal as to render the trade free as
the wind to all but the wealthiest individuals that were engaged
in the business. The import duty from England and the United
States are now both the same; namely, four per cent.

In this state of public feeling, the single prosecution of an
interloper in the fur trade caused, as we have already related,
a considerable degree of popular excitement, on the part of the
French settlers. From words they flew to arms, chiefly, as they
alleged, in consequence of believing, whether right or wrong,

that Major Caldwell had threatened to call out his pensioners against them. In this struggle, legality, in a certain degree, carried the day; but in such a way that public opinion was left as dissatisfied on the point as before, and the law as vague as before. Hence, it has happened, through a dread of the renewal of such a conflict between reason and force, that we have, since then, been deprived of the advantages of Mr. Thom's ability, public spirit, and independence. Such a result, clearly traceable to this gentleman's perverse use of his talents, by constantly exercising them to support his own opinions in opposition to all others, is deeply to be regretted.[1]

---

[1] Adam Thom's unpopularity was so great in 1849 that he lost his place as Recorder of Rupert's Land. Instead he was appointed Clerk of the Council of Assiniboia, a post he held until 1854. [Swainson]

Annual Routine In Red River Settlement

Joseph James Hargrave

The starting of the Northern Packet from Red River is one of the great annual events in the colony. It occurs generally about December 10, when, the ice having been thoroughly formed and the snow fallen, winter travelling is easy and uninterrupted. The packet arrangements are such that every post in the Northern Department is communicated with through its agency. The means of transit are sledges and snowshoes. The sledges are drawn by magnificent dogs, of which there are three or four to each vehicle, whose neatly fitting harness, though gaudy in appearance, is simple in design and perfectly adapted to its purposes, while the little bells attached thereto, bright looking and clearly ringing, cheer the flagging spirits of men and animals through the long run of the winter's day.

In the course of the long distances traversed by the winter runners, every pound weight laid on the sledges tells. So jealously was all excess in the amount of mail matter transmitted through the packets guarded against in the old times, before the institution of Red River mails, that the carriage of newspapers was disallowed, with the exception of an annual file of the Montreal *Gazette*, forwarded to head quarters for general perusal. Newspapers were then rare and highly prized, but now the bulk of the contents of the Company's inward bound packets consist of newspapers addressed to private individuals.

A pair of stoutly constructed wooden boxes, measuring about three feet in length by eighteen inches deep and fourteen wide, when well packed, contain an astonishing amount of printed and written matter. These receptacles are secured to the dog sledges, and the party sets forth on its journey, the dogs running at a gentle jog trot from about daylight till dusk, and the drivers accompanying them on foot. To walk over the snow the latter require "snowshoes." These are composed each of a

SOURCE: Joseph James Hargrave, *Red River* (Montreal, 1871), pp. 155-73.

light wooden frame, about four feet in length, tapering from a width of about fifteen inches at the centre to points at either end, the toes being so turned up as to prevent tripping. Over this frame netting is stretched for the foot of the runner to rest on. The object of the appliance is by a thin network to distribute the weight of the wearer over so large a surface of snow as will prevent him from sinking. The invention is an Indian one, and, like that of the canoe and other Indian instruments, it is so perfectly suited to the object to be compassed as not to be susceptible of improvement from the whites.

In traversing the frozen lakes the parties skirt their shores from point to point, selecting their camping places for the night in the more sheltered spots, where firewood can be obtained. A quantity of snow having been cleared away, sometimes with the aid of a snowshoe used as a shovel, the members of the party set themselves to work in collecting all the dry wood they can find, and a long fire is lighted. Supper having been prepared and eaten, and the dogs fed, the fire is replenished, and the members of the party, arranging their blankets so that each lies with his feet to the blaze, fall asleep. Some time before sunrise they are again awake and, after finishing their breakfast of pemmican and tea, resume their journey. Forty miles a day is considered not an extraordinary run. A halt of one or two hours is made towards noon for dinner.

The winter packet generally runs from Fort Garry over the whole length of Lake Winnipeg to Norway House at its northern extremity, in eight days. The distance thus travelled is about 350 miles. At Norway House the entire packet is overhauled and repacked so as to separate matter going north and west from that going eastward towards the coast of Hudson's Bay. The Red River runners return from Norway House, bringing with them to the settlement the packet from York Factory on the Bay, which is run to connect with the one they have brought from the settlement.

A new set of packet bearers travel from Norway House to Carlton, near the eastern extremity of the great Saskatchewan valley. Their route runs across Lake Winnipeg and up the river Saskatchewan on which Carlton is situated. The distance is about six hundred and fifty miles, and is performed in twenty-two days. At Carlton the process of unpacking and redistribution is again performed, matter directed to the north being separated from that directed to the west, including the posts in the districts of Swan River and Saskatchewan. Carlton, although not the chief post in the Saskatchewan district, is the grand centre of the winter packet arrangements. The runners who come from Edmonton down the river Saskatchewan, and those whose journey from Norway House I have just traced, wait there the arrival of the outward bound express from the northern districts, strictly so called, being those of Mackenzie River and Athabasca. When the runners coming from these three different directions have met and exchanged their burdens, the last grand link in the operation is completed. The express which has come down the river returns to Edmonton, the Norway House men retrace their steps eastward, while the great Northern Packet journeys onwards in charge of the men who have come to meet it from the remote regions to which it is consigned.

Men engaged at Carlton are then dispatched overland to Red River, through the Swan River district, with the matter consigned to posts within the latter, and the collected correspondence of the north and west to be mailed for the outside world, as already described, by the agency in Red River settlement. This outwardbound express usually reaches Fort Garry in the last week of February. Its arrival forms one of the chief events of the winter. For some days after its receipt the Company's office is a scene of comparative bustle, maintained by a succession of inquiries for letters from friends inland. Occasionally very sad news is brought out by such opportunities. Death and other causes of change operate even among the scanty population of the north, and the accumulated incidents of six months often present at least one or two topics of general interest. The ramifications of relationship in the country are so complicated that events of importance which affect any family are felt by a wide circle of more remote connections. The great majority of the settlers, too, have been themselves connected with the fur trade or have near relatives stationed at some of the Company's posts, scattered up and down the country. All these causes combine to render the receipt of a large quantity of news from the interior a very interesting event in the colony.

The arrival of the Northern Packet in February is closely followed by the dispatch of subsidiary expresses of minor importance, but chiefly intended for the convenience of the Company in its trading operations. The men from Carlton, after a few days' rest, return overland by the same route through Swan River District along which they had come to Red River, and a packet called the "Red River Spring Packet" is sent to Norway House *en route* to York Factory, whence another express called the "York Factory Spring Packet" comes to meet it.

The striking difference in the contents of outward and inward packets lies in the presence of newspapers and other printed matter in the latter, while in the former the whole contents consist of letters, the white envelopes of which contrast strongly with the soiled, stamped, and postmarked appearance of their inward bound neighbours. Correspondence of a private nature is much indulged in throughout the Indian country where a great part of the year is spent in idleness. The chief drawback to letter-writing at a remote post is the total absence of any thing to write about. This difficulty is overcome by the ingenious expedient of writing one letter, a copy of which is forwarded to each friend whom the author is desirous of laying under the obligation to reply to him. The excitement caused at a remote post by the arrival of the packet with all its news from home is very great.

The runners, whose duty it is to carry these packets, are, of course, not unimportant men either in their own eyes or in those of other people. When they can manage to be at one of the Company's posts on Christmas or New Year's Day, they are handsomely welcomed, and, under all circumstances, their recognized character as newsbearers secures for them a certain amount of flattering consideration. They certainly pass through a strange scene in their journeys. To their accustomed eyes, however, all is monotonous enough in the appearance of the withered woods through which the wind howls and shrieks shrilly in the night, or in the endless expanse of snow the glare of whose unsullied whiteness blinds the vision of the Lake traveller. The solitude of the regions they traverse is described by travellers as very striking, and, indeed, save when the occasional dog sledge with its peals of little bells in winter, or the swiftly passing boat brigade, resonant with the songs of the summer *voyageurs*, intrudes, with its momentary variation, on the shriek of the all-penetrating wind, the ripple of the stream, the roar of the thunder-toned waterfall, or the howl of the wild beast of the woods, the vast expanse is abandoned to the undisturbed possession of the Indian hunter and his prey.

On the outbreak of spring the hibernal torpor, which has influenced a large portion of the settlement population, gives way to the active life generated by the vigorous prosecution of several branches of important and laborious business. Of these the freighting operations are among the most important. They are conducted by land and water. At the latter class of work we shall first glance.

The water carriage of the country is performed by means of what are called "inland boats." Each of these is worked by nine men, of whom eight are rowers and the other is steersman; it is capable of carrying about three and-a half tons of freight. Brigades composed of numbers varying from four to eight of these craft are kept plying in various directions, throughout the season of open water, on the inland lakes and rivers between those points to and from which goods have to be carried. The tripmen who man these boats are Indians or half-breeds engaged at the place where the brigade is organized, and paid a stipulated sum for the performance of the trip. Between Red River Settlement and York Factory such brigades pass and re-pass throughout the whole season of open navigation. They are organized in the settlement, both by the Company and by such private settlers as have capital and inclination to invest it in that description of business. The cargoes sent to York are made up of furs and other country produce consigned thither by the Company for the purpose of shipment to England; the return freight from York to the settlement is partly composed of goods imported by private merchants and partly of those imported by the Company for use in its trading operations. These goods have all previously been shipped from England to York by the Company's annual vessel.

The route between Red River and York runs north through Lake Winnipeg to Norway House, thence eastward along a rugged line of streams and lakes by Oxford House to the Bay coast. The voyage both ways, including all stoppages, occupies about nine weeks, and the rates of pay allowed men belonging to the respective grades of steersman, bowsman, and middleman are £8, £7, and £6 for the journey. The employer, in addition to the above pay, of course, furnishes the brigades with food, consisting of pemmican and flour.

The greatest and most important of the brigades organized at Red River Settlement is that commonly known as the Portage La Loche Brigade. The chief objects of this organization are to convey inland the English manufactures intended for barter with the Indians in the remote and valuable districts of Athabasca and Mackenzie River; to bring out the furs already traded in these districts for shipment to England from York Factory; and to transport from the latter place to the settlement as much of the freight deposited at the factory for conveyance to that part of the country as the boats can carry.

Of late years this brigade has subjected the Company to considerable loss and inconvenience through mutinous conduct. The description I shall give of it refers less to what it has now become than to what it was so recently as 1866. Till that year, from 1826, when first organized, it served its purpose in a satisfactory manner. It consisted of about fifteen boats arranged in two minor brigades, each of which was under the charge of an experienced guide, whose boat, sailing at the head of the line, guided the rest through rapids, shoals and other obstacles to the navigation of the route. During the first week, in June, the ice in Lake Winnipeg having disappeared and spring completely set in, the leading brigade of seven or eight boats usually starts. About a week afterwards it is followed by the second brigade. The interval is allowed with the object of preventing the brigades meeting and creating undue bustle and confusion at any of the halting places along the route.

The first of these halting places is Norway House, to which depot is conveyed a vast quantity of agricultural produce from Red River Settlement. At Norway House there waits the arrival of the boats the outfit of English goods previously brought from York and stored there to be taken onward by them for the use of the trade in Athabasca and Mackenzie River districts. Having discharged their Norway House freight, and shipped that intended for the north, the boats resume their journey. Their new route runs in a westerly direction across Lake Winnipeg, up the River Saskatchewan, and northwards past Forts Cumberland and Isle à la Crosse, to Methy Portage, called also Portage La Loche . . . ["the Height of Land separating the waters flowing into the Arctic Sea from those draining into Hudson's Bay"].

This is the extreme limit of the course traversed by "the Portage Brigade." Here it is met by brigades travelling south from Mackenzie River and bringing the furs already traded. The Portage is about twelve miles in length. Efforts have been made to facilitate the transport across it by means of oxen and carts; but the men belonging to the boats are often necessarily employed here, as on all the other Portages, in carrying the packages on their backs. When the latter course is adopted it is usual to make the Red River men take their "pieces" half way across the Portage, where they deliver them over to the men from the North, receiving in exchange the fur packs brought to meet them by the latter. The new cargo shipped, they retrace their course down stream and, passing Norway House, run eastward to the Bay, with the object of delivering at the factory for shipment to England, the furs they have brought from Portage La Loche. Should the Company's ship have arrived at York before them, they immediately return to the settlement; but, if not, they wait for her and receive what freight she brings for them to transport to Red River.

Besides the goods, the Portage La Loche brigade carries a packet. The opportunities offered by it in summer and by the "Northern Express,' whose course has been already traced in winter, are the only two available to parties living north of Portage La Loche for communicating with the civilized world.

The time occupied by the trip just described is about four months, the boats starting early in June and returning to the settlement early in October, thus being employed during all the summer. Detailed average rates of travel may be taken as follows. The boats leaving the settlement on June 1 may arrive at Norway House on June 10, leave it on the twelfth, and pass Cumberland on June 24, and Isle à la Crosse on July 9, reaching Portage La Loche on the seventeenth of the same month. Leaving the Portage on the return trip on August 1, they will pass Isle à la Crosse on the fifth, Cumberland on the fifteenth, Norway House on the twenty-first, and arrive at York Factory on August 31. Leaving York on September 10 they will reach Norway House on September 30, and Red River Settlement about October 8.

The probable duration of the voyage, as a whole, may be relied on as above stated; but great uncertainty necessarily prevails as to the date of arrival at each post on the route. The above estimate is meant merely to indicate probability. In passing through the lakes the sail is used when the wind is fair; but, should it be otherways, it often happens that a detention of several days occurs. The difference of time occupied in ascending and descending rivers will also be observed. The upward trip from Norway House to Portage La Loche will occupy thirty-six days, the return will be executed in twenty-one days; that from Norway House to York will be performed in ten days, while the laborious ascent will require the efforts of twenty days. The rapidity and strength of the currents in the rivers cause the delay in ascending, and aid the efforts of the crews in descending the streams.

On the rivers traversed by these brigades, there are many interruptions to the navigation of so serious a nature that the boats have to be unloaded and, along with their freight, carried by the crews occasionally for a considerable distance overland, to be re-launched at the nearest spot where the obstruction is at an end. This process is called "making a portage." Where the interruption is not of a character sufficiently formidable to render a portage necessary, the crew, going ashore, pull the vessel along by means of lines. This is called "tracking."

The vast amount of handling necessary in passing goods over the numerous portages which intervene between Hudson Bay and even the nearer inland districts, renders the packing of the merchandise a matter of very great importance indeed. The standard weight of each packet used in the Company's trade is one hundred pounds. Such a bale or case is termed an "Inland piece." Each of the above described boats is supposed capable of containing seventy-five pieces as a fair cargo. It is the country method of estimating tonnage. The facility with which such pieces can be handled by the muscular tripmen is very perfect; a boat can be loaded by its crew of nine men in five minutes, and the compact, orderly appearance presented on completion of the operation is beyond praise.

The arrangement of the duties of the various grades of men belonging to these brigades is well calculated to suit its purpose. The steersman attached to each boat is the captain. Seated on an elevated flooring at the stern of his boat he steers, either with the common helm or, where the situation is critical, with his long and powerful sweep, with one stroke of which an expert workman will effect an instantaneous change in the course of his skiff. It is an important duty of the steersman to lift the pieces from their places in the boat, and lay them on the backs of the tripmen at the portages. The process of raising seventy or seventy-five pieces, each weighing a hundred pounds, from a position beneath the foot to a level with the shoulders, is one requiring a man of considerable strength to perform efficiently and with expedition.

Of the eight men composing the crew, one is called the "bowsman." The special duty of this person is to stand at the bow of the vessel at all portions of the route abounding with rapids, shoals or sunken rocks, and, while advising the steersman by voice and sign where such obstructions exist, himself, with the help of a long light pole, to aid the motion of the boat into the safer channel. While not occupied in this distinctive duty, the bowsman works at the oar like any other man of the crew.

The "middlemen" are the rowers. When a favourable breeze blows their duties are relieved by the substitution of the sail. At portages they transport the boat and goods overland. Each man is considered competent to carry two "pieces" on his back at a time. These are maintained in position by a leather contrivance termed a "portage strap," by which the weight of the burden is brought to bear on the forehead of the porter.

After the performance of a few voyages over the Portage route, the ordinarily intelligent middleman gains such knowledge of the details of navigation as to become capable of acting as bowsman. After further service, should he turn out a man fit to command others, and likely to be careful of the property composing his ladings, he is eligible for promotion to the position of steersman.

Over each brigade, as already mentioned, there is placed a guide. This functionary may be described as the commodore of the fleet. His special duty is to show the route in all parts where it is doubtful, or to lead the way where rapids or other obstructions intervene. He supports the authority of the steersmen and transacts the business of his brigade at the posts where it touches on the route. He is a most important official, and, when properly qualified, exceedingly useful. He is generally advanced in life, having necessarily risen from the position of middleman to that which he holds. His knowledge of every rapid and shoal throughout the long course of his run is generally perfect, and the two men who have been at the head of the Portage La Loche brigades since 1833 and 1848 respectively, named Alexis L'Esperance, and Baptiste Bruce, know their way so well that, even in a dark night, with a favouring breeze, they will press forward through treacherous waters when economy of time becomes an object.

On the Portage La Loche brigades, being those now specially under consideration, the pay of a guide for the entire trip, occupying the four summer months, has been £35, of a steersman, £20, bowsman, £18, and middleman, £16. When efficiently performed, the work done, though of a healthy nature, is extremely severe.

Until the year 1848 the Portage La Loche brigade consisted of only seven boats under one guide. The extension which gradually took place in the northern trade, however, necessitated the employment of increased means of transport. In that year the brigade was subdivided, and placed on the footing already described in detail. In the year 1866 a third subdivision was organized, so that, at the time I write, the concern really consists of seventeen boats in three brigades. Since 1866, however, the whole thing has got into so disordered a condition that I have selected a period anterior to that date as the one in respect to which my description holds good.

The manner in which the disorganization comes to be felt is in the mutiny of the crews and their refusal to complete the required voyage. Having delivered their outfits at Portage La Loche, they bring the furs which constitute their outward ladings as far as Norway House. Here the mutiny begins in a refusal to carry their furs to the Bay, and is followed up by a return to Red River with empty boats. The result is that a large quantity of valuable furs, comprising all those traded during the previous year in the vast northern districts, are stored up at Norway House, where no means exist of forwarding them to the seaboard for shipment to England, and consequently delay ensues in bringing them to the European market, and arrears of freight are stored up against the ensuing summer, when all the efforts which can be brought to bear are not much more than adequate to suffice for the evil proper to the day.

A check upon this method of doing business might be brought to bear on the men, were it not for the system of advancing wages on the trip, necessary in dealing with the class of which, for the greater part, these crews are composed. The men may be literally said to exist for the year on the proceeds of their summer work. On their return they do not betake themselves to any regular mode of industry, but vary seasons of hunting and fishing with longer intervals of total idleness. Towards mid-winter they find themselves and their families in a condition nearly allied to starvation. Early in December the books are opened in the Company's office for the enrolment of men to serve on the trips of the ensuing summer, and the needy crowd comes forward. At first all is anxiety to be enrolled. An advance is given in money at the time of engagement, and afterwards, at stated intervals before the commencement of the voyage, further sums are paid. Towards spring the crowd assumes a higher tone, and threats are used that, unless new demands are complied with, the threateners will not start on the voyage at all. The counter threat of imprisonment for breach of contract is superciliously smiled away with the remark that the period of imprisonment will be less than the time occupied by the trip. Of course no concession is ever made by the Company to such demands, or the undertaking would be indeed a failure. The result is that a few of the men engaged are not to be found when the day of embarkation arrives, and those who do start have received about one half of their wages in advance. At Norway House they receive a few necessary supplies on account, and, were they to perform the voyage, would receive more at York. During their absence their wives and families draw on the amount still "coming to them" to provide themselves with the necessaries of life, so that the sum forfeited by mutiny, and a premature return from an unfinished voyage is quite inadequate to restrain the men. Excuses also are trumped up as to the lateness of the season at which they arrive at Norway House, rendering it impossible for them to go to the coast and return with open water. Although this has a feasible look, the alleged lateness of the season is owing to the delay and want of energy on the part of the men themselves in performing the upstream voyage to the Portage in the early part of the summer. The experience of years proves the sufficiency of the time allowed for the execution of the work.

It was a matter of regret that even during the time the voyage was properly performed the use made by the drawers of the balance paid them on their return was often a bad one. The possession of a few pounds led, as a natural cause, to the investment of a large part of the sum in liquor, and disgraceful scenes often occurred during which those who had not spent all their available cash frequently lost it no one knew how. Then succeeded the season of alternate rest and partial occupation, until the necessities of the new winter caused an application for a fresh engagement. The continuance of this system has been caused by the necessities of the men whom it preserves from absolute starvation, and the undoubted fact that the laborious nature of the work to be done renders it difficult, if not impossible, to secure men in spring, when many other opportunities exist of gaining a livelihood through other and less-trying channels. As a class the Portage La Loche tripmen rank very low indeed in the colony. They are principally French half-breeds and Indians. Their priests profess a certain influence over them, but they confess their flock is disreputable, and not to be prevailed on to fulfil their voyaging contracts.

The land transport of the country is carried on in carts. . . . Something like fifteen hundred of these are employed on the route between Red River Settlement and St. Paul, giving employment to perhaps four hundred and fifty men. Of these carts about five hundred make two trips each season. At the commencement of summer, when the Plains have become dry, and the grass grown, the first parties start, taking with them the furs collected for exportation; the return trip bringing the manufactured articles from the civilized world is the one which pays best. Each cart will carry eight hundred pounds weight, the through freight on which will average £7. Cart, harness, and ox cost about £15. To this must be added the wages of a driver for each three carts, for six weeks, occupied by the journey at the rate of £4 per month, and an allowance for spare oxen before an estimate of the profits on Plain freighting can be obtained. The allowance of spare oxen varies from one-tenth to one-fifth of the total number of vehicles. The autumn brigade of carts leave the settlement late in August and return in October.

Since the Saskatchewan district grew into importance, and the Hudson's Bay Company altered the route, by which goods intended for its trade were imported, from the old one by way of Hudson's Bay to that by St. Paul, considerable cart traffic has existed between the settlement and the region in question. About three hundred carts, employing one hundred men, and making one trip each season, travel over that road. The ultimate point to which the Red River vehicles travel is Carlton, although a well beaten track exists all the way between Fort Garry and Rocky Mountain House, comprehending a distance of about eleven hundred miles. The time usually occupied by parties going to Carlton and returning is seventy or eighty days.

Conspicuous in importance amongst the annual events in the colony are the journeys made to the Plains by the Buffalo hunters at different periods of the year. The parties belonging to the summer hunt start about the beginning of June, and remain on the Plains until the beginning of August. They then return for a short time to the settlement for the purpose of trading their pemmican and dried meat. The autumn hunters start during the month of August, and remain on the prairie until the end of October, or early in November, when they usually return bringing the fresh or "green meat," preserved at that late season by the extreme cold. Those hunters, of whom there are many who remain on the Plains during the whole winter, employ themselves in trapping the fur-bearing animals, and hunting the buffalo for their robes. The pemmican, which forms the staple article of produce from the summer hunt, is a species of food peculiar to Rupert's Land. It is composed of buffalo meat, dried and pounded fine, and mixed with an amount of tallow or buffalo fat equal to itself in bulk. The tallow having been boiled, is poured hot from the caldron into an oblong bag, manufactured from the buffalo hide, into which the pounded meat has previously been placed. The contents are then stirred together until they have been thoroughly well mixed. When full, the bag is sewed up and laid in store. Each bag when full weighs one hundred pounds. It is calculated that, on an average, the carcase of each buffalo will yield enough of pemmican to fill one bag. This species of food is invaluable as a travelling provision. There is no risk of spoiling it as, if ordinary care be taken to keep the bags dry and free from mould, there is no assignable limit to the time the pemmican will keep. It is the travelling provision used throughout the north, where, in addition to the already specified qualifications, that of its great facility of transportation renders it exceedingly useful. The dried meat is the flesh of the buffalo, which, when it has been cut in thin slices, is hung over a fire, smoked and cured. It is packed in bales weighing on an average about sixty pounds each, and is also much used as a travelling provision. The fresh or green meat supplied by the late fall hunt is consumed in the settlement, and is not much used in travelling.

The operations connected with these Buffalo hunts give employment to somewhat over one thousand men and twelve hundred Red River carts. The people go to them with their families, who are employed in preparing the meat after the animals have been killed. The whole of those connected with the business may be divided into two sections, of which one leaves the settlement by the road leading to Pembina, and the other by that passing the spot on the river Assiniboine, called the White Horse Plain. The former proceeds in search of buffalo in a southerly, and the latter in a southwesterly direction. They act quite independently of each other. The carts leave the settlement in straggling parties without any bond of union, but, when once out on the prairie, they collect and choose a captain, who appoints subordinate officials of different grades, each of whom is charged with the performance of important and well-defined duties. They act as the police of the camp. Thenceforward all is conducted in admirable order. A system of penalties, to which all must submit, is strictly enforced, and perfect harmony of progress exists in the camp. Each evening all the carts are formed in a vast circle, into the centre of which the horses and oxen are driven, with the object of preventing thefts by prowling Indians and losses through cattle straying. After the camp has entered the country in the neighbourhood of which the buffalo are known to be, no gun is permitted to be fired until, in sight of the herd, the word of command is spoken by the captain authorizing the opening of the chase. The word given, the horsemen start in a body, loading and firing on horseback, and leaving the dead animals to be identified after the run is over. The kind of horse used is called a "buffalo runner," and is very valuable. A good one will cost from £50 to £70. The sagacity of the animal is chiefly shown in bringing his rider alongside the retreating buffalo, and in avoiding the numerous pitfalls abounding on the prairie. The most treacherous of the latter are the badger holes.

Considering the bold nature of the sport, remarkably few accidents occur. The hunters enter the herd with their mouths full of bullets. A handful of gunpowder is let fall from their "powder horns," a bullet is dropped from the mouth into the muzzle, a tap with the butt end of the firelock on the saddle causes the salivated bullet to adhere to the powder during the second necessary to depress the barrel, when the discharge is instantly effected without bringing the gun to the shoulder. The excitement which seizes the bold huntsman on finding himself surrounded by the long sought buffalo renders him careless in examining too curiously whether the object fired at is a buffalo or a buffalo runner mounted by a friend, but I have never heard of any fatal accident having happened, resulting from the pell-mell rush and indiscriminate firing. Guns, however, as a result of the careless loading, often explode, carrying away part of the hands using them, and even the most expert runners sometimes find their way into a badger hole, breaking or dislocating the collar bone of the riders in the fall. The breach-loading rifle is used in running buffalo by the wealthy amateurs who come from Europe to enjoy the sport, but the hunters of the country still almost universally use the old muzzle loaders.

The serious decrease in the number of buffalo which has been perceptible of late years is producing a very disastrous effect on the provision trade of the country. Pemmican, which formerly cost three-pence a pound, can now be procured with difficulty for a shilling, and dried meat formerly costing two-pence now costs eight-pence. This is a circumstance which threatens the transport business of the Company with the most alarming complications.

The rivers usually set fast toward the beginning of November, and the ice breaks up early in April. In winter, after the first snow has fallen, and before the tracks have been beaten, the roads are bad, but the inconvenience undergone by passengers at that season is as nothing to that caused by the melting snow in spring, when the ground is usually, for nearly a month, so saturated with water as to render locomotion, except on horseback, almost impracticable. The change from the summer buggies and carriages to the winter equipments of cutters and carrioles with their warm furs and chains of bells is agreeable. The monotony of mid winter is broken by the Christmas holidays, during which a good deal of festivity prevails in the settlement. The amusements are of course chiefly of a private and home kind, theatres and Christmas pantomimes not being yet known at Red River. Much driving about and visiting take place, and balls, family parties, and celebrations of a kindred nature are set on foot. Processions of perhaps twenty cutters and carrioles set out for a long drive over the snow, and the occupants generally arrange to call at some friend's house in a body and have a dance. This is called a surprise party, and the dissipation has its charms.

One of the principal events of the holidays is the celebration of a midnight mass in the cathedral of St. Boniface, on Christmas eve. The large church is brilliantly lighted with several hundreds of candles, the decorations are as gaudy as can be procured, and the music, which is performed by the nuns, and such of the scholars and priests as have any skill in that way, has always been well studied beforehand and is effectively rendered. The congregation begins to gather from all quarters about an hour before midnight, and the numerous carrioles and cutters, with their bells clearly ringing in the frosty air, create quite an excitement in the dead silence of the winter night. The unusual nature of the solemnity no doubt constitutes the groundwork of its popularity. The advanced hour at which it takes place gives rise to some inconvenience occasionally through the arrival of some noisy worshipper who has been spending a convivial evening with his friends. The doorkeepers, however, usually succeed in dissuading such parties from persevering to effect an entrance.

Easter season is also observed in the colony, where Good Friday is one of the very few recognized holidays of the year. At St. Boniface, and by the whole French population, the weeks of Lent are observed with punctuality, and religious services of a nature special to the occasion are usually attended by crowded houses. Of late years the Anglican churches have also been opened for special services during Lent, and the attendance has given satisfactory proof of their popularity.

Although the route by St. Paul is now the recognized channel by which goods intended for use in the colony are imported, the facilities offered to the officers and servants of the Company for importing articles for their private use by way of York Factory are so considerable as to render the latter route preferred by the parties in question. The annual supply of "Private Orders" therefore arrives toward the beginning of October, and their receipt marks quite an epoch in the year. The orders for shipment have to be made out and forwarded to Europe early in spring as the ship leaves England at the beginning of June in order to reach Hudson Bay *viâ* Stromness some time in August. Amusing anecdotes are current in the country relative to mistakes made by men unaccustomed to the work of ordering supplies from home. One French gentleman desirous to possess a swimming belt, most properly wrote for a life-preserver, and his astonishment was described as great when on receipt of his box he extracted therefrom an instrument composed of leather and lead, the use of which he could not without assistance imagine. Another veteran officer, whose knowledge of English spelling was defective, puzzled himself for years in trying to guess why his agent persisted in forwarding him a fine new clock. He certainly succeeded in selling all the articles at a profit, but his curiosity to ascertain the motive of the consignments led him to consult a friend who discovered the mistake to have risen from faulty spelling on the part of the consignee, the article really desired by the latter being a new cloak for his wife.

With regard to orders on a large scale I have heard of a very ludicrous mistake having been made by the Governor-in-Chief, Sir George Simpson. That gentleman during the later years of his administration finding his eyesight weakening transacted most of his reading and writing business through a secretary. One day a clerk in his office was reading over to him an indent or order for goods requested for a very remote post in the Southern Department, when he came to the item "20 metal kettles" of the large kind used for rendering whale oil at the posts in East Main where the whale fishery is carried on. Moved by a consideration of the difficulties attending the transport of heavy articles in the remote regions whose supplies he was considering, or by some other reason to me unknown, Sir George remarked to his assistant "Put a nothing to that, boy," meaning to disallow the item. The man did as he imagined he had been ordered, and thought no more about the matter, nor was the attention of any one at Lachine further called to it until about eighteen months afterwards, when Sir George was advised by the gentleman in charge of the post for which the articles had been required that, in consequence of some misunderstanding, the grounds of which his correspondent was unable to explain, a consignment of two hundred large kettles in lieu of twenty of the same kind requested as per indent, had been received in good order and condition, though after the expenditure of considerable trouble in the way of transport.

The only annual occurrences of much public interest in the settlement other than those already alluded to are, I think, the spring and autumn goose hunts. The former occurs in April, when the birds are on their way to their breeding grounds in the north, and the latter in September when they are emigrating southwards to their winter quarters about the Gulf of Mexico. The autumnal hunt, which occurs after the heats of the long summer have passed away and the weather has become cool, is the most enjoyable. Many families leave the settlement and go off a distance of sixty or eighty miles to the neighbouring lakes to live for a few weeks a camp life in the open air. The geese which fly with almost incredible speed and at great height come down to drink from the lakes and rivers, on the shore of which the hunters are encamped, and are despatched by the latter in great numbers. They also form a welcome addition to the fare of the Indian hunters, who watch for their periodical returns with the anxiety of interested men.

The Battle at the Grand Coteau, July 13 and 14, 1851[1]

W. L. Morton

On July 12, 1851, a small band of Métis buffalo hunters from Saint François-Xavier on the Assiniboine River in the Red River Settlement encountered and (on July 13 and 14) fought and defeated some hundreds of Sioux warriors on the first slope of the Grand Coteau of the Missouri southeast of Minot in what is now North Dakota. This was the most formidable, as it was the last, of the encounters between the buffalo hunters of Red River and the Sioux of the American plains.

It is the purpose of this paper to assemble the surviving accounts of the fight and to narrate how this action came to be fought and in what manner it was fought.[2]

SOURCE: *Papers Read Before the Historical and Scientific Society of Manitoba*, series III, no. 16 (1961), pp. 37-49. Reprinted by permission of the author and the Manitoba Historical Society.

[1] As there is some doubt as to the year of the fight, I am glad to be able to say that there was, as Rev. L. F. R. Laflèche reported, an eclipse of the moon on the night of July 12-13, 1851.

[2] The surviving accounts, so far as they are known to the author and to Mrs. A. N. MacLeod, are as follows:

1. A letter from Rev. L. F. R. Laflèche, dated September 4, 1851, and published by Arthur Savaete *Vers L'abîme* (Paris, n.d.), pp. 182-84.
2. A letter of Father Albert Lacombe, O.M.I., dated March 11, 1852, and published in *L'Echo de Saint-Justin*, X (10), August, 1931.
3. To this, on pp. 193-201 of *Vers L'abîme* is a supplementary account "based on the knowledge of" Abbé Georges Dugas.
4. A passage in the "Journal of Rudolph Friederich Kurz" published in Bulletin 115, Bureau of Ethnology, Smithsonian Institute, pp. 191-92.
5. A letter from Father Lacombe, dated January 1852, published in *Les Cloches de Saint-Boniface*, 1917, p. 61.
6. Francois-Xavier Falcon's account of a battle, seemingly that of 1851, but said to have taken place in 1853. This was written in 1940.
7. The account of Abbé Georges Dugas in his *Histoire de l'ouest canadien* (Montreal, 1906), pp. 119-30. Dugas does not give his sources, but his abundance of vivid detail makes it clear he had talked to those who had been present.
8. A. S. Morice, *Dictionnaire historique des Canadien métis* (Québec, 1908).

These will be referred to hereafter as:

Laflèche, Lacombe 1, Lacombe 2, Dugas 1 (L'histoire etc.), Dugas 2, Kurz, Falcon.

First, however, it is to be noted that the fight at the Grand Coteau is also the most remarkable military feat of the "new nation" of the Métis and exhibits the peculiar tactics of their plains fighting at their highest development. To tell the story of the battle is therefore to comment on the whole military history of the Métis from the "fur trade war" on the Assiniboine and the Red from 1815 to 1817 to their defeat by the Canadian militia at Batoche in 1885.

The Métis of Red River was a hunter and a trapper, a fisherman, a *voyageur*, by boat or cart brigade, even perforce a farmer – but above all, he was a horseman and a buffalo hunter. The buffalo hunt was his most characteristic occupation. As an occupation, particularly in the great summer hunt, it was highly organized and disciplined.[3] On the hunt, the Métis was a "soldier." He called himself so, thought of himself so, and in his own manner so behaved. As has been often recounted, the hunt was organized, at rendezvous at Pembina or along the Pembina valley, before moving out on to the plains, by the election of a captain, or president of the hunt, of a council made up of ten captains, and by the choice by each captain of ten soldiers.[4] The captain of the hunt had complete authority on the march or in the hunt. Each of the captains acted in rotation as what might be called "officer of the day," and, with his men, policed the camp that day. All matters of regulation and discipline were settled in the council of the hunt, and a serious offence, such as running the buffalo alone or betraying the presence of the camp to the Sioux, might be punished by being turned loose on the plains without horse or bridle, a possible death sentence. Scouting for the Sioux and for buffalo, the conduct of the march, the making of camp, the approach to the herds, and the running of the buffalo were all carried out as an inbred drill, from which no serious departure was allowed, by a people naturally reckless and impatient of any restraint.

The discipline and conduct of the great hunt on the buffalo plains of the Sioux was the first thing that made the Métis a "soldier." But the first generation of the Métis had also been taught to think of themselves as soldiers, and the teaching had pleased them. When the partners of the North-West Company

---

[3] See, for example, the admiring account in Isaac Cowie, *The Company of Adventurers* (Toronto, 1913), pp. 324-25.

[4] The two best accounts are in Alexander Ross, *The Red River Settlement* (London, 1857), pp. 241-63, and in Henri de Trémaudan, *La Nation Métisse* (Winnipeg, 1935), pp. 438-39, an account by Louis Riel.

decided in 1814 that Selkirk's colonists must be harried out of
Red River, they turned to the Métis as their instrument. They
had long used them, or their fathers, as bullies to harrass rival
traders. But to destroy the Selkirk colony was a bigger operation. The war of 1812, in which the Nor'Westers had recap-
tured Michilimackinac and the Wisconsin country as far as
the Mississippi, gave them military ideas, some spare military
uniforms and equipment, and the chance to pose as military
officers themselves.

There followed Duncan Cameron's parading as a uni-
formed officer in Red River in the spring of 1815, and the
deliberate harrying of the colonists until those who had not
agreed to go to Canada were forced to leave. When Colin
Robertson restored the colony that fall, the reply of the
Nor'Westers was to proclaim Cuthbert Grant, the educated
halfbreed son of a Nor'West *bourgeois* as "Captain-General of
all the halfbreeds of the northwest." Young Métis were collected at Fort L'Esperance on the Qu'Appelle under Grant in
the spring of 1816. After the capture of the Hudson's Bay
Company's pemmican on the Qu'Appelle, Grant led his men
in two bands under two "captains" to the capture of Brandon
House and the collision with Governor Robert Semple and his
men at Seven Oaks.[5] The whole operation was conducted
roughly on military lines, and the Métis acted at Seven Oaks
in two bands, one of which fought like the militia of New
France, firing from the shelter of their ponies and throwing
themselves on the ground to re-load,[6] and the other from horseback, runing the fleeing colonists like buffalo.

Even more striking, perhaps, in their military character
were Grant's operations against Fort Douglas after its recap-
ture by Miles Macdonell and the de Meurons in the winter of
1817. Twice Grant led expeditions down the Assiniboine, the
first to try to force Macdonell to surrender the fort, the second
to await at the "passage" of the Assiniboine the coming of the
North-West partners.[7] But the Canadian fathers of Métis sons

[5] Authoritative accounts are to be found in Chester Martin, *Lord
Selkirk's Work in Canada* (Oxford, 1916), pp. 70-89 and in A. S.
Morton, *A History of the Canadian West to 1870-71* (Toronto,
[1939]), pp. 569-78. A more detailed study of the collision at Seven
Oaks will appear in a forthcoming study of Cuthbert Grant by
Margaret Arnett MacLeod and the author. [See Margaret Arnett
MacLeod and W. L. Morton, *Cuthbert Grant of Grantown: Warden
of the Plains of Red River* (Toronto, 1963) — Swainson.]

[6] As their Canadian forebears did in the battle of the Heights of
Abraham; see C. P. Stacey, *Quebec, 1759* (Toronto, 1959), p. 147.

[7] *Public Archives of Manitoba*, Selkirk Papers, microfilm.

had heard of the Prince Regent's Proclamation ordering a cessation of the fighting, and were reluctant to have their boys join Grant. Grant accordingly had one of the young men court-martialled for failing to obey his summons. Heurter, the de Meuron sergeant who told the story, gives few details, but as an old soldier he would know a court-martial when he saw one.[8] One thinks at once of the Métis court-martial which tried and condemned Thomas Scott in 1870. Were there others in between those dates? It is to be presumed that the council of the hunt, in fact, acted as a court-martial to try infractions of the laws of the hunt, and punished offending "soldiers" as a military court and by what was, in some sense, a form of military law.

Thus the people who in 1869 and 1885 were to oppose in arms the annexation of the North West to Canada had by 1851 considerable of what may be called discipline and of what may even more properly be called military tactics. This nation in arms was the instrument Riel was to use to win provincial self-government for Red River in 1870 and which he was to try to use for some muddled version of the same in 1885.

In 1851, however, Canada had not yet looked beyond the lakes and the Pre-Cambrian plateau to the Red River valley and the prairies of the North West. The Métis were still pursuing their old occupation of the buffalo hunt and their hereditary feud, as sons of Cree and Saulteaux mothers, with the Sioux of the plains. From this pursuit of these established occupations came, in 1851, the fight at the Grand Coteau.

In June of that year, the Saint Boniface, or "main river" party accompanied by Father Albert Lacombe (going for the first time to the plains where he was to serve out his ministry) travelled south to a rendezvous with the Pembina party. From Pembina the combined parties set out west on June 16 to a rendezvous with the buffalo hunters of Saint François-Xavier. The parties numbered three hundred and eighteen hunters. With them were the able-bodied women, with children too small to be left in the settlement, for it was the women who cut up and dried the meat, made the buffalo-hide sacks and prepared the pemmican.[9] The total number of persons was thirteen hundred, with eleven hundred carts.[10]

[8] *Ibid.*
[9] Margaret Arnett MacLeod, "A Note on the Red River Hunt," *Canadian Historical Review* (June, 1957), pp. 129-30.
[10] Lacombe 1.

On June 15, the White Horse Plain party had left Saint François-Xavier, accompanied by its missionary, Rev. Louis François Richer Laflèche, grand vicar of Bishop Provencher and himself later to be famous as Bishop of Three Rivers. The party was small, numbering only two hundred carts and sixty-seven hunters, with an unknown number of women.[11] It was led not by the chief of the White Horse Plain settlement, Cuthbert Grant, but by a nephew of his, Jean Baptiste Falcon, a son of the bard of the Métis.[12]

It seems evident that the Métis of Saint Boniface and Pembina, and those of Saint François-Xavier, were acting independently of one another, as Hind says they were in 1852.[13] It may be conjectured that the cause of the separation was the rejection, by the Métis of Saint Boniface and Pembina, of the leadership of Cuthbert Grant of Saint François-Xavier in the troubles surrounding the Sayer trial of 1849.[14] But the parties had to plan mutual support in the event of attack by Sioux. It was known that the Sioux were planning to attack the hunt, and it was important therefore to give them no advantage.[15]

The rendezvous was kept safely on June 19. A general council was held, not only for the usual election of officers but also to discuss "the route the two 'camps' would have to follow to keep apart sufficiently from one another so as not to injure each other's hunt."[16] The decision was made to divide, but to move, as a single camp moved in parallel columns, along parallel routes at twenty to thirty miles from one another. The parties were to keep in touch and come to one another's help in the event of attack by the Sioux. There was an express agreement, clearly something novel, that no Sioux on whatever pretext would be allowed to enter either camp.[17]

After the council, both parties advanced out into the plains towards the southwest, veering off a little from the lands of the

[11] Laflèche; Dugas 1; Dugas 2.
[12] Falcon. It is usually said that the captain of the White Horse Plain camp was unknown, but Falcon's evidence is accepted here as probably true. It is certain that Cuthbert Grant was not present.
[13] H. Y. Hind, *The Red and Assiniboine Exploring Expedition, II*, pp. 179 and 283-84.
[14] See the author's *Introduction to the Letters of Eden Colville, 1849-1852* (Hudson's Bay Record Society, 1957), pp. lxxxii-lxxxvi.
[15] Dugas 2, p. 120.
[16] Lacombe 1.
[17] *Ibid*.; Dugas 1.

Sioux in doing so.[18] According to Father Lacombe, they travelled and hunted together, or in close proximity, for some days,[19] until perhaps June 28. When they did separate, it does not appear whether the White Horse Plain party was to the south or north of the main party. It would be natural to suppose that it would have taken the northern route, as the one less exposed to attack by the Sioux, and the rest of this narrative rests on that assumption, which admittedly could be erroneous. The main party did encounter some Sioux shortly after parting company, but according to the previous agreement with the small party, did not allow them into camp and chased them away.[20] The Saint François camp was warned at once.

For some days after that encounter, which must have taken place about June 30, the two parties travelled and hunted without incident. Their parallel routes must have now been towards the land between the headwaters of the Sheyenne River and the big bend of the Souris. The main party was travelling near the *Maison du chien*, or Dog Den Butte, a well known land mark on an outlying ridge of the Coteau de Missouri, which

[18] Lacombe 1. The movement of the two parties has been estimated as follows for this paper:

Saint François-Xavier Party leaves Saint François on June 15 and reaches rendezvous in four days, i.e. on June 19.

Saint Boniface and Pembina Parties leave Pembina on June 16 and goes to rendezvous.

That is, the first marches three days and the latter four.

Allowing a march of 15 miles a day, the parties would meet near the traditional rendezvous of Calf Mountain or Star Mound (Note that St. F. party was there first, i.e. the smaller party moved faster.)

A council was held here; perhaps also later. This would consume June 20, and perhaps another day later.

The three parties then travelled and hunted together for some days, but had been separated, it would seem, for two weeks before July 12.

Say, then, they hunted and travelled together June 22 to June 28.

Allowing an average day's march of 7½ miles, hunting and travelling, this would take them 60 miles southwest from Calf Mountain.

The St. F. party then separated from the two larger parties.

The larger party had travelled and hunted 14 days to reach a point near the Dog House. At 7½ miles a day, this would be 150 miles further, a total march of 280 miles from the present site of Winnipeg (by Pembina). The distance from Winnipeg to the region of the Dog House is 200 miles.

The St. F. party, not having gone by Pembina, would possibly be some miles farther west, having travelled 235 miles since June 15, not having gone by Pembina.

Thus the days and route of travel, so far as they are accounted for in the documents, roughly agree with the actual distance.

[19] *Ibid.*

[20] Dugas 1.

was commonly called the Grand Coteau. They were on the march on Sunday, July 13, by permission of Father Lacombe, in order that they might run, on Monday, some buffalo which had been reported to be near. While the camp was on the march, a small party of Sioux tried to cut off some stragglers.[21]

The evening before, Saturday, July 12, the Saint François camp reached a spot on the Grand Coteau of the Missouri which cannot now be determined precisely.[22] On the assumption made above, that it had followed a northern route, and assuming also that the two parties had kept roughly parallel after their separation, it would be twenty to thirty miles northwest of the Doghouse.

The scouts had just topped the first "buttes" and the party had just climbed to the top of the first terrace of the Coteau when they sighted a large camp of Indians. They at once signalled a warning to the carts below. Falcon promptly ordered camp to be made on a spot which could be easily defended and sent five hunters forward with a spy glass. These rode boldly and carelessly, Métis-fashion, to the top of the nearest high bluff.[23] There they saw that the camp was that of a very large band of Sioux (the number of warriors is estimated in the various accounts at from two thousand to twenty-five hundred).[24] These figures are no doubt greatly exaggerated, but serve to indicate how impressed all the Métis and their companions were by the size of the band.

The five scouts, having scorned concealment, now scorned any other precaution. They proceeded to ride towards the camp. At once a party of twenty Sioux rode out to meet them. When the two met, the Sioux surrounded the Métis and invited them to go to the camp in a way that left no doubt that they were considered prisoners. There seemed to be nothing for it but to go peacefully. But two Métis suddenly kicked their buffalo-

---

[21] Lacombe 1; E. Coues (ed.), *New Light on the Early History of the North West, I*, p. 406 — "At three o'clock we came to the ridge of high land, which runs from E. to W., and separates the waters between the Missourie and Rivière la Souris. This ridge adjoins the Dog's House, which we could plainly see about three leagues eastward — supposed to be the highest hill for many miles. It stands nearly due S. from the S. E. bend or elbow of Rivière la Souris, and may be seen at a considerable distance. We could also discern the banks of that river to the N. about five leagues distant; and had the weather been clear, doubtless we could have distinguished the Snake's Lodge, which bears S. about 20 leagues."

[22] Dugas 1.

[23] *Ibid.*

[24] Dugas and Lacombe say 2,000, Kurz about 2,500.

runners into a gallop, and broke away and escaped under fire back to the carts. Three – James Whiteford, one of the three McGillis boys in the party, and one Malaterre[25] – were held by the Sioux.

The Métis camp, when they saw the fugitives riding hard down the slope, sprang to arms. Falcon and Laflèche called the hunters together; with the boys of twelve years old, there were seventy-seven men who could handle a gun.[26]

The Sioux who had pursued the two Métis who escaped then approached the camp of the Métis and parleyed with some of them. They insisted that they had no warlike intentions and that the three captives would be freed on the morrow. They protested that they were hard up, and in need of help. They would come the next day with the prisoners and only a small party, in the hope of receiving some presents.[27]

With that they rode off, but Laflèche and the Métis were convinced that they were insincere and meant trouble. They therefore began to make ready to receive an attack, and, when three Sioux horsemen were seen approaching, they sent ten mounted men to meet them and keep them from observing the camp and its defences. The customary courtesies were exchanged, but the Sioux were kept at a distance and departed. The Métis were convinced that a surprise attack had been intended then, and that they had foiled it.[28]

The decision was now taken to fight without further parley, even if this meant, as they feared it did, that the three captives would be killed. It was thought better to sacrifice them and save the party than to risk all.[29] While they did not know how many Sioux they faced, they knew the camp was a very large one; it seemed to them unlikely, careless as the Métis customarily were of odds in conflict with the Sioux, that they would be able to beat off the attack of hundreds of the boldest fighters on the plains.

They therefore resolved to sell their lives dearly, and, if possible, to hold out until succor came from the main party. The carts were placed in a circle, wheel to wheel, with the shafts tilted in the air. The poles carried to make the frames on which the buffalo meat was dried were run through the

---

[25] Dugas says Malaterre, Falcon says Whiteford.
[26] Dugas 2.
[27] *Ibid.*
[28] Dugas 2.
[29] Dugas 1, p. 123.

spokes to make the carts immovable.[30] Packs, hides, saddles, and dried meat were piled between and under the carts to complete the barricade.[31]

The purpose of the barricade of carts was not to form shelter behind which the hunters would fight. It was meant to fence in the cart ponies and oxen, and to break up the charge of the Sioux horsemen.[32] The carts formed a corral but gave little protection against gunfire or arrows. For that purpose, trenches were dug under the carts, and here the women and children took shelter. But the men dug trenches, or rifle pits (here one meets the rifle pits of Batoche) out in front of the barricade. Their purpose was to hold the Sioux out of range of the carts and of the draft animals.[33] The women and children were reasonably safe in their trenches, but if the draft animals were killed, the party would perish on the plains without further attack by the Indians.

After darkness, two men were sent to carry the news of the threatened attack to the main party and to ask for help. The camp police kept an especial guard that night, but Laflèche and the hunters stayed up to watch the eclipse of the moon, of which he had warned them, spread its black shadow over the silver slopes of the Coteau.[34]

The next morning, Sunday, July 13, "having exhorted and confessed all those who presented themselves, Laflèche celebrated Mass and distributed the sacrament to all who desired to die well."[35]

When these final preparations were completed, the scouts were seen to signal that the Sioux were coming. When they appeared along the crest of the Coteau, it was not the few horsemen promised the night before, but an army, the whole manpower of the great Sioux camp, their war ponies of piebald and pinto and chestnut vivid on the skyline, their gun barrels and spear points glinting in the fierce sunlight of the plains.

At a signal the Sioux host halted. Was it possible they did not mean to attack? The Métis had held their buffalo-runners ready in the cart circle for a sally. Now thirty of the hunters rode out to accost the Sioux and warn them to keep their distance from the camp.[36]

[30] *Ibid.*
[31] Kurz.
[32] *Ibid.*
[33] Dugas 1, p. 123.
[34] Laflèche.
[35] Dugas 2.
[36] Dugas 1, pp. 123-4.

In the midst of the Sioux the three prisoners could be seen.
McGillis, on seeing the thirty approach the front of the Sioux,
suddenly kicked his horse into a gallop and escaped from the
startled Sioux, and joined the Métis band. Daring as was his
action, he was in terror and besought his friends not to laugh
at his being afraid. There were, he gasped, two thousand Sioux
who meant to attack them.[37] The Métis rode up, however, to
the advance guard of the Sioux, made them some presents and
requested them to go away.

The Sioux ignored both the presents and the request. They
could and would take all the camp had to yield, and brought
out some carts to haul away the booty. They began to push
forward. The Métis at once wheeled away and rode hard for
the camp. The Sioux tried to head them off, hoping to over-
whelm the camp by entering with the hunters in their retreat.
But they were too slow, and the hunters re-entered the cart
circle, left their horses, and ran for their rifle pits.[38]

The Sioux came charging in, hoping to brush aside the
flimsy barrier of the carts and break up at the circle. At their
head rode a young chief, "so beautiful," Falcon said in after
years, "that my heart revolted at the necessity of killing him."[39]
He shouted to the Sioux brave to turn away, but the Indian rode
on, the war cry ringing from his lips. Falcon shot him off his
horse, and the Métis hunters fired in volley. Here and there a
Sioux warrior whirled from his saddle and tumbled into the
grass; the others pulled their ponies around and galloped back
to the main body.

Inside the circle, Laflèche had donned his surplice with the
star at the neck and had taken his crucifix in his hand. His tall,
white figure passed around the carts as he encouraged the warriors and soothed the children. All through the fight he prayed
amid the fighting and exhorted his people from a cart rolled
into the centre of the circle, a prairie Joshua. He did not, he
told a friend later, take a gun himself, but he had a hatchet
handy, resolved that if the Sioux reached the carts he would
fight beside his Métis warriors.[40]

A brief pause followed the first charge, but was ended
almost at once. Whiteford and Malaterre were guarded by an
American living with the Sioux.[41] This man now told them to

[37] *Ibid.*, p. 124.
[38] All these details are from Dugas 1, pp. 124-5.
[39] Falcon.
[40] Dugas 1; Laflèche.
[41] Falcon says a Frenchman.

make a dash for it. He would, he said, only pretend to shoot at them. Whiteford suddenly put his horse, perhaps the best runner on the plains, to a run and rode, weaving and swaying through a poplar grove, down the slope towards the camp. Malaterre, knowing his horse was too poor to carry him clear, first shot at the nearest Sioux and actually hit three. He then rode for his life, but was soon brought down by a storm of balls and arrows. His body, bristling with shafts, was dismembered and mutilated, and his remnants waved at the Métis to terrify them. But Whiteford escaped unharmed; and with true Métis bravado, he checked his flight and shot down a pursuing Sioux. Then he was welcomed wildly within the cart circle, where he joined the defenders. His old mother, who had been weeping for a son she believed doomed, ran to him and said: "My son, if you are tired, give me your gun and go and get some sleep. Let me fire a shot at those rascals out there!"[42]

There was no time for sleep for anyone. The mass of the Sioux now closed in and surrounded the camp, as Laflêche wrote, like a waistband.[43] Indian-fashion, they did not charge in a body. They crept forward, sniping; they made sudden dashes; now and then, excited braves would come charging in on horseback and swerve off shooting from the saddle or under their horses' necks. It was exciting, it was dangerous, but it was not the one thing that might have brought victory to the Sioux, the overwhelming of the Métis by their numbers. The Métis were, therefore, able to hold them off from the cart circle, firing steadily as targets offered, themselves offering no target. Most of the Sioux bullets fell short of the cart circle; all their arrows did. Only occasionally did a horse rear, or an ox bellow as a shot went home. And up the sun-scorched slope, the Sioux began to feel the bite of the telling Métis fire. Warrior after warrior, "like choice game" writes Dugas, "was offered up with the sure hand of the priest practised at the sacrifice." Some of the stricken warriors turned over quietly in death, some leaped in their death throes, "strewing the yellow prairie with their heaving bodies."[44]

The fight was too hot for them. Indians, and even the warlike Sioux, would never suffer casualties as Europeans would. It was not a matter of courage, but of the conventions of warfare. In battle the Indian saw no merit in death, however brave. The Sioux now drew back to take account of the nature of the

[42] Dugas 1, p. 126.
[43] Laflêche.
[44] Dugas 2.

contest they had engaged in. Their shame grew as they viewed the small numbers of the Métis and the fragility of their defences. Their shame turned to anger. Whooping and yelling, the infuriated warriors charged in on their straining ponies, swerving, checking, striving always to kill or stampede the stock in the corral. But their fury produced no giving way. Laflèche still cheered his people from the cart in the corral. Falcon, steady, earnest, fired with his men, and moved among them to keep them steady. With him was his sister Isabella; when he went around the rifle pits, she took his gun and fired for him, not without effect.[45]

The second assault failed like the first, and still the Sioux had not used their numbers to make a mass charge and overrun the gun pits and the barricade of carts. Sullenly, the Sioux began to withdraw, one by one or in small groups. The more stubborn or more daring kept up a sniping fire and tentative sallies from time to time. But after six hours, all were wearied of the unrewarding battle. A chief was heard to cry: "The French have a Manitou with them. We shall never come to the end of them. It is impossible to kill them."[46] Such was the effect of Laflèche's courage. And, in fact, not a Métis had been killed in the action, although they had lost twelve horses and four oxen.[47] The Sioux had suffered losses they thought heavy, and now began to load their wounded into the carts they had brought to carry away the plunder of the Métis camp. They had also to regain their courage and replenish their ammunition.[48] A heavy thunderstorm completed their discomfiture, and it was followed by a mist which made it impossible to shoot.[49]

Moreover, their scouts, thrown out towards the main Métis body at the Doghouse, had brought in reports that had to be considered.[50] The two hunters sent on Saturday night had encountered the Sioux scouts and returned to camp. But two young Métis had panicked and fled from the camp towards the main party.[51] Would they bring the main party to the help of the besieged camp?

The Métis themselves had the same question foremost in their minds. But when the Sioux withdrew, the hunters rode out

[45] Falcon.
[46] Dugas 1, p. 127; Laflèche.
[47] Kurz; it is assumed they were lost on July 13 because better precautions were taken on July 14.
[48] Dugas 2.
[49] Lacombe.
[50] Dugas 2.
[51] Dugas 1, p. 128.

over the battle field, where they saw many traces of the hurt inflicted on the attackers. Eight Sioux had been killed and many wounded, as was shown by the blood-stained grass and the waters of two nearby ponds.[52] They also found the mutilated body of the unfortunate Malaterre pierced by three balls and sixty-seven arrows. They buried him there on the prairie.[53]

On the next day, July 14, the Sioux were expected to attack. A council was held and the decision was taken to try to join the main party as they had not withdrawn far. The Sioux kept raising the war whoop around the camp during the darkness of the night.[54]

It was a decision to retreat in the face of an enemy yet undefeated and in overwhelming numbers, one of the most dangerous operations of war. The Métis planned and executed it brilliantly. Four mounted parties were sent out a mile from the line of march, one ahead, one behind, and two on the flank towards the Sioux. They were to signal any approach of the Sioux by two scouts galloping past one another on a butte, the best known of all the plains signals of the buffalo hunters. The carts were to advance in four columns, so placed that by two columns wheeling quickly, one left and one right, a square could be formed rapidly. Then the cart corral could be formed, the barricade stiffened with the poles, and the hunters fan out for the fight.[55]

After an hour's march, the scouting party behind was seen to make the signal of two horsemen crossing on a butte. The Sioux, who had been shouting around the camp during the night, were in pursuit. At the signal, the columns halted and wheeled into position, the ponies and oxen were taken out of the shafts, and the carts were run into the circle. The Métis had learned even more vividly from the loss of stock they had suffered in the first day's fight the need to conceal their stock and hold the Sioux at a distance. The cart ring was now formed of two lines of carts, then, at three chains from the barricade of carts, the hunters hastened to throw up their rifle pits well out from the cart ring.[56]

The Sioux were perhaps less numerous and less fiery than

[52] Falcon.
[53] Dugas 1, p. 128.
[54] Ibid.
[55] Ibid.
[56] All details are from Dugas 1, p. 129, and show how he must have got them from an eye-witness who thoroughly appreciated the significance of every feature of the Métis defence.

the day before, but they closed in, none the less, on the cart corral, and pressed the attack for five full hours.[57] Once more Laflêche exhorted his people to remember their faith and their ancestry; once more Falcon and Isabella aided the Métis marksmen in the heat and dust and drifting smoke.

Finally the firing slackened, and the war cries died away. Once more a thunderstorm was rolling up over the Coteau.[58] A Sioux chief rode up, upraised palm out in the gesture of peace, and demanded to be allowed to enter the camp. He was told to leave quickly, if he did not wish to be left on the prairie. He replied with dignity, before retreating, that the Sioux had had enough, that they were going away; that, henceforth and forever, they would never again attack the Métis.

Then the whole war party, mounted and yelling a last defiance, war plumes flying and lances waving, put itself at a gallop, and charged in single file around the cart ring, firing a last tremendous volley of gun fire and arrows from the backs of their straining ponies. It was the heaviest volley of the two day battle.[59] Then the cloud of horsemen streamed over the shoulder of the Coteau and vanished. As they vanished the rain broke in torrents.

The weary Métis thought that they must have suffered losses from the tremendous discharge, but as the men ran in from the rifle pits, it was found that only three were wounded, and those but slightly. As they rejoiced, the first party of hunters from the main party, warned by the fugitives, came pounding over the prairie.[60] They had been despatched early that morning, fasting, by Father Lacombe.[61] The main body came up later.

With the three hundred and eighteen fresh hunters of the main party were as many Saulteaux warriors. With those of the White Horse Plain camp, they numbered seven hundred men, a force sufficient to scatter the enemy. The Sioux, it was known from their increasing use of arrows, were short of ammunition as well as discouraged by their defeat. Many of the hunters demanded that they should be pursued and chastized. But Laflêche and Lacombe, with the majority of the hunters, were against further fighting. Better to be merciful and complete the hunt was the decision.[62] The Métis resumed their hunt, but first

[57] *Ibid.*
[58] Lacombe.
[59] *Ibid.*, Dugas 1, p. 129.
[60] *Ibid.*
[61] Lacombe 1.
[62] *Ibid.*; Dugas 1.

they raised a tall pole on the plain with a letter to the Sioux. What was in the letter, no one has recorded.

In the whole adventure they had lost only the unhappy Malaterre and, in the two actions, not one man, woman, or child. They had lost, it is true, twelve horses and four oxen, but not enought to prevent them moving over the plains. The Sioux, it was reported later, had lost eighty men, besides many wounded and sixty-five horses.[63] By the standards of Indian warfare, this was a heavy defeat, and in fact it ended the long warfare of the Métis and the Sioux.[64]

The Métis, thereafter, were masters of the plains wherever they might choose to march. The action of the Grand Coteau showed that they could fight and move on the plains even in the face of superior numbers of Sioux, perhaps the most formidable warriors of all the North American plains tribes. Their conduct of the march of the cart brigade, their plains craft, their battle tactics, from the firing from the saddle to the use of the rifle pit, were brilliant by any standard of warfare. What wonder that the British officers who knew them spoke admiringly of their virtues as cavalry.[65] What wonder that veteran of Europe's wars, Captain Napoleon Gay, after his service with Riel in 1870, tried to train his volunteer cavalry in the Franco-Prussian war as Métis mounted riflemen![66]

The battle of the Grand Coteau was perhaps the proudest memory of the Métis nation.[67] It symbolized their highest achievement as a people. Nothing more conclusively proved their mastery of the plains by which they lived. It stands midway between the collision at Seven Oaks and the black day of Batoche, when the Canadian militia did what the Sioux had not, and overran the Métis rifle pits. And finally it demonstrates that the boundary of Canada and the United States was not a mere astronomical line, but a real boundary marked by the clash of peoples and cultures, the border of the park belt and the grassland, of the prairie and the plain, where the Métis of Red River continued the old feud of Cree and Saulteaux with the Sioux, and helped, in the blind and primitive working of history with geography, to prepare for the different histories in western North America of Canada and the United States.

[63] Kurz; Lacombe 2 says that only eighteen Sioux were killed. It is probable the Métis never really knew. To the Indian mind even eighteen was a heavy loss.

[64] Falcon; but not of the Sioux and the Saulteaux.

[65] See Cowie's reference, *Company of Adventurers*, p. 170.

[66] P.A.M., Riel Papers, Gay to Riel.

[67] See the account in Henri de Trémaudan, *La Nation Métisse* (Winnipeg, 1935), pp. 143-45.

John A. Macdonald, Confederation, and the Canadian West

Donald Creighton

Today, January 11, 1967, is the one hundred and fifty-second anniversary of the birth of John A. Macdonald; the centenary of Confederation is less than six months away; and in only three years from now the Province of Manitoba will be a hundred years old. It is appropriate for students of history to re-examine these major events of the past; and it is particularly important to do so at the present moment, for we are now confronted by a radically new interpretation of their meaning. Historians, of course, are always busy revising and modifying the accepted historical record; but I am not thinking of such minor changes in detail or emphasis.

The version of Confederation which has become current during the past few years is much more than this. It amounts, in fact, to a new theory of Canadian federalism, a theory which rests on the basic assumption that ethnic and cultural values are and ought to be recognized as fundamental in the life of the Canadian nation. The real essence of the Canadian federal union is thus the cultural duality of Canada. And Confederation becomes a compact between two cultures, two nations, English and French.

This interpretation, I have already suggested, is fairly new. The point deserves to be emphasized. In fact, the new version has been given expression mainly during the last six or, at most, the last ten years. Its increasing popularity among historians, writers, and journalists may, of course, be attributed in part to the interest in Canadian federalism which has been growing steadily as the centenary of Confederation approached. But though the centennial would naturally have revived an interest in Confederation, it would not necessarily have inspired a radical new interpretation of it. The real origins of the new theory are political; they lie in the rapid rise of French-Cana-

SOURCE: *Historical and Scientific Society of Manitoba Transactions*, series III, no. 23 (1966-67), pp. 5-13. Reprinted by permission of the author and the Manitoba Historical Society.

dian nationalism which has come about since Jean Lesage in 1960 assumed power in Quebec. For the last half-dozen years a group of politicians, lawyers, historians, and journalists, mainly French-Canadian but with some English-Canadian associates, have been disseminating a radically new view of Confederation and of French Canada's place in it. Their aims are varied and in some degree contradictory. On the one hand, they have tried to improve the status and enlarge the rights of French Canadians in the nation as a whole; on the other, they have sought to emphasize the separateness and strengthen the autonomy of the Province of Quebec. At one and the same time they seem to believe in a bilingual, bicultural, but united Canada, and a virtually independent Quebec, which, if it decides to remain in confederation at all, will have to be given a "special position" and may even become an "associate state."

Obviously, the realization of either or both these aims would mean a revolution in the present structure of Confederation. But Confederation, embodied in the law and custom of the constitution, is an inheritance from the past; and inevitably therefore, the French-Canadian nationalists and their English-Canadian associates have had to cope with the intractable problem of history. Like everybody who desires social and political change, or is merely interested in its possibility, they had to make up their minds about the past. Revolutionaries have realized this necessity long ago, and they have evolved two different and indeed quite contradictory methods of coming to terms with history. The "quiet revolutionaries" of Quebec appropriated both. The first method is to dismiss the past as irrelevant and meaningless for the present; the second is to identify the past with the revolutionary aims of the present. In other words, history can be rejected as a useless obstacle to the revolutionary programme; or it can be re-interpreted to provide a justification for it.

The case for the dismissal of the past is not our business tonight. But the historical re-interpretation of Confederation which the Quebec nationalists have been so persistently offering for the last six years is certainly worth examining. This is an historical society, and I am an historian; and we are – or should be – interested in the use, or misuse, of history. Revolutionary re-interpretations of the past usually have a purpose. In this case, the object of the "quiet revolutionaries" was to back up a political programme with a new theory of federalism. The old view of confederation as a political union of several provinces must be broken down and discredited; and the conception of

Canada as a cultural duality, as a partnership of two different cultures or "nations," must be established in its place. The fiction of duality was to be substituted for the fact of plurality. The true meaning of confederation, the French-Canadian nationalists argued, has been misunderstood and its essential spirit forgotten. Only on the surface can it be regarded as an agreement among several provinces; in reality it was a compact between the two cultures, the two nations, English and French, of Canada.

There is very little aid or comfort for the believers of this theory in what we know of the aims and intentions of the Fathers of Confederation. There is no support for it at all in the lean, spare phrases of the Quebec resolutions or the British North America Act. It is obvious that the last thing the Fathers of Confederation wanted to do was to perpetuate duality; they hoped, through confederation, to escape from it forever. They had seen enough, and more than enough, of duality in the old province of Canada. There it had paralyzed governments and prevented progress for a quarter of a century. The new Dominion of Canada was to be organized, as the arrangements for the Senate make quite clear, not as a duality but as a triumvirate of three divisions: Quebec, Ontario, and Atlantic provinces as a group. The distinctive cultural features of French Canada – its language, civil code, and educational system – were confirmed in those parts of Canada in which they had already become established by law or custom. But that was all. They were not extended in their application to Ontario or to the Maritime provinces. There was nothing in the Quebec Resolutions or the British North America Act which remotely approached a general declaration of principle that Canada was to be a bilingual or bicultural nation.

The evidence against the two-nation theory of Confederation is so overwhelming that some of its advocates have been driven back upon a secondary line of defence. The bicultural compact, they admit, was only a "tacit" or "implicit" agreement, or a "moral" commitment, when the British North America Act was framed. But later, when Canada expanded westward and the Hudson's Bay Company territories were taken over, the Fathers of Confederation honoured the moral commitments and took care to provide that the new western domain should become the joint possession, on equal terms, of both English and French-speaking Canadians. The first Conservative government after confederation established Separate Schools and gave legal status to the French language in Manitoba. The first Liberal government after confederation did exactly the same for the North-West Territories. It was a basic national policy, deliberately adopted, carefully carried out, concurred in by both parties.

This, in short, is the theory of confederation as a bicultural compact applied to Manitoba and the North-West Territories. What is its truth when tested by the actual events of the time? This is the problem which I should like to examine with you tonight.

II

John A. Macdonald was, above everything else, a nation builder. The union of the original British North American colonies was the first of his two greatest achievements; the expansion and integration of the new Dominion on a continental scale was the second. He was an expansionist; but he was also a realist. His purpose was to ensure that Canada would not be despoiled of her great territorial inheritance on the North American continent; he was absolutely determined that, as he himself put it, "the United States should not get behind us by right or by force and intercept the route to the Pacific." In his mind there was no doubt about Canada's ultimate destiny; but at the same time he was equally convinced that Canada should assume its great heritage slowly and prudently, a step at a time, by one firm stage after another. Even as late as March, 1865, he would have preferred to see Rupert's Land and the North-West Territories remain a crown colony under imperial control. He soon realized, however, that the march of events could not be so deliberate as he had hoped. Great Britain's urge to withdraw from her North American commitments, the British government's desire that Canada should take over its responsibilities in the North-West, and the threat of American northward expansion all helped to convince him that there could be no more delay. In the spring of 1869, the bargain with the Hudson's Bay Company was finally concluded and Canada prepared to assume the assets and liabilities of its new western Dominion.

At this point it should be emphasized that Macdonald was still trying to hold fast, as far as he was able, to his original policy respecting the North-West. He had been compelled, far earlier than he had wanted to, to assume responsibility for Rupert's Land and the Territories; but he knew very well that the problem of their government and future development was a difficult one, and he had no intention of risking a hasty solution to it. The bill which he introduced in the Canadian House of Commons late in May, 1869, was characteristically entitled "For the Temporary Government of Rupert's Land." It deserves far more attention than it has yet received. It is the only document that embodies the Conservative cabinet's original policy respecting the North-West; it expresses Macdonald's original intentions, his first tentative provisional plans. And it is obvious from its few brief clauses that he was trying to keep as closely as possible to the idea of a Crown colony, the idea which he had proposed as little as four years before. The North-West was to be governed not as a province but as a territory, by a lieutenant-governor and a small nominated council. The existing laws were to continue until altered; the public officers were to retain their posts until it was ordered otherwise. Nothing was to be changed in a hurry. Nothing new was to be introduced at once. There was no mention of either schools or languages.

Now it is usually assumed that this whole provincial plan of government was invalidated by the Red River Rising of 1869-70. It is also usually taken for granted — even less justifiably, it seems to me — that the Manitoba Act of 1870 was the only natural result, the logical and inevitable constitutional consequence of the rising. Both those assumptions, I am convinced, badly need a critical examination; and the examination ought to begin by making a clear distinction between the Red River community on the one hand and the military dictatorship of Louis Riel on the other. There is no doubt whatever about the kind of government which the Red River community would have liked to see established in the North-West. Their wishes were democratically determined in the debates of the Convention which met at Fort Garry in mid-winter 1870; and the results were embodied in the resolutions of the second "List of Rights." If this second list — the one document in which the constitutional preferences of the whole Red River community are faithfully recorded — had formed the basis of the negotiations at Ottawa, the Manitoba Act of 1870 would have been a very different statute. The Convention, against the opposition and to the intense indignation of Riel, decided against provincial status, at least for the time being. It requested equality for the English and French languages in the legislature and the courts; but it made no mention of separate or confessional schools. If the wishes of the Convention and the terms of the second "List of Rights" had been followed in drafting the Manitoba Act, there would have been no very serious departure from Macdonald's *Act for the Temporary Government of Rupert's Land* of the previous year.

But this moderate and sensible constitutional settlement was not to be. Riel was determined to prevent it. An adroit and ruthless dictator, he had no intention of permitting democracy to have its own way at Red River. His terms for the union with Canada had been openly and emphatically rejected by the Convention; but at the same time, as a final reluctant concession in the interest of political conciliation in the Settlement, the Convention had confirmed the provisional government and elected Riel as its president. At once and with purposeful energy he took over control of the negotiations with Canada. He quickly nominated Ritchot and Alfred Scott, who, he felt confident, would support his own private plans for the future of the North-West; and he persuaded the reluctant Convention to accept them as two of the three emissaries to the Canadian government. He then proceeded to make short work of the Convention's "List of Rights." The wishes of the Red River community, where they differed from his claims for his own people, the Métis, meant nothing whatever to him. In two quite new and increasingly detailed "Lists of Rights," drawn up in private by Riel and his lay and clerical advisers, the delegates sent to Ottawa were instructed to insist that the North-West should enter Confederation, not as a Territory, but as a Province. It must have, they demanded, an elaborate provincial constitution with an absurdly top-heavy bi-cameral legislature, including a little senate on the model of Quebec. It must also have a system of sectarian or confessional schools, again on the Quebec model. This, if you like, was a demand that biculturalism should prevail on the prairies, and that French and English institutions should be combined in the government of the North-West; but it was neither a demand that was made by the community at Red River nor a plan proposed by the government of Ottawa. It was a claim exacted by Riel's dictatorship.

Why did Macdonald accept it? Why did he consent to impose such an elaborate constitution upon such an immature colony? How was he persuaded to settle all the basic institutions of a community which had not had time to develop its real and permanent character? The answers to these questions can never be absolutely certain, for the conclusive evidence is lacking; but the probabilities, at all events, are very clear. The pressures in favour of a quick settlement in the North-West were inescapable and compelling. Macdonald's foremost aim was to ensure, at almost any cost, Canada's continental destiny, her unobstructed expansion from the Atlantic to the Pacific Ocean. His greatest fear was that the United States, by deliberate policy or tragic accident, might prevent the achievement of these natural limits. He knew only too well that the acrimonious disputes which had arisen between Great Britain and the United States during the American Civil War had not yet been settled. There was evidence that both President Grant and Secretary of State Hamilton Fish were annexationists, prepared to use any method short of war to acquire all or part of British America. And finally it was clear from the beginning, that the American expansionists at St. Paul Minnesota – the "Yankee Wire-pullers," Macdonald called them – were eager to exploit the rising at Red River, and that American citizens in the settlement were deep in Riel's councils. So long as the provisional government continued, so long as the future of the British American North-West remained uncertain and confederation was still incomplete, the threat of American intervention hung over Canada's future.

A quick settlement was urgently necessary. And its character by this time was fixed and virtually unalterable. Appeasement on any terms meant in fact appeasement on the terms demanded by the fanatical emissaries from Red River, backed up by Cartier and his French Canadian "Bleu" followers, and supported by Sir Clinton Murdoch of the British Colonial Office. It is true, of course, that the Canadian government refused to yield to Riel's vainglorious and incredible demand that the entire North-West enter Confederation as a single province; and it is also true that the request for provincial control of public lands was likewise rejected. Macdonald could limit boundaries and withhold lands, but within the restricted area of the new Province of Manitoba he had to accept a bilingual and bicultural system of rights and institutions. "The French," Sir Stafford Northcote observed, "are earnestly bent upon the establishment of a French and Catholic power in the North-West to counteract the great preponderance of Ontario." Their purpose was to fix the character and institutions of the new province at a time when French-speaking Roman Catholics formed a large part of its population, and therefore at the most favourable moment for preparing defences against the approaching influx of Protestant, English-speaking settlers.

III

The Manitoba Act did not represent the carrying-out of a solemn commitment to biculturalism which had been made at

Confederation. It was not drafted in fulfilment of an ideal conception of what Canada should be; it was, to a very large extent, imposed simply by the force of circumstance. In 1869-70, a particular set of circumstances, including some very frightening external circumstances, had practically dictated a hasty policy of appeasement. But these circumstances were exceptional and transitory; they did not reappear in quite the same powerful constitution; and as a result the main argument in favour of biculturalism lost most of its force. This would not have mattered, of course, if the Fathers of Confederation had really felt morally committed to the ideal of a bilingual and bicultural Canada, to the conception of two nations in the Canadian national state. But the simple truth is that they did not. The French language and French-Canadian institutions had not been given legal status in any province of the original union outside Quebec; and no attempt had been made to establish the equality of the two cultures in any of the provinces that entered Confederation after Manitoba. The Manitoba Act did not lay down a national bicultural pattern which was solemnly confirmed and carefully followed thereafter. When British Columbia and Prince Edward Island joined the union, nobody so much as mentioned the great moral commitment to biculturalism.

The exception to this consistent record is, of course, the North-West Territories. And it is a very dubious exception which effectively proves the rule. It was not until the session of 1875, nearly five years after this passage of the Manitoba Act, that the Parliament of Canada finally got around to setting up a system of organized government in the western territory beyond the new province of Manitoba. The main feature of the North-West Territories bill, which the new Prime Minister Alexander Mackenzie introduced in the Commons, was a rather complicated set of clauses providing for the gradual introduction of elected members in the North-West Council as the population of the region increased. The bill contained no reference to separate or confessional schools, and no provision for the French language. If this silence could have been made to appear as a betrayal of a recognized bicultural compact, it is obvious that the Conservative opposition, in which several of the Fathers of Confederation were sitting, would have been quick to grasp the opportunity of so doing. But the Conservative members sat silent. And it was left to Edward Blake, who was not a Father of Confederation, and knew nothing whatever at first hand of its purposes or principles, to move, in amendment, that separate or confessional schools should be established in the territories.

Why did Blake take up the cause of what he called "religious instruction" in the North-West? On the record, there was no reason to expect him to show any particular sympathy for the Roman Catholic Métis of the prairies; on the contrary, he was thought to share the critical views of *Canada First* and its representatives at Red River, Mair and Schultz. In 1871, when he had been leader of the opposition in the Ontario legislature, Blake had moved a resolution demanding that the "murderer" Riel should be brought to justice; and in the following year, after he had formed the first Liberal government in Ontario, he introduced a similar resolution offering a five thousand dollar reward for the arrest and conviction of the "murderers" of Thomas Scott. Undoubtedly he had gained a good deal of political capital from these astute moves; and political capital may well have been what he was after in the session of 1875. He was not a member of Mackenzie's government; he had been angling deviously for Mackenzie's post as Prime Minister; he was critical of Mackenzie's policies and determined to block his railway bill; and he was embarrassing him at every turn.

It was in this curious way, and with this unexpected sponsorship, that separate schools found their way into the *North-West Territories Act* of 1875. The grant of legal status to the French language, which was made when the statute was amended in 1877, came about in an even stranger and more accidental fashion. It was not a government amendment at all; it was proposed by a private member in the Senate. And the speech with which David Mills, the Minister of the Interior, greeted this amendment when it was brought down to the Commons effectively destroys the odd notion that the promotion of biculturalism on the prairies was the settled policy of Liberal as well as Conservative governments. Mills reminded the members that the dominant language of the region was Cree; he thought the North-West council was the only body that could properly settle the question of official languages. He regretted the Senate amendment; and he reluctantly accepted it because otherwise it would be impossible to get the revised statute through Parliament before the end of the session.

We are now in a position, it seems to me, to come to certain conclusions. The bicultural compact theory of Confederation as applied to Manitoba and the North-West Territories cannot be sustained. The idea of a solemn commitment to biculturalism, accepted in principle and deliberately implemented by both parties, is simply not borne out by the facts. The west did not get its institutions in accordance with the provisions of some long-range plan; on the contrary, the process was characterized throughout by accident and improvisation. The pressure of circumstances, the influence of certain powerful political interests, and the ambition of a few key personalities, all combined to force a series of hasty and ill-considered decisions; and the result was the abandonment of Macdonald's plan for the gradual development of government in the North-West and the premature establishment of an elaborate and cumbrous constitution. This attempt to fix the political institutions of the west before immigration and the growth of population had determined its true and permanent character was a mistake for which the whole of Canada paid dearly. By 1890 — only twenty years after the Manitoba Act and fifteen years after the North-West Territories Act — the West had outgrown the inappropriate constitution that had been imposed upon it. It began suddenly and uncompromisingly to change the status of the French language and the character of its schools. The violent controversy that followed lasted for more than a quarter of a century; and it ended in the virtual extinction of biculturalism in the Canadian West.

This is an episode in our history which should not be forgotten. We should all remember it when we come to read the forthcoming report of the Royal Commission on Bilingualism and Biculturalism. The commission may possibly recommend constitutional changes designed to improve the position of the French language and of French-Canadian culture throughout the nation, including the West. These proposals should be judged critically in the light of history; and with the aid of the same clear light, westerners should examine the historical theory by which these proposals will probably be justified. The idea of a bicultural compact, of the two-nation state, has got much of its currency and its vogue during a period of profound revolution in Quebec; and this very fact ought to make it suspect. New historical interpretations which make their appearance in revolutionary times are usually the result, not of the search for truth, but of the need for historical justification. They are invented — or partly invented — to supply historical authority for a program of radical changes. Canadians on the whole are badly equipped to protect themselves against this kind of propaganda. For they are not as historically minded as the English, and, unlike the Americans, they have not been brought up in a thorough knowledge of their own history. They cling to old myths, and are easily sold new and spurious inventions. It would be a tragedy if, at this most critical period of their history, they were led to damage their future irretrievably through a serious misunderstanding of their past.

Big Bear, Indian Patriot

W. B. Fraser

On April 2, 1885, at Frog Lake, one hundred and twenty-five miles east of Edmonton, Indian Agent Thomas Trueman Quinn and eight other white men were killed by a group of Indians belonging to Big Bear's band of Plains Cree. Word quickly spread that the chief, long considered by many government officials to be the most troublesome Indian leader on the Canadian prairies, had led his people onto the warpath in support of Louis Riel's ill-conceived rebellion. For years, this view was so widely held that even W. B. Cameron, a surviving witness to the events involving the Big Bear band, and one of the chief's few contemporary defenders, found it convenient to capitalize on the popular prejudice and publish his personal account of the troubles under the title *The War Trail of Big Bear*. More recently, however, the trend has been to portray the Cree chief as a simple old man, an innocent victim of events he neither understood nor influenced. Neither portrait does him justice.

In spite of long-held misconceptions, the clatter of rifle fire that accompanied the Frog Lake massacre proclaimed the end, not the beginning, of Big Bear's resistance to the white man. Even as the old chief rushed forward shouting at his young men to stop their bloody work, he must have realized that his ten-year struggle to prevent the complete subjugation of his people had been in vain.

Maybe he had even foreseen the violent finale. Once, some years earlier, when camped on the Missouri, Big Bear's sleep had been troubled by an ugly dream. He saw a spring of water spout up through the ground and, when he tried to stop the flow with his hands, the water turned to blood and spouted through his fingers. On April 2, 1885, the dream had come true; once again the chief was unable to stop the flow of blood.

Big Bear never planned armed resistance to the whites. Whatever he was, the Cree chief was no fool. He was not ignor-

SOURCE: *Alberta Historical Review*, vol. 14, no. 2 (Spring, 1966), pp. 1-13. Reprinted by permission of the author and the Publishers.

ant of the power of the white man and he knew that the Indian had everything to lose and nothing to gain by fighting. Unlike Louis Riel, he was neither fanatic nor mystic. Unlike Gabriel Dumont, he was no hot-head.

What and who, then, was Big Bear? What made Indian Commissioner Edgar Dewdney call him the most influential Indian on the plains? Was it accurate to elevate him to such lofty rank when his contemporaries included men like Crowfoot, Red Crow, Piapot, and Poundmaker? W. B. Cameron observed that

Big Bear had great natural gifts: courage, a keen intellect, a fine sense of humour, quick perception, splendid native powers of expression and great strength of purpose. . . . Big Bear was imperious, outspoken, fearless[1]

Indian Commissioner Dewdney reported:

I have not formed such a poor opinion of Big Bear, as some appear to have done. He is of a very independent character, self-reliant, and appears to know how to make his own living without begging from the Government.[2]

Neither of these men had reason to err in Big Bear's favour. Cameron suffered much at the hands of the chief's followers, and Dewdney was charged with the responsibility of carrying out a policy that Big Bear was attempting to frustrate.

In neither appearance nor in dress did Big Bear personify the "noble savage." From photographs and descriptions come the picture of a man short of stature with a homely but strong face. He affected none of the foppish styles of dress popular among the Plains Indians of the day. To the contrary he appears to have shown such a lack of concern for appearance as to be untidy. Certainly he felt no need to trust his reputation to superficial appearance. And in his case his people seem to have agreed.

Little is known about Big Bear's early years. He was born sometime around 1825, probably in the vicinity of Fort Carlton. At least he was trading into that fort when he first came to public attention. There is even some doubt as to his tribal origin. Once, Rev. George McDougall referred to him as a Saulteaux

---

[1] W. B. Cameron, *The War Trail of Big Bear* (1927), pp. 243-44.

[2] Report, Department of Indian Affairs, *Sessional Papers of Canada, 1889*, p. 77.

and, although all other accounts identify him as a Cree, there may have been some justification for the missionary's allegation. There was a strong Saulteaux mixture in all the Cree bands along the North Saskatchewan.

Nevertheless, when Big Bear comes to the attention of the historian, he was identified with the River People, a tribal division of the Plains Cree which wintered along the North Saskatchewan from the Elbow west to the Vermilion River. In the summer some bands of River Cree, known as Prairie People, ranged as far south as the Cypress Hills, mingling with the Lower Plains Cree and Young Dogs (Cree-Assiniboines also known sometimes as Prairie People). The most westerly bands frequently hunted with the Beaver Hills Cree southeast of Fort Edmonton.

Prior to the early 1860s, Big Bear and his family wintered at Jackfish Lake, north of the present city of Battleford, and traded into Fort Carlton. Even then the Cree recognized him as one of their leading head men and in the large gatherings on the plains he was sometimes accepted by several bands as head chief over the entire camp. Then, around 1865, Big Bear moved west and began trading into Fort Pitt. There he headed a small band of his relatives with a permanent following of somewhere around one hundred souls and began to become increasingly important as a Plains Cree leader.

At the time Big Bear moved west, the Fort Pitt Plains Cree apparently divided into two broad groups. One centred on Sweetgrass, a chief recognized by the Hudson's Bay Company, while the other gathered around the independent leaders whose influence was strongest in the large camps far out on the plains. These were the Prairie People. The fact that Big Bear was never recognized as a chief by the Hudson's Bay Company indicates his position of independence. From the start he was no Company lackey. This did not mean that he was antagonistic to the men of the Company; in fact, when members of his band started killing Company cattle during a famine in 1872, he put a stop to it.[3]

Not only was Big Bear reluctant to concede any authority to the Company or other white men, he also refused to stand in awe of the Métis. An example of this occurred in a mixed Métis-Indian camp in 1873 when Big Bear and some of his followers clashed with Gabriel Dumont and his uncle over their enforcement of the hunt laws. The Cree chief disputed the Dumonts'

[3] Edmonton Bulletin, May 2, 1885.

assumption that they could legislate Indian behaviour. When the Métis majority forced Big Bear and his people to submit, Big Bear's resentment caused a lasting breach between himself and the Dumonts.[4]

Because of his reputation for independence, Big Bear attracted a following from among like-minded families of River Cree. Many were aggressive and belligerent, and for this reason his band soon came to be regarded with disfavour in some quarters. The members were known to the Blackfoot as notorious horse thieves, to the Hudson's Bay Company as shiftless trouble-makers, and to the missionaries as unrepentant pagans. Among his own people these vices were regarded as virtues and in the large camps Big Bear was soon equal in stature to both Little Pine and Piapot and, as the government was soon to discover, a force to be reckoned with.

By 1870, when Canada assumed sovereignty over the North-West, it had become evident to Indian leaders that the old days of unrestricted freedom were coming to an end. Already the tribes were beginning to be pushed westward by the advance guard of civilization. There were signs that the buffalo would not be around forever and that the country was becoming devoid of fur-bearing animals. Fearing for their future, the Company chiefs from the Fort Pitt and Edmonton districts petitioned the Canadian government for help and, at the same time, pleaded for a recognition of Indian rights. As the petition was sponsored by the influential whites in the district, it is hardly surprising that the signatories were all Hudson's Bay- and missionary-approved leaders. What was going through Big Bear's mind at this time there is no way of knowing for certain; but during the next several years, as the treaties were being signed with the Indians living to the east and to the south, Big Bear's voice was being raised in words of caution. In 1875, Rev. George McDougall reported to Lieutenant-Governor Morris that "Big Bear was trying to take a lead in their [the Indians'] councils."[5] McDougall obviously disapproved and reported that Big Bear was a "troublesome fellow."

It wasn't until 1876 that the Great White Mother's representatives came to the North Saskatchewan with a treaty pre-

---

[4] Constance K. Sissons, *John Kerr* (1946), p. 153. Kerr lived with Dumont for some time and believed that the breach between the men never healed.

[5] Letter, October 23, 1875, quoted in Alexander Morris, *Treaties of Canada with the Indians of Manitoba, the North-West Territories and Kee-wa-tin* (1880), p. 174.

pared for the Indians' approval. The first gathering took place at Fort Carlton, and the loyal Company chiefs, after making a few petty demands, made their X's and shook Lieutenant-Governor Morris' hand. However, in spite of this good will, considerable discontent was evident. The first objections came, not from the local chiefs, but from a group of Qu'Appelle Saulteaux who advised Chief Beardy and his Willow Crees to think seriously about the treaty terms before signing. Their leader, *Nus-was-oo-wah-tum*, who had been involved in the negotiations at Qu'Appelle two years earlier, made the issue plain when addressing Morris:

. . . it is true we told them [the Cree] 'do not be in a hurry in giving your assent'; . . . all along the prices have been to one side, and we have had no say . . . through what you have done you have cheated my kinsmen.[6]

Later Poundmaker touched on the same point when he proclaimed: "This is our land, it isn't a piece of pemmican to be cut off and given in little pieces back to us. It is ours, and we will take what we want."[7] But Poundmaker, in the end, acted with the majority and placed his mark on the treaty. The promise of an immediate feast and the distribution of a few presents, blankets, and beads was too much of a temptation for a people who had little experience in looking very far into the future.

It wasn't until the treaty party reached Fort Pitt that real signs of resistance appeared. First, the independent chiefs were absent with the majority of their followers, the Prairie People. Those of the Plains Cree who did attend chose as their head spokesman, Sweetgrass, a man who owed much of his prestige to his acknowledged ability to work harmoniously with Europeans. However, the government was soon to learn that in spite of what it had been told by the Hudson's Bay officers or the missionaries, Sweetgrass' influence over the River Cree was exceedingly limited. Most of the Thickwood Cree accepted the annuity payments, but Sweetgrass was able to induce only 317 Plains Cree, the majority being his own personal following, to take the Queen's money.[8]

[6] Morris, *op. cit.*, pp. 223-24.
[7] Henry T. Thompson, "Buffalo Days and Nights," the life of Peter Erasmus. Manuscript.
[8] The number of bands and gatherings has been taken from the Annuity Lists. The Plains Cree from the Fort Pitt area numbered around 1,500 at the time of treaty.

Many of the River People from the Fort Pitt area were out on the plains. They had, however, chosen Big Bear to go in to Pitt and act as their spokesman, and he arrived at the fort towards the close of the proceedings. Following the farewell speeches of Sweetgrass and Keehewin, Big Bear rose and addressed the assembly: "Stop, stop, my friends," he warned, "I heard the Governor was to come, and I said . . . when I see him I will make a request that he will save me from what I most dread, that is: the rope to be about my neck, it was not given to us by the Great Spirit that the red man or white man should shed each other's blood."[9] When Big Bear had finished speaking, both Sweetgrass and Seenum (the first, a Catholic convert, the second, a Methodist and both wearing the Hudson's Bay seal of approval) advised him to sign, saying that the treaty was good for the Indian people. Big Bear rejected their advice.

Historians have referred to that portion of Big Bear's speech related to hanging. It has usually been explained as a personal fear of execution and accepted literally as a major reason for the chief's refusal to sign the treaty. However, Big Bear was never accused of cowardice by any man who knew him. Nor did he ever raise the issue again during the six years that he remained outside of the treaty. It is far more plausible to believe that he used this dramatic example to illustrate the one-sidedness of the treaty; if the white man could legally shed Indian blood, why couldn't Indians shed whitemen's blood? There is no reason to believe that he had any intention of signing the treaty when he came to Fort Pitt, consequently he was not speaking for the benefit of Lieutenant-Governor Morris but was addressing his remarks to the Indians present. He was voicing his opposition to the entire spirit of the Canadian treaty terms. Like the Saulteaux chief, and like Poundmaker, he was telling his people that they were giving up their birthright, their independence, and their land, for a mere pittance.

Until the Fort Pitt signing, every chief and head man had accepted the various western treaties presented by the government. Most had even thanked the Queen's representative for making so generous an offer. The rank-and-file may have been motivated by a short-sighted desire for immediate gain, but the same could not be said of all the leaders, many of whom were men of considerable character. They succumbed because of fear – fear of approaching starvation. When the great

⁹ Morris, *op. cit.*, p. 240

northern buffalo herd was finally destroyed, who but the Queen would be able to feed the poor Indian? Big Bear was not ignorant of the rapid decline of the northern herd, but his reaction was characteristically different from that of the treaty chiefs. He wanted his working arrangements on better terms than were being offered, something better than the complete subjugation of his race.

The centre of the rapidly diminishing buffalo range was between the Cypress Hills in Canada and the Judith Basin in Montana Territory. Little Pine, the only other treaty holdout of any significance, generally hunted towards the Cypress Hills in the summer, and Big Bear frequently joined him in his southward journey. So, in 1877, the two free leaders, their bands increased by numerous stragglers, once again headed south — this time to take up year-round residence at the Cypress Hills.

That was the same year the most westerly Plains Cree signed their adhesions to Treaty Six, and the year that saw the capitulation of the mighty Blackfoot. Crowfoot, Red Crow, and the other chiefs all took the Queen's money and almost outdid the Cree Company chiefs in praising Her Majesty's generosity. So, if the Plains Indians were to get better terms, the only ones left to do battle for their rights were Big Bear and Little Pine and that hard-headed group of Crees who surrounded them.

When Big Bear and Little Pine reached the Cypress Hills they found a considerable gathering of kindred spirits. It is true that the chiefs already gathered around Fort Walsh had accepted the Queen's annuities but they had no intention of settling down. Almost all of the Canadian Assiniboines were there; most of them had called the Cypress Hills their home for years. Then there was Piapot, Little Pine's brother-in-law, a leader who had never enjoyed or needed the recognition of the Hudson's Bay Company. His band of Young Dogs also considered the Cypress Hills to be within their hunting territory. Cowesses, the Saulteaux from Qu'Appelle, was there with a sizable following, and there was a growing group of stragglers coming from the east after deserting those chiefs already settling on reserves. All told, there were more than 2,000 allied Indians including the new arrivals from the north.

Later that same year, Sitting Bull, the Sioux leader, brought his reputation and several thousand followers into the area and, for a time, attracted most of the panicky attention of Canadian officialdom. When the chief crossed the International Boundary, his people had just wiped out George Armstrong

Custer and most of the U.S. 7th Cavalry on the Little Big Horn. It is known that Big Bear met and talked with Sitting Bull and other Sioux leaders several times. This must have added greatly to his education. Here were men who had held out against any surrender to the white man's authority; men who were willing to fight to maintain their independence yet who found their greatest military victory had ended only in disaster for themselves.

By 1878, the buffalo herd was so reduced that those Indians who had remained around Battleford, Pitt, and Edmonton found it necessary to go further out onto the plains in search of food. Many of these people remained out at annuity payment time; consequently the government decided to make payment at Sounding Lake to accommodate them. Big Bear attended, warned once again that the terms were not satisfactory, and asked that the Indians refuse to co-operate until he could get them better terms. But once again the attraction of "cash in hand" was great, and even some of his own band signed under another chief. However, when Big Bear left Sounding Lake, he took many of the families away with him, including those of his followers who had taken treaty. Sweetgrass was dead, and when his band started breaking up, some former members also joined Big Bear's band.

Big Bear returned south and found that the big allied camp had moved west to the Medicine Hat area. When he joined it, the huge assembly included Cree, Assiniboine, Saulteaux, and even some Sioux. Nearby were Blackfoot, Bloods, and Peigans, and to the east was a camp of government surveyors. Here was an explosive situation and trouble wasn't long in coming. Some of the young men compelled the surveyors to quit work, the police were called, tempers ran high, and for a time it looked as if blood might be spilled with even the Blackfoot getting into the trouble. It was Big Bear who settled the dispute and acted as spokesman for the allied camp.[10]

The chief's stubborn refusal to accept the treaty terms and his acknowledged leadership of the Fort Walsh Indians soon

[10] In an account written in 1909, Col. A. G. Irvine, the N.W.M.P. officer who was called to the scene of the trouble, inferred that Big Bear was responsible and had consented to allow the surveyors to proceed out of fear of a N.W.M.P.-Blackfoot attack. However, an 1878 account in the *Saskatchewan Herald* blamed the Assiniboine and credited Big Bear for settling matters peacefully. The latter account, unlike Irvine's reminiscence, would have been unaffected by the prejudicial attitude which developed against Big Bear after the 1885 rebellion.

became a source of concern for the Mounted Police and Indian Department officers. They could not help but view any unity as dangerous and regard any unifying leader with distrust. Soon rumour spread of conspiracies involving Sitting Bull, Crowfoot, and Big Bear — although in his report for 1878, Colonel James Macleod reported that his investigations had found the rumours to be exaggerations.

Big Bear was not ignorant of these rumours. Evidence as to how well informed he was about attitudes of the white people appeared in an 1882 edition of the *Saskatchewan Herald*. Big Bear sent a message, which the paper published, refuting a report that he was holding secret meetings and plotting against the whites. This he strongly denied and mentioned that he had refused to listen to the council of Riel and others as well as Indians from across the line to commit acts designed to embarrass the government.[11]

The year 1879 saw the last Canadian buffalo hunt, followed by three more years of indifferent hunting in Montana. Then the whole economy of the prairie tribes simply vanished from the face of the earth. With starvation becoming reality, many of the non-treaty Indians decided to accept the annuity in 1879. Most of them had no intention of settling down as long as there were any buffalo to hunt, but the treaty payments were too much to resist, even for a large section of Big Bear's band. These families went into treaty under Lucky Man, one of Big Bear's head men, at the same time that Little Pine signed his adhesion to Treaty Six.

Big Bear alone held out. He had a number of interviews with Edgar Dewdney that summer, and the Indian Commissioner mentioned to Big Bear that his band was deserting him and he soon would not be able to claim the status of head chief. Apparently he also reached the conclusion that Big Bear was going to sign during the treaty payments in August. In this he was mistaken.

This must have been one of the great times of decision for Big Bear. Although he still had a large personal following, the government was now officially recognizing Lucky Man as head chief over those of his band who were inside the treaty. There was some truth in Dewdney's warning. On the other hand his own relatives led by his nephew, Little Poplar, formed the hard core of a sizable group who still refused to sign the treaty. If he stayed out he would retain a unique position and in spite of

[11] *Saskatchewan Herald*, August 5, 1882.

the government's attitude there was no reason to believe he would lose his influence in the Fort Walsh area.

Big Bear really had only two alternatives. He could settle on a reserve, under the terms of a distasteful treaty and thereby surround himself with a following of the meek and pliable. Or, he could remain with the fearless and the free and wait. If he settled, he would discredit himself in the eyes of the very people who were the best material for opposing the govrnment. If he followed the second course, he could do little else than prepare them for action at a future date. Certainly nothing could be effected as long as a sizable herd of buffalo remained on the plains.

In the north the treaty chiefs who stayed and accepted reserves were able to retain only a small fraction of their followings. Most members of the three Plains Cree bands from Fort Pitt moved to Fort Walsh where they attached themselves officially to Lucky Man and Little Pine but followed Big Bear. They were joined by families from every band along the North Saskatchewan and from as far west as Buffalo Lake.

One of these small groups of River Cree which came south was headed by a man destined to make his mark on Western Canadian history. He became a head man and war chief of Big Bear's band, although as a treaty Indian he took his annuity payments under a group of Cypress Hills stragglers. This was *Kahpaypamachakwayo*, Wandering Spirit.

Not only were the northern bands reinforced but Piapot and Cowesses were joined by portions of practically every southern band of Plains Cree and Plains Saulteaux. Many of the Fort Qu'Appelle Cree joined together in a new band under the leadership of Foremost Man.

In 1880 the buffalo failed to come north of the International Boundary; some say the Americans fired the prairies to stop the northward migration. It scarcely mattered, because the Canadian Indians went south to the buffalo range and Montana Territory became unwilling host to Canadian Cree, Saulteaux, Assiniboine, Blackfoot, and Blood hunters. Hundreds of Métis also followed the herds south.

There was little doubt who was the most influential chief in this great gathering. In 1879, the *Saskatchewan Herald* called Big Bear "the head and soul of our Canadian Plains Indians."[12] In 1881 Indian Commissioner Dewdney called him "a non-

¹² *Saskatchewan Herald*, March 24, 1879. The newspaper was paraphrasing a letter from Father Lestanc.

treaty Cree but to whom all the Crees look up to as their chief
. . . who has more influence than any Indian on the plains."[13]
When in 1881 Sitting Bull removed himself from the scene and
became a "reservation Indian," and when Crowfoot went home
to settle, there was no doubt about it: Big Bear was the un-
disputed leader of all the free Indians left on the Northern
Plains.

Thunderchild, one of his head men, abandoned hope, made
his peace with the government, and took a few families north
to settle on a reserve near Battleford. But Big Bear gained
other leaders; Four Sky Thunder from the Qu'Appelle district
and Wandering Spirit from Fort Carlton. Both became head
men. Unavoidably he gained trouble as well, for his lodge
became the rallying point for the disaffected, some of whom
were simply unruly troublemakers. Both Big Bear and his white
neighbors had reason to wonder how this class could be held
in line once there were no buffalo left to chase.

They were soon to find out, because by 1882 the great
northern herd had vanished. Apart from a few straggling bands,
the buffalo were gone from the plains for good, and the Indians
faced starvation. Some of the Assiniboines and a few Cree
under Little Poplar remained in the south searching for the
remnants of the once mighty herd, but the rest turned their
faces north and headed for Fort Walsh. Soon over 5,000
Indians were camped in the Cypress Hills under Big Bear,
Little Pine, Piapot, Foremost Man, Cowesses, and Lucky Man.
For the treaty Indians there were at least the meagre government rations; for Big Bear's non-treaty Indians there was
nothing.

Big Bear had no alternative now. His first duty as a chief
was to assure the basic needs of his people, so after several
interviews, one lasting the greater part of the night, he signed
his adhesion to Treaty Six on December 8, 1882. At this time
his personal following numbered 247.

All of the Fort Walsh chiefs decided to take reserves in the
Cypress Hills, but Big Bear announced his intention of moving
back to his old home at Fort Pitt. Why he made this decision
remains a mystery. In the south at this time there were over
five thousand of the very Indians who looked to him for leadership. Yet he seemed suddenly to have moved in a direction
diametrically opposed to the policy he had persistently pursued.

[13] Letter, Dewdney to D. L. Macpherson, August 4, 1881, Macdonald Papers, Dewdney Volume, p. 244. P.A.C.

Possibly he was temporarily discouraged, but would not have actually left when the time came. No one will ever know, because, at that moment, the government decided to force all Indians to follow Big Bear in his planned exodus from the hills.

Fear of border incidents caused by such a large concentration so close to the old Montana haunts induced Ottawa to decree that the Indians would have to settle towards Qu'Appelle or the North Saskatchewan. If they failed to depart, they would be taken out of treaty and all government assistance would be cut off. For people with no means of support, this was a convincing argument. Only the Foremost Man band ignored the order and stayed.

Thus, in 1883 the Fort Walsh concentration came to an end. Two bands of Assiniboines, Little Pine, Lucky Man, Big Bear, and assorted stragglers headed north for the Fort Pitt-Battleford area.

When he arrived at Fort Pitt after almost seven years absence, Big Bear had with him a band of 351 people. The government wanted him to settle on a reserve; in fact Indian agent Thomas Quinn told the chief to locate his land and move there at an early date or have his assistance withheld. Big Bear was not intimidated; he ignored the official threat. He wanted time to find out how matters were progressing along the Saskatchewan, to find out the temper of those Indians who had stayed in the north and who had already settled on reserves.

Most bands had tried to start a new life for themselves but things had not gone well. The experiences of Poundmaker had been typical. Originally he had been a head man in the Red Pheasant band but when his chief, an example of the white man's "good" Indian, took a reserve in 1878, Poundmaker left him and went to the plains with some of the more independent families. Shortly afterwards he changed his mind, decided to give the new way a fair trial, chose his reserve, and encouraged his people to make an honest effort. The *Saskatchewan Herald*, which had a sympathetic interest in the Indians, singled out Poundmaker as the chief doing the best job in the area – and ironically, Red Pheasant as the one doing the worst. However, by 1883 Poundmaker was thoroughly discouraged.

The reason for the discontent was not hard to find. The government expected to bridge a thousand years of history overnight and their policy was designed to force rather than assist the transition. The general attitude was that the Indians were inferior "wards' and this soon caused a rift between the proud warriors and the government employees. Ottawa also had a rare knack of staffing the Indian Department with people who knew nothing of Indians or Indian values; they were expected to learn on the job, and the training period usually proved disastrous to future relations.

Big Bear spent the winter of 1883-84 at Fort Pitt. The long winter nights provided time to consider a plan of action. He came to the conclusion that he must force concessions from the government before the Indian became an insignificant minority in his own land. He was well aware of how much more respect was shown the Blackfoot, who were settled on large reserves containing thousands of people, than was given to the Cree, Saulteaux, and Assiniboines who were divided into tiny units scattered through the country. Therefore he wanted to draw as many of his people together as he could so that they could act in unity.[14]

Big Bear must have known the dangers of such an undertaking. Among so many bold, truculent, and dissatisfied warriors, any spark could set off an explosion that would defeat his purpose and bring violent reaction from the Canadian Government. Yet he had to hold the Indians together in a manner that posed a threat of trouble for Ottawa. Big Bear had one advantage in that Ottawa was particularly vulnerable at the time. Settlement of the west depended on peace, and if settlement was delayed, John A. Macdonald's dream of empire could vanish, for Uncle Sam's policy of "manifest destiny" was not entirely dead. If Ottawa thought that an Indian uprising was a real possibility, it might be willing to grant major concessions in return for a decade of peace.[15]

In the spring of 1884, Big Bear set out from Fort Pitt on what was to be his last campaign. He moved with his band, now swollen to about 450 people, and settled on the outskirts of Battleford where most of the River Cree and Eagle Hills Assiniboines were gathered. Mounted Police Inspector L. N.

---

[14] See "Incidents of the Rebellion, as Related by a Fine Day," in *The Cree Rebellion of 1884*, Canadian North-West Historical Society pamphlet No. 1 (1926), pp. 11-18.

[15] Big Bear was not ignorant of international affairs. He was informed as to the views of the territorial press, as indicated by his letter to the *Saskatchewan Herald*, and by his own admission he had discussed native problems with Riel. The Métis leader certainly knew of Canadian fears and American ambitions and how to work both to his advantage. Big Bear also had several good friends among the leading members of the white community – men like James Simpson of the Hudson's Bay Company who respected his intelligence – and he must have discussed such matters with them.

Crozier ordered the Indians to depart, but they refused. He then ordered Big Bear to return to his agency at Fort Pitt but the chief retorted that he had been invited to Battleford, was doing no harm and would go only when he was good and ready. Crozier was furious but uncertain of the Indians' temper, so he did nothing and the Indians stayed. Poundmaker had informed the inspector that Big Bear was the head chief of the two thousand assembled Indians. He was still the leader and he had defied the police successfully.

Shortly afterwards Big Bear travelled east as far as Fort Carlton. There, in front of a large gathering of Indians, he pleaded for united action. He told them that runners were visiting all of the Indians on the plains, even their old enemies the Blackfoot, and soon they would have a movement that the Queen could not ignore. Following the Fort Carlton gathering, he returned to Battleford and went to the adjoining reserves of Poundmaker and Little Pine where a Sun Dance was to be held. Every band in the area was present, and, following the dance, a huge council of the attending chiefs was planned to formulate a joint plan of action. Without a doubt this was the biggest organized effort ever held by Indians on the Canadian plains. Unfortunately it was doomed.

The failure of the council was due to the impetuous actions of a young man named *Kahweechetwaymot*, one of the malcontents whom Big Bear had so much reason to fear, as well as to the obstinacy of an unfeeling Indian Department employee. *Kahweechetwaymot* demanded food, was refused, and, after administering a beating to the farm instructor with an axe helve, helped himself. When the Mounted Police arrived to arrest the offending Indian, an uprising almost occurred and bloodshed was prevented only because of the level heads of the police officer and the chiefs. In the end the culprit was surrendered but it was obvious that the young men were spoiling for a fight.

The Mounted Police report credited the chiefs with trying to get *Kahweechetwaymot* to give up and mentioned that, at the height of the uproar, Big Bear had shouted for "peace." But the people were losing patience with controlled agitation and many were prepared for a showdown with the white "soldiers."

Little Pine died some time after the trouble, and some say he was poisoned because of his stand for peace. His band came under the control of Sailing Horse and the war faction. Young Sweetgrass lost his influence as well, and Fine Day, his war chief, became the ruling spirit. Poundmaker, more of a hot-

head than some of the other chiefs, retained his position, and
Big Bear seemed to have lost none of his power. But appear-
ances were misleading.

Shortly after the sun dance, Big Bear and Lucky Man combined once again under the leadership of Big Bear, moved to
Fort Pitt for the 1884 annuity payments. Little Poplar had returned from Montana, and the strength of Big Bear's band was
now somewhere around 750 people — the biggest personal following of any chief on the plains. But, although some families
were attracted by his past reputation, many were following the
more violent head men around him. Real control had passed
into the hands of the Rattlers — the River People's Soldier
Society — as was to be proven by the events that followed.

The band still refused to take a reserve in spite of the government's efforts to get them settled, but there is evidence that
the members were becoming divided on the issue. Big Bear himself had promised to settle in the spring, and he may well have
decided he would have to locate or see the band break up. Little
Poplar was opposed to taking a reserve or even accepting treaty,
but seems to have opposed outright war. He decided to move to
Battleford for the winter and took close to ninety people with
him. Tatwasin and Big Bear's peacefully-inclined son, Twin
Wolverine, moved to Buffalo Lake in Alberta with 150 followers; many were former members of the Bob Tail band from
that district. Whether they were moving away from suspected
trouble or simply wintering with relations will never be known.
In addition, a handful of families were wintering with relatives
on various reserves and Big Bear, with approximately 520 followers, moved up to Frog Lake to winter on Oneepowayo's
reserve.

So the band was divided during the winter of 1884-85, with
the main body still being with Big Bear. With this body, too,
were the seeds of destruction — Big Bear's son Imasses, Wandering Spirit, the war chief, and the hostile core of the Rattlers.

What followed has been told many times. Discontent
smouldered throughout the winter along the entire length of the
North Saskatchewan, and the St. Laurent Métis led by Louis
Riel and Gabriel Dumont fanned the embers. Runners were
sent to the reserves preaching some form of resistance, with the
Indians and Métis united in a common cause. It is hard to believe that Big Bear was overly receptive to the Métis plans.
He had rejected Riel's wild talk on the Missouri, and he bore no
good will to Gabriel Dumont. On the other hand, many of the
young men must have liked what they heard; they were being

offered action, and this was what they wanted.

Riel was dreaming if he thought he could get united action from the Indians on short notice. All he succeeded in doing was stirring up the discontent in the Soldier's Lodges to the breaking point. When trouble erupted in the spring of 1885, he had no control over any band outside the Carlton area. The Indians acted "all together, one at a time" in true Indian style.

What really led up to and caused the Frog Lake massacre is one of those mysteries so often existing behind Indian outbreaks. W. B. Cameron believed that Imasses was the instigator. One of the Indian participants laid all the blame on Wandering Spirit, claiming that he was "jealous of those who wished to take a reservation. After killing Quinn [the Indian Agent] he was afraid and wished to drag the others into it."[16] Why did he kill Quinn? Was it because Quinn was related by marriage to his inveterate enemy, the Lone Man? Possibly Quinn had used his influence to support his in-law in a personal quarrel: History has turned on pettier issues.

Once started, the trouble soon got out of hand, and all of the Indians in the neighborhood, even the peaceful Thickwood Cree, were drawn in. One fact is certain, Big Bear was not involved in any plot. Apart from the fact that violence was contrary to his interests, he was absent hunting for several days prior to the outbreak, arriving back in camp only the preceding night when he immediately went to bed.

But once the trouble started he remained with his people. He could have run away to hide in the bush like the "loyal" head man from the Red Pheasant reserve, but he did not desert his people in their time of trouble. Besides, there was much good that he could do. After the massacre, he used what influence he still possessed to prevent any prisoners from being killed. When the Indians besieged Fort Pitt he was able to arrange for the evacuation of the fort without the loss of lives. And when Wandering Spirit attempted to stir up hate against the prisoners he pleaded on their behalf. "I pity every white man we have saved!" he cried, his voice tremulous with emotion. "Instead of speaking bad about them, give them back some of the things you have taken. See; they are poor! Naked! And they are not, like us, often hungry; they do not know how the teeth of the cold bites! They have always worn warm clothes. Have pity!"[17] These were hardly the words of a blood-thirsty savage bent on a war of extermination.

[16] Cameron, *op. cit.*, p. 229.
[17] Cameron, *op. cit.*, p. 131.

Big Bear's band made no serious attempt to join Pound-maker or Riel. His River Cree won all their battles and lost the war. At Frenchman's Butte, Big Bear's people showed that they were more than a match for the white soldiers, but, at last, short of ammunition and food, they scattered. There was nothing left to do but run for the United States or surrender, so Big Bear returned to the place of his youth and surrendered at Fort Carlton. The wheel of life had turned full circle for the old Plains Cree chief.

Big Bear was tried for treason-felony and, in spite of evidence to the contrary, was found guilty. Prejudice and a complete misunderstanding of the authority vested in an Indian chief by his people were among the reasons. Another, no doubt, was the antagonism Big Bear had built against himself in the white community and among officials by his refusal to act like a "good" Indian. When he was given the opportunity to speak at his trial, it was for his people not himself, that he pleaded. To the end he remained the unselfish patriot.

Big Bear, like Poundmaker, received a three-year sentence to be served in Stony Mountain Penitentiary. While in prison both chiefs accepted baptism into the Roman Catholic Church. Under the circumstances, the sincerity of these conversions can be doubted, but Big Bear, who had been forced to surrender to an alien government, now submitted to an alien God. Once the government got what it wanted — his complete subjugation, physical, and spiritual — it commuted his sentence and released him along with Poundmaker. His old band was broken up and scattered, so he went on to Little Pine's reserve where in 1887 he was listed on the annuity sheets as chief. But chiefs were nothing now — simply tools of the Indian Department permitted to retain their positions provided they pleased the administration and furthered the government's Indian policy. It was no life for Big Bear so, in the winter of 1887-88, with nothing left to live for, he died.

During the long history of European settlement of this continent, there were many conflicts between the natives and the intruders. Most were the result of impulsive reaction against injustice. Planned, organized, and sustained resistance was seldom achieved. Of the Indian leaders who succeeded in organizing effective movements only Pontiac, Tecumseh, Sitting Bull, and Big Bear were involved with Canada's history — Sitting Bull only as a refugee — and in the West only Big Bear rose to make a rational attempt to change the course of history for the benefit of his race. It is unfortunate that he has attracted so little attention from historians.

Riel has become the centre of the recent interest in the western Canadian rebellions, yet in 1885 Riel led his people into a madcap bloodbath they could never hope to win. Big Bear, on the other hand, was a proponent of the only form of protest that could possibly have benefitted his people: passive resistance. His hope was to force concessions before the Indian became a minority in his own land. He was still working to effect greater Indian unity when the outbreak at Frog Lake shattered his plans. The vengeful violence was not of his doing.

Big Bear foresaw the humiliating subjugation of his people and made a tremendous effort to prevent it. History made his failure almost inevitable, but left him no honourable alternative other than the course he took. His name belongs with those Canadians who have resisted tyranny and opposed injustice, for Big Bear was not only a great Indian, he was also a great Canadian.

Canadian Nationalism In Western Newspapers

R. Craig Brown

The historians of the Royal Commission on Dominion-Provincial Relations concluded their summary of the first thirty years of Confederation with the judgment that "the period was one of trials, discouragements, and even failure."[1] Even before the first flush of glowing nationalist sentiment had worn off the face of the infant Canadian Dominion, the existence of the child was sorely tested. The first thirty years were a period of economic depression, relieved only briefly between 1880 and 1884 and after 1894. They were the years of Dominion- Provincial rivalry for power and of renewed strife between English- and French-speaking Canadians, and they were the years of renewed difficulties between Canada and the United States.

Somehow, at the end of the first thirty years, the Canadian infant had emerged from the period of trial, disappointment, and failure as a healthy and confident adolescent already demanding the responsibilities of adulthood. Less than five million people had put a railway across the length of the North American continent, had defied geography to tie together distant regions of a nation composed of people of widely varying cultural backgrounds. By 1897, trade and commerce had expanded enormously and the diversification of Canadian trade patterns had begun. By 1897, the hopes of 1880 were being fulfilled; the Canadian West was experiencing a population explosion as immigrants rushed to the prairies from the United States, Great Britain, and Europe. The trials and the failure, then, had to be balanced by a measure of success. It is true that the ringing prophecies of 1867 had not all come to pass. But it is also true that Sir Wilfrid Laurier could confidently look to the future as "Canada's century."

SOURCE: *Alberta Historical Review*, vol. 10, no. 3 (Spring, 1962), pp. 1-7. Reprinted by permission of the author and publishers.

[1] *Report of the Royal Commission on Dominion-Provincial Relations* (Ottawa: Queen's Printer, 1954). Book I, p. 65.

Certainly the politicians from Sir John Macdonald to Sir Wilfrid Laurier were in no small way responsible for the growth of Canada between 1867 and 1897. It was their determination, in the face of depression, inter-sectional and cultural friction, and overt pressure from the United States, which made growth possible. But more than the determination of politicians was needed. Politicians could not lead where people would not follow, and, without a faith in the destiny of Canada on the part of the people, the task of the politicians would have been hopeless. More fundamental, then, was the belief of the people of Canada that they lived within the boundaries of a nation which they had created, which they intended to develop in status and in stature, and which they would preserve in the face of threats from the gigantic power to the south.

In short, Canadian nationalism, an expression of fidelity and loyalty to the Dominion of Canada by its inhabitants, was the foundation stone upon which the politicians built their national policies. Yet it was precisely this concept which was implicitly challenged in the disputes between Canada and the United States. The challenge was not, basically, political. Rather, the two nations which shared the North American continent were both anxious to exploit the economic wealth of the continent. And each nation had adopted a policy of economic nationalism replete with protective tariffs, railway building, and plans of settlement of virgin land. Between 1867 and the turn of the century, Canada and the United States engaged in an intense competition of economic nationalism. Two of the most serious disputes were the North Atlantic Fisheries question, and the debate over Canadian-American trade relations.

At first glance it would appear improbable that the newspapers of Western Canada should be concerned with the first of these problems. Of what interest was it to western Canadians whether or not American fishing vessels were allowed to ply the inshore fishery waters of Canada? As a matter of fact, as the history of the North Atlantic Fisheries dispute throughout the nineteenth century reveals, western interest in the dispute was both immediate and practical.

By the first article of the Anglo-American Convention of 1818, United States fishermen were barred from the Canadian inshore waters of the North Atlantic fisheries except "for the purpose of shelter and of repairing damages therein, of purchasing wood, and of obtaining water, and for no other purpose whatever."[2] But the inshore fisheries were the source of mackerel, the bait fish essential to the cod-fishery. Further, access to the Canadian inshore waters for commercial purposes, to ship crews, ice, bait, and supplies, and to trans-ship catches was very valuable to the American fishermen. By the Treaty of Washington, 1854-66, the Americans had been granted access to the inshore waters in return for Canadian-American reciprocity in natural products. From this point forward the North Atlantic Fisheries question was irretrievably tied to the extension of freer trade between Canada and the United States. Again, the Treaty of Washington, 1871, granted access to the inshore waters in return for American trade concessions; though the concessions were severely limited in contrast to those of 1854.

When, in 1883, the United States Government announced its decision to abrogate the fishery articles of the Treaty of Washington, 1871, the Macdonald government was determined to return to a policy of protection of Canada's inshore waters, including the exclusion of American vessels from those waters except for purposes of shelter, repairs, wood, and water. Further, the Canadians would do all in their power to secure a broad reciprocity agreement with the United States in return for re-opening the inshore waters to American fishermen. In fact, Sir John Macdonald and his colleagues viewed the Canadian inshore waters and the commercial privileges that could be secured therein not simply as an asset of the Maritime provinces but, rather, of the nation. Their policy was not to surrender the asset to the United States but to reopen it to joint Canadian-American exploitation in return for trade concessions on the part of the United States that would benefit the whole Canadian nation.[3] Thus, western Canada would benefit along with the rest of Canada from an equitable settlement of the North Atlantic Fisheries question. It was not surprising then, that western Canadian newspapers echoed the sentiments of their Maritime and central Canadian brethren in demanding that Canadian rights in the inshore fisheries be protected.

"The fisheries are a valuable property," proclaimed the *Calgary Herald* in January, 1887.

[2] C. C. Tansill, *Canadian-American Relations, 1875-1911* (New Haven: Yale University Press, 1943), p. 5.

[3] R. C. Brown, "Canadian-American Relations in the Latter Part of the Nineteenth Century" (Ph.D. Thesis, University of Toronto, 1962), ch. 1.

Anything consistent with reason we are willing to grant to our neighbors; but it is rather hard to threaten to cut us off from the American continent simply because we are not prepared to yield them equal rights in a source of wealth which, on their own admission, belongs exclusively to us.[4]

The *Manitoba Free Press* observed that the exchange of free fishing for free fish would be a "paltry price" for Canada to pay for a settlement of the problem. In turn for opening the fisheries to American vessels, Canada at least should get a market in the United States for her agricultural produce and animals, lumber, coal, and metallic ores.[5] The *Victoria Daily Times* noted that "all Canada wants is a fair and square deal." That paper's concept of such a bargain was "a return to reciprocity as it existed between 1854 and [1866]."[6] The *British Weekly Colonist* of Victoria commended the Ottawa Government for having "taken time by the fore-lock and shown our big sister across the way that we do not propose that our *rights* shall be trampled on."[7]

The prospect of economic benefit could not, however, obscure the fact that under any circumstances Canada's inshore fisheries belonged to Canada, and invaders were not welcome. "This would be a good time to let the world see that Canada is worthy of the stock from which she comes, and that such rights as she has in the fisheries she means to maintain," commented the *Victoria Daily Times*. "American fishermen must keep off the grass!"[8] "Let England and Canada stand to their rights and Uncle Sam will condescend to be honest," noted the *Regina Leader*.[9] It was the *Edmonton Bulletin* which came to grips with the fundamental question – the preservation of a Canadian identity on the North American continent. In an editorial on the fisheries question the *Bulletin* said that "if the principle is once admitted that because the United States wills Canada must, then the prospect of a Canadian nationality is lost and the name Canadian becomes a reproach."

Unfortunately, the hope that Canada's national asset might be opened to joint Canadian-American exploitation in return for trade concessions benefitting all of Canada could not be fulfilled. The Joint High Commission of 1887-88 did arrive at a settlement by way of a new treaty, but it was largely limited to

4 *Calgary Herald*, January 28, 1887.
5 *Manitoba Free Press*, January 19, 1886.
6 *Victoria Daily Times*, June 12, 1886.
7 *British Weekly Colonist*, May 21, 1886.
8 *Victoria Daily Times*, May 6, 1886.
9 *Regina Leader*, June 1, 1886.

opening the inshore fisheries to Americans and allowing them commercial privileges in Canadian harbours in return for a free market for Canadian fish in the United States. The Canadian Parliament duly ratified the treaty, but the United States Senate considered even these meagre terms too generous and rejected the treaty in September, 1888. Fortunately the Joint High Commission had foreseen this possibility and provided for an alternative settlement by way of executive agreement to a *modus vivendi*. The *modus vivendi* was also a compromise on the basis of free fishing for free fish — or a license system in lieu thereof — and it provided for a temporary settlement of the North Atlantic Fisheries question until a final decision was given by the Hague Tribunal in 1910.[10]

Western Canadian reaction to the abortive Treaty of 1888 and the compromise settlement was mixed. The prospect of reciprocity with the United States in agricultural produce and animals, perhaps even reciprocity in some manufactured goods such as farm implements, had been alluring. The failure to secure reciprocity was a disappointment. The *Edmonton Bulletin*, which was disposed to criticize the Macdonald Government whenever occasion arose, viewed the treaty as an evidence of Ottawa's weakness. "A treaty which gives up such a large part of the contentions of the administration which negotiated it can only be termed a surrender, not a treaty."[11] On the other hand, the staunchly Conservative *Calgary Herald* rallied to the defence of Sir John and his colleagues. Even though a large measure of reciprocity was denied, the important point was that "we have sustained our interpretation of the Treaty of 1818." Undeniably, the Treaty of 1888 confirmed this view. "We have secured a victory on this important matter," the *Herald* concluded, "a fact all true Canadians will hail with immense satisfaction."[12] And, interestingly enough, despite the disagreement between the *Herald* and the *Bulletin* in their interpretations of the Treaty of 1888, both papers agreed on the main point, the preservation and protection of a Canadian national asset. The point of the *Bulletin*'s comment was that the Ottawa Government was wasting its asset by opening the inshore fisheries for too little compensation from the United States.

The circumstances of the times made the failure to secure a large measure of reciprocity all the more galling The federal

---

[10] R. C. Brown, "Canadian-American Relations . . . ," *op. cit.*, chs. 3 and 11.
[11] *Edmonton Bulletin*, March 10, 1888.
[12] *Calgary Herald*, February 29, 1888.

budget of 1884 had shown a healthy surplus, but by 1886 the cloud of depression had descended on Canada once again and it remained there until the middle years of the next decade. In depressed times western Canadians could see only burdens in Macdonald's National Policy Tariff which was geared to protect the infant industries of eastern Canada. Western Canadians believed the National Policy Tariff was taxing them unjustly for the benefit of a commercial and industrial minority in the St. Lawrence valley. In 1886 the Manitoba Liberal Association resolved that "the present tariff is especially oppressive to the farmers of Manitoba while it gives no advantage to any class of its settlers, and justice to the Province urgently demands its modification."[13] The *Free Press* sprang to the defence of the Liberals with the observation that "freedom of trade relations between this country and United States is both natural and desirable."[14]

As the *Free Press* hinted, reciprocity in trade with the United States would lessen the burden of the depression. And even in good times all Canadians believed in the advantages of reciprocity with the Republic. This had been the aim of the Conservatives in 1871 and 1887-88 and of the Liberals in 1874. Indeed, in 1879 the Conservatives argued that the National Policy Tariff — reciprocity in tariffs — would force the United States into reciprocity in trade. Where Canadians disagreed was on the extent of reciprocity and on the price they were willing to pay for reciprocity.

With the onset of renewed depression in the middle years of the 1880s an extreme solution was put before Canadians with the proposal of Commercial Union. The essence of the proposal was a complete economic union of the North American continent with a common tariff against the outside world and a pooling of the customs receipts of the United States and Canada. Sentiment in favour of Commercial Union was centred mainly in Ontario under the guiding hand of Goldwin Smith and, to a lesser extent, in Nova Scotia where the Province's Attorney-General, J. S. Longley, carried the banner. The proposal posed a serious question for Canadians to ponder. The preponderant position of the United States in such an economic union would inevitably dictate that the American tariff would be adopted against the outside world and that the United States would determine the distribution of pooled customs receipts.

[13] *Manitoba Free Press*, March 17, 1886, advertisement, p. 3.
[14] *Ibid.*, January 26, 1886.

In short, the fiscal independence of Canada which had only been won in 1859 after decades of struggle, would have to be surrendered. Was Canada willing to pay such a price? Was Canada willing to give up her economic and probably also her political autonomy in North America?

Commercial Union, said the *Regina Leader*, was a proposal for a treaty "between the bully and the bullied. This is not the temper of the mass of Canadians who believe in their country and are determined she shall be great, prosperous and free."[15] The *Edmonton Bulletin* believed that Commercial Union was "commercial robbery" and went on to point out that it was not free trade at all but rather increased protection. It was true that the commercial boundary on the continent would be wiped away, but at the cost of an even higher tariff against the rest of the world and especially Great Britain.[16] The *Medicine Hat Times* concluded that the prophets of Canadian doom who preached salvation through Commercial Union "would cut down the twig because it is not a tree."[17] Plainly, the proponents of Commercial Union were asking too high a price. Western Canada had no desire to sacrifice its Canadian identity.

Still, the depression continued and deepened, and the Liberal party, under its new leader, Wilfrid Laurier, sought a solution to the problem which might also, incidentally, bring the party to power in Ottawa. With appropriate fuss and flurry Sir Richard Cartwright proposed a new Liberal trade policy, Unrestricted Reciprocity, to the House of Commons in March, 1888. Unrestricted Reciprocity was a compromise with Commercial Union designed by J. D. Edgar, Toronto Liberal, which would give Canada complete free trade with the United States yet also allow Canada to establish its own tariffs against the outside world and hence preserve Canada's fiscal independence. But many Canadians believed that Unrestricted Reciprocity was just another name for Commercial Union. The *Regina Leader* noted that only "the consumptive Grit organs" supported it and that wise Canadians would have "none of it . . . they will ally themselves with no party that does not carry the flag and keep step to the music of a great Canadian nation."[18] The Liberal party's program naïvely assumed, said the *Edmonton Bulletin*, "that the tail can wag the dog." "If our resources are not being developed as fast as they should be, at least they

[15] *Regina Leader*, November 1, 1887.
[16] *Edmonton Bulletin*, July 2, 1887.
[17] Cited, *Edmonton Bulletin*, September 3, 1887.
[18] *Regina Leader*, July 26, 1887.

are still ours, to be developed for our benefit when the time comes."[19]

The issue between retention of the National Policy and the adoption of Unrestricted Reciprocity was fought out in the general election of 1891. The *Victoria Daily Colonist* viewed the election as "the most important ever fought in this Dominion. The people of Canada were called upon to decide whether they were willing to remain the subjects of Queen Victoria or whether they were ready to become citizens of the United States."[20] The *Edmonton Bulletin* quoted with approval a note from the *Winnipeg Commercial* saying that free trade would suit Manitoba, "but any commercial union compact which would restrict our trade relationship with other countries, or bring Canada into a tariff combination with the United States, would certainly prove obnoxious to this country."[21] And the *Manitoba Free Press* echoed these sentiments; "we would be glad to have free trade itself, but we do not want annexation."[22] When the polling was done, the Old Man and the Old Party had been narrowly sustained.[23] Canada had been saved for Canadians by Canadians.

The narrow defeat of the Liberals in 1891 might well have encouraged the party to retain its policy of Unrestricted Reciprocity. Though the Government had a majority of about thirty seats in the House of Commons, it had only garnered 51.1 per cent of the popular vote and apparently 48.9 per cent of Canada's voters had favoured the Liberal trade policy.[24] But a number of factors led the Liberals away from Unrestricted

---

[19] *Edmonton Bulletin*, December 24, 1887.

[20] *Victoria Daily Colonist*, March 6, 1891.

[21] *Edmonton Bulletin*, March 7, 1891.

[22] *Manitoba Free Press*, March 2, 1891.

[23] See E. P. Dean, "How Canada Has Voted: 1867 to 1945," *Canadian Historical Review* XXX (1949), pp. 227-48.

[24] R. C. Brown, "Canadian-American Relations . . . ," *op. cit.*, p. 300. Significantly, western Canada showed a much less favourable attitude to Liberal policy than the Dominion as a whole, as the following indicates.

Percentage of Popular Vote:
Government (with Opposition in brackets):
Manitoba, 53.5 percent (46.5 percent); North-West Territories, 65.4 percent (34.6 percent); British Columbia, 73.1 percent (26.9 percent); Canada, 51.1 percent (48.9 percent).

Seats Won:
Government (with Opposition in brackets):
Manitoba, 4 (1); North-West Territories, 4 (0); British Columbia, 6 (0); Canada, 123 (92).

Reciprocity. On March 6, the day following the election, Edward Blake's West Durham letter was printed in the *Toronto Globe* and revealed that the former party leader strongly disapproved of the party's trade policy. Agricultural exports, cut out from the American market by the McKinley tariff, found a ready and expanding market in Great Britain. Canadian trade increased significantly, and, by the mid-1890s, the Dominion appeared to have conquered the depression. Most important of all, the Liberal party discovered that much of its key financial support in Toronto business circles was withdrawing from the party because of its trade policy.

At the Great Convention of 1893 in Ottawa the Liberal party announced that it had abandoned its flirtation with continentalism. The new trade policy was "freer trade with all the world, especially Great Britain and the United States." (The order is significant.) The *Manitoba Free Press* spoke for all western Canadian newspapers when it congratulated the Liberal party for its return to the banner of Canada and Empire.

Those who wish the Liberal Party well in the next election will congratulate it on the abandonment of unrestricted reciprocity. This country could not afford to throw down all the customs barriers between it and the United States, while maintaining them against Great Britain. It would be entirely too revolutionary. . . . The time may come to sever the connection with the mother country, but it is not yet nor is it in sight. We would rather endure our present afflictions than raise a hand to hasten the separation.[25]

The attempt to sort out a clearly nationalist position in eastern Canadian newspapers in the latter part of the nineteenth century must be made with caution. Many of the outstanding eastern papers, the *Toronto Globe*, the *Empire*, the *Montreal Gazette*, *La Minerve*, the *Halifax Morning Chronicle* and others, had been founded as party organs and had been engaging in political warfare for decades. Often, though not always, their comments on national issues were heavily laden with partisan bias. Often they would sing hymns of praise when the party of their favour took a given stand on a national issue, only to launch into the most bitter criticism when the opposite party took a similar stand.

The same argument can be applied to the western Canadian

newspapers though I find it much less convincing. It is true that a few western papers – the *Calgary Herald* is an obvious choice – did proclaim themselves as staunch supporters of one or the other of the national parties. But this did not preclude them from taking a broad view of national issues regardless of party. Political organization in the Canadian west was weak, if it existed at all. The western provinces, almost without exception, tended to support the party in power at Ottawa regardless of its name. And this was as true of the newspapers of the west as it was of the voters of the west on election day. In 1896 the *Calgary Herald* noted with approval that a candidate had said "let a man be either a Liberal or a Conservative, he must be a North West man first and for party afterwards." As the *Herald* put it, "Country before party."

It may be argued this was really an expression of regionalism rather than nationalism. And, as in the case of the western support of a strong stand on the fisheries question, at least part of that support resulted from a hope of regional economic relief from the depression. But it is also implicit in the argument that the west was dependent upon Ottawa for much of the development of its regional interests. And, as was true in the case of the west's spurning of Commercial Union or Unrestricted Reciprocity, the Canadian west much preferred dependence on Ottawa to dependence on Washington. The Canadian west realized that Ottawa's National Policy did not always benefit western interests, but it further realized that – as the continual stream of agrarian protest south of the border revealed – probably Washington's national policies would be even less beneficial.

In short, the people of the Canadian west and their newspapers were determined to work out their regional and immediate problems within the broader framework of the Canadian nation. The fate of the region was dependent upon the fate of the nation. And when the nation was threatened as it was during the years of "trial, discouragements, and even failure," the western Canadian newspapers rallied to its support to sustain it and to hope, with the rest of Canada, for its greater growth.

A Mennonite Community In the East Reserve: Its Origin and Growth

William Friesen

In 1875, J. C. Hamilton, a visitor to Manitoba from Ontario, heard frequent mention of the newly-arrived Mennonites. On his way down the Red River to Winnipeg by Red River steamer, he saw several groups of them. On his way back by stage coach as far as St. Paul, he made the personal acquaintance of two of them.

In the following year, he published an account of his visit in a book entitled *The Prairie Province*. The main purpose of this book was to describe the resources of Manitoba and to report the progress of settlement in various parts of the province. However, it also contained interesting references to various people whom he met during the course of the journey.

He was apparently impressed by the large number of Mennonites that were coming to settle in Manitoba, for he mentions them at some length in several places in his book. The more important of his references to the Mennonites are given in the quotations that follow. They indicate the impression the Mennonites made on the author and should serve also to give some idea of the reaction of the local inhabitants to the arrival of these strangers from a distant land.

The broad faces and stout forms of Menonnites, dressed in brown homespun — men, women, and children, here greet us in numbers. . . . The purser informed us that several parties of them passed in by boats this season. They have generally large families — children of every age up to puberty. One man had his second wife and twenty-three children.

The Rat River settlers broke about three thousand acres of land, and sowed the same last spring, but suffered greatly from grasshoppers. The thirty families that settled at Scratching River

SOURCE: *Papers Read Before the Historical and Scientific Society of Manitoba*, Series III, No. 19 (1962-63), pp. 24-42. Reprinted by permission of the author and the Manitoba Historical Society.

*had good crops. The Pembina Reserve has only recently been
made and has upon it about three hundred families.*

In his description of the return journey, Hamilton makes
reference to a number of passengers on the stage coach in addition to the two Mennonites already mentioned. Among them
were an American business man, a Canadian senator, an exferryman, and a young man whom he describes as "the smart
boy from Ontario."

*We are now joined in company by . . . , and two Mennonite
gentlemen, intelligent, plainly dressed, having broadcloth over-
coats lined with dressed sheepskin, the wooly side next to the
person. They were on a business trip to St. Paul, but would soon
return.*

*Our two companions passed the time in chat, or with their
pipes and a religious book which one of them had. We asked
how they liked Manitoba. "O," said they together, brightening
up, "A guttes-land, schönes-land." "A guttes-land" you say and
I believe you old Mennons," said the exferryman, rousing himself, "and you broad brims have the best of it; you get a free
passage from Quebec, and then squat close to the river, with one
hundred and sixty acres, a free gift to each of you, and the railroad soon to pass your doors. Then you have no fighting, no
lawyer's bills, and I guess but little doctor's stuff to swallow or
pay for, you'll soon make this a land of Goshen." "How's that
about fighting and doctors?" put in the smart boy, while the two
Mennonites looked on half understanding and much amused.
"Why these old sober-sides are a sort of Dutch Quakers," replied
the ferryman, "but I would not advise you to tackle any of their
boys without taking their measure well. If they don't strike from
the shoulder they may squeeze like the bears of Russia, from
which they came, being invited to leave because they won't go
soldiering for the Czar. I'm told they settle their disputes by
friendly arbitration, hate the smell of gunpowder and as to
physic the very women are stronger than our average American
men. When I was coming down the Old International, one of
the fraus borrowed a mattress, disappeared down the hatchway
about noon but was up again before sunset with a little Mennon
in her arms, whose first squall was heard about the Pembina.
Ask purser Smith and he'll tell you all about it."*

The smart boy . . . broke out with a rattling ditty as follows:

The Mennon Bold

A beautiful home has the Mennon bold
His harvest he reaps and he sells it for gold
From lawyers' bills and from doctors' pills
He is free as the wind of the western hills.
The prairie land is a beautiful land
The chosen home of the Mennon Band.

He never would fight for Gortchekoff,
And the word of the Czar was "drill or be off!"
O'er Gitchie Gumu, then away came he
With his frau and his kind, to the land of the free.
The prairie land is a beautiful land
The chosen home of the Mennon Band.

The Metis may laugh by the River Rat,
At his sheepskin coat and his broad-rimmed hat,
But he drives his steer and he drinks his beer;
And a happy home is the home he has here.
The prairie land is a beautiful land
The chosen home of the Mennon Band.

Hamilton's light-hearted but sympathetic and fair-minded references to the Mennonites, and the comments and views expressed by his fellow travellers probably reflect fairly well how the man on the street felt about the Menonnites and the limited extent to which he had learned to know them.

Who were the Mennonites? In the following pages I shall deal briefly with this question before proceeding to my topic proper. Then after telling the story of the origin and growth of Steinbach, I shall spend some time in discussing a topic that has always been important to the Mennonites, the education of their children. For the source of much of the material on Steinbach I am indebted mainly to three local historians of the Steinbach area, Mr. G. G. Kornelsen (deceased), Mr. K. J. B. Reimer, and particularly Mr. John C. Reimer.

Who are the Mennonites? How and where did they originate? Most of the Mennonites who live in Manitoba today are descended from Frisian farmers and Flemish artisans who formed Anabaptist groups in the early years of the Reformation, beginning about 1530. As time went on they were joined by Anabaptist refugees from various parts of Germany and a few from Switzerland. The Anabaptists were Protestant sects who felt that the reforms of Luther and Zwingli did not go far enough. They believed in complete separation of Church and State, abstention from taking of the oath, and non-resistance. They would not accept the infant baptism of the Roman Catholic and Protestant churches and rebaptized converts upon confession of faith. It was this which resulted in their enemies' calling them Anabaptists; they referred to themselves as "The Brethren."

To explain how they came to be called Mennonites requires a brief reference to the life and work of Menno Simon. He was born in 1496 and was educated for the Church and in due course became a Roman Catholic priest. Observing the stuanchness and zeal with which "The Brethren" faced imprisonment, torture, or death for their faith, he felt there must be some basis for their strong conviction and began a thorough study of their teachings. This led to a careful rereading of the scriptures and, finally, to his joining the "Brethren" and soon becoming one of their outstanding leaders. So completely and whole-heartedly did he throw himself into his work, with all its attendant dangers and hardships, that he shortly became the recognized leader of the whole Anabaptist movement in Holland and northwest Germany, and his fellow religionists came to be known as Mennonites.

Under the rule of the Spanish Catholic Duke of Alva, persecution of the Mennonites in the Netherlands was intensified. They were imprisoned, tortured, drowned, buried alive, and burned at the stake. All told, at least 18,000 lost their lives during this period of persecution. *The Martyr's Mirror* tells the story of the deep faith, fortitude, and courage of these people and of the unspeakably cruel means employed to stamp out their so-called heresy. Large numbers left the country and sought a haven elsewhere. This was not always easy to find. However, there was a need for good farmers to reclaim the low-lying lands adjacent to the Vistula and Nogat Rivers, and the rulers of this area, many of them Catholic, were willing to be tolerant to these Dutch dissenters who knew how to do it.

Here the Mennonites lived for 250 years, the farmers in villages which they established in the area and the artisans in the city of Danzig. For most of this time, they continued to use the Dutch language in their church services, while in their homes they spoke their Frisian or Flemish dialects, which were similar to the Prussian Low German or *Platt Deutsch* spoken by the local inhabitants. However, near the end of this long period they discontinued the use of the Dutch language in favour of High

German in their churches, and their speech in the homes became more or less identical with that of their Low German-speaking neighbours.

In time, all of the land occupied by the Mennonites fell under the rule of Prussia. As this nation became more powerful and more nationalistically inclined, the Mennonites, never popular with their Lutheran neighbours, were forced to undergo various restrictions. One of the most serious was a regulation prohibiting them from acquiring land. Added to this was the ever-increasing threat of the possibility of being required to serve in the Prussian army. Consequently, when Catherine of Russia, who had heard of their success as farmers and needed colonizers to settle the large stretches of land left uninhabited as a result of her wars with Turkey, sent an invitation to them to come to Russia, a goodly number of the Mennonites decided to accept it.

In 1789, the first group of emigrants, mostly of Flemish persuasion, which consisted mainly of families who had been unable to acquire land because of government restrictions, left Prussia. They established their settlement on the steppes lying on both sides of the Chortitza River, a tributary of the Dnieper. That this group's main reason for leaving was largely economic rather than religious is attested to by the fact that no ministers accompanied it and that for some time they were without any minister to serve them. Conditions in the new land were extremely difficult at first, but the Russian government helped with food and other aid until they were reasonably well-established in their new homes.

Conditions continued to worsen for the Mennonites in Prussia, especially with respect to the military service requirement. As a result another large group left in 1803 to form a second colony. This group passed through the first or old colony to locate on the Molotschna River not far from the Sea of Azov. The members of this group were wealthier and better educated than the Chortitza settlers and also somewhat more liberal in outlook. Being fairly well-to-do and having the experience of the Chortitza settlement to guide them, these newcomers were able to establish a thriving colony in a very short time. They were also favoured by a milder climate and a better soil.

When the settlement at Chortitza became crowded, new areas for settlement had to be located and purchased. The first of these was the Bergthal colony which was set up as a daughter colony of the old colony at Chortitza and consisted of five villages, the largest of which was Bergthal (1836-52). It was located in the Mariepol district south of Chortitza and almost due east of the Molotschna colony. A second daughter colony was established in an area known as the "Fuerstenland," land of the Prince (1852 and later).

Under the colonial system employed by the Russian government, these colonies were largely left to manage their own affairs, secular as well as religious, with what, on the whole, seemed beneficial results. They flourished materially, education gradually improved, and cultural interests grew.

However, prosperity and ease may lead to worldliness and selfishness, especially when oppression ceases. In the Molotschna colony there arose a group under the leadership of a certain Klaas Reimer who felt that the church membership, generally, was getting too worldly in its outlook and too lax in its morals and in its adherence to the traditional rules and procedures of the church. This resulted in the formation of a minority church which came to be known as *Die Kleine Gemeinde* (the small congregation). The descendants of this group will play an important part in our story later, which is the reason for introducing it here.

By 1870, modern progressive trends in the Russian Empire resulted in two movements which did not favour the benevolent paternalism which had up to this point prevailed in the establishment and maintenance of foreign colonies as more or less autonomous and separate communities. The Liberals wanted equal rights for all and the pan-slavic element was not particularly sympathetic towards special privileges for these flourishing Germanic settlements. They advocated establishing a national educational system and national military service from which no one would be excluded.

These new trends caused a good deal of concern to the Mennonites, especially those of more conservative outlook. Various negotiations took place and various attempts were made to make sure that the old privileges would be retained. Some compromises were finally reached, but many Mennonites refused to accept them as satisfactory and started making preparations to come to America. A delegation of twelve was sent out in 1873 to "spy out the land" and to decide on the best place in which to settle. Among other places, they visited Manitoba; but most of the delegates, when they saw the conditions which prevailed here, considered them too harsh and decided in favour of the United States. However, the delegates of the more conservative groups chose Manitoba. They felt that the privileges they asked for would be more permanent under the rule of a monarch than in a republic. They remembered how Catherine had invited them to come to Russia and now in this invitation to come to Canada they saw a parallel situation and felt that history was repeating itself. They did not realize that Queen Victoria might be completely unaware of what was about to happen in this remote part of her empire.

The delegates, Heinrich Wiebe and Jacob Peters, representing the Bergthal colony, and Cornelius Toews and David Klassen, representing the *Kleine Gemeinde* group, and indirectly the Fuerstenlander who had sent no delegates of their own, saw Manitoba in company with eight others. They visited what was to become the East Reserve on a route that followed closely its eastern boundary. Near the end of the route they came to the home of a settler, Mr. Mack, who had a German wife. Here they stayed for a meal and learned at first hand about the land that was to be their new home. Although they found the mosquitoes almost unbearable and the soil not of the best, they persisted in their determination to make this the new home for themselves and their people.

Next year, 1874, the exodus began. Homes and personal effects were sold, sometimes at much below cost. Within two years, all the 500 families living in the five Bergthal villages sold out completely and most of them moved to Manitoba, settling first in the Rat River or East Reserve. The Fuerstenlander, beginning their migration in 1875, settled on the open prairie east of the Pembina Hills just north of the American boundary, which was part of the West Reserve. About half of the Bergthaler, dissatisfied with the poor soil and drainage of the East Reserve, moved west after a few years and established themselves in the unoccupied part of the West Reserve, east of the Fuerstenlander. The *Kleine Gemeinde* group which was the smallest, some 700 persons in all, established the villages of Blumenort, Blumenhof, Gruenfeld and Steinbach in the East Reserve and the villages of Rosenhoff and Rosenort on the banks of the Scratching River near Morris.

In their manner of settlement and in the management of their affairs, such as local government, fire insurance, and banking, the Mennonites continued as closely as possible the system they had begun to develop in Prussia and had perfected in Russia. Most of the settlers grouped themselves in villages of about twenty to twenty-five families. Usually the village followed the course of a stream, which insured suitable drainage and could provide water for the cattle. The plan of the village of Steinbach was quite typical. A lot of sixteen acres was allotted to each owner (*Wirt*) for every quarter-section of land owned, six acres were on one side of the road and ten on the other. In time, each owner built a substantial house and barn, joined together, on the yard lot (*Feuer Statte*) of six acres.

One village in the settlement served as the capital. Here the reeve (*Ober Schulze*) resided, and the books and papers of the settlement were kept. Here also the council, consisting of the headmen or mayors of the villages, met to decide the affairs of the settlement such as the building of roads and ditches, road levies, and other secular matters of general concern. A secretary kept the books and looked after the correspondence.

The church was served by a number of ministers under the leadership and direction of a senior minister known as *Der Aelteste*, elder or bishop. In addition to presiding at the meetings of the Church Board (*Lehrdienst*), the bishop was the only minister authorized to administer the rites of communion and baptism. The church in each colony was more or less autonomous. Even though two colonies might belong to the same branch of the Mennonite church they were run separately. However, in Russia, for example, when questions of common concern arose, such as the pending legislation relating to military service, representatives from the various colonies would meet in conference to decide on a common policy.

In the East Reserve there were two distinctly separate churches from the beginning; the Bergthaler, who, having lived in a somewhat isolated colony for a number of years, had developed an outlook and point of view different from any other group; and the *Kleine Gemeinder*, who had formed a separate church organization shortly after the founding of the Molotschna colony in Russia. Not only had these two groups different views on religion from each other, they also had different backgrounds that went back almost a hundred years to 1789 when the first colony was established in Chortitza. Moreover, most of the Chortitza colonists were originally of Flemish extraction and persuasion while many of the Molotschna were Frisian.

As a result, there was little mixing of the two groups in Manitoba. They lived in separate villages and attended separate church services. In matters of education, the Bergthaler, at least those who stayed in the East Reserve, were inclined to be even more conservative than the *Kleine Gemeinde* group. In secular matters, however, the whole colony in the East Reserve acted as a unit and the village of Chortitz, a Bergthaler village, served as the capital. Here the records were kept and the secular issues of common concern decided.

When almost half of the Bergthaler moved to the West Reserve they elected a bishop to direct church matters there and had little contact with their brethren in the East Reserve. It soon became evident within the group that moved to the west, that there were a few among them who were much more liberal-minded and progressive than the rest, especially in matters of education and religion. They did not feel that one's religion depended on maintaining old customs, or old styles of clothing, or other minute observances, and they were anxious to learn the language of the land of their adoption. One of the leaders of this group was the newly-elected bishop, Rev. Johann Funk. When he and others of the same mind co-operated with the Manitoba Department of Education to bring in H. H. Ewert from Kansas to become the principal of a Mennonite High School at Gretna and to act as the government inspector of Mennonite schools, a serious rift developed in the Bergthaler church in the West Reserve. The majority broke off, formed a separate church and selected a bishop of their own. This bishop lived in Sommerfeld, and, consequently, this new group came to be known as the Sommerfelder. The remnant that stayed with Bishop Funk retained the name of Bergthaler. Even more conservative than the Sommerfelder were the Fuerstenlander, the first settlers in the West Reserve, who in Manitoba were generally referred to as the *Alt Colonier* (people from the Old Colony). They refused to have anything to do with the new school or even with any of the Bergthaler. The Bergthaler who had stayed in the East Reserve consisted almost purely of the conservative element. They continued under the leadership of Bishop Gerhard Wiebe, who had originally led them to Canada. They were in close sympathy with the new Sommerfelder in the West Reserve. Bishop Wiebe, himself, was very much upset by the course taken by the progressive Bergthaler and in a pamphlet written a few years later attacked them bitterly for their worldliness and ungodliness. In time his followers came to be known as Chortitzer because he lived in the village of Chortitz.

The Bergthaler under Bishop Funk continued in their progressive views. Eventually, because of some internal disagreement they established a second private school in Altona. Both schools served a very useful function in providing high school education for prospective teachers for the elementary schools, at first only for the West Reserve, but later also for the East Reserve.

After this brief sketch of the origin of the Mennonites and

their establishment in Manitoba, it is now my purpose to deal more specifically with the Mennonites who settled Steinbach.

The original settlers of Steinbach were all members of the *Kleine Gemeinde* Church, and Steinbach was the last but one of the six villages founded by the *Kleine Gemeinder*. People have wondered why such an out-of-the-way place and such swampy and bushy land was chosen for the site. One reason that has been given is that the founding fathers wanted to get as far from any future railway as possible. Another, that they were rather late in getting started and that all the better land had already been taken up. They might have settled in the area immediately south of their coreligionists in Blumenort but for the fact that the English or Scottish settlement of Clear Springs, three miles square, occupied this area. Consequently, they chose a site for their village just south of the boundary of the Clear Springs settlement. The close proximity of this isolated Scottish settlement, already established, may have had quite an important effect on the peculiar nature of the development of Steinbach in the years that followed. Another factor that may have helped to shape this development was the fact that Steinbach was on the edge of the prairie land next to a wooded area which stretched south and east for many miles.

It was in the fall of 1874, that seventeen men, accompanied by their wives and children numbering eighty in all reached the site of the present town of Steinbach and pitched their tents, preparatory to the erection of more permanent shelters. First of all a plan of the village was laid out. The village street was drawn to follow a route almost due southeast, paralleling a creek bed some hundred yards to the left of it. A rectangular block of land consisting of some 320 acres was marked off into twenty sixteen-acre lots, about six acres of which lay on the northeast side of the road and ten on the southwest. The space allowed for the road was ninety-nine feet wide. The lot on the north side of the road was to become the *Feuerstelle* or homestead, that on the south the *Kattstelle*. On the *Feuerstelle* the buildings were to be erected and sufficient room was also allowed for gardens and a small enclosure for cattle. The lots on the south side would later serve as homes for residents that might move in or for the children growing up and marrying, and continuing to live in the village. In the meantime, it was cultivated by the villagers whose property it had become. Each villager was entitled to as many sixteen-acre lots as he had taken out quarter-sections in the blocks of land assigned to the village. Hence, Klaas Reimer and Franz Kroeker, who had each taken out two, had two lots, the former, numbers 9 and 10 and the latter, 19 and 20.

The shelters erected for the first winter had to be built hastily and varied in form and structure. Most common, perhaps, was a shelter known as a *semlin*. It was made by digging a rectangular hole three or four feet deep to serve as the lower half of a dwelling sufficiently long and wide to accommodate a family at one end and a few head of stock at the other. To make the walls, sods were piled up to a height of at least three feet above the ground around the edges of the hole. Light was provided by inserting two windows at ground level. Across the sods, poles or rafters were laid close together and covered with earth to serve as a roof. Above this hay might be piled for further warmth. A strong partition was built to shut off an area assigned to the cattle. The interior of the dwelling area was then lined with boards by those who had the money to purchase them in Winnipeg or were able to saw them from logs before the winter set in.

Hay had to be cut for the cattle by hand. Since much of it was frozen before the settlers found time to cut it, it was not very palatable and the cattle gained little nourishment from it. As a result of the lack of food, the cattle did not withstand the first winter very well. Many lost ears or horns or tail. Some had to be destroyed because they were so badly frozen. The production of milk under these conditions, of course, was very limited indeed.

Many of the settlers were quite poor and could spend very little money for food. In any case it was hard to obtain. The food for every meal was made mainly of flour, and the flour was of very poor quality. Variety in the menu depended on the ingenuity of the housewife in preparing various forms of baking or cooking this one ingredient. A sort of coffee was made from roasted barley, ground fine.

An interesting account of his early experiences in the founding of Steinbach was given by K. W. Reimer at the celebration of the sixtieth anniversary of this event. In the translation from the German that follows an attempt has been made to retain the homely flavour and simple but terse style of the original.

We bought the following articles at Duluth — a cookstove, an axe, a ham, and five pounds of lard. Drove by rail to Moorhead and took the Red River steamer from there. Reached Niverville, September 15, 1874. Pitched our tent and spent the night on shore. It rained practically all night. My brother and I found shelter at a half-breed Indian's home. Next morning we set out for the immigrant houses. We stayed there a week. Then our fathers came from Winnipeg with wagons and oxen and we set out for Steinbach. We learned that Canadian oxen stopped for "ho, ho" (In Russia they had used a similar sounding expression to get the oxen to start).

When we reached Steinbach each one's lot had been decided upon. On ours stood a large tree. Under it we pitched the tent and tied it to the tree. Then father hung the ham and his watch on the tree and began to build.

Here was our father with his sick wife, our mother, and eight children between heaven and earth [under the open sky] and winter was at the door. We built the house as follows: First we dug a hole in the earth, thirty feet long, fourteen feet wide, and three feet deep. The sods we piled up at the sides three feet high. Then we put in two small windows just above the level of the earth. Then we went to the bush to get rafters. It is the bush that still stands on John W. Reimer's farm. We had to carry the felled trees out of the bush. Father took the thick end and Abram and I the thin one. The roof of the house was thatched with rushes. Fifteen feet of the roof had boards underneath it, but only rushes covered the rest. [Apparently, in their case, a gable roof was built: this type of hut was usually referred to as a Serrei]. *That was for the cattle.*

After this we made a little hay. It was all frozen.

One evening we were surprised by a prairie fire. To protect ourselves against it we hastily ploughed a strip of land in its path. Many of the sods had to be turned over by hand. However, we were able to save the house.

That winter our cattle refused to eat the hay because it was too badly frozen. Fortunately, we were able to buy some better hay to save them from starvation. In addition to the hay we gave each ox and cow a slice of bread daily and in this way managed to bring the cattle through the winter.

Our food throughout the winter consisted of potatoes "fried" in water, salt, black bread and "prips" [roasted barley coffee substitute]. For a bag of flour father had to work six days making fence posts. For one load he received a bag of flour.

In spring, each man began cutting down the light brush and plowing. Those who did not possess two oxen used one ox and a cow. Many people spent their last dollar for seed.

In 1876, we built a better barn for the cattle, but continued to live in our hut [serrei] for another winter. In the spring of '76 many had lost courage because of the grasshoppers and wondered if they should put in seed for another year. [Grass-hoppers had completely destroyed the crop sown in '75.] One Sunday my grandparents, uncles and aunts were all gathered at our place. Several of my uncles wanted to move to the States. Then grandmother said, "We must not do that, for the dear God has heard my prayer. He protected us during the voyage and brought us safely here. We do not want to go farther. Much rather we shall go to work faithfully with God's help and not lose courage. I trust in God, I trust that He will bless us and that we shall have our bread."

These words encouraged our parents so much that, filled with new hope, they ordered their seed. A heavy rain on the 24th of May, accompanied by cold weather and snow, killed the eggs laid by the grasshoppers the previous year. They got much rain that summer. In places they had to cut their grain in the water and carry it to a dry spot.

My father had been a blacksmith in Russia. He needed coals to carry on this occupation here. Then John Peterson came and helped him make charcoal out of green poplarwood. In the years that followed we often had too much water [rain] and the grain drowned out. Often it froze. The roads were bad. A trip to Winnipeg required five days. There were many mosquitoes and many strawberries. In places the main street of Steinbach was so overgrown with scrub and trees that the ox drivers had to walk ahead of the oxen.

John Peterson and John Carleton [Clear Springs settlers] owned the first threshing machine that was used to thresh the grain in Steinbach. The separator had only two wheels. The power take-off was driven by four pair of oxen. Sometimes the sheaves were frozen together so badly that they had to be cut apart with an axe.

Our father started a store in 1877. He had gone to Winnipeg with products of the farm and happened to enter the dry goods store of R. J. Whitla. He asked father whether he would not like to take some goods with him and sell it among our people. He agreed to sell him $300 worth to be paid for later at father's convenience. The chest containing the goods became the counter and it was used as such until the store was built that still stands on Main Street and carries the name "Central Store" [1934].

I built my first home in 1885 and sold it in 1887 to John Thiessen for $400 all in $20 gold pieces. My own occupation was that of cheesemaker. In 1889, I built my first cheese factory in Steinbach. In 1892, I built the second in Blumenort and in

1896, the third in Hochfeld. In 1897, the total production of the three factories was 150,000 pounds of cheese. Before I began making cheese I had taken a six months' course in Winnipeg in the making of cheese and butter.

In 1897, I made cheese for the exhibition and received the first prize – $40.00 cash and a certificate for No. 1 cheese.

After the first year or two, the people of Steinbach, like the settlers in the other villages, began building substantial homes. They followed a Frisian pattern of joint house and barn that had been used by the Mennonites in Europe for many generations. In the East Reserve this structure was built by first making a heavy framework that consisted of squared timbers approximately six inches by six inches crossing each other vertically and horizontally at three-foot intervals. The spaces in each frame were blocked in with squared poles of similar dimensions. The chinks were filled in with homemade mortar. Later, many of these buildings were sided with boards, or with shingles, which lent themselves more readily to covering the rather uneven surface. The steep gable roof was thatched during the early years with bundles of rushes, lapped neatly and securely tied in place. The barn section was somewhat wider and higher than the house and was flanked on the side facing the back by a large shed. The barn door led to the backyard and the house door to the front. The ceiling of the house was supported by heavy joists or rafters eight inches deep and four wide, placed some three feet apart. The upper story under the steep gable roof was used for the storage of grain, which had to be carried up very steep stairs in two or three bushel bags.

The house was heated by a large brick stove or furnace so located in the walls separating the living room, bedrooms, and backroom (*Hinterstube*) that it heated all the main rooms without benefit of forced air ventilation or open doors. It was stoked from the backroom through a large door. In areas where wood was not readily available, hay or straw was used for fuel. Flax straw was especially suitable for the purpose. Above the fire box was a large baking oven which could hold many loaves of bread. Once fired and thoroughly warmed up, this type of stove retained its heat for many hours.

In the first years, a few small windmills were dragged into the East Reserve to grist flour and saw wood. However, in 1877, A. S. Friesen, a man of some means and a great deal of initiative, made use of some heavy logs hauled into Steinbach by men in the employ of Mr. Hespeler to build a large Holland-type windmill. When completed it towered sixty feet into the air and had sails which spread forty-six feet from tip to tip and were five feet wide. The studding for the main tower consisted of eight of the best logs hauled out by Hespeler's men. They were flattened on two sides to receive the siding. Then they were set up in the traditional pyramid style of architecture and covered with siding. The cross braces and other lighter timbers were cut by means of a light saw mill driven by oxen power. The shingles, steel shaftings and bearings, and the mill stones had to be hauled from Winnipeg. The long haul was complicated by seven sloughs in each of which the oxen invariably got stuck. The loads had to be unloaded and carried by manpower out of the slough. In this operation A. S. Friesen – who, in addition to his many other talents, was the local strong man – came in very handy.

The drive shaft of the mill to which the sails were to be attached was made of four twelve-inch squared oak timbers securely bolted together. Considerable ingenuity was required to devise a method of rounding the ends of this massive beam. Pins were put into each end. By means of these the beam was suspended in a frame. Then a rope was wound around the beam and drawn out by a team of horses thus causing the beam to turn. While it turned the builders used their axes, draw knives, and chisels to make a good neck bearing at one end. The wings were firmly screwed to this end and a large wooden wheel, twelve feet in diameter, was bolted to the other. To it were fastened large wooden cogs, and around the wheel were placed wooden brake shoes by means of which it might be stopped or allowed to turn. The cogs on the wooden wheel engaged the cogs of a large iron cog wheel that was attached to a long perpendicular oak shaft that extended to a lower story where it was fastened to a wooden wheel which turned an iron wheel attached to a five-foot upper millstone.

This mill was used to saw wood and to crush feed as well as to make flour. Because the surrounding trees checked the flow of the wind it was found that the mill was not sufficiently dependable to provide all the power needed to meet the demand. Consequently, Mr. Friesen was forced to install a steam engine to serve as an auxiliary source of power when the wind was low. Peter K. Barkman, who had been a mill builder in Russia, was in charge of the construction of the mill and Klaas Reimer, a blacksmith by trade, did the necessary iron work. Barkman's pay was fifty cents per day.

At first, the land surrounding the villages was farmed under the open field system. In this system the arable land was set out in large fields, each of which was divided into strips, varying in size from ten to twenty acres. Every owner in the village was entitled to one strip in each field per quarter-section of land owned. Those who had taken out pre-emptions as well as homesteads accordingly had two strips in each field instead of one. Crop rotation was practised with an alternation of wheat and feed crops followed every three years or so by summerfallow.

As the years passed, the population of Steinbach slowly increased, and it came to be the chief trading village of the area. Its growth continued to be slow until the building of the first all-weather roads in the thirties. At this time a number of activities were begun that considerably increased the cash returns for the people of this community. One was the growing of raspberries. This gave employment to a number of people, many of them children, during the picking season. Trucks came in the morning to pick up the crates of baskets filled with berries and whisk them to Winnipeg where the fruit found a ready market. Another source of income was the growing of potatoes for the early summer market. In time, the producers learned to market their produce in orderly fashion and thus lengthened the period during which the potatoes commanded the early market price. A third development was the feeding of poultry and livestock with balanced-ration feeds. This greatly accelerated poultry and livestock production and resulted as well in the rapid expansion of the production of special feeds by local millers and feed crushers. Furthermore, to meet the rapidly growing demand for poultry chicks several local hatcheries were established and began to thrive.

Advances came also in merchandising. Local merchants, many of whom had their own transportation system, became expert buyers and were able to provide their customers, extending in the course of time far beyond the original Steinbach trading area, with a ready supply of consumer goods at competitive prices.

Local manufacturing enterprises, originally begun with very modest investments, began to grow and expand. This was manifested especially in the establishment of two successful sash and door factories, one of which branched out into manufacturing a variety of products made from wood and also entered into the production of bee supplies, which were sold from coast to coast and even abroad. A machine shop, well-equipped with metal lathes and other power tools used in the machining of metal has given expert and faithful service for many years and thus continued the tradition of service and craftsmanship brought to Steinbach by the original settlers. A local sheet-metal firm started a foundry and began casting metal for various purposes.

Local automobile agencies and repair shops owned by men like J. R. Friesen, P. T. Loewen, and the Penner Brothers, as well as several others, had established thriving businesses in the forties; some, especially J. R. Friesen, many years earlier. Penner's Electric was ready when rural electrification reached its stride in Manitoba and did wiring in many parts of the province. J. T. Loewen's building-moving firm developed means of moving extremely large buildings safely and economically over large distances and was soon engaged in operations extending far beyond the boundaries of this province. Barkman, more recently, established a concrete plant which produced septic tanks, porch steps, and various other articles made of concrete in large quantity. Other important developments took place in the fields of transportation, earth moving, and construction. A firm, originating in Steinbach, Reimer Transport, operates daily from Edmonton to Montreal, but now has its head office and base depot in Winnipeg.

Education

The Mennonites had always been firm believers in education. They considered it essential that each person should learn to read and write in order to be able to read the Scriptures. However, of those who came to Manitoba few saw any need for education beyond the elementary level. They feared that an education which went much beyond the rudiments of reading, writing, and simple arithmetic could become a threat to their way of life and would undermine their religious faith. Consequently, in Steinbach many years were to elapse before opportunities for higher education were provided. As has been mentioned earlier, in the West Reserve there was a relatively small number of progressive-minded Bergthaler who saw the need for higher education, especially for the training of future teachers, almost from the beginning.

Although both the *Kleine Gemeinde* group and the Chortitzer in the East Reserve continued for many years to hold very conservative views with respect to education, the six *Kleine Gemeinde* villages, including Steinbach, were more ready to accept provincial grants and, in general, took more interest in maintaining the educational standards they were accustomed to from Russia. From the very first year, the children in Steinbach and indeed in all the villages, Bergthaler (Chortitzer) as well as *Kleine Gemeinde*, were sent to school. The Board (*Lehrdienst*) of the *Kleine Gemeinde* Church drew up a rather interesting set of rules and regulations for the establishment and maintenance of schools that in some respects are not too dissimilar from the regulations in effect in this province today. In the translation that follows an effort has been made to keep as close as possible to the style and content of the original German. In the interests of space some of the less relevant clauses have been omitted or condensed. It reads:

Because it is necessary that every one in his occupation should be able to read, write, and figure [do aritmetic] every village is required to establish an elementary school [Klein Kinderschule], in which the children, before they are old enough to do regular work or carry on an occupation, are to receive the most essential elements of an education. For this purpose the Church considers it necessary to establish the following regulations:
1. The school is under the direction and control of the Church Board [Kirchenvorstand] and its first responsibility is to see to it that a qualified teacher is appointed, who in his moral behaviour will serve as an example to the children entrusted to his care at all times, and who will prevent anything that might lead them astray from finding its way [Einschleichen] into the school.
2. The subjects that the teacher is required to teach are, to read correctly, to write, and to do arithmetic, also as time permits, to give instruction in grammar and composition. In addition, singing according to ciphers should be taught in order that, having learned to read music written in ciphers, each one will be able to learn many melodies which he did not have time to learn in school later on himself. However, it is necessary only to learn those melodies which may be found in our Mennonite Hymnal. Part singing we do not consider to be in accord with our standard of simplicity.
3. The school may be held either in the community meeting house or in a building specially rented for that purpose. It must in any case be supported by every member of the village community, without exception, regardless of whether he has children of school age or not, since the school is required not only for the children of today, but for all that follow in the future. It is the responsibility of the Board [Vorstand] to see to it that no child is unable to attend because of poverty.
4. In view of the fact that some arable land is set aside for the use of supporting the teacher, it is required that such provision

and the labour pertaining thereto be divided equally among all the homesteads in the village. The actual cash payment, however, providing the amount is not too high, is to be collected at an equal rate per child.

5. *The school attendance age for boys is set at seven to fourteen and for girls at seven to thirteen. During this age they shall be kept on the school register, and the school fees for each one must be paid regularly. Feeble-minded or otherwise incapacitated children are excluded from this ruling.*

6. *Those who do not live in a village are at liberty to teach their children themselves and are not required to pay to the support of any school or to pay pupil fees. However, a parent that neglects his children and fails to give them the necessary instruction, is duty bound to find some way of bringing them to a village school, in order that they may receive instruction equal to that of the others.*

7. *Instruction shall be given from the first of November till the first of May in every village school, five days a week and from five to six hours daily. Apart from illness or some other valid reason no absence from school will be permitted during the above-named period.*

8. *It is the duty of the school teachers to hold three conferences during the school term, one each, in the months of November, January, and March in order that they may exchange ideas and demonstrate methods. The children are required to be present at each conference.*

9. *Before the end of the school in April a general examination or achievement day* [allgemeine Prufung] *shall be held by the church leadership* [Kirchenvorstand] *in every school. The teacher should know a year in advance what his obligations are. In order that this may be so he should be engaged for the next year by the 1st of March. A frequent change of teachers is very harmful to a school. However, if a village hopes to improve a situation by a change, before such a change is made, the Church Board should make a thorough investigation to insure that changes are not made rashly or for trivial reasons.*

10. *The salary is to be paid the teacher in two instalments, namely, on the first of January and on the first of April. If for acceptable reasons any parents sends his child for only part of the school term, he is required to pay in proportion only.*

The *Kleine Gemeinde* regulations give a fairly adequate picture of the Mennonite belief in order and system as well as justice and fair play. However, they restrict as well as guide;

they serve as a limit as well as a goal, and, for the first thirty years, there was little change in the educational program of the East Reserve or in Steinbach itself. However, the *Kleine Gemeinde* teachers did try to improve themselves in their knowledge of subject matter and teaching method through attending H. H. Ewert's institutes and teachers' conferences and through private study as well. Most of the Chortitzer teachers, because of the opposition of their church to any innovation or outside influence, failed to do even that. In many cases there was actually a deterioration in the education of the children under their care. Only a few of the teachers who came to Canada from Russia had received high school education. Others had learned through self-study and experience and had thus improved themselves in their profession. However, busy making a living and overcoming the problems that face all pioneers in a new land, most of the Mennonites had no time to give thought to the need of providing qualified teachers. When their teachers retired or entered more profitable occupations, there were no qualified or even semi-qualified persons to take their places. As a result many of the children received a much poorer education than their parents had had in Russia.

In Steinbach this deterioration did not actually take place. Instead there was a very gradual improvement. In time some geography was taught and by very slow degrees English was introduced into the program. Steinbach, in company with other *Kleine Gemeinde* schools, accepted government grants and this helped to meet the costs of operation. Government inspectors of Mennonite schools usually reported quite favourably on the conditions they found in Steinbach. After 1900, students from the East Reserve began attending the private schools in Gretna and Altona, and around the years 1910 to 1914 educational progress began to accelerate. The Steinbach teachers made rapid strides in improving their qualifications. J. G. Kornelson, son of veteran Steinbach teacher, G. E. Kornelson, took Grade VIII in Gretna in 1911 in three months. Next year, he took Grades IX and X. Then he took Third Class Normal. In 1914, he took most of Grade XI in Gretna. In 1915-16, he and A. P. Friesen, who had commenced his high school education somewhat earlier, both took Grade XII in Gretna.

Coincident with this rapid improvement in qualifications of the teachers was a rise in the academic level of courses offered in Steinbach. In 1912, a third teacher was added to the staff, a change greatly needed, for enrolment had passed the hundred mark in 1909. Grade VIII was taught for the first time in 1913 with two students enrolled. High school instruction was begun next year, but at first the number of high school students increased slowly. By 1920, it had risen to thirteen out of a total enrolment of 209. In 1923, Grade XI was offered for the first time with one student in the class and a total high school enrolment of twenty-eight. A Grade XII class was begun in 1937 and numbered thirteen. The total enrolment at this time was 387 and of this number seventy-three were in the high school. By now, the staff had risen to nine teachers with three, presumably, in the high school. Most of the teachers needed for the East Reserve were now able to get their academic training in Steinbach, and every year a large number of candidates for the teaching profession came from this school.

Shop, Commercial, and Home Economics courses were added to the Steinbach curriculum in the late thirties or early forties. In 1945-46, these were given in addition to a full matriculation program. In addition to these extra courses there was a mixed choir, a girls' choir, and a boys' chorus. A school paper was published regularly, and there was an annual yearbook. A three-act play was also produced every year. Despite these extra activities, the pass rate was high, especially in 1945. Enrolment continued to rise and reached a total of 572 in 1945-46, of this number, 131 were in the high school with eighteen in Grade XII.

Three of the students in the 1944-45 classes have since become professors in the University of Manitoba and every year a large percentage of Steinbach Collegiate graduates enter the teaching profession. By 1946, many of the students went on to continue their studies at the University. All of the boys in the 1946 Grade XII obtained degrees in due course at various universities of the United States and Canada. All the girls of this class went directly into teaching after taking a year of professional training. Some continued their studies later and at least one graduated with a B.A. A Grade XII student of 1947 won the Gold Medal in Science at the University of Manitoba a few years later. A graduate of the Grade XII class of 1945 had the honour of navigating the plane that took Prime Minister St. Laurent around the world.

Education has by now been accepted as desirable and necessary by all the Mennonite churches in the East Reserve and the increase in the academic level and educational achievement has been tremendous as a result.

Expansion of Settlement In Manitoba, 1870-1900

John Friesen

This paper sets out to describe some of the forces at work in the period 1870 to 1900 which helped create rural Manitoba of today. I would like to deal with this topic under three main headings: Transportation and Settlement, 1870-1880; The Railway Era, 1881-1891; and Settlement Follows Railways, 1891-1900. First, however, I will discuss the system of land division which was a prerequisite to any activity in settlement.

Three systems of land survey are in common use in the agricultural portion of Manitoba. The parish or the river lot system of survey, though revised from time to time, is still in effect in the areas of early settlement. These extend from near Lake Winnipeg on either side of the Red River as far south as Emerson, west along the Assiniboine River to approximately four miles southwest of Portage la Prairie, and in other isolated portions of the province on river or lake frontages. The river lot system was modelled after the survey used in Lower Canada. This served the settlers who, besides working for the Hudson's Bay Company and supplying it with farm produce, were also engaged in fishing, hunting, and trading.[1] The river at their front door represented something more than a convenient base for surveys, it was also an essential element of the settlement and the survey was oriented towards it.

The second system of survey was devised by Colonel J. S. Dennis, an Ontario Provincial Land Surveyor. He made little use of the long narrow lot survey of that province; rather the American survey scheme, with some alterations, was used as a prototype for the prairie survey.

The proposed system was to consist of townships of sixty-four squares of eight hundred acres each and to contain, in

SOURCE: *Papers Read Before the Historical and Scientific Society of Manitoba*, series III, no. 20 (1965), pp. 35-47. Reprinted by permission of the author and the Manitoba Historical Society.

[1] John Warkentin, "Manitoba Settlement Patterns," *Papers Read Before the Historical and Scientific Society of Manitoba*, series III, no. 17, pp. 62-4.

addition, five per cent of the area in each section as an allowance for public roads. This scheme was modified when field survey work was interrupted by the Riel Uprising in 1869-70. The townships were changed to contain only thirty-six sections each approximately one mile square with a road allowance one and one-half chains wide. It was felt that townships in the original system were too large and that immigrants would be more familiar with the latter. Thus the townships measured six miles on each side, plus the road allowances. This system covers most of Southern Manitoba (south of Township 27) and extends into Eastern Saskatchewan. In 1881 this system was modified making the road allowances one chain wide and placing them on each alternate east and west line, though retaining them on all north and south lines. This revision was introduced to increase the amount of land allotted for cultivation and to decrease the cost of survey.

Thus, a large area of the province was surveyed using a "system which had for its primary consideration, the rapid and accurate division of the prairie region into farm holdings."[2] The survey proceeded well ahead of settlement as it rapidly superimposed a rigid stereotyped pattern without any regard to the physical characteristics of the land. No attempt was made to conform to topography, soils, drainage, and vegetation, and this system has been criticized by rural sociologists for the isolated life which it induced.

With these criticisms in mind and in seeking the best agricultural adjustments to the local physical conditions, planners attempted to introduce schemes within the official survey, usually the township. One such scheme was superimposed over the sectional survey at Birch River.[3] It was intended to alleviate social isolation with a planned village for the community center and park reservations along the River. Thomas Adams, the planner brought to Canada by the Commission of Conservation, suggested a number of village settlement schemes designed to provide for a more integrated form for farm building sites, a more convenient and direct access to the trading center, a reduction in land reserved for services, and the use of non-agricultural land as a source of timber.[4] In addition, some radical

---

[2] Canada, "Report of the Department of the Interior, 1892," *Sessional Papers*, xxv, no. 13.

[3] Thomas Adams, *Rural Planning and Development* (Ottawa, 1917), p. 59.

[4] *Ibid.*, p. 62. There were 54 miles of roadway reserved to service one township and the alternate scheme proposed by the Commission reduced this to approximately 40 miles.

plans were advocated which could be incorporated within the existing six mile township. One such scheme, put forth by Sir William Van Horne, provided for roads converging on a common center in each township or larger area.[5] In regard to these and other proposals, F. H. Peters, Surveyor-General of Canada, said in 1941 that "none of them seemed to be particularly attractive. It was very difficult to find any scheme of laying out a system of roads that would be as economical as the system which is followed in the Western Provinces."[6]

It is evident that every survey system which was employed or projected revealed some defects. Some appeared to be right in theory but did not work out satisfactorily in practice, and perhaps no system could have been advanced which would have been suitable for general application. In Beresford's evaluation of the rectangular system, he states that the survey is

a system which has received the highest praise wherever known, a system of survey which has been the greatest single factor in the successful development of Western Canada and one that has caused perhaps less litigation over land boundaries than any other in the world.[7]

With the completion of the survey in the Red River Valley and the western highlands, the first prerequisite to settlement was an accomplished fact. Law and order was provided by the Legislature of the province and by the North West Mounted Police. A succession of treaties with the Indians placed them on reservations as wards of the Queen. Certain lands were designated as half-breed reserves which subsequently were changed to half-breed scrip lands. The lands not affected by pre-1870 claims and not designated as reserves were available for homesteading, outright sale, or as grants to railways. The Canadian Pacafic Railway alone received a total grant of twenty-five million acres of land. Approximately two sections in every township were set aside for the Hudson's Bay Company for one-twentieth of the fertile belt south of the North Saskatchewan River was the company's reservation. Two sections in every township were designated as school lands.

[5] *Ibid.*, pp. 53-4.
[6] Quoted from F. H. Peters in L. Z. Rosseau, "Surveys and Land-Use Planning in the Province of Quebec," *Proceedings of Thirty-fourth Annual Meeting of the Canadian Institute of Surveying*, 1941, p. 31.
[7] H. E. Beresford, "Early Surveys in Manitoba," *Papers Read Before the Historical and Scientific Society of Manitoba*, series III, no. 9, p. 12.

In 1872 the Federal Government passed an *Act Concerning the Public Lands of the Dominion* whereby any person twenty-one years of age or over could apply for a homestead right to 160 acres of Dominion land. Title to the property was granted at the expiration of three years, provided the homesteader had resided on the property and made specified improvements.

The pre-emption privilege which was enacted at this time allowed a homesteader to make preferential claim to purchase a quarter-section or a part of a quarter adjoining the homestead for the price of one dollar per acre.[8] Due to land speculation, as well as the inability of the homesteader to pay for his pre-emption, this right was abolished in 1889.[9] The effects of the pre-emption right, according to the "Unused Lands" report of 1926, were such as to produce a "somewhat scattered population in the settlements and the natural result was excessive cost of construction and maintenance of roads, schools, public buildings, bridges, etc."[10] Two other results of this land policy were: first, the farm unit in districts settled during the "pre-emption period" was established as 320 acres, and second, a large number of people took advantage of this privilege with a view to land speculation on a small scale.[11]

With respect to incoming settlers, it was suggested that a prospective homesteader contact the agent at the Land Registry Office and have him arrange with his "Land Guide" to locate the vacant sections and to give information regarding the quality of the soil, the presence of water, and the availability of wood and hay lands.

TRANSPORTATION AND SETTLEMENT, 1870-1880

Prospective settlers entering Manitoba before 1878 followed three main routes: the Hudson Bay-Lake Winnipeg route; the Dawson route *via* Lake of the Woods and the Great Lakes; and the United States route by railroad to Moorehead and by steam-

---

[8] In a region where summerfallowing was to become a conspicuous form of land use this provision to acquire a second quarter had something to recommend it.

[9] The settler would mortgage his homestead quarter. All too often he would lose both his pre-empted and the homestead quarter.

[10] R. W. Murchie and H. C. Grant, *Unused Lands of Manitoba*, Manitoba Department of Agriculture and Immigration (Winnipeg, 1926), p. 60.

[11] To counteract this speculation the provincial government, in 1886, stipulated that farms should be assessed for taxation purposes as if they were in their unimproved state.

boat on the Red River to Emerson or Winnipeg.[12] In 1878 Winnipeg was connected to the American railway system *via* Emerson, thus removing a very serious obstacle to immigration.

Emerson and Winnipeg developed into the two main dispersal points for settlers. The Pembina Hills area had two lines of approach: one, *via* the International Boundary Commission Trail, and the other, by way of the trail to the Missouri River from Headingly. The move westward from Winnipeg was along the north and south branches of the Saskatchewan trail. The settlers found their way to their homesteads on the plains by following trails which were in use right up to the time railways superseded them.

During the years from 1876 to 1881, excessive spring rain made movement over the trails extremely difficult, and this tended to encourage navigation on the Assiniboine River. In 1876, the *Prince Rupert* displaced the stagecoach between Winnipeg and Portage. In 1879, and again the following year, the *Marquette* made the voyage through the sand hills past the Grand Rapids, eight miles above the mouth of the Souris, to Fort Ellice.

Prior to 1870 settlement was confined mainly to the river lots along the Red and Assiniboine Rivers; however, the machinery was being set up, and agricultural technology for the successful settlement of the prairies was being developed. Not only was a system of land disposal inaugurated and a form of law enforcement established, but technology in farming was advancing to the degree where the vast prairie expanse could be settled. The tough prairie sod could be cut by the steel plow introduced by John Deere. Barbed wire had made its appearance as the answer to the problem of fencing a country where trees were a scarce commodity. Another restraint to the development of the West was overcome when Red Fife Wheat made its appearance. This variety was well suited to the Manitoba environment; it matured in from 115 to 125 days, while the earlier varieties took over 130 days to mature. Red Fife rose to premium ranks when in the 1870s, the La Croix purifier was introduced and the traditional millstones were replaced by chilled iron rollers. A new method of tillage had evolved to meet the needs of the semi-arid environment. Summerfallowing

[12] The all-Canadian Dawson route was a combination of trails and steam launches.

Railroad connection to Moorehead from St. Paul was made in 1870.

had come to be an essential part of the dry farming practices in the plains area of the United States by 1860, and was definitely a part of the Western Canadian scene in the 1880s. According to the Manitoba Department of Agriculture Crop Reporting Bulletins, there were 47,728 acres in fallow in 1884 and 68,559 acres in 1885.[13] There are some sources which claim that summerfallowing was introduced by chance at Indian Head when General Middleton, in 1885, required the horses during the North West Rebellion. The horses were returned to the farm too late for springwork and consequently the land continued fallow for the whole of the summer of 1885. In 1886, under drought conditions, crops grown on the fallow fields returned a good yield whereas crops grown on stubble were almost a complete loss.[14]

A converging of these factors, that is, technological advances in farming on the prairie type of environment together with the exhaustion of the better land in the United States and Ontario and improved transportation facilities, was ultimately to inaugurate a new era in the Canadian West. By 1871 Manitoba had been well advertised in Ontario, and those who undertook the difficult and slow move to the Red River began to occupy the prairie and parklands in the Stonewall, Prairie Grove, and Springfield areas. In the following three years, new settlements grew steadily; however, very few settlers were willing to homestead on the open prairie, much of it being barren of both wood and running water.[15] The settlement around Emerson became the dispersal point for settlers pushing west and some east along the International Boundary Commission trail. Trails from the Kildonans towards Shoal Lake gave rise to settlements such as Grassmere, Argyle, and Woodlands. Immigrants followed the north branch of the Saskatchewan trail and established the Westbourne, Woodside, Palestine, and Livingstone settlements. To the southwest, Boyne and Nelsonville settlements sprang up. Settlement was checked by a severe plague of grasshoppers in 1876. When immigration increased in 1877, its distribution was affected by a succession of springs having high precipitation. Settlers discovered that south of the Assiniboine River the lands above the escarpment were as

---

[13] *Manitoba Crop Bulletin*, No. 6, Department of Agriculture, Statistics and Health (1884), p. 15.

[14] A. S. Morton, *History of Prairie Settlement* (Toronto, 1938), p. 84; H. G. L. Strange, *A Short History of Prairie Agriculture* (Winnipeg, 1964), p. 27.

[15] William L. Morton, *Manitoba: A History* (Toronto, 1957), p. 158.

fertile as, and better drained than, those in the valley and that this area provided a considerable growth of wood. This gave rise to settlements such as Darlingford, Somerset, Snowflake, Beaconsfield, Crystal City, Clearwater, and Swan Lake. The traffic along the Assiniboine River called attention to the lands adjacent to the valley. From points of debarkation along the river settlers proceeded to the Rapid City area, to the area surrounding the Brandon Hills, as well as to Odanah, Minnedosa and Birtle. By 1881 settlements in more or less direct relation to the North or South Saskatchewan trails appeared, giving rise to Wellwood, Oberon, Osprey, Neepawa, and Eden.

In the years 1874 and 1875, group settlement was begun; for in these years the Federal Government, by Order-in-Council, set aside blocks of land on which group colonists homesteaded. The first group settlers were the French from Quebec and Massachusetts who took up land in reserves in the Letellier, St. Pierre-Jolys, and St. Malo areas, as well as in the old settlements of the Ste. Anne-des-Chênes, Ile-des-Chênes, and the reserves set aside for the Métis. The first Mennonites came to Manitoba in 1874 and settled in the "East Reserve" located north and east of the Rat River. A second reserve was established west of the Red River, along the border towards the Pembina Mountains, in 1876. These two areas were set aside for the sole use of the Mennonite settlers. This was the first major demonstration of settlement on the open plain removed from wooded areas. In these two reserves, they superimposed upon the sectional survey, the pattern of the agricultural village carried forward from Russia. During this period, a reservation of more than six townships was set apart for a colony of Icelanders. The reserve extended for thirty miles along the west shore of Lake Winnipeg, with Gimli as its center.

According to A. S. Morton and James Trow, the system of reservations tended to retard settlement.[16] Trow claimed that many of the reservations (including railway reserves, Hudson's Bay Lands, Indian reserves and School Lands) were not in the interest of the Province and would retard legitimate colonization, unless thrown open for settlement. These reserves together with the holding of land by speculators, created a "landlock" which was vigorously denounced. This factor, plus flooding, caused by heavy precipitation during 1877, encouraged

---

[16] A. S. Morton, *History of Prairie Settlement*, p. 56; James Trow, *Manitoba and North West Territories,* Department of Agriculture (Ottawa, 1878), p. 17.

settlers to push beyond the escarpment and the Assiniboine delta.

Until the eighties, Manitoba was largely the market for its own agricultural products, but, beginning in 1877 a small amount of wheat was being shipped east by steamboat. In the main, however, settlement up to this time had been a speculative venture in anticipation of the railway.

In 1881, the Trans-Continental Railroad reached Brandon and during the same year, by an Act of Parliament, the boundary of the province was changed on the west to its present boundary and on the north to 53° of latitude.

THE RAILWAY ERA, 1881-1891

Settlement in the 1870s followed trails leading in different directions, and, when the Canadian Pacific reached Brandon in 1881, its single line running across the province was already inadequate. This was borne out by the various charters granted by the province for the construction of additional lines.

The C.P.R., according to Clause 15 of the *Canadian Pacific Act*, had a practical monopoly to build rail lines on the lands south of their Trans-Continental line. This right was disputed by the province, however, and several charters passed by the Manitoba Legislature were disallowed by the Dominion as conflicting with Clause 15. This clause was cancelled in 1888.

During the decade of the 1880s, the Manitoba North Western Railway was built as a feeder from Portage to Gladstone, Minnedosa, Birtle, and into the North West Territories. The C.P.R. continued westward from their Winnipeg-Gretna line (1882) at Rosenfeld to Manitou and Deloraine (1886), by-passing the village of Nelsonville by five miles. Another line from Winnipeg to Brandon was commenced by the Manitoba and South Western Co. as far as Elm Creek. The C.P.R. bought out its charter and continued the line through Glenboro to Brandon. In 1889, the Northern Pacific and Manitoba Railway Co. built a line from Morris to Greenway and to Brandon which gave rise to the towns of Miami, Somerset, and Wawanesa. According to studies carried out, it was generally agreed that the distance within which producers could economically haul their grain to market was in the vicinity of ten miles, although some farmers were known to haul their produce a distance of fifty miles. The distance and cost of grain movement to the shipping point depended on the alternative uses to which the farmer's time and equipment might be put. This left many a farmer beyond the economic limit for grain transportation.[17] In 1885 it was reported that there was a "great want of railway facilities" especially in the counties of Turtle Mountain, Souris River, Shoal Lake, Russell, Rock Lake.[18] This acute shortage resulted in homesteads being abandoned and prepared land left unseeded.

Trouble also resulted from inadequate facilities such as platforms, warehouses, elevators, and grain cars to handle the mounting surplus of grain.[19]

During the years 1882 to 1887, immigration was at a low ebb. These were years of depression, of severe frost damage to crops, and of drought. It was during 1883 that the duties on agricultural implements were substantially increased. It was during this period also that methods of dry farming were adopted and that earlier maturing varieties of wheat, notably Red Fife, were being developed.

Even though the frontier of settlement had moved westward beyond Manitoba during the 1880s, there remained areas of empty land in the southern portion of the Province. There was the scantily settled wet lands between Morris and Carman, and the sandy lands along Middle Assiniboine. The largest area of relatively unoccupied land was in the southeast where poor soils and poor drainage effectively retarded settlement.[20] The rough and wooded lands in the vicinity of Turtle Mountain, and Riding Mountain discouraged settlement in that area, and much filling in of settlement remained to be done in districts already occupied.

SETTLEMENT FOLLOWS RAILWAYS, 1891-1900

By 1890, the rapid railway construction of the past decade had come to a pause. The basic pattern of the railway network was laid, with Winnipeg emerging as the nodal point for goods and people moved by rail. During the latter part of this decade, however, two major railway lines were added to the network, as well as some minor branch lines and extensions. During 1896, Mackenzie and Mann commenced construction on a line from

---

[17] William L. Morton, *Manitoba: A History* (Toronto, 1957), pp. 209 ff.

[18] *Manitoba Crop Bulletin*, No. 10, Department of Agriculture, Statistics and Health (June, 1885), pp. 18-19.

[19] Prior to the advent of the modern grain elevator flat warehouses were used for grain handling. The first elevator was built in 1879 at Niverville. The first square standard elevator was built in 1881 at Gretna by the Ogilvie Milling Company.

[20] *Economic Atlas of Manitoba*, p. 28.

Gladstone to the Dauphin area. With the completion of this line, Manitoba had gained a new booming frontier to the northwest. To the north of this new frontier lay the country of the Swan River Valley which was reached by the rail line in 1899. Dauphin was used as a base for settlers moving into this valley. The same two energetic railway projectors constructed another line from St. Boniface to Marchand. This project was begun in 1898 and reached Fort Frances in 1901. It passed through the forested lands of the southeast that by and large were too sandy or too poorly drained for agricultural use.

During the first half of this decade there was a slackening of the inflow of immigrants. The reasons for this decline seem to have been related to the subnormal precipitation from 1886 to 1897 (excluding 1887), to the fact that most of the good land south of the Riding Mountains had either been taken up by actual settlers or was being held by speculators, and to the depressed economic situation which resulted when the price of new land was comparatively high relative to the low produce prices.

The wooded slopes of the Turtle and Riding Mountains were avoided by the settlers; however, they became an important source of wood for building and fuel. In 1895, the Government of Canada designated them as "Timber Reserves" along with the Spruce Woods area. The latter was partly settled by this time and the Dominion Government purchased the privately held land as well as the remaining C.P.R. lands. Another timber reserve was established in the West Lake area; this was cancelled by the Canadian Forestry Act of 1911.[21]

Settlement in the Dauphin area began in 1886, with settlers coming in from the west. Settlement in this fertile frontier area, where first quality land was cheap, had passed beyond the railway. By 1888 settlers were following the Arden Ridge up into this fertile district and with the increase in settlement and in crop surpluses, there grew the need for communication with the outside world. With a means of communication established, the best lands in this area, as well as in the Swan River district, were soon occupied. This area was settled largely by Canadians or Anglo-Saxons, and for many of them this was a second frontier, as they had already sold their original improved homesteads at high prices. With the settling of these two frontiers the last of the better agricultural land was occupied. This left untouched

[21] Oral report from C. B. Gill, Forestry Branch, Department of Mines and Natural Resources, 1963.

the marginal lands which demanded a greater investment for their development and promised lower returns than any of the lands hitherto settled. These lands, extending from south-eastern Manitoba through the Interlake area and past Dauphin as well as land adjacent to Riding Mountain Park and Duck Mountain Forest Reserve, had been avoided by earlier immigrants. The major part of the task of settling the bush country was left to the Slavic people who began to migrate to Manitoba during 1896 when most of the good land had already been settled.

At the threshold of the twentieth century the basic pattern of railway transportation was almost complete. Manitoba during the past thirty years had developed pretty well into a grain-growing province; the growing and shipping of wheat were its two main occupations. With the immigration of the settlers from eastern Europe during the turn of the century the province increasingly turned into a polyglot mosaic of diverse people. And in many cases the various ethnic groups settled in definite zones or in reserves set aside for a particular group.

The Hutterians: History and Communal Organization of a Rural Group

Victor Peters

There are over twelve thousand Hutterians[1] in North America. A little over eight thousand of them live in Canada, the others in the United States. They all live in cluster-type colonies known as *Bruderhöfe*. Manitoba has over thirty of these colonies, Alberta almost twice as many, and Saskatchewan has six of them. The forty colonies in the United States are largely confined to South Dakota and Montana.

In Hutterian doctrine, one cardinal article of faith is the belief in common ownership of all their property. This is known as *Gutergemeinschaft*, which may be translated with the phrase "community of goods." The Hutterian interpretation of Christ's teachings is that the spiritual community must be made tangibly visible in a community of goods, where spiritual and temporal blessings are shared equally.[2] Since the Hutterians have subscribed to this ideal for over four centuries, it is necessary to deal at least briefly with their history in order to understand them and their ways.

The Hutterian church had its origin in the turbulent Reformation years. Barely had Luther and Zwingli broken away from the Catholic church, when some of their closest supporters pressed for still greater changes. Many of the leaders of these radical reformers were humanists like Conrad Grebel and Dr. B. Hubmaier. In time, these reformers became known as Anabaptists. They were especially numerous in Southern Germany, Austria, and Switzerland. The Anabaptists endorsed adult bap-

SOURCE: *Papers Read Before the Historical and Scientific Society of Manitoba*, series III, no. 17 (1960-1961), pp. 6-14. Reprinted by permission of the author and the Manitoba Historical Society. This paper was originally entitled: "The Hutterians – History and Communal Organization of a Rural Group in Manitoba."

[1] The Hutterians are more generally known as "Hutterites." Their own constitution, as incorporated by Act of Parliament, however, refers to them as "Hutterian Brethren."

[2] *Cf.* Peter Riedemann, *Confession of Faith*, English translation from the original German edition of 1565, in the British Museum (England, 1950), p. 88.

tism and rejected the use of the sword and the oath. They also stressed the elected lay ministry.

To the Catholics the Anabaptists were heretics, and to their fellow-Protestants they were seditionists because of their refusal to bear arms. In either case the punishment was death. Many of the Anabaptists escaped the imperial and princely sheriffs by fleeing to the Eastern borderlands.

The most accessible of these borderlands in the sixteenth century was Moravia. Thousands of Anabaptists fled there to find sanctuary on the estates of powerful German and Moravian nobles. Several of these Anabaptist groups introduced common ownership of goods. Though the pooling of their worldly resources created many problems of human adjustments, the congregations gained a strong leader in a young Tirolean minister, Jakob Huter. Huter, an uncompromising believer in the community ideal, welded together a small but strong church. Huter died a martyr's death at Innsbruck, in 1536, but he left an indelible impression on and his name to the congregations. Henceforth, they were known as Hutterian Brethren.

The following century saw an extraordinary growth of Hutterianism; the church membership rising to over fifty thousand. According to Hruby, a Czech historian, the Hutterians were unsurpassed as millers, farmers, clock-makers, and weavers.[3] The museums of Vienna, Prague, and Brünn to this day exhibit samples of Hutterian ceramics of unusual craftsmanship. The Hutterian schools had an excellent reputation. The Hutterian school regulations of 1578 indicate that schools and teachers were far in advance of their times.[4] Mention should also be made of Peter Riedemann, an early Hutterian Elder. Next to Huter no man contributed more to Hutterian thinking than this man, who wrote his *Confession of Faith* in a Marburg gaol in 1540. To this day this book is found in every Hutterian colony, and no student of Hutterian history can ignore it.

The Thirty Years' War (1618-1648) almost exterminated the Hutterian congregations, and wiped out every one of their colonies in Moravia. Some Hutterians, however, succeeded in escaping to Slovakia, others to Transylvania. The scope of this paper does not permit an account of the development of their

[3] Frantisek Hruby, *Die Wiedertäufer in Mahren* (Leipzig, 1935).

[4] English translation by H. S. Bender, "A Hutterite School Discipline of 1578 and Peter Scherer's Address of 1568 to the Schoolmasters" appeared in the *Mennonite Quarterly Review* (Goshen, Indiana, October, 1931), pp. 231-44.

communities here. Marginally, I will only mention that though the Hutterians would seem to have been far removed from Western Europe, they, nevertheless, had contact with various kindred groups. George Fox (1624-1691) knew of them, and there is evidence that their ways influenced the development of Quakerism in England.[5]

The death blow to the Hutterian communities in Slovakia and Transylvania was dealt to them during the reign of Maria Theresa, in the eighteenth century. The Empress, a devout Catholic, had given the Jesuits a free hand in this matter. This phase of Hutterian history is amply documented by the Austrian historian Josef von Beck, himself a Catholic.[6] What followed was not a bloody persecution, but children were permanently removed from their parents, and, indeed, the older people themselves were placed in monastic institutions. All worship outside the prescribed state churches was forbidden. Hutterianism was blotted out, except for a small party of sixty souls, which fled across the Transylvanian Alps to Wallachia. Wallachia was then under Turkish suzerainty, and here the Hutterians were accepted and permitted to settle near Bucharest. This was in 1767.

The following year war broke out between Turkey and Russia. Unexpectedly, the brethren found themselves in the vortex of retreating and advancing armies, with no peace in sight. When the Russian commander-in-chief, Count Rumiantsev, offered them free land on his estates in the newly-acquired Ukraine, the Hutterians willingly accepted the offer. In 1770, they made the long trek from Bucharest to the Desna River, a tributary of the Dnieper.

For over one hundred years the Hutterians lived in Russia, or, rather, in the Ukraine. During this period they enjoyed complete religious liberty, control over their schools, and exemption from military service. But it seemed that this very freedom produced dissension within their own ranks. In time the practice of community of goods was discarded, and the Hutterians moved to the Mennonite settlements to the south. The Mennonites and Hutterians had a common Anabaptist heritage, except that community of goods had never been a Mennonite doctrine of faith. Also, in matters of dress, the Mennonites were much

---

[5] Cf. Joseph Besse, A Collection of the Sufferings of the People Called Quakers (London, 1752), pp. 420-32.

[6] Josef von Beck, Dei Geschichtsbücher der Wiedertäufer in Osterreich-Ungarn, Fontes rerum Austriacarum, II. Diplomatica et Acta, XLIII (Vienna, 1883).

less conservative. There were also some ethnic differences. The Mennonites spoke the Low German of their North German homeland, while the Hutterians spoke a Tirolean dialect. The language in church of both groups was German. The common religious heritage and church language had a powerful impact on the Hutterians who formed by far the smaller group. But before any great changes in Hutterian ways occurred, external developments intervened.

In 1870, the Russian government introduced universal compulsory military service. Many Mennonites and all Hutterians decided to leave the country. Ten deputies, two of them Hutterians, were sent by their congregations to explore the conditions of settlement in North America. The group visited many parts of the United States, as well as Manitoba. The eighteen thousand Mennonites who left Russia divided, with approximately one-half of them settling in the United States, and the other half in Manitoba. All the Hutterians, on the other hand, settled in the Dakota Territory, in an area that subsequently became the State of South Dakota. There were about five hundred Hutterians in all. But about one-half of them decided to relinquish community of goods and to settle as individual landholders. Descendants of these Hutterians are almost indistinguishable from other Americans. Some of them have served as elected legislators in the State House and Senate.

The community Hutterians on their arrival, in 1874 and in the years immediately following, settled on three colonies. This was of some significance as there are today three major congregations among the colonies, with minor differences among them. The minister of the first colony was by trade a blacksmith, and his group became known as the *Schmiedeleut* (the blacksmith people). All the Manitoba and South Dakota colonies belong to this group. The minister of the second group was named Darius Walther, and they became known as *Dariusleut*. The leader of the third colony was a teacher, and his group became known as the *Lehrerleut*. The colonies of Alberta, Saskatchewan, and Montana belong to these two latter congregations.

The Hutterians fared well until 1917, when the United States entered into the war. War fever ran high, and this led to many wild charges against the colonies. The Hutterians, for instance, operated many flour mills. One charge was that they committed acts of sabotage by mixing ground glass with the flour. It was also maintained that they did not contribute enough to the war effort. Their cattle and sheep were driven off their lands and sold to neighbouring farmers at ludicrously low prices. At least two Hutterian boys, who were conscientious objectors, died as a result of mistreatment at an army camp. The Hutterians felt that, under these conditions, it would be better for them to leave and they approached the Canadian immigration authorities with the request that they be permitted to migrate to Canada.

As early as 1873 the Canadian government had been prepared to accept the Hutterians and to grant them the same terms that were extended to the Mennonites; namely, exemption from military service. This offer was renewed during the Spanish-American War, when the Hutterians established a colony in Manitoba, in the Dominion City area.[7] Repeated flooding of their lands caused the Hutterians to return to South Dakota in 1905. In 1918, the Canadian West faced an acute manpower shortage. The war was still in progress, and the European allies relied on Canada's agricultural output. Since the Hutterians were known to be very productive farmers, the Canadian government did "What it could to encourage the Hutterite immigration."[8]

All but one of the American colonies, thereupon, transferred to Canada, settling in Alberta and Manitoba. The first colony in Manitoba established itself on land purchased from Senator Benard in the Elie district. During the first two decades, the growing number of colonies was not considered a problem. With their almost self-sufficient economy the Hutterians were better prepared to ride out the Depression of the thirties than the individual farmer. Especially in Alberta, municipalities and towns wooed the Hutterian colonies to settle in or near them, for the colonies were in a position to pay their taxes on land and they also paid in cash for purchases in stores. On the other hand, the Hutterian remained what he had been. In many ways he was an alien, marked by his speech, dress, and beard, staying away from the neighbourhood social or dance, and refusing to be drawn into the melting pot.

During the Second World War, with the resurgence of national emotions and the upsurge of the national agricultural economy, the Hutterian colonies became the targets for public criticism. This feeling survived the war. In Alberta the legis-

[7] Copies of correspondence are on file with the records of Mr. E. A. Fletcher, Q.C., Winnipeg, solicitor for the Hutterians. The letter from James A. Smart, Deputy Minister of the Interior, is dated Ottawa, October 27, 1899.

[8] *Winnipeg Free Press*, October 16, 1919.

lature passed the restrictive *Communal Property Act* that prevents Hutterians from purchasing land within forty miles of an existing colony, and also limits their land holding. In Manitoba we have a so-called voluntary "Gentlemen's Agreement" between the colonies and the Union of Rural Municipalities that also restricts indiscriminate Hutterian expansion. Here I would like to break off the first part of my paper and devote some time to a description of a Hutterian colony and of colony life in general.

The Hutterian *Bruderhof*, or colony, is an organic whole in which it is difficult to segregate the part played by such accepted institutions as the church, the family, the school, or the industrial enterprises.

The colony is the temporal base for the spiritual church. The colony may or may not have a special building for church services. The school or the community dining hall serve the purpose equally well. There is a lengthy morning service on Sunday, and a short evening service every day of the week, summer or winter. Attendance is not compulsory, but members and children attend fairly regularly. To the Hutterians colony life itself constitutes divine service. In this sense the instruction of the child, the almost silent meal, the evening spent with the famliy at home, the day spent at work, are all forms of worship, marred of course by human frailties, failings, and shortcomings.

The population of a colony ranges from eighty to two hundred adults and children. The colony consists of a nucleus of buildings placed on a landholding of from three to four thousand acres. In Alberta the acreage of a colony may run to ten thousand. The dwellings are built around a spacious community kitchen and dining hall. Beyond these are the farm buildings, barns, granaries, implement sheds, carpenter and blacksmith shops, the public school, the hatchery, the killing plant, the poultry houses, the turkey compounds, and numerous buildings required for the different farm enterprises. The whole pattern of the colony resembles that of a cluster-type village, but the arrangement of the buildings is more functional than beautiful.

The outsider who penetrates beyond the barns and community buildings of the colony is perhaps most deeply impressed by the religious conviction common to its people. "Twentieth century America," wrote Dr. Clark some forty years ago, "knows little of that sort of piety which makes the enveloping atmosphere of all Hutterian life."[9] And more than thirty years later, two American researchers, Kaplan and Plaut, again reported, "The [Hutterian] people as a whole are religious to an unusual degree, and there is hardly a doubter among them."[10]

Within the larger brotherhood each colony constitutes an autonomous, economic unit, but is ready to extend help and assistance to another, less well-to-do colony. The help may be in the form of an interest-free loan, a direct cash contribution, a contribution in kind, or the dispatch of a team of workers to help in urgent work, be it harvesting or the building of a new barn, or canning for winter.

The administration of a colony is democratic. The entire baptized, male congregation is the final authority in all major undertakings. It also elects a council of five or six members, known as *Zeugbruder*, who hold their positions for life. Indeed, all elective offices are for life, but an occupant may forfeit his position if he is guilty of a serious misdemeanour, or he may be elected to a different office, and then would relinquish his former post.

The spiritual head of the colony is the *Diener am Wort* (minister), who occupies the most respected position. If the colony is large, he may have an assistant. Candidates for this are nominated by the male congregation of the colony, but the final selection is made by the drawing of lots. The colony manager, known as the *Haushalter* or *Wirt* (householder or steward) is the secretary, the treasurer, and the co-ordinator of the various economic enterprises. He is assisted by the *Weinzierl* (farm-manager). No position entails any special favours or privileges. Even the minister has his specific manual duties, be it as a gardener, bee-keeper, or carpenter.

In addition to these positions every enterprise has its elected head. There is the *Hennemann* (poultry-man), the *Viehwirt* or *Kuhmann* (cattle-man), the school-master, the head carpenter, blacksmith, turkey-man, the usually elderly *Brotmann* (bread-man), who supervises the dining hall, and many others, each one in charge of specific tasks. Generally outsiders refer to these men as "bosses," the farm-manager as the farm-boss, the stew-

[9] B. Clark, "The Hutterian Communities" in *The Journal of Political Economy* (Chicago, 1924), xxxii, 3 and 4, pp. 357-74, 468-86, page 363.

[10] Bert Kaplan and Thomas F. A. Plaut, *Personality in a Communal Society*, Analysis of the Mental Health of the Hutterites (University of Kansas, Lawrence, Kansas, 1956), page 12.

ard as the colony-boss, the pig-boss, etc. The Hutterians disapprove of this terminology, but some are beginning to use it themselves.

Then there are the positions occupied by the women. These are elected to their posts by the male congregation of the colony. There is the *Haushalterin* or *Küchenfrau* (stewardess or kitchen-woman), whose chief duties are in the kitchen, planning the meals and establishing the order of rotation in which the colony women are required for kitchen duties. The *Zuschneiderin* (seamstress), who works in close co-operation with the stewardess, is in charge of the purchase and distribution of cloth. Almost all the clothes worn on the colony are made by the women at home, each woman sewing for her family. The *Gartenfrau* is in charge of the gardens and of winter canning. The *Hebamme* (mid-wife), the *Kinderweib* or *Kinderangela* (kindergarten teacher), are each responsible for the work in their domain.

Since the average colony has a population of about 120, and more than half of it are children fourteen years and younger, and at the other end of the age scale are the retired members, it becomes evident that practically every adult, male or female, occupies some position of responsibility in the administration and operation of the colony.

The Hutterian family itself may be termed as patriarchal, but does not differ markedly from the Western European family pattern. Divorces are not permitted, and illegitimacy is almost unknown.

Marriage generally takes place between the ages of twenty to twenty-four, that is, shortly after the marriage partners have been received in church through baptism. Both parties have to be members of the church. The man may select his bride from the home colony, or from any other colony. Marriages with outsiders are rare, but are permitted, provided the outsider joins the Hutterian church. The wedding itself takes place in the groom's colony. It is marked by a church service, followed by a modest celebration. Hutterian rules permit moderate drinking of alcoholic beverages, but smoking is forbidden. There is some singing at weddings, but *Buhlenlieder* (frivolous songs) are not tolerated. Except for a Bible and perhaps some other books, there are no gifts. Invariably the wife moves to her husband's colony. The newly-married couple is assigned one or two rooms, but transfers to a larger home as the size of the family increases. Hutterian homes have no kitchen, as the food is prepared in the community kitchen, and consumed in the common dining-hall.

As a rule Hutterian families are large, averaging ten to twelve children. The family relationship is wholesome, and violent quarrels are practically unknown.[11] Indeed, the whole community resembles in many ways an outsize family, in which the atmosphere is happy and cheerful.

The clothes worn by adults and children are plain. Ornaments are forbidden. Sometimes the girls and young women chafe under these restrictions. Boys and young men sometimes acquire musical instruments or radios, both in violation of colony ordinances. Older women may show a weakness for idle gossip, and a man may occasionally take one drink too many or smoke a cigarette. These weaknesses carry with them the strong disapproval of the church and the community members. Generally a visit from the minister persuades the delinquent to conform to colony ways. In more serious cases a member may be punished in that the congregation "takes his peace" (*seinen Frieden nehmen*). He is shunned, a practice known as the *Meidung*, and isolated, whether at work, or at the table. And, indeed, he may be assigned living quarters separate from those of his family. He is re-admitted into the congregation when he shows repentance. If the member refuses to make his peace, he may be placed under the ban. This may go so far as exclusion from the colony. There are only a few instances of this in Hutterian history. In 1928, one Hutterian in Manitoba became a member of the Jehovah Witnesses. He was permitted to remain on the colony provided he did not attempt to proselytize among the community members. When the estranged member felt that he could not abide by his promise, he was asked to leave.

The aged in the Hutterian society are not required to work, but will help voluntarily whenever they can. Their opinions on all matters are valued and respected.

The Hutterian school plays an important role in colony life. The kindergarten is perhaps the most attractive feature of any colony. It is headed by a female teacher, who may have one or two assistants. From the kindergarten the children proceed to the public school. The latter is administered by a senior government official, and staffed by non-Hutterian teachers. Here the

[11] *Cf. Clark*, "The Hutterian Communities"; L. E. Deets, *The Hutterites — A Study in Human Cohesion* (Gettysburg, Pa., 1939); W. D. Knill, "Hutterian Education . . ." (unpublished Master's thesis, Montana State University, 1958); Joseph Eaton and Albert J. Weil, *Culture and Mental Disorders, A Study of the Hutterites and Other Populations* (Glencoe, Illinois, 1955).

English language and the prescribed curriculum of the province is used. However, one hour before the opening and one hour after the closing of the public school is devoted to religious instruction by a Hutterian teacher. Attendance at colony schools is exceptionally good, averaging over 90 per cent. The schools are located on the colonies, and transportation and bad weather are no problems here. The Hutterians are not opposed to elementary education, but do not favour education beyond junior high school. However, there is no rule against it. Once the child leaves the school his education continues in the form of apprenticeship in the different colony enterprises.

The economic basis for the colony is provided by a highly diversified form of agriculture. The Hutterian belief makes it practically mandatory for its members to be farmers. When the colony population grows beyond a certain number, a branch colony is set up on newly-purchased land. A division takes place, and half the community moves to the new location. Both colonies, after that, function as fully-independent units.

The assets of a colony, depending on the land, the machinery, the buildings, etc., may represent the cash equivalent of from one-half to one million dollars. A colony will generally have pigs, cattle, chickens, ducks, geese, turkeys, and may raise diversified crops ranging from canary seeds to feed grains. The colony's own economy supplies the major needs of the community, whose greatest problem is to feed, clothe and shelter a population that doubles within every sixteen to twenty years.

Spiritually, the colony provides a sanctuary, a "Noah's ark," where the members of the brotherhood find safety from what they consider the sins and temptations of the outside world. Economically, the colony provides its members with complete security from the cradle to the grave. "These people," says the *Scientific American,* "live a simple, rural life, have a harmonious social order and provide every member with a high level of economic security from the womb to the tomb. They are a homogenous group, free from many of the tensions of the American melting-pot culture."[12]

For centuries the Hutterians resisted state-demanded, religious conformity. Canada and the United States provide them with full religious liberty, but there are strong elements in both countries which insist on the cultural assimilation and uniformity of all citizens. But in the complex Hutterian pattern,

[12] J. W. Eaton and Robert J. Weil, "The Mental Health of the Hutterites," in *Scientific American,* vol. 189, no. 6 (December, 1953).

the religious and cultural values are so interwoven that the group feels that a compromise, or displacement of old values, is a threat to its existence.

What the future holds for the Hutterians in Canada is difficult to foretell. It is possible that they will in time be accepted, with their peculiarities, as a component of the Canadian mosaic. In turn, they too may change in some ways. Their qualities and characteristics are not incompatible with the ideals of the larger society around them. Their colonies function on democratic principles; there is a marked absence of crime among them; the people lead sober, frugal lives. They emphasize family life, and take good care of their children and the old people. The public school is accepted without a protest.

On the whole the Hutterian communities show remarkable vitality. Moreover, they continue to hold the loyalty and devotion of their young people.

The Patrons of Industry in Manitoba, 1890-1898

Brian R. McCutcheon

There were at least three different farmers' organizations that arose in Manitoba before the birth of the Patrons movement in the 1890s. The first of these was the Grange imported from the United States by way of Ontario – the first lodge being established in Winnipeg in 1874 as a political caucus.[1] Others were established at High Bluff (which quickly disappeared), Carberry, Mekiwin, Wellwood, Florenta, Gladstone, Arden, and Eden;[2] but the movement was never strong in the then sparsely settled West.

The second group to arise, the Manitoba Farmers' Protective Union, is of more fundamental importance, patterned as it was in part on the native radicalism of the North-West. The Manitoba Railway Boom of the early 1880s based on many of the same premises as the American boom to the south, bred a false sense of confidence. Between 1876 and 1881, forty thousand immigrants entered the province, mainly from Ontario. With them came the necessary technological knowledge for the breaking of the prairie sod and the successful cultivation of the open plains.[3] This sudden interest in the future of the West was the occasion for the Great Boom and "Manitoba fever." Winnipeg grew from a small village to a small city, and several outlying rural towns sprang into existence. All of them, fed on inflated prices for land, planned too much too fast. Emerson, for example, was chartered as a city and assumed a large debt in anticipation of growth that never came. In the provincial capital, the rate of growth quickened to the point where lots

SOURCE: *Historical and Scientific Society of Manitoba Transactions*, series III, no. 22 (1965-66), pp. 7-25. Reprinted by permission of the author and the Manitoba Historical Society.

[1] W. L. Morton, *Manitoba: A History* (Toronto: University of Toronto Press, 1957), p. 210.

[2] Aubrey Wood, *A History of Farmers' Movements in Canada* (Toronto: The Ryerson Press, 1924), p. 65. Wood states that the first lodge was established at High Bluff in 1876.

[3] Morton, *op. cit.*, p. 181.

on Main Street were exchanged for higher prices than those then commanded on Michigan Avenue in Chicago.[4]

The boom, artificial as it was, could not last, and, in 1883, there followed a general business collapse which affected not only the small urban population but the rural agricultural settlers as well. Coupled to the collapse of the boom were problems endemic to the whole of Western North America. Freight rates and elevator charges in any frontier area proved to be high, but in Manitoba the farmers had a special complaint — the famous monopoly clause of the C.P.R. guaranteed that no line could be built between the main line of the C.P.R. and the American border for twenty years after completion of the transcontinental line. At the same time, world wheat prices had declined drastically, cutting the farmers' margin of profit.

Nor were credit conditions good at any time. The chartered banks were slow in moving into newly settled areas, and, consequently, in a society which depended upon credit, the void was filled by locally organized banks which charged interest excessive in the farmers' eyes. In Gladstone, the only bank until 1896 was that owned by W. S. Bailey, and the rates of interest on loans were double those charged by the chartered banks.[5] Thus in 1883 Manitoba had a generally indebted population, bearing at the time heavy civic and municipal liabilities for hastily conceived public works, and facing a general economic depression.

Economic discontent resulted in the formation of the Manitoba Farmers' Protective Union organized at Manitou on December 5, 1883. The objects of the Union were:

1. To concentrate the efforts of the agriculturists of Manitoba and the Northwest in securing the repealing of laws that militate against their interests.
2. The removal by agitation and other lawful means of the railway and all other monopolies that prevent the securing of a free market for the products of the soil.
3. The securing of the cheapest freights possible to the markets of the world.
4. The removal of unjust restrictions upon trade, and generally, to guard the interests of the people against unjust aggression from any quarter whatsoever.

[4] *Ibid.*, p. 200.
[5] Margaret Morton Fahrni and W. L. Morton, *Third Crossing* (Winnipeg, 1946), p. 90.

5. The formation of subordinate unions in every portion of the province.[6]

In December, a provincial convention was held at Winnipeg where a Declaration of Rights patterned on the earlier Bill of Rights adopted by the Conventions of the Métis and Red River Settlers at the time of the *Résistance* in 1869 was accepted. This document dealt with the railways, tariff, public lands, and grain inspection, laying down the basis of a program that was later to be taken over by the Patrons and later still by the Manitoba Grain Growers' Association.[7]

The movement was short-lived, however. It became a political football for such aspiring young Liberal politicians as Clifford Sifton and R. P. Roblin. Thomas Greenway, the leader of the Liberal opposition in the provincial legislature, partially adopted the program of the Union and seized upon its strong provincialism. Before long the Union was branded as another Grit organization, and thus it lost its non-partisan nature.

At the same time, Charles Stewart, who had taken over the leadership of the Union at the Brandon Convention in December of 1883, pursued a more radical course. The convention held in Winnipeg during March of 1884 passed a resolution recommending that, until the grievances of the North-West had been remedied, any further immigration into the Prairie region should be discouraged. Added to this was an ill-chosen threat by Stewart that if redress did not come quickly, Manitoba would secede from Confederation.[8] Not surprisingly, by 1886, the Farmers' Protective Union had disappeared.

The final organization to appear before the rise of the Patrons was the Farmers' Alliance. It crossed the border from the North-Central states in the winter of 1890-91 and established itself at Balmoral, north of Winnipeg. Sub-lodges were set up at Foxton, Greenwood, Alliance, Stony Mountain, Brant, and Clandeboye, the membership reaching about 500. With the advent of the Patrons, it appears that the Alliance was absorbed into the new protest movement which swept the province.[9]

---

[6] *Manitoba Free Press*, Thursday, December 6, 1883, p. 4.

[7] *Ibid.*, Thursday, December 20, 1883, p. 4. Alexander Begg, *History of the North-West*, Volume III (Toronto: Hunter-Rose & Company, 1895), pp. 85-6.

[8] W. L. Morton, *op. cit.*, pp. 212-13.

[9] Aubrey Wood, *op. cit.*, p. 124.

We now turn to the Patrons of Industry. Originally an American organization, it crossed to Canada at Sarnia in 1887, and was promptly Canadianized by the farmers of Western Ontario. Founded by Reverend F. W. Vertican, a retired Presbyterian Church minister, Dr. David Campbell, a physician, and F. W. Krauss, a printer, its object was to give members a chance to discuss matters of an economic and scientific nature.[10] In both Canada and the United States, it quickly became more an organized protest than an educational movement. And, particularly in the former country, it acted as the Farmers' Alliance did for the majority of American farmers, having strong political overtones from the outset in the Eastern provinces. In the West it functioned somewhat differently at first.

During the spring of 1891, A. L. McLachlan, an American under the direction of the Grand Officers of the Supreme Association in Michigan, set to work to organize the farmers of the Canadian prairies.[11] On May 6, the *Weekly Review* of Portage la Prairie noted:

The Patrons of Industry are becoming very strong on the Portage plains as there are already six associations. This work will be pushed forward as quickly as possible. This is a society that every farmer will find it his interest to join. A free lecture will be given in the various district schools by the Provincial Organizer.[12]

By the fall of 1891, the Patrons were strong enough to call a Convention to organize a provincial association. On Wednesday, November 11, 1891, the Convention met at Portage la Prairie.

During the first day, elections were held. Charles Braithwaite of Portage la Prairie was elected as Grand President, James Burland of Brandon as Grand Vice-President, H. C. Clay of Minnedosa as Grand Secretary, H. A. Sturton of Lorne

---

[10] *Ibid.*, pp. 110-11.

[11] *Ibid.*, p. 124.

"Grain Growers of the 90's." *The Grain Growers Guide*, March 1, 1916 (Vol. IX, No. 9), p. 21. In an interview H. C. Clay noted that the first organizers came from the United States and that they organized all over the province not just at Portage.

[12] *Weekly Review*, Wednesday, May 6, 1891.

Number of associations was revised to five in the Wednesday, May 20, 1891 issue.

County as Grand Treasurer, George Underhill of Minnedosa County as Grand Guide, and J. A. McConechy of Brandon County as Grand Sentinel. The Grand Trustees were W. M. Creighton of Norfolk County, W. J. Curtis of Brandon County, and J. H. Martin of Minnedosa County.[13] Of the successful candidates for the various offices, Braithwaite, Clay and to a lesser extent Underhill, took the most active part in the Order.

Braithwaite is by far the most important. The first President, he was continuously re-elected to office until 1897, and was a tower of strength to the organization. Barely literate and possessing the rudest fundamentals of a formal education, he was, nevertheless, a spell-binding orator.[14] And it was in this latter capacity that he did his greatest work for the Lodge. Throughout the spring and summer for the next six years, he attended picnics organized by the various sub-associations, attacking the vices of the great moneyed trusts and exhorting the farmers to unite to oppose the giant combines intent on cheating the farmer and his family.

It is unfortunate that really very little is known about Braithwaite. Outside of the fact that he was a farmer from the Portage district and that he had been a Liberal before becoming a Patron and a one-time Conservative,[15] there is not much on the record before 1891 nor after 1897. However, it is known that there were two sides to his character. Aubrey Woods describes him as "a romantic figure, masterful and shrewd, though dwelling for the most part in the realm of the emotional."[16] This is well demonstrated by his speeches and in his letters to the various newspapers of rural Manitoba. On the one hand, there is his energy and his oratorical skill; on the other, instability and his almost child-like trust in the promises of the Winnipeg business community and the provincial and national politicians which helped to weaken and discredit the organization.

H. C. Clay was very much like Braithwaite. An Ontario immigrant, he settled at Rapid City in 1879, and in the 1880s founded the *Marquette Reporter*.[17] Strong-willed and of an

---

[13] *Ibid.*, Wednesday, November 11, 1891.

[14] Aubrey Wood, *op. cit.*, p. 126.

[15] Ellen Gillies Cook, "The Federal Election of 1896 in Manitoba" (unpublished M.A. thesis in History, University of Manitoba, 1943), p. 118.

[16] Aubrey Wood, *op. cit.*, p. 126.

[17] *Grain Growers' Guide*, vol. IX, no. 9 (March 1, 1916), p. 21.

equally emotional nature,[18] he was too much like Braithwaite to get along with him well. The internecine quarrel between Clay and Braithwaite over the editorial policy of the *Patrons' Advocate*, the official organ of the movement, paved the way for the eventual collapse of both, and the failure of both men's dreams. But in the early stages of the Patrons' growth, the two men complemented one another's talents. Largely through their efforts, the organization grew and flourished.

Besides electing the first slate of officers, the Convention established work committees to draft an overall policy statement. The major plank in the platform, unanimously agreed upon, was "Manitoba for Manitobans."[19] It was a strong plea for provincial rights from a province which was, in the delegates' eyes, a second-class participant in the Confederation pact of 1870. The clause bound up the whole of the agitation surrounding the public lands question, the bitterness surrounding the boundaries award, and the Canadian Pacific Railway monopoly, which had erupted five years earlier in the Manitoba Farmers' Protective Union. On these points, no one including the members of the Greenway ministry would seriously disagree. But it implied something else as well. The fourth clause explicity defined the further importance of the major plank:

That we mutually agree as farmers and employees to band ourselves together for self-protection and for the purpose of obtaining a portion of the advantages that are now almost exclusively enjoyed by the financial, commercial and manufacturing classes, who by a system of combines and monopolies are exacting from us an undue proportion of the fruits of our toil and that we may have more time to devote to education, and secure for ourselves and [sic] equitable share of the profits of our industry.

That our endeavour be to place the farmers and laborers of

[18] This is very well illustrated by a quarrel with L. A. Burbank of the *Carman Weekly Standard*. Since the *Marquette Reporter* has been lost for this period, Clay's side of the story is not available. However, it seems that Clay did not always reciprocate in the exchanges of news articles that were so essential to the successful operation of rural newspapers during this period. Burbank expressed his annoyance in print. Clay replied in a manner that outraged the former who in turn printed a diatribe on the character of the editor of the *Reporter*.

[19] *Weekly Review*, Wednesday, November 11, 1891.

Manitoba in unison with the manufacturing laborers of the east to the exclusion of the middle men.

That we advise and aid each other in acquiring business and commercial habits, and assist in placing as quickly as possible our trade on a cash basis, believing that it will greatly conduce to the benefit of every member of our order, and the prosperity of Manitoba.[20]

This statement of class solidarity in the face of class conflict between industrial workers and the agricultural class was important. Whether the farmers of Manitoba grasped its full implications is doubtful, although, when the Patrons published their political platform two years later, it was with the statement that "When the law Compels me to Contribute my just Quota to the Support of the Government, it is Taxation, but When it Compels me to Contribute to the Support of Private Enterprise, it is Robbery."[21] The ideas themselves were probably borrowed from the American example through the intervention of the Provincial Organizer, McLachlan. And many of the delegates would have come into contact with these ideas through the newspapers which published long extracts from either side in the controversy between Populism and the Establishment in the United States.

It must be remembered that these were the same people who organized the Manitoba Farmers' Protective Union five years previously. At that time there was no question of class conflict or united action with the workers. And it is interesting to note that after McLachlan drops from sight, there is less emphasis on this philosophy. The Patrons of Industry became an agrarian pressure group in Manitoba imbued with a sense of righteousness which had its origin in the conditions of the frontier and as a result of the policies pursued by businessmen and politicians in the urbanized centres of the East. There are attacks on the eastern manufacturing interests and their brethren in the grain trade in Winnipeg, but there is no formulation of a struggle between the exploiters and the exploited.

The Committee on Printing and Publication recommended that an official organ "devoted to the interests of the Patrons of Indutsry" be established in the province. The Convention accepted the proposal, and it was decided by the Executive,

[20] *Ibid.*
[21] *P.A.M., Greenway Papers*, W. C. Graham to Bro. McNaught, February 17, 1894, no. 6381.

perhaps somewhat hastily, immediately after the meeting, that H. C. Clay of Minnedosa should be given the contract.[22]

Moreover, the Convention accepted the Report of the Committee on Co-operation which recommended that negotiations be opened with the "some two or three"[23] other organizations that had the same objects as the Patrons and already existed in the province. Nevertheless, the report does not seem to have passed without considerable debate — "a warm discussion" the official report reads.[24] A compromise of sorts was eventually hammered out. Because the Patrons were the first to organize a Provincial Executive, it was reasoned, it was resolved to invite all organizations to send delegates to the next annual meeting of the Grand Association where they would be fully accredited delegates. Any local association of another group was invited to be chartered as a sub-association of the Patrons.[25] There were only two possible groups to which the resolution could be referring: the Farmers' Alliance and the Grange. The importance of the resolution is that it indicates that another group was (or other groups were) actively soliciting support from the farmers in the Province at the same time as the Patrons, and that the delegates to the Convention had come in contact with them.

The three months between the founding convention and the first annual meeting were ones of great activity. The Executive appointed A. L. McLachlan as Provincial Organizer with a roving commission. He was instructed to push the work of organizing with all possible speed as it was hoped by the Executive that the membership would have increased to 5,000 by the middle of February.[26]

The appointment of McLachlan as Provincial Organizer proves that there was no direct break with the American parent organization as there was in Ontario.[27] The means of separation were more subtle. The actual organizing in the province was accomplished by "several assistants" appointed by the Provincial Executive.[28] Nothing further is recorded of Mr. McLachlan.

The Patrons were quickly patriated not only to Canada but to the West. In Manitoba they became the expression of a discontent which sprang from causes which bore greater similarity

[22] *Weekly Review*, Wednesday, November 11, 1891.
[23] *Ibid.*
[24] *Ibid.*
[25] *Ibid.*
[26] *Ibid.*
[27] Aubrey Wood, *op cit.*, p. 112.
[28] *Weekly Review*, Wednesday, November 11, 1891.

to those that led to the Farmers' Alliance in the Western states than to those that accounted for the strength of the Patrons movement in Ontario. But the Patrons were born of the Ontario democracy that had spawned the Clear Grits and the Liberal-Conservative coalition. And although the Patrons continued to profess their loyalty to this democracy, they were radically altering the principles underlying it as they adapted to the circumstances of a new environment, so that they were creating a movement that, while in many respects similar to those in Ontario and the United States, was unique.

The annual meeting held in February indicated just how much they had become absorbed by the earlier Western Canadian agrarian protest movements. The Grand President, Charles Braithwaite, ignored the theme of the conflict of class interests and returned to themes expounded by the Farmers' Protective Union in condemning the binding twine and implement combines, the unfairness of the duty on machinery and implements purchased from American manufacturers, and the lack of agricultural representation on the board which established grain standards. On the positive side, he advised that farmers own and operate their own elevators; and more radically, that the government establish banks in central locations where, "upon sufficient security," loans could be obtained by farmers at 5 percent.[29]

The meeting also brought to light the first of the major difficulties that were to arise between the Executive and the general membership, and between the organization and the public at large, which were to contribute to the failure of the movement. The scheme of publishing a journal in the interests of the Patrons of Industry was opened again, pointing up the fact that the settlement arrived at between Clay and the rest of the Executive was not entirely to the satisfaction of the delegates. It was understood at the November Convention that tenders were to be let. According to the report submitted by Clay himself to the *Weekly Review*, the Executive let the contract to him at a meeting held immediately after the Convention without asking for competitive bids.[30] Any possibility that this action would sit well with the general membership was destroyed when it was revealed that it was necessary to increase the membership dues in order to undertake publication of the journal. In the resulting

[29] *The Brandon Sun*, February 25, 1892.
[30] *Weekly Review*, Wednesday, November 11, 1891.
    Clay wrote the newspaper report. *Morden Monitor*, Thursday, November 19, 1891.

debate, no agreement could be reached, and the matter was finally referred to committee.[31] Eventually, the *Patrons Advocate* appeared, published by H. C. Clay, but not without having left scars upon the movement. The incident, while it might appear trivial, was the first in a series that suggested to the general public that the leaders of the Patrons were either extremely naïve or none-too-honest. And it was such incidents that made the public only too willing to believe the wild tales that the organization's enemies told of the Executive's personal aggrandisement.

The two years succeeding the first annual meeting were critical in the development of the new farmers' movement. Where in Ontario they had engaged in politics shortly after their formation,[32] in Manitoba and the Territories the Patrons proved to be somewhat reluctant to take this step. The reason can be seen in the fact that Manitobans were convinced that self-help was the solution to their problems. Ontario members of the Order, on the other hand, had experimented with the Grange and failed to achieve any lasting economic success through co-operation. In the West, the Grange had established itself in a number of rural communities, but it had not been strong enough to have any real impact. Of course, many of the farmers in Western Canada would have come in contact with the Grange before leaving Ontario, but the movement collapsed after they had emigrated. Therefore the farm leaders of the Patrons undertook a program of co-operation among themselves and lobbying in the old political parties to achieve the ends of Western agriculture.

Exactly when the decision to enter the political arena was taken, it is difficult to know. The minutes for the annual meeting held in the last week of February, 1893, are not available, but at the 1894 annual meeting, Braithwaite championed the cause of political intervention. Somewhere, then, between January, 1892 and the beginning of 1894, this momentous decision was made.

The failure of the original principles upon which the organization had been built is a difficult process to trace, for the newspapers of the province tend to ignore the activities of the Patrons as much as possible; and in most cases when reference was made to them, it was unfavourable. The brief honeymoon with the *Weekly Review* is typical. Although the editor agreed with

---

[31] *The Brandon Sun*, February 25, 1892.
[32] Aubrey Wood, *op. cit.*, p. 113.

many of the farmers' complaints, he was not so sure about the solutions proposed by the leadership for the difficulties in which Western Canadian agriculture found itself. Farmers' organizations were not to meddle in political or economic affairs. When they did, they were overstepping the bounds set by society. His comments on the monetary policy then being pursued by the Farmers' Alliance in the United States are revealing. Certainly the lack of easy credit was a problem, but the methods proposed to supply the people with "more money" were deplorable. Sound money was sound economics.[33] And as the Patrons tended to become more preoccupied with the evils of the credit system, his opinion of the movement correspondingly declined.

Moreover, leading members of the Grand Association did little to further good relations with the press. In August of 1891, H. C. Clay, then editor of the *Marquette Reporter*, had accused the *Weekly Review* of refusing to publish a letter favourable to the formation of the Patrons of Industry, commenting that the editor of that publication had little use for farmers.[34] The reply was indignant: a warning to be more careful; a denial of ever having received such a letter; and a declaration that the "*Review* is, and always has been, the Farmer's Friend."[35]

Furthermore, when Clay was elected to the position of Grand Secretary in November, 1891, the action was hardly likely to convince the owners and editors of the newspapers in the province of the responsibility of the movement. It was generally agreed in the publishing fraternity that the editor of the *Marquette Reporter* was a very hot-headed gentleman. According to the editor of the *Carman Weekly Standard*, L. A. Burbank, who it must be admitted in all fairness, was not unlike Clay, even the term gentleman was inappropriate.[36] And when Clay became editor of the official organ of the Patrons, *The Patrons' Advocate*, the movement as a whole was given a bad press among the rest of the provincial newspaper editors.

The rapid deterioration of press relations was not entirely the fault of Clay. The unpolished roughness of men like Charles Braithwaite and John Forsyth[37] did nothing to improve the situ-

---

[33] *Weekly Review*, Wednesday, May 13, 1891.

[34] *Ibid.*, Wednesday, August 26, 1891.

[35] *Ibid.*

[36] *Carman Weekly Standard*, Thursday, June 18, 1891, p. 2.

[37] He was Grand Vice-President of the Order in 1893. An itinerant preacher and farmer, he was elected M.L.A. for Beautiful Plains in 1894. He was chiefly noted for his skill as an orator.

ation. To receive a letter from the Grand President was an experience many editors would rather have done without. Spelling and punctuation were unbelievable. This fact coupled with a certain dislike for "book-learning" on the part of several prominent Patrons among whom Forsyth but not Braithwaite could be counted, created the impression that the Patrons were ignorant farmers led by uneducated demagogues.

One final factor should be noted in the deterioration of press relations, and this is the secrecy that surrounded most Patron gatherings. No one was quite sure what went on behind the closed doors at these meetings. Official press releases were prepared by the Secretary of the sub-association or the Grand Association as the case might have been. Much speculation inevitably followed as to what actually did take place.

By 1895, only three newspapers in Manitoba supported the organization.[38] All were owned and operated by members. When the Patrons decided to enter politics in 1894, this indifference or outright hostility on the part of the press was to play a large role in the collapse of the movement.

To return to the main thread of the argument, the years between 1892 and 1894 saw the emphasis laid on co-operation. In 1892, the Patrons Commercial Union was organized. It was a supply company incorporated under the laws of the Province, and it began to do business at Portage la Prairie with W. C. Graham,[39] Secretary of the Grand Association, as manager. Goods were sold by mail order, most of them being distributed from Winnipeg. The Union handled such things as agricultural implements and binder twine, particularly the latter, and to a lesser extent it functioned as a selling agency for the farmers' produce.[40]

In its first summer of operation, the Commercial Union ordered binder twine in bulk, and by this expedient was able to save its members a cent and a half a pound on over 72,000 pounds of twine.[41] By 1894, it was handling over 500,000

---

[38] *Patrons' Advocate, Russell Chronicle, Marquette Reporter.* Of the three, the first and last were edited by H. C. Clay and later by William King; the *Chronicle* was owned and operated by Senator C. A. Boulton who was a strong Patron supporter.

[39] William Creighton Graham, who had received a B.A. from the University of Manitoba in 1889, and who was descended of an early Portage la Prairie family, succeeded Clay as Grand Secretary in the spring of 1892.

[40] Aubrey Wood, *op. cit.,* p. 125.

[41] *Weekly Review,* Wednesday, November 2, 1892.

pounds annually at the remarkably low price of seven and a quarter cents a pound.[42]

The year 1892 also saw the Patrons attempt to market their grain in bulk directly to the millers. This was less successful than the sale of binder twine. Although the scheme was a forerunner of the later Pooling system, it suffered in that too few farmers took advantage of the facilities provided for the Patrons to get a significant premium. Moreover, farmers were unwilling to commit themselves to sell their wheat through the Union.[43] Unable to guarantee delivery of specific quantities of grain, the Union was placed in a weak position in dealing with the milling companies. In view of these circumstances, it is hardly surprising that the attempt at co-operative marketing was a failure.

The Patrons also entered the elevator business. New elevators were built at Boissevain, Holland, Glenboro, Rathwell, and Alexander by the fall of 1892.[44] These were relatively successful. But it should be pointed out that this was not a radical departure. Farmers' elevator companies had been established at various points in the Province at least as early as 1890 and probably earlier.[45] These were joint-stock companies owned and operated by the farmers. They were not co-operatives, and it is fair to assume that the Patrons' elevators were organized on similar principles.

At the same time, a major attack on the credit system was begun. Patrons were urged to do all of their business on a strictly cash basis. This admonition was rather unrealistic. Despite the constant emphasis upon frugality, it was next to impossible on the frontier not to do business on credit. The capital investment needed to undertake the moderately mechanized agriculture of the Canadian West was beyond the immediate grasp of most prospective farmers. And with the deepening of the Depression, with correspondingly low prices for wheat and other produce, many established farmers as well were forced to borrow in order to meet expenses.

It was the Depression that was the actual motivating factor in the Patrons' decision to enter the political arena. In large measure it accounted for the failure of the Patrons' attempts to remedy the farmers' economic problems by means of co-operation, and yet it made the solution of these difficulties of paramount importance.

---

[42] Aubrey Wood, *loc. sit.*
[43] *Manitoba Free Press*, Thursday, January 18, 1894, p. 7.
[44] *Weekly Review*, Wednesday, December 14, 1892.
[45] *Carman Weekly Standard*, Thursday, December 11, 1890, p. 2.

The leaders of the Patrons became convinced that the tariff wall and the trusts were at the root of the trouble. The C.P.R. is a case in point. In the 1890s, it possessed a virtual monopoly in Western Canada and set rates at its own discretion. The provincial government, although it had been more successful than its predecessors in this area, had not been able to force the railway to make sufficient concessions. Pressure was applied to both the provincial government and the company by the Patrons. From both the response was not heartening. The government ignored the farmers, being preoccupied with the schools issue; the railway begged that its financial situation was at best precarious west of the Great Lakes.[46] Neither answer was particularly satisfactory. As redress was impossible to obtain through existing channels, the Patrons were forced to the conclusion that the only way to save the country from the trusts was to enter Parliament themselves and to force the changes necessary upon the nation.

It must not be imagined that the Patrons did not face opposition. On the contrary, bitter hostility to the movement emerged early. It came from those quarters one would suspect most – merchants, grain traders, and elevator operators. But it emerged among those engaged in agriculture as well. This opposition usually took the form of personal indictment of leaders of the movement. An attack levelled by "Outsider" in the *Weekly Review* was typical. He insinuated that the Grand Secretary was paid to establish lodges and that the executive disposed of the membership fees collected for their own benefit.[47] The *Emerson Enterprise* charged Braithwaite with opening an office in the Winnipeg Grain Exchange and furnishing it comfortably for himself at the membership's expense. More damning, he was accused of getting at least a cent a bushel for handling Patrons' wheat.[48]

In 1894, the Order grew into a full-fledged protest movement. Newspapers sat up and took notice, and politicians began to give the Patrons more than their fair share of attention. More important, leading citizens in the rural communities of the province, where in the past they had sat and watched, somewhat detached from the workings of the Lodge, now undertook the active leadership of the organization.

---

[46] *Manitoba Free Press*, Thursday, January 18, 1894. p. 7.
[47] *Weekly Review*, Wednesday, December 7, 1892.
[48] *Patrons' Advocate*, October 17, 1894.

This interest on the part of the leaders in the rural communities was not sudden. The same factors were at work with regard to the successful and established farmers as on the newcomer. As the Depression deepened, radical solutions to problems seemed to be the only solutions. This was especially true for Liberal-Conservatives in the West. The policies of the great Liberal-Conservative coalition which had determined the destiny of the nation, also ensured certain consequences. The two keystones in the Liberal-Conservative governments' policy of national development were the National Policy and the trans-continental railway system of the C.P.R. To complete the task of nation-building it was essential for Canada that these policies be adopted. It was also essential that, as Canadians, the people would have to make sacrifices if they hoped to create their Empire of the North. To the farmer in Western Canada it was manifest that he was making too many of the sacrifices demanded. He pointed to the prosperity of the American farmer to the south, not realizing that his plight was continental rather than regional, and demanded that something be done to remedy his situation. As long as there was prosperity, even relative prosperity, the issues could be safely ignored by the politicians. But when Depression set in – mild Depression after 1883, severe Depression after 1890 – then it was an entirely different matter.

The experience of Prairies bred certain responses. With this in mind, the artificial labels of party politics of Eastern Canada came to mean less in the West. By 1894, a consensus among members of both the national parties was evident. For example, Liberal-Conservatives from the West such as Senator Boulton of Russell,[49] who attacked the government's tariff and railway policies in the Senate, agreed more with the Opposition than with the Cabinet.

A Liberal was not confronted with so difficult a choice as a Tory. His party had a long tradition in the defense of free trade. And as the English-speaking wing had its origins in the agrarian regions of Western Ontario, a distrust of the monopolistic corporations supported by the Macdonald government followed.

What happened, then, was simply that while a number of Liberals found themselves to be more radical than their party, most continued in their allegiance to it, for the provincial party was a farmers' party and the national Liberal party's principles

---

[49] Senator Boulton was appointed to the Senate in 1887. He had long been connected with the West, having been involved in the Red River Resistance on the side of the Canadian Party.

went a long way towards meeting their demands. For the Liberal-Conservative from Ontario who shared in the general experience resulting from the frontier conditions and the one-staple economy, there was not the same opportunity to reconcile his views with those held by his party. In an age when party feeling ran deep, it was not of minor consequence to change one's allegiance. The Western Tories' goal was to reform their party from within not to abandon it. When that party, as the government, refused to listen to their pleas, they were, in the light of their economic circumstances, ready to join a new organization which was essentially to become the party of the "radical" Conservatives. Disgruntled Liberals never became more than a minority in the political movement launched by the Patrons, but their contribution of the agrarian radicalism of rural Ontario provided a link with the Canadian radical tradition. In the Patrons we see the union of the Prairie experience and the democracy of Ontario to lay the foundations of the twentieth-century "radical" tradition in the West.

The annual meeting of the Patrons in 1894 was held as usual in Brandon. Between 100 and 150 delegates were present from the province and the Territories, representing in all a membership of 3,172.[50] The keynote address of Grand President Braithwaite was an indictment of the membership for not supporting the Order's co-operative activities, and the announcement of his retirement. The question is just how much did he mean of what he said. One is impressed by the fact that the more he stressed the failure of the movement's original purposes, the more likely he was to convince the delegates that political action was necessary. His intention to resign, on the other hand, was sincere. In the first place, he was no longer a farmer, and, second, he no longer had an income outside of the Order.[51]

The Convention debated at length the necessity of political action, and of Braithwaite's retention as President despite his obvious reluctance to continue in that position. There is no indication by what margin the delegates agreed to the former proposal, or when, but, by the second day, they were outlining a platform. The committee on legislation reported that the cost of justice was too high and that limits should be set on interest received on mortgages, while the committee on railways recommended a general reduction of rates, the abolition of preferen-

[50] *Manitoba Free Press*, Friday, January 19, 1891, p. 1.
[51] *Ibid.*, Thursday, January 18, 1894, p. 7.

tial rates, and rebates, and the construction of a Seaway to make Port Arthur a seaport.[52] And on the last day, Braithwaite was prevailed upon to remain as President after a committee which he had personally requested had exonerated him of any wrongdoing.[53] Provision was made that the organization pay him a salary.[54]

The summer of 1894 was the high point of the movement. Braithwaite travelled from rural community to rural community preaching the gospel of the Patrons. The meeting held in Carman in March was similar to those held across the Province. Braithwaite lashed out at the excessive freight rates charged by the C.P.R. and the high tariff. It was absolutely essential that the cost of carrying the crop to the Eastern markets should be reduced – either that, or the whole country would become bankrupt. This reduction in rates could be accomplished by the completion of the Hudson's Bay Railway, which the Dominion government refused to build not because the route was unsatisfactory, but because it would be injurious to the Eastern Provinces. As the Northwest sent only seven members to Ottawa, it was not in a position to bring any pressure upon the government. Another project was the deepening of the Canadian waterways, which would entail the expenditure of $50,000,000, but which would reduce the cost of shipping wheat from the West to England from 35c to 20c a bushel. The tariff came under equally close scrutiny. "All classes in the Province" were interested in its reduction. Why should 95 percent of the people, he asked, be taxed for the 5 percent who make up the manufacturing class. And then he went on to show how the government had a higher tariff on necessities than on luxuries. To remedy these evils, he proposed that the farmers of Dufferin County join with the Patrons in placing candidates in the field or supporting those pledged to a similar program in the forthcoming elections.[55] The speaking tour across the province and the hard work of the local organizations had the desired effect. By July, Grand Secretary Graham was claiming that the movement had from 6,000 to 7,000 members and 300 lodges.[56]

By mid-summer the Patrons were nominating candidates for the federal elections expected at any time. James Morrow of Pilot Mound was nominated for Lisgar, Charles Braithwaite

[52] *Ibid.*, Friday, January 19, 1894, p. 1.
[53] *Ibid.*, Saturday, January 20, 1894, p. 2.
[54] *Grain Growers' Guide*, vol. IX, no. 9 (March 1, 1916), p. 21.
[55] *Carman Weekly Standard*, Thursday, March 15, 1894.
[56] *Ibid.*, Thursday, July 12, 1894.

for Macdonald, James Fisher of Springfield for Selkirk, W. Postlethwaite for Brandon, and T. Young for Marquette. Provencher and Winnipeg were the only two Manitoba constituencies in which the Patrons did not nominate. And then John Forsyth was nominated for the provincial constituency of Beautiful Plains in a by-election. To everyone's surprise he won handily, thereby encouraging the Order in its efforts. Furthermore, the victory served to convince many of those who doubted the ability of the Patrons to win of the widespread popular support it enjoyed among non-members.

The period of success and harmony was brief. No sooner was the election won, and the movement for political action launched, than a quarrel broke out between the Executive Board and H. C. Clay of the *Patrons' Advocate*. The Executive Board had finally come to the conclusion that the editorial policy of the paper and the fiery nature of its manager had to be curbed. Clay had attacked practically every government organization that dealt with the farmer, and every leading local, provincial, or national politician. It can be said in his favour that he showed no discrimination, but he did not show any political sense either.

If he had confined his attacks to the established political parties, it is likely that no difficulties would have arisen, but when he began to criticize Patron policies and the actions of the Executive, he passed beyond the pale of what was acceptable and what was not. In the issue of November 21 he severely criticized the financial condition of the Farmers' Mill and Elevator Company at Portage which was owned and operated by the Patrons.[57] Then, in a series of articles on freight rates beginning in the same issue, he condemned local governments and the freight rate commission for not taking stands on the issue of rates.[58] Finally in the December 4 issue in an article headed "Provincial Patrons Candidate" he, in the words of the Executive, "advocated the claims of one old party over the other and laid the whole order open to the construction. . . . of being in sympathy with and working for the Liberal party, thus having lost our independence and substituting instead a partizan bias."[59] Clay disagreed with the Patrons' policy of placing candidates in the forthcoming provincial elections. The Greenway

[57] *Patrons' Advocate*, November 21, 1894.
[58] *Ibid.*, November 21, 1894. This was particularly annoying to the Patrons because several of the leading members of the Order at the local level were leading figures in the local governments.
[59] "Patrons of Industry," *The Manitoba Liberal*, December 11, 1895.

government was essentially a farmers' government. Nationally, he took a different view entirely.

Each of these articles had been picked up by the provincial press, and unfavourable publicity had followed. Braithwaite wrote to Clay and his editor, William King, in December. He stated that the public considered the Executive Board responsible for utterances about which they had not been consulted.[60] When this did not have the desired effect, a public repudiation of Clay's stand was prepared by the Executive and published under the authority of the Grand Secretary. In part it read:

> *Patrons do not and cannot consistently recognize either of the old parties and such an utterance being contrary to our principles of independence we do hereby repudiate it.*
>
> *Had an official outline of the Patron action been given it would have been to speedily place candidates in all the local constituencies where a fair chance of success be possible.*[61]

In reply, Clay published the above-mentioned letter of the Grand President with all its grammatical mistakes and an appropriate paragraph-by-paragraph commentary, as well as a front-page editorial attacking the Executive Board's stand as interfering with the freedom of expression of the Lodge's members.[62] Thereupon the Executive Board servered its connection with the *Patrons' Advocate*. The quarrel between the official organ of the Order and the Executive centred on the fact that the former Liberal-Conservatives in the Patrons organization, while they were willing if not anxious to break with their own party, were not willing to support a Liberal government even if that government had accepted as its program basically the same solutions to the overriding economic problems as they themselves advocated.

At the annual meeting in January, 1895, the differences among the members were not apparent. This time in his state of the union message, Braithwaite spoke confidently of the future. The movement had strengthened, and its accomplishments had increased. The Grand President claimed the following successes: a reduction in freight rates, a larger percentage of grain graded No. 1 hard, a reduction in the tariff and in the cost of such necessities as binder twine and fence wire, and

---

[60] *Patrons' Advocate*, December 12, 1894.
[61] "Patrons of Industry," *The Manitoba Liberal*, December 11, 1895.
[62] *Patrons' Advocate*, December 12, 1894.

increased government efficiency.[63] Admittedly, although some improvement had taken place by the Patrons' standards, it was not so much because of their action as the result of a combination of economic and political factors over which the Patrons had no control. Braithwaite's speech seems to have been for public consumption, as the committee reports prove that progress during the year had been disappointing. The main plank in the platform remained free trade, while the legislative committee recommended the discontinuance of pauper immigration, abolition of elevator privileges, abolition of the Senate, women's suffrage, and a series of legal reforms.[64]

Furthermore, the Convention was significant in that Senator Boulton of Russell, appointed to the Red Chamber by Macdonald, attended and openly supported the Patrons, becoming Grand Auditor. It must be noted that he did not entirely agree with the resolution passed by the Order dealing with the Senate,[65] but in general he was sympathetic. And his presence lent an aura of official approval. Long a member of the radical wing of the Liberal-Conservative coalition, he had become a spokesman for the Tories in Western Canada. The transfer of his allegiance to the Patrons was an indication of the extent to which the Conservative was compelled to seek a new political home on the Prairies.

The Convention also invited all mechanics and industrial workers to join the Association, but refused to join with any organization other than one whose interests were agriculture.[66] In effect, the invitation was worthless, and the Patrons in Manitoba remained an occupational interest group.

During the first six months of the new year, the movement continued to grow. In February H. C. Clay was forced to resign from the *Patrons' Advocate* and the Order. Under William King that publication was reinstated as the official organ by the Executive Board.[67]

At the same time, Braithwaite travelled to Toronto where in meetings with the Dominion Executive, a national platform was drawn up.[68] This platform was more national in name than in fact. Enclosed with a letter of W. C. Graham dated February 17, 1894, is a copy of the Patrons' Platform adopted in Janu-

---

[63] *Ibid.*, January 16, 1895.
[64] *Ibid.*
[65] *Ibid.*
[66] *Ibid.*, February 6, 1895.
[67] *Ibid.*, February 20, 1895. *Grain Growers' Guide, loc. cit.*
[68] *Patrons' Advocate*, March 13, 1895.

ary of that year at the annual Convention of the Grand Association of Manitoba and the Northwest held in Brandon. It is identical with the national platform with the sectional variations for the West adopted in the first months of 1895 in Toronto.[69]

The first plank stressed the permanence of the British connection. Those following enumerated the various proposals of the movement. Public lands were to be reserved for actual settlers. This applied primarily to Manitoba and the Northwest. Representatives of agricultural communities were to be farmers chosen for ability, integrity and independence. This plank was to apply to Manitoba and the Northwest only. Rigid economy was to be practised in every department of the public service, while simplification of the laws and a general reduction in the administrative machinery were demanded. This meant the abolition of government house, superannuation grants, the military college, subsidies to railways and other corporations, and reductions in civil servants' salaries, the number of Cabinet ministers, and in the expenditures of the Militia Department. There was to be a revenue tariff only, with a number of goods essential to agriculture admitted duty free as agriculture was the principle industry of the Dominion. Anti-combines legislation was sought, as was the principle of "one man, one vote" and the disfranchisement of all civil servants. The Senate was to be abolished, women admitted to the franchise, and an end put to the liquor traffic. Unofficially, support was to be given to the Western Patrons in their demand for the Hudson's Bay Railway and in a general reduction in freight rates.[70]

Comparison of the Bill of Rights adopted by the Manitoba Farmers' Protective Union and the platforms of the Patrons of Industry and the United Farmers of Manitoba shows a striking similarity in provisions. The response to conditions that in essence did not change from 1885 to 1920 and the continuity in leadership provide the basis for this similarity. This does not mean that the platforms were completely in agreement. There is a growing sophistication and an expansion of views that can be traced, and, in a number of instances, the solution to specific problems varies. But, underlying all three platforms, there are a number of basic principles. Agriculture, as Canada's basic industry deserved special consideration. This entailed the abolition of the protective tariff and government regulation if not

[69] *P.A.M., Greenway Papers*, W. C. Graham to Bro. McNaught, February 17, 1894, no. 6381.
[70] *Patrons' Advocate*, March 13, 1895. The platform is set beside a paragraph by paragraph commentary by Braithwaite.

ownership of the transportation industry. And both the Patrons and the U.F.M. stood for sweeping changes in parliamentary institutions and administration.

In 1895, the Patrons in Manitoba came to represent three important reform movements: agricultural reformers, prohibitionists, and those in favour of woman suffrage. In July, the Patrons and Prohibitionists agreed to a joint platform upon which they would contest the forthcoming national and provincial elections.[71]

And then disaster struck. On September 25, Herbert D. Cartin of Neepawa wrote to the *Patrons' Advocate* accusing the Patron member of the legislature, John Forsyth, of using a railway pass.[72] The Grand President ordered an immediate investigation which substantiated the charges.[73] On October 23, the Executive Board ordered Forsyth to resign all his offices in the Order, and expelled him from the movement.[74] The enemies of the organization, meanwhile, were watching the proceedings with great interest and pounced upon the incident as proof of what they had long claimed – the Patrons were in politics for what they could get out of it personally. Further credence was given to their charges in December when Philip Thomson, Sessional Clerk to the Patron members in the Ontario Legislature, confiscated the passes of the Patron members in that House.[75] Although the Order had purified itself, the damage was done. The public never entirely believed the Patrons' promises again. As the party of general moral perfection, they had been found out as hypocrites, no better than the members of the older parties which they had so bitterly opposed.

One further problem came to a head in 1895. The Manitoba Schools issue divided the members of the Order into Protestant and Catholic factions, and alienated the latter after the Patrons accepted the government's stand on denominational schools.

It was in this state that the Patrons were forced to meet the Manitoba electorate in January of 1896. The major issue was the Schools Question. It was so important that there is considerable doubt as to whether it would have made much difference to the Patrons if the scandals had not taken place. It is known, however, that a number of strong Tories reverted to form after the railway pass affair; this did much to weaken the

[71] *Ibid.*, July 24, 1895.
[72] *Ibid.*, September 25, 1895. Cartin was a Patron.
[73] *Ibid.*, October 2, 1895.
[74] *Ibid.*, October 23 and October 30, 1895.
[75] *Ibid.*, December 4, 1895.

movement locally. Neither provincially nor federally could the Patrons count on the support of ex-Liberals. Thus it was essential that the Patrons garner the Tory vote. The failure to do so proved disastrous, and undoubtedly the scandals played their part in this failure.

The Patrons nominated twelve candidates of which number two were elected – W. J. Sirrett in Beautiful Plains and W. Crosby in Dennis.

The decline of the Order was more apparent at the Provincial Convention. Just sixty-four delegates attended.[76] The Dominion Parliament was nearing the end of its life, and a decision had to be made whether or not to contest that election in view of the defeat in Manitoba. It was decided to support the candidates already in the field.

The election campaign which began in May proved to be the end of the movement as a major force in the Province. Five candidates were nominated as has been indicated. Of these, three withdrew by the end of the first month – James Morrow in Lisgar, James Fisher in Selkirk, and Thomas Young in Marquette. Only in the latter constituency was the Order strong enough to bring forward a replacement in G. A. J. A. Marshall.

As has been noted, the Patrons in Manitoba relied on the dissatisfaction of the Tories with their federal and provincial parties. Sir Charles Tupper in the opening speech of his campaign at Brydon Rink in Winnipeg, revealed a platform that went a long way to meeting the Patrons' demands. Instead of free trade, preferential trade with England was advocated for commercial reasons and for strengthening the bonds of Empire. Agricultural reforms were promised, and a promise to intensify efforts to increase immigration was made. And finally, Tupper made a firm commitment to complete the Hudson's Bay Railway to the Saskatchewan within two years.[77] This, linked to the scandals and better economic conditions, led to large numbers of Tories returning to the fold. The result was a rout.

With the defeat, the Patrons rapidly declined into political obscurity. The Territorial Patrons severed their connection with their Manitoba brethren in the summer of 1896, and the 1897 Convention saw the movement trying to stave off the inevitable. Membership was thrown open to lawyers, doctors, and merchants. The ritual of the Lodge was abolished and the terminology changed – Provincial Convention instead of Grand Con-

[76] *Patrons' Advocate*, January 29, 1896.
[77] E. G. Cook, *op. cit.*, pp. 33-4.

vention, etc. — and the *Patrons' Sentinel* which had succeeded the *Patrons' Advocate* as the official organ was discontinued.[78] Braithwaite retired as President and took a job with the provincial government as inspector of noxious weeds.[79] C. J. Green succeeded as President and W. C. Graham continued as Secretary-Treasurer.[80]

In 1898, the Patrons of Manitoba formed themselves into an Independent Industrial Association. This body died overnight. The Commercial Union changed its name to the Farmers' Trading Company and continued in business until 1912.[81] The movement itself was reborn in 1903 as the Manitoba Grain Growers' Association out of which grew the Manitoba Non-Partisan League and the United Farmers of Manitoba. But the actual influence on western Canadian and national policies was greater than can be seen in the succession of farmers' movements. Diefenbaker's agrarian Toryism has its roots much deeper than the 1930s. Western Conservatives have tended to be radical. The response to the conditions of the western American agricultural frontier has been of greater importance than the development of an abstract Conservative philosophy on the Prairies.

---

[78] *The Brandon Sun*, Thursday, January 28, 1897.
[79] Aubrey Wood, *op. cit.*, p. 129.
[80] *The Brandon Sun*, *loc. cit.*
[81] Aubrey Wood, *op. cit.*, pp. 129-30.

W. R. Motherwell:
The Emergence of a Farm Leader

Allan R. Turner

The name of William Richard Motherwell has become almost a legend in Saskatchewan. A stone cairn on the Trans-Canada Highway at Indian Head, an impressive federal government building in Regina, a northern lake – all bear his name. They perpetuate the memory of a man who, after heading the powerful Territorial Grain Growers' Association, became Minister of Agriculture for Saskatchewan (1905-1918), then for Canada (1921-1930). Motherwell brought to public office in 1905 an experience of over twenty years in pioneer farming, community activities, politics, and the farmers' movement. His early career illustrates many of the trials and triumphs of prairie agriculture; moreover, it provides an insight into the policies which he was to pursue in his ministerial career.

Motherwell was born in 1860, the son of an Irish farmer near Perth, in Lanark County, Ontario. His boyhood was spent in the pattern of rural Ontario life. He went to the country school during the winter months and worked on the farm in the busy summer season. After reaching the age of sixteen he combined farm work with attendance at the Perth Collegiate Institute (where he completed his matriculation in 1879). He then enrolled in the Ontario Agricultural College at Guelph and graduated with high-class honours in 1881. Thereupon he and two of his fellow students headed West to see the country and to investigate the possibility of homesteading. They spent some time in exploring southern Manitoba, secured work in the harvest fields of Portage la Prairie, and returned to Ontario for the winter. In the following spring of 1882, Motherwell came west to the end of the rail at Brandon and then travelled by wagon and ox-team to Fort Qu'Appelle where he engaged a land surveyor to help him locate a homestead. There being no land

source: *Saskatchewan History*, vol. XI, no. 3 (Autumn, 1958), pp. 94-103. Reprinted by permission of the author and publishers.

available south of the Qu'Appelle, he chose a site north of the river in the Pheasant Hills country, thus becoming one of the first settlers of the Abernethy district.

Motherwell had made a wise choice. The Dominion land surveyor responsible for the outline survey of township 20, range 11, west of the 2nd meridian, described its soil as a first-class, rich clay loam, well adapted for settlement.[1] Pheasant Creek crossed the south-east portion of the township, and wood was in plentiful supply immediately to the east. This township was sub-divided in 1883, and Motherwell filed his homestead entry for the north-east quarter of section 14 on March 26 of that year. At the same time he made entry for the adjoining southeast quarter as a pre-emption. He then embarked on the careful program of husbandry that was to make his farm, later called Lanark Place, one of the finest in the province. By 1889, in making application for his homestead patent, he was able to report that he had broken 100 acres and had enclosed seventy-five acres with a pole fence. His modest house, eighteen by twenty-four feet in size, was valued at $400, and he had erected a log stable, thirty by sixty feet, valued at $100. He then had thirty head of livestock, a marked increase over the yoke of oxen and three horses with which he had begun. He was granted letters patent for his homestead on December 3, 1889,[2] and completed the purchase of his pre-emption on May 31, 1890.[3]

Subsequent improvements to his farm included the building of an impressive house of cut field stone in 1897 and a stone barn in 1907. The material, obtained from nearby coulees, was gathered stone by stone for several years before enough was assembled for building. This substantial program was under-taken on the earnings of the farm, without any outside financial assistance. The planting of shelter belts and shrubbery began with cottonwood cuttings obtained from the Indian Head Experimental Farm. Motherwell told of "cutting off branches from the cottonwood trees and of tying them together with the halter shank and bringing them home in the waggon on the return trip from Indian Head where he had been drawing grain

---

[1] C. F. Miles, in *Descriptions of the Townships of the North-West Territories* (Ottawa: Dept. of the Interior, 1886).

[2] Archives of Saskatchewan (hereafter cited as AS), Dept. of the Interior Homestead File No. 215741.

[3] Entry in Township General Register, Sask. Dept. of Agriculture, Lands Branch. Mr. Motherwell acquired additional property in later years but his farming operations were always carried out from the original homestead on which he continued to reside.

a distance of about twenty-five miles."[4] Many of his trees were planted from seed. The carragana hedges were eventually strong enough he said, "to turn a bull or stallion."[5]

Motherwell's name has frequently been associated with the discovery of the dry farming technique of summerfallowing. At least one account[6] states that the discovery was made on his and a number of other farms in the Indian Head district in 1886, as a result of fields having been left fallow while the men were absent during the North-West Rebellion the previous year. Evidence now available indicates that, while Motherwell engaged a man to drive his team in transporting supplies for the troops, he managed to sow his land in 1885. He broadcast the seed by hand and harrowed it in with a two year old Shorthorn bull![7] This situation is confirmed by his application for homestead patent in which he showed that in 1885 he cropped all the acreage he had broken by that year. In a letter written many years later, Motherwell stated: "Eighty-six was our first experience of a real dry year . . . . Where an occasional fallow had been made the year previous – 85 – the resultant crop of wheat thereon ran from 15 to 25 or 30 bush."[8] Another resident[9] of the Abernethy district relates that Tom Rogers, who homesteaded the south-east quarter of section 28, left his farm, on which he had broken and cropped a few acres in 1884, to take advantage of the lucrative pay for transport drivers in the Rebellion. He made arrangements with neighbours to plant his field. Apparently it was prepared for seeding, but, owing to the scarcity of labour, some or all of it was left fallow. In 1886, this acreage produced a crop which yielded much better than neighbouring fields. Motherwell was much impressed by this phenomenon and drew it to the attention of his friend, Angus MacKay, of Indian Head. The latter investigated the conditions under which the grain had been grown, and this was the basis for the experiments he proceeded to undertake at the new Do-

[4] AS, Motherwell Papers, Sask. Dept. of Agriculture file (1): F. H. Auld to J. G. Rayner, June 13, 1917.

[5] Personal Papers of Dr. F. H. Auld: Motherwell to F. H. Auld, September 17, 1934.

[6] W. J. Rutherford, "Economic Resources of Saskatchewan," in Canada and Its Provinces (Toronto: Publishers' Association of Canada, 1914), vol. xx, part 2, p. 560.

[7] AS, Office Files: R. T. Motherwell to L. H. Thomas, April 10, 1955.

[8] AS, Motherwell Papers, Sask. Dept. of Agriculture file (1): Motherwell to F. H. Auld, December 28, 1934.

[9] Ralph P. Stueck, see AS, Office Files: R. T. Motherwell to L. H. Thomas, op. cit.; Stueck to L. H. Thomas, March 26, 1955.

minion Experimental Farm. The discovery of dry-farming, whether confined to the Rogers farm or originating on several, led to the almost universal application of the method on the plains of western Canada.[10]

Motherwell commenced to practice summerfallowing and was rewarded in the dry year of 1889 with a crop of thirty bushels to the acre on his summerfallow. In 1894 he began to grow brome grass seed which he had imported directly from Austria. This proved a profitable crop, with the advantage over wheat that it did not lodge, ripened ahead of frost, yielded a seed that was worth seven times as much as wheat and, since it weighed so lightly for its bulk, required fewer trips to market. In 1904, when the railway station was built within two miles of his farm, Motherwell went into oat-growing extensively, and still later he began to grow winter rye because of its advantages in the western climate.

Motherwell's interest in improved farming practices led him to take an active part in the work of local agricultural societies. In 1887 he took prizes for seed grain at the Fort Qu'Appelle, Wolseley, and Indian Head fairs. He entered an essay contest sponsored by the Indian Head Agricultural Society and won a first prize. His paper, entitled "Oat Growing for the Qu'Appelle Valley," was published in the *Nor'West Farmer* in April, 1901. In this practical discussion he stressed the need for proper preparation of the soil and the use of sound, well-cleaned and treated seed. His conversion to the "gospel of dry farming" was reflected in his counsel: "Do not begrudge a nicely prepared plot of fallow for a portion of your oat crop at least."

In the Abernethy community, Motherwell was an elder of the Presbyterian church, clerk of its Session for a time, and chairman of the Church Building Committee. He was active in financial support and volunteer labour when construction of a stone church was begun about 1900. He also served on the committee which undertook the organization of the local school district. When Abernethy S.D. No. 300 was erected, February 20, 1894, Motherwell was elected a trustee, served as secretary-treasurer for seven years, then was chairman of the Board of

[10] Dry farming techniques may be traced into antiquity. In Canada a form of summerfallowing was known to the Red River settlers who left their fields fallow one year out of five or six. The re-emergence and adaptation of the practice to semi-arid regions in North America in the 1880's appears to have been independent of earlier experiences and occurred almost simultaneously in a number of districts in the United States as well as at Indian Head.

Trustees until he entered the government. He also was a Justice of the Peace for the North-West Territories from 1892. In 1894 he took part in the organization of his township as a Statute Labour and Fire District.[11]

In 1891 Motherwell made an abortive foray into politics. He was one of the organizers of a meeting at Fort Qu'Appelle to select a candidate to oppose William Sutherland, the sitting member for the electoral district of North Qu'Appelle in the Legislative Assembly of the North-West Territories. The meeting drew only a small turn-out. Motherwell, whose name was proposed as a candidate, declined to stand on the grounds that the meeting was not representative of the constituency. The invitation to delegates had been mishandled with the result that some districts, including the town of Fort Qu'Appelle, had been overlooked. The local paper, the *Vidette*, commented editorially:

Mr. W. R. Motherwell . . . gave his reasons for refusing to accept the honor at their hands in a most manly and straightforward manner, and by so doing he proved himself to be a man of strong convictions and honest intentions, and well qualified to look after the interests of all of his constituents should he at any time be honored with the confidence of his neighbors as their representative in the Assembly or any other position of trust, and should he at any future time allow his name to be placed in nomination as an independent candidate he may be sure of the support of very many of all shades of politics.[12]

Three years later he undertook his first election campaign. A general election to select a new Legislative Assembly had been called for October 31, 1894. At a public meeting in Fort Qu'Appelle, William Sutherland appealed for re-election and was opposed by G. F. Guernsey who had announced his candidacy. In brief speeches following those by the candidates, A. Hamilton and W. R. Motherwell "alluded to a number of irregularities in the performance of certain work in the Balcarres and Abernethy districts."[13] At that time, public works expenditures in the North-West Territories were administered

---

[11] *The North-West Territories Gazette*, September 1, 1894. The Statute Labour and Fire District was a rudimentary form of local government in the N.W.T. See A. N. Reid, "Local Government in the North-west Territories," *Saskatchewan History*, vol. II, no. 1 (Winter, 1949), p. 4.

[12] *Qu'Appelle Vidette*, October 29, 1891.

[13] *Ibid.*, October 18, 1894.

by the sitting member in each electoral district. Sutherland replied to the charges at the meeting by promising to look into the matter and to discontinue contracts with parties who might have accepted payment for work which they had not satisfactorily completed. On nomination day, October 24, Motherwell was nominated in addition to Sutherland and Guernsey. At the public meeting that day Motherwell "reiterated two or three cases of boodling, and stated that these not being explained to his satisfaction was the grounds for his coming out at this late hour."[14] The *Vidette*, despite its comments on Motherwell at the time of the 1891 election, strongly supported Sutherland and made light of Motherwell's candidacy. In one column it printed an uncomplimentary bit of verse, which avoided the use of names beyond the rather obvious title, "Smotherwell's Soliloquy," and in another column concluded its report of a public meeting at Abernethy at which the candidates had spoken with this note: "The meeting . . . closed with cheers for Sutherland and groans for Motherwell, both of which were given with a will and considerable spirit."[15] Nonetheless, the electors of the Abernethy poll gave Motherwell a majority, as did neighbouring Balcarres, but he trailed behind in the other eleven polls in the riding. Sutherland won handily with 312 votes; Guernsey polled 183; Motherwell received only 71.

Motherwell published a card of thanks in these words: "Thank you, friends, you fought nobly, but defeat is not necessarily disgrace, nor victory honorable."[16] The wording was prophetic. Suggestions of irregularities in the North Qu'Appelle expenditures continued. Motherwell took the lead in pressing for an official investigation with the result that, in 1895, Premier Haultain was appointed a special commissioner to enquire into the charges. Motherwell expressed his strong feelings over delays in the matter in a letter to Haultain:

. . . your policy on this question has been from the first (to use a hackneyed phrase) one of masterly inactivity . . . . You have seen fit to treat us with contempt and indifference, as if we were a lot of soreheads clamoring about nothing. While admitting that external circumstances might probably point in that direction for a time, you are surely now persuaded that such grave

---

[14] *Ibid.*, October 25, 1894. Elections for members of the Territorial Assembly were non-partisan, so that candidates were nominated on a personal basis rather than as the representative of a political party.

[15] *Ibid.*

[16] *Ibid.*, November 1, 1894.

offences have been committed that the safety of the public interest demands a remedy.[17]

Motherwell stated bluntly that should Haultain persist in balking the investigation he would "refer the whole subject to the Dominion government and ask for a thorough enquiry on their part."[18] However, Haultain, in his report to the Assembly in 1896, confirmed the charges, although he exonerated the member of personal complicity therein. Sutherland promptly resigned. A by-election was called for December 1, 1896. While D. H. McDonald, a Fort Qu'Appelle banker and businessman, early announced that he would be a candidate, rural demand for a public meeting to consider nominations resulted in a gathering of seventy electors in the town hall at Fort Qu'Appelle on November 14. Three men – Messrs. Miller, Nicholls, and Motherwell – were proposed. Motherwell framed the principal issues in three questions:

(1) Is it your wish to perpetuate the painful past in regard to the expenditure of public money in the district? (2) Has the time not come when the great agricultural interests of this district demand such recognition and representation of their views in the Legislature as their importance justify? (3) Would it not be in the interest of good government to assist in organizing an energetic though fair opposition to the present Executive?[19]

McDonald also addressed the meeting and then withdrew with his suporters while a ballot was taken. Motherwell was declared the choice of the meeting.

Attendance at the ensuing Motherwell-McDonald campaign meetings was hampered by extremely cold weather, but both candidates found space in the local paper to publish an "Address to the Electors." Motherwell's was brief. He appealed for support "as one whose interests are entirely the same as your own, and believe that in justice to yourselves you will determine that the Farmer's Candidate shall be your next representative in the Assembly."[20] The *Vidette* took a neutral position and stated:

[17] AS, Motherwell Papers, 1890s Sutherland-Boyd case: Motherwell to Haultain, June 27, 1896.
[18] *Ibid.*
[19] *The Vidette* (Fort Qu'Appelle), November 19, 1896.
[20] *Ibid.*

Naturally the contest has become more or less a question of the relation of either candidate to the past history of the constituency and the claims of each from a personal and business point of view to the support of the electors. Whichever candidate is successful, his majority will not, we think, be a very large one.[21]

Motherwell polled 157 votes, far short of the total 382 received by D. H. McDonald.

Following this second defeat at the polls Motherwell abandoned any personal political ambitions for a time, although in Dominion politics he appears to have supported James M. Douglas more or less actively,[22] and worked on behalf of the Liberal party in his immediate district. Shortly he turned to other means of advancing the interests of the farmers which he had sought to represent in the Territorial Assembly.

The circumstances surrounding the formation of the Territorial Grain Growers' Association have been described by a number of writers.[23] The Manitoba Grain Act of 1900, drafted to carry out the recommendations made the previous year by the Royal Commission on the Shipment and Transportation of Grain, provided for general supervision of the grain trade by a warehouse commissioner and granted the farmer the right to ship his own grain and build flat warehouses to facilitate loading. It required the railway to furnish loading platforms where necessary. These provisions were expected to end the monopoly in grain handling extended to elevator companies by the railway and which had been attended by such evils as low grades, short weight, excessive dockage, and unfair prices. However, the crop of 1901 proved to be the largest the country had yet known; the railway was quite unprepared to move it. Elevators plugged up; farmers could not deliver their grain. The frustrations of the farmers were expressed in the Indian Head district at a meeting

---

[21] *Ibid.*, November 26, 1896.

[22] AS, Motherwell Papers, 1890s: F. W. Pinkess to Motherwell, July 11, 1896. James Moffat Douglas was supported by the Liberals and the Patrons of Industry in the election of 1896, and ran as an Independent Liberal in 1900. See Gilbert Johnson, "James Moffat Douglas," *Saskatchewan History*, vol. VII, no. 2 (Spring, 1954), pp. 47-50.

[23] e.g. H. J. Moorhouse, *Deep Furrows* (Toronto: George J. McLeod, 1918); H. S. Patton, *Grain Growers' Co-operation in Western Canada* (Cambridge: Harvard University Press, 1928); L. A. Wood, *A History of Farmers' Movements in Canada* (Toronto: Ryerson Press, 1924). See also *Saskatchewan History*, vol. VIII, no. 3 (Autumn, 1955), pp. 108-112, for Mr. Motherwell's personal recollections of the early history of the organization.

called by John Sibbold and John Millar. Motherwell attended but deplored the violence which was threatened by the more radical farmers. Nevertheless, some sort of concerted action was indicated.

Motherwell and his neighbour, Peter Dayman, got together to discuss the situation. They met in the living room at Lanark Place which might thus be said to be the cradle of the grain growers' movement in Saskatchewan. It was a cheerful, well-lighted room, with simple but comfortable furnishings and a few Victorian adornments – a hanging lamp, two stuffed owls on the mantel over the fire place, and enlarged portraits of Motherwell's parents on the white plaster walls. Motherwell, dressed in overalls and flannel shirt, heavily bearded, and wearing a walrus moustache, made use of the table-height stone window sill to draft notice for a meeting of farmers to be held in Indian Head on December 16, 1901. Dayman, a Conservative, and Motherwell, a Liberal, both signed the notices to avoid the possibility of partisan interest being attached to the undertaking.[24]

The date of the meeting was chosen to coincide with the much heralded debate between premiers Haultain of the North-West Territories and Roblin of Manitoba, on the proposed extension of the Manitoba boundary. With many people in town for the debate in the evening, the afternoon meeting in the fanning mill factory drew a sizeable turn-out of some seventy-five farmers. The aroused farmers agreed to form a Grain Growers' Association.[25] Motherwell was elected provisional President, and a meeting to draft a constitution was set for Indian Head on January 2, 1902. At this second meeting, Motherwell recapitulated the causes leading to the formation of the association:

There could be no doubt that there were many grievances to correct and he had every faith in the solution of many difficulties through the combined wisdom of the farmers of the West. The eastern papers had recently conveyed the news of the completion of the grain blockade. It was a most serious state of affairs and one which affected not alone every grain grower, but also every merchant, mechanic and professional man in the

---

[24] This was to avoid the fate of the Patrons of Industry, an American movement transplanted to Canada, which flourished in western Canada in the mid-90s but disintegrated before the end of the decade due to political candidacies and internal quarrels. See Wood, *op cit.*, ch. 11.

[25] See Moorhouse, *op. cit.*, pp. 49-52, for a description of the Indian Head meeting of December 16, 1901.

country. Cessation in moving the grain practically meant cessation of business. The aim of the association would be to indicate and press for a practical solution of as many problems now before them as were susceptible of solution.[26]

Motherwell and other members of the Board of Directors proceeded to address local meetings in eastern Assiniboia with the result that several branch associations were organized. The Directors then convened the first annual convention of the Territorial Grain Growers' Association at Indian Head on February 12, 1902. In his presidential address, Motherwell reiterated his belief in the efficacy of concerted action and voiced the traditional agrarian antipathy to "big business":

The day has gone by for our remaining scattered, unbanded communities, a tempting bait to the ambitious designs of others. No one can deny that the farmer extracts the wealth from the soil by his industry and skill, in conjunction with the forces of nature, and no one can deny that in the past his rights have been ruthlessly trodden upon by dealers and transportation companies. It is a fact that in other branches of agriculture such as dairy, fruit, and stock interests, all have recognized organizations, and it seems strange that grain growers have not before this realized the importance of organizing also.[27]

He went on to suggest practical steps that would alleviate the difficulties in grain handling. Changes should be made in the Grain Act to require the railways to supply loading platforms within a reasonable time after demand and to grant the right to load cars from vehicles whether there was a platform or not. These proposals were incorporated in resolutions of the convention, together with another which would require the local railway agent to apportion cars, where there was a shortage, in the order in which they were applied for, and in cases where such cars were misappropriated by applicants not entitled to them the penalties of the act should be enforced. The resolutions, pressed upon the federal government and debated in Parliament, were adopted as amendments to the shipping clauses of the Manitoba Grain Act at the 1902 session.

The crop of 1902 surpassed the bountiful harvest of 1901. Despite the new provisions of the Grain Act, the C.P.R. was un-

[26] *The Nor'-West Farmer* (Winnipeg), January 6, 1902, p. 22.
[27] *Ibid.*, March 5, 1902, p. 187.

willing or unable to revise its practices in line with them. Elevator companies continued to command the available supply of cars. Loading platforms without cars were of no help to the farmers. Motherwell and Peter Dayman went to Winnipeg on behalf of the Grain Growers' Association and secured promises from c.p.r. officials that they would carry out the intent of the car-distribution clause of the Grain Act. The promises, however, were not translated into action at the local stations. The Association then took the more drastic step of laying a charge against the c.p.r. agent at Sintaluta for an infraction of the Grain Act in his allocation of cars. The celebrated case, tried before three magistrates at Sintaluta, resulted in the agent being fined fifty dollars and costs. The c.p.r. appealed the case to the Supreme Court of the North-West Territories but that body upheld the magistrates' decision.[28] Speaking at a Grain Growers' meeting in Regina, March 27, 1903, Motherwell said, "The c.p.r. has got to keep the law no matter how many prosecutions we have to enter."[29] The company, however, bowed to the inevitable with good grace and instructed its agents to distribute cars in the order in which they were booked.

In his Regina speech Motherwell warned that the farmers must not relax their vigilance. "So long as the farmers of the West grew a product like wheat," he said, "it would be necessary to have an organization."[30] While the elevator companies realized they would now have to conduct their business differently, the farmers should not depend upon them, he warned. They must avoid the "ruinous way" of selling by the load. It was better to sell in bulk or through farmers' elevators. The latter should provide only handling facilities, since, he maintained, if they bought grain, they would be in the same position as the other companies, and their prices would be governed "by the same combine."

The Sintaluta test case publicized the T.G.G.A. Its membership grew rapidly and spread into Mantitoba, where Motherwell assisted in forming the first local association at Virden on January 3, 1903. Two months later a Manitoba Grain Growers' Association was formed. Their strength augmented by two members of this organization, Motherwell and Gillespie of the T.G.G.A. proceeded to Ottawa to confer with representatives of the grain dealers and the railway companies with the result that

---

[28] See Paton, *op. cit.*, pp. 35-36 for details of this case.
[29] *The Leader* (Regina), April 2, 1903.
[30] *Ibid.*

further refinements in the shipping clauses of the Grain Act were made at the session of 1903. The principles of direct shipment and equality in car distribution were thus firmly established. The Grain Growers' then turned to effecting improvements in the grading and inspecting of grain shipments, meeting again with success. Motherwell continued as President of the T.G.G.A. until his resignation following his entry into the Scott cabinet.[31]

While party politics had not, nominally at least, entered into the make-up of the Territorial Assembly, with the passing of the Alberta and Saskatchewan Acts in 1905 the Dominion political parties began to organize on a provincial basis. Motherwell attended the Liberal provincial convention held at Regina in August, 1905, to elect a leader and adopt a platform. He was appointed to the Resolutions Committee and moved the resolution respecting agriculture and ranching.[32] He was also elected to the provincial executive as the representative for the North Qu'Appelle constituency. The Regina *Leader* interviewed Motherwell "as to the report that he was likely to be a candidate in North Qu'Appelle in the Liberal interest at the forthcoming provincial election." He replied that "so long as he held the position he now does as President of the Territorial Grain Growers' Association he had no intention or thought of entering political life."[33]

On August 30, Walter Scott, who had been chosen Liberal leader, wrote to Motherwell: "There will likely be quite a number of the friends gathered here next Monday, and if at all possible I wish you would make a point of being here. A number of things require to be discussed."[34] The occasion of course was the inauguration ceremony of the province. On September 5, Lieutenant-Governor Forget asked Scott to form a government. In a public statement, Scott said that he at once invited Calder, Lamont, and Motherwell to join him. "Messrs. Lamont and Motherwell requested me to give them until the end of the week for consideration, to which I consented. All rumours as to

---

[31] Motherwell's resignation became effective at the annual meeting of the Saskatchewan Grain Growers' Association, February 6-7, 1906.

[32] *The Leader* August 23, 1905. The brief resolution read: "Resolved that, inasmuch as the progress and prosperity of the Province will depend almost entirely upon the development of its agricultural and ranching industries, the Provincial Government should assist these industries in every possible way."

[33] *Ibid.*

[34] AS, Scott Papers: Scott to Motherwell, August 30, 1905.

friction and difficulty which have been in circulation are, so far as I know, quite baseless. Each of the gentlemen had consented to join the Government and this morning [Sept. 12] the full cabinet was sworn in . . . "[35] The rumours had been associated with Lamont; there is no record of the considerations Motherwell may have taken into account in the few days which elapsed before he made his decision.

Motherwell's prominence as a leader of the grain growers, combined with his professional training in agriculture and practical experience as a farmer, made him an eminently satisfactory choice as Commissioner of Agriculture[36] for the new province.

[35] Quoted in *The Leader*, September 13, 1905.
[36] The office was known as Commissioner of Agriculture until December 18, 1909, when the designation of Minister of Agriculture was adopted. Motherwell also held the portfolio of Provincial Secretary, September 12, 1905, to August 19, 1912.

Liberal Politics, Federal Policies, and the Lieutenant-Governor: Saskatchewan and Alberta, 1905[1]

John Tupper Saywell

The lieutenant-governor is both the representative of the federal government in the Canadian provinces, appointed, instructed, and dismissable by it, and the representative of the Crown in so far as the working of cabinet government is concerned. Since these two aspects are so completely fused in the one office, it is often impossible to clearly separate them, and the discretionary powers of the representative of the Crown may on occasion be used in the interests of the federal government. Moreover, since the central government is formed from a political party, it is often difficult to separate the interests of the government from the interests of the party. The formation of the first provincial governments in Saskatchewan and Alberta in 1905 is an excellent illustration of the general problem; the discretionary power of the lieutenant-governor to select his ministers was definitely exercised in the interests both of the federal government and of the Liberal party, then in power in Ottawa.

By 1905 the demand for provincial status had long been in the air, although only after the turn of the century did it become a matter of immediate political importance. The Laurier administration had no desire to impede this inevitable development, but even the most unobservant could see that any solution would be a thorny one. The evils that had followed the premature entrance of Manitoba into the federation had not been forgotten, and many people were inclined to question the grant of provincial status to two more provinces in the West. Unquestionably, territorial society was sufficiently mature, as the event proved; the doubts were, nonetheless, legitimate. Further-

SOURCE: *Saskatchewan History*, vol. VIII, no. 3 (Autumn, 1955), pp. 81-88. Reprinted by permission of the author and publishers.

[1] The author would like to record his appreciation for grants from the Social Science Research Council, the Canadian Social Science Research Council, and the Humanities Research Council, that made possible a study of the office of the lieutenant-governor of which this essay is a byproduct.

more, serious disputes were bound to arise, both in the West and in the East. Unlike the other provinces (except Manitoba), the new ones would be the creations of the federal government, which naturally considered itself empowered to decide upon the terms of creation; negotiation in fact might properly be said to have been a courtesy extended to the territorial government, rather than a stern necessity. The federal government could gain little: terms unacceptable in the Territories would affect Liberal power in the West; terms acceptable there might easily be criticized in other parts of the nation, particularly those concerning finance and education. This unenviable position was to some extent improved by the irresistible pressure from the West; Laurier could answer his eastern critics by pointing out that he had acted solely in deference to the wishes of the people, for was not local self-determination basic in the Liberal creed? As Walter Scott observed, "Haultain was really playing into Laurier's hands, just as the Tories elsewhere have been doing with Dundonald, the Tariff, the G.T.P. and generally. As effectively as he could do it he has made inevitable action easy on Laurier's part."[2]

The creation of two provinces necessitated the establishment of two governments where there had been one previously. The constitutions of the provinces were set out in the acts passed by Parliament, but the actual initiation was left to the lieutenant-governors. It was universally agreed that A. E. Forget, the lieutenant-governor of the Territories, would be re-appointed, and that he would stay in Regina, thus becoming the first lieutenant-governor of Saskatchewan.[3] The other appointment was less foreseeable. There were, however, very good reasons for the selection of George H. V. Bulyea.

The Liberal party in the West owed Bulyea a good deal. He had been a prominent member of the territorial government. As the autonomy question came more and more to the fore, he grew restless and wished to resign, but, at the request of other Liberals, he remained in the government. The reason was later divulged by Scott:

When the pinch came in 1903 I expected a general federal elec-

[2] Archives of Saskatchewan (AS), Walter Scott Papers, Scott to T. M. Bryce, February 2, 1905.

[3] *Regina Leader*, March 22, 1905, Scott to Laird. Scott later felt that it might be best if Forget went to Alberta to give that province "the advantages of his knowledge of constitutional procedure." (AS, Scott Papers, Scott to Calder, June 17, 1905). This was impossible, as will be seen, when Haultain decided to stay in Saskatchewan.

tion that coming winter. It is easy now after the event to gauge public sentiment regarding autonomy. It was not so easy then. Bulyea's resignation would have necessitated local general elections and would have saddled the Liberals with the onus of bringing in a party division, and I feared that autonomy would in the melee become an exciting issue, that is to say that people would become exercised over it to a degree that might injure us in the later federal fight.[4]

To prevent the characterization of the Liberals as opponents of autonomy, Bulyea stayed in the government, which thus retained its non-partisan composition, and in 1905 he was a delegate to Ottawa when the terms were being discussed. The Liberal party was certainly obligated to him, yet at the same time his "standing in the breach" had injured his reputation and political position in the Territories, and it was doubted whether he could successfully carry either province in the first election.[5] He had, therefore, to be shelved. What would it be? the Senate or the lieutenant-governorship of Alberta? Laurier and his western colleagues decided on the latter. The Prime Minister's offer emphasized not that his political usefulness had ceased, but that Bulyea might find it difficult to openly fight Haultain, with whom he had been associated for such a long time, "with all the firmness which a political contest means in this country. . . . "[6] Bulyea was not deceived; he agreed that his record would seriously hamper the party in both provinces.[7]

As soon as possible after September 1, 1905, these two men — Forget and Bulyea — would ask someone to form a government. Whom would they call? At first there seemed to be no problem at all; when Haultain and Bulyea came to Ottawa in January, 1905, Laurier thought,

. . . and indeed everyone thought, that as soon as the two provinces came into existence, the then existing government of the territories would naturally become the government of Saskatchewan.[8]

[4] AS, Scott Papers, Scott to Bryce, January 17, 1905. See also: Public Archives of Canada (PAC), Laurier Papers, vol. 377, Bulyea to Laurier, August 5, 1905.
[5] AS, Scott Papers, Scott to Calder, June 17, 1905; G. W. Brown to Scott, June 28, 1905.
[6] PAC, Laurier Papers, vol. 377, Laurier to Bulyea, confidential, July 25, 1905.
[7] *Ibid.*, Bulyea to Laurier, August 5, 1905.
[8] *Ibid.*, Laurier to Bulyea, confidential, July 25, 1905.

Hautain would then have become the first premier. Unquestionably that recognition would have been well earned: since 1897 he had been the territorial premier and, for almost a decade before, he had been a member of the Advisory Council and Chairman of the Executive Committee; his government had been non-partisan, but his own position had been unchallenged; he had been returned in 1902 with the support of twenty-four of the thirty-five members; he had led the struggle for autonomy and was thus really the "Father" of the new province. Yet Haultain was not asked to form the first provincial government of Saskatchewan.

The story of the autonomy negotiations has been often told.[9] It is sufficient to recall here that, on each of the major propositions, Hautain and Laurier differed: Hautain desired one province and provincial control of public lands and education; Laurier insisted on two provinces, federal control of public lands, and a compromise on the schools question; they also disagreed on the financial terms. Negotiations almost foundered on the educational question; faced with the resignation of Clifford Sifton and the threatened wholesale revolt of the western M.P.'s, Laurier incurred momentary unpopularity in Quebec by agreeing to compromise.[10] This compromise was accepted by

---

[9] See C. C. Lingard, *Territorial Government in Canada – The Autonomy Question in the Old North-West Territories* (Toronto, 1946); John W. Dafoe, *Clifford Sifton in Relation to His Times* (Toronto, 1931); O. D. Skelton, *Life and Letters of Sir Wilfrid Laurier* (Carleton Library, vols. 21 and 22).

[10] Scott throws some interesting light on the crisis. "I am convinced myself that but for what is either unpardonable stupidity or unpardonable selfishness, or both, these measures would have gone through with a very minimum complaint or disturbance. As you know I was always willing to stand for continuance of the schools constitution the way they had it since 1875. The North-West Members were united in this position. In all the conferences we had with the Government we were given to understand that they intended to provide just that and nothing more. The education clause itself has been very carefully framed to appear innocent on the surface but careful analysis of it shows that it is the most comprehensive clause providing for a separate school system that could be devised.

Of course Sifton is out now and is not committed to anything. When a man once breaks out it is hard to tell how far he will go. I may say to you, however, confidentially that I am positive that he was willing to stand with us for the separate school as we have it in the North-West to-day. Even yet I am hopeful that if the Bill is modified to meet our views in this respect that Sifton will be found ready as a private member to support it. This is the solution which I think there is some reason to hope can be found." (AS, Scott Papers, Scott to Brown, March 2, 1905).

the western Liberals and by Sifton, although the latter refused to re-enter the cabinet. With Haultain, however, it was otherwise. As the western Liberals swung into line behind Laurier's Liberal government, Haultain moved further into opposition. In federal politics he had always been a Conservative. Now, on February 14, 1905, he declared his unrelenting opposition to the educational clause.[11] Several weeks later, after the compromise had been arranged, Haultain openly denounced the whole scheme; it was, he said, the complete ruination of provincial autonomy.[12] His statement "was recognized as a gauntlet of defiance to the Federal authorities and an indication that he would do what was possible to fire the Western heather against the Autonomy legislation."[13] Not only did he oppose the Bill but also he willingly allied himself with the Conservative party; he was "in all the secrets of the enemy and helping them to the extent of his ability."[14]

Since Haultain, although the leader of a non-partisan government, was a Tory in federal politics, western Liberals had always been reluctant to admit that he would have to be asked to form one of the two governments in the West. They admitted, however, that "by following precedent" his selection was almost inevitable.[15] In which province would Haultain stake his future? Alberta Liberals felt sure he would play the political game there, and agreed that he should be accepted as premier if the other members of the cabinet were to their liking; in other words, the old non-partisan government was to be retained in the province.[16] When it became apparent that he planned to remain in Saskatchewan, the Liberals in that province became concerned. Walter Scott, member of Parliament for Assiniboia West, broached the idea of having Haultain called in Alberta; presumably he would refuse, but there could be no argument that he had been overlooked.[17] However, nothing came of this suggestion.

The chief difficulty faced by the western Liberals was less

[11] University of Alberta Library (UAL), Rutherford Papers, Talbot to Rutherford, confidential, February 24, 1905; Lingard, *op. cit.*, p. 174.

[12] Toronto *Globe*, March 13, 1905; Lingard, *op. cit.*, pp. 174 ff.

[13] *Canadian Annual Review* (1905), p. 57.

[14] UAL, Rutherford Papers, Talbot to Rutherford, confidential, March 22, 1905.

[15] *Ibid.*, February 24, 1905.

[16] *Ibid.*, March 22, 1905.

[17] AS, Scott Papers, Scott to Bulyea, private and confidential, May 20, 1905.

the stirrings of their tender consciences than the opposition of Laurier, who for a long time was unwilling to approve any suggestion that Haultain be by-passed. The Prime Minister's determination on this count — soon to become hesitation and finally surrender — was the result not of his political scruples but of his philosophical beliefs regarding the Canadian federal system. Although his actions when in power belied his principles when in opposition, Laurier had, throughout his career, stood out for the non-interference of both the federal government and federal politicians in provincial affairs. To issue an order that Haultain was not to be summoned would, of course, be an open interference in a matter which, although of immense importance to the federal government and the Liberal party, could hardly be termed a legitimate exercise of his power.

The decision was taken from Laurier's hands. When Haultain campaigned vigorously and viciously on the Conservative behalf in two Ontario by-elections in June, 1905, and stated emphatically that if he won power in the West, he would go to any length to secure a revision of the settlement, the Liberals decided against him. Frank Oliver, by this time the western representative in the Laurier cabinet, refused to have him summoned in either province under any circumstances, on the ground (as Scott put it) that his recent activity "is about all the reason that is needed to excuse passing him over."[18] Laurier was finally convinced:

When in the early part of the struggle which followed the introduction of the bills, Haultain went out of his way to openly take side with the opposition, I am free to admit that I was keenly disappointed but even then I did not come to the conclusion that the breach was irreparable. When, however, he threw himself into the contests of London and North Oxford and especially when he announced his intention of carrying on provincial elections on the avowed policy of destroying the school system . . . he left us no alternative, but to accept the declaration of war.[19]

If Laurier had arrived at this decision during the by-elections, he did not at once let his colleagues know. Early in July, Scott informed a close political friend that

Laurier still sticks in some degree to the idea that, notwithstanding all that has occurred, our best policy will be to call Haultain

[18] *Ibid.*, June 17, 1905.
[19] PAC, Laurier Papers, vol. 377, Laurier to Bulyea, confidential, July 25, 1905.

in Alberta. So far as I know no other man here holds that opinion any longer and in face of the unanimous opinion which prevails I fancy that Laurier will be compelled to relinquish the idea.[20]

Laurier did indeed; but it is apparent that he regretted "the impossibility of doing what, under ordinary circumstances, would have been the obvious thing."[21]

The decision had been made. Two Liberals were to be called, and two Liberal governments formed. It is singular that no mention was made of the personal prerogative of the lieutenant-governor; it was taken for granted that his personal discretion would be exercised as the party and the federal government saw fit. The representative of the Crown was to be neither impartial nor independent; he was to act as a federal officer (in an unusual and hardly legitimate sense) and a party member. If the federal government did not instruct the lieutenant-governors to call on acceptable Liberals, both government and party would "simply stultify themselves, and give an exhibition of weakness,"[22] and, at the same time, show "little regard for the provincial Liberals . . ."[23]

All that remained was the selection of provincial Liberal leaders. In Saskatchewan there were only two candidates, Walter Scott and J. A. Calder. Scott was one of the leading Liberals in the West. After Sifton's resignation, he had hopes of entering the cabinet, but when Laurier, probably on Sifton's advice, asked Frank Oliver instead, he became the obvious choice.[24]

[20] AS, Scott Papers, Scott to Brown, private and confidential, July 4, 1905.

[21] *Ibid.*, Scott to Bulyea, private and confidential, July 25, 1905.

[22] *Ibid.*, Scott to Calder, private and confidential, July 12, 1905.

[23] PAC, Laurier Papers, vol. 393, C. W. Cross to Talbot, personal, July 3, 1905.

[24] See Dafoe, *Sifton*, p. 301n. As early as March 2 Scott had mentioned his own appointment to the cabinet: "Naturally there is much speculation with regard to Sifton's successor. I have no intimation as to Laurier's intention but of course will not be very greatly surprised to be sent for myself. Just what my answer would be in this case it is yet too early to say excepting that no western member could possibly accept office or support the education clause as it stands." (AS, Scott Papers, Scott to Brown, March 2, 1905). Talbot wrote that Scott and Oliver were rivals, but felt that Scott would get it: "I don't think Sifton will go back as Min. of the Interior. I think Scott is booked for that position and I fear Oliver will be disappointed. There may be a row . . ." (UAL, Rutherford Papers, Talbot to Rutherford, confidential, April 2, 1905; also *Ibid.*, March 28, 1905.)

For a long time, Scott continued to press Calder to accept the provincial leadership, but leading Liberals were quite convinced that Scott was the man. The Liberal convention in due time chose Scott, and Forget asked him to form a government.

Once Oliver became Minister of the Interior, the choice in Alberta boiled down to two people, Peter Talbot and Alex Rutherford. Talbot, a member of the House of Commons, was the overwhelming favourite; Laurier, Scott, Bulyea, Brown, Forget, and numerous others agreed that he was better qualified and more likely to suceed. Talbot himself was not much concerned, and declared his willingness to do whatever the interests of the party called for. Rutherford, on the other hand, a member of the territorial legislature since 1902, was determined to secure the leadership, and the office that would go with it, at any cost. At Laurier's request, Talbot went west in July to size up the situation. He reported that as far as political strength was concerned, there was little to choose between them, but added that since Rutherford had committed himself to the headship it would be best to let him have it rather than split the party.[25] Talbot did not let his name go before the party convention, and Rutherford was elected. Laurier was not particularly pleased and may perhaps have hoped that Bulyea would select Talbot anyway.[26] Rutherford was asked to form a government soon after the provinces had been created.

Rutherford's selection passed without much comment; protests were voiced throughout Canada when the selection of Scott was announced. Laurier had previously stated in the House of Commons that the choice of the first premiers was the exclusive concern of the lieutenant-governor, but few were deceived.[27] The Montreal *Gazette* was brief and blunt:

In passing Mr. Haultain over, and selecting for the premiership one of his principal political opponents, a gentleman who was not a member of the late territorial legislature, Lieutenant-Governor Forget made himself a part of the Federal Liberal machine, and sacrificed in part his title to the respect his office

---

[25] PAC, Laurier Papers, vol. 377, Talbot to Laurier, August 7, 1905; Bulyea to Laurier, August 5, 1905.

[26] He believed Talbot was by far the best man for the job, but informed Bulyea that this was "a matter as to which of course, your better judgement must prevail." (PAC, Laurier Papers, vol. 377, Laurier to Bulyea, August 11, 1905).

[27] House of Commons *Debates*, 1905, p. 7744.

should secure him, and which his record gave reason for thinking he would maintain.[28]

Forget later referred to his action as "the only one . . . which . . . had met with severe criticism," but added that "despite all that has been said . . . he felt sure, in his conscience, that he had done his duty. But whether he had made a mistake or not . . . , his mistake, if it was a mistake, was then and has since been approved by a great majority of the Province."[29]

The selection of Scott had indeed been overwhelmingly approved, (although it could be argued that whoever was chosen would have been approved); the government won seventeen of the twenty-five seats in the legislature, and, under various leaders, remained in power until 1929. The election was fought in great part on the autonomy Acts: while denying any subservience to Ottawa or to Laurier, Scott fully endorsed the settlement; Haultain formed a Provincial Rights party, the program of which centered around complete provincial autonomy, better financial terms, and a separation of federal and provincial politics.[30] Haultain attempted as well to make an issue of the lieutenant-governor's action, asking the electors if they wanted a federal and a Liberal puppet in Government House. Scott openly admitted that Haultain had been the logical choice until he decided to wreck the settlement: "That the Crown acted upon Liberal advice is a charge I shall not try to refute."[31]

This advice, however, was not that of any provincial advisers, but of the Laurier administration; it was not given through constitutional channels, but through political ones. This was the point emphasized by Robert Borden, the Conservative chief, when the House of Commons next met. Laurier denied any interference at all; Forget had every right to bypass Haultain if he so desired; he had the constitutional right to call on any man in Saskatchewan he thought could form a government. Frank Oliver threw in a red herring by arguing that Haultain was from Alberta; Bulyea, not Forget, he suggested, should be criticized, if criticism there must be.[32] Later in the year, with

[28] September 7, 1905.

[29] Regina *Morning Leader*, October 15, 1910.

[30] In this latter point Haultain was reflecting a genuine western political tradition.

[31] Cited in the House of Commons *Debates*, 1906, p. 111.

[32] *Ibid.*, 1906, pp. 43 ff, 52 ff, and 118 ff.

more information at hand, (including a letter from Scott, which had somehow slipped into his hands, indicating that Laurier had only reluctantly, and after much hesitation, agreed that Haultain was not to be called), Borden again brought the matter to the attention of the Commons.

What has the Prime Minister of Canada to do with passing over Mr. Haultain? Is that not the business of the Lieutenant-Governor of Saskatchewan? Have we not a constitution in this country under which we are supposed to have lieutenant governors who act independently of the federal authority? Is not the whole basis of our constitution dependent upon that principle?[33]

Borden observed that Laurier's action was in complete contradiction to his beliefs, so ardently espoused while in opposition, for he had then been a staunch upholder and guardian of provincial rights. As for the lieutenant-governor,

He is not an officer of the federal government; he is the direct representative of the Crown, and any attempt to undermine the dignity and independence of such an officer is in my opinion a blow aimed against the spirit and indeed against the letter of the constitution.

Similar criticism has been made in more recent years, by scholars as well as politicians; Dr. C. C. Lingard, for example, declares without qualification that Forget "left himself open to the charge of being the willing instrument of a federal party machine. The Crown, according to constitutional custom, was above and beyond party politics, and so far as His Honour could judge Mr. Haultain still retained the confidence of the people."[34]

These arguments are only in part correct. The lieutenant-governor is a federal officer, appointed, paid, dismissable, and instructed, by the federal government. His position as a federal officer was in principle identical to that of the colonial governor as an imperial officer. The extent to which the colonial governor was entitled or advised to use his discretionary power in the interests of the imperial government was never reduced to definition, nor has it been in so far as the lieutenant-governor and federal interests are concerned. Even a cursory reading of Ca-

[33] *Ibid.*, 1906-7, pp. 26-7.
[34] Lingard, *op. cit.*, p. 250.

nadian history in the 1860s, for example, will reveal how often such powers were exercised and how important they were. Dr. Lingard refers to this period and suggests that passing over Haultain was as unjustified as passing over John A. Macdonald in 1867 would have been. This seems sound on the surface and is an attractive argument, but it should be remembered that Macdonald was the prime mover and the staunchest upholder of the settlement that had brought Canada into being. Haultain was the determined opponent of the settlement of 1905.

Furthermore, a good constitutional argument can be set forth to justify the selection of Scott and Rutherford. Although the territorial government had been non-partisan, there was a general desire, once provincial status had been achieved, to establish the two-party system in each of the provinces; Haultain's action had made this inevitable if it had not already been so. One can safely say that the old territorial government was in fact dissolved before it formally came to an end. Under such circumstances, the clear duty of the lieutenant-governors was to select the leader of the party that had the support of the people. As Forget declared, "les Lieutenants-Gouverneurs n'ont donc, à mon avis, d'autre alternative, que de choisir leur premier Ministre dans celui des deux partis politiques qui, pour le moment, semble avoir la majorite."[35] The question was, of course, which of the two parties had the majority.

Judging from the affiliations with federal parties listed in the *Parliamentary Guide*, the majority of the members of the territorial legislature were Liberals. There was, however, an even surer guide: the federal elections of 1904 that had been fought on strict party lines. Seven of the ten members sent from the Territories were Liberals. This, declared the lieutenent-governor, "ne laisse aucune doute."[36] The danger and illogicality of gauging political strength in the provinces by the vote in a federal election is at once apparent. Given the peculiar circumstances of 1905, however, it was less open to censure, for it was, after all, the policy of the federal government that was at issue and upon which the electorate would be asked to express their opinion.

When all is said, the truth remains that the decision to pass over Haultain, whose claims — politically and constitutionally — were indeed substantial, was a political act. The decision was

[35] PAC, Laurier Papers, vol. 374, Forget to Laurier, confidential, July 10, 1905.
[36] *Ibid.*

forced on Laurier by Haultain's indiscreet opposition to federal policy – opposition that threatened to re-open, with all its bitterness and viciousness, the whole racial, religious, and linguistic question in Canada – and the pressure of the less principled western Liberals, who, regardless of Haultain's course had wanted to overlook him from the beginning. To suppose that the federal authorities, with the means at hand to secure a sympathetic government in the new provinces, would have neglected to use whatever power or influence they possessed, legitimately or otherwise, is to credit men with a too respectful concern for the forms of political life; politicians are interested essentially in the forces that give these forms life. In Canada, at least, it would have been an unprecedented and unexpected act of abnegation.

History of the Saskatchewan Stock Growers' Association

John H. Archer

There has always been an aura of adventure, danger and glamour associated with the western plains of the United States and Canada. Indians, fur traders, buffalo hunters, cavalry, and Mounted Police crowd the early pages of history. Then came the cattle kingdom and with it, the cowboy – kingpin of a world of cattle drives, stampedes, round-ups, ropes, branding irons, and broncos. No doubt there was more of danger and hardship than of glamour and adventure in all this. The cowboy will tell you that riding the range is a job, not a role. The rancher will tell you that ranching is hard work, a precarious living. True, all true, but the aura of a colourful era persists.

The cattle kingdom had its origin in Texas before the Civil War. It arose at that place where man began to manage cattle on horseback. The use of the horse primarily distinguished ranching in the West from stockfarming in the East. The place was the Nueces Valley where Mexican cattle came into the presence of the mounted Texan, armed with rope and six-gun. Following the Civil War, a shortage of cattle in the northern states opened up a new market for beef. Railways pushing westward across the plains offered rail facilities to eastern markets. Cattle from the south and southwest were driven north in great herds to shipping points on the railway. There came a time when surplus cattle were held on the northern range. They did well on the northern grass, and the cattle kingdom spread west to the Rockies and north into the southerly grass lands of the North-West Territories of Canada.

In the early days of ranching, the land itself had no value, grass was free, and water belonged to the first comer. The unit of production was the ranch, which included the house and all

SOURCE: *Saskatchewan History*, vol. XII, no. 2 (Spring, 1959), pp. 41-60. Reprinted by permission of the author and publishers. [This article was reprinted as a pamphlet by the Saskatchewan Stock Growers' Association in 1963. It is this slightly abbreviated version that is reprinted here.]

the range of the cattle, whether fenced or unfenced. There was little thought of any serious competition from farmers for the aridity of the plains appeared to be an effective deterrent to settlement. As R. T. Coupland writes:

Spread of farming into the region from the east was impeded by the early description of the area as the "Great American Desert." After settlement started about the middle of the century, the droughts of 1860-62, 1870-73, 1883-89 and 1893-95 impeded farming and resulted in emigration from the Plains. Not until methods of dryland farming were perfected (1885-90) was it clear that the Great Plains would be used for crop production.

When settlement did spread over the American plains, the settlers came somewhat as interlopers into a cattleman's world where range law, tradition, and practice were well established.

In western Canada there were no cattle on the open range prior to the disappearance of the buffalo, as the buffalo bulls would kill the range bulls and the cows would drift off with the herd of buffalo. By 1874, however, the buffalo were disappearing. In 1877, conditions had so changed that cattle could be turned out on the open prairie, marking the first step in the ranching industry in what is now the Province of Alberta. The imminent disappearance of the buffalo by 1879 gave the federal government much concern. Efforts were made to encourage the raising of cattle in the Territories so that supplies of meat would be available for feeding the Indians. Leaseholds were granted on single tracts of land up to 100,000 acres, at a rental of one cent per acre per year. The federal government contracted for beef and tried to arrange for delivery at convenient points. Ranching on the Canadian prairies seemed to have made an auspicious start.

This encouraging beginning quickly gave way to leaner years. In 1885, the transcontinental railway was completed. Dry farming techniques developed in the United States appeared to promise success in the Canadian West. Governmental leaders in Ottawa looked to the day when the parkland and prairies of the North-West Territories would support millions of settlers. Railway land grants, colonization schemes, veterans' grants, squatters' rights, homesteading – all these terms were heard in official circles and each, when effected, cut into the free grass. The Indians were persuaded to retire to reservations where they were encouraged to raise their own food supply.

Before the ranching industry in the Canadian West could establish its roots and effectively delineate its bounds, land hungry settlers attracted by the homestead policy of the Canadian government were encroaching on the grass lands.

Ranchers in the Territories were soon caught in an inexorable squeeze. In 1886, rentals were raised to two cents an acre. In 1887, all leases greater than four sections were thrown open for purchase by tender. In effect this placed a capital value on lease rights in these lands, in addition to the regular rental fee. In 1887, also, twenty-one-year leases were provided for, terminable at any time for homestead entry or pre-emption. In 1892, it was announced that all leases held under the old form, which did not provide for homestead purposes, would terminate on or after December 31, 1896. This regulation did include an option to purchase up to ten percent of a leasehold at $1.25 per acre. Finally, in 1905, a regulation was passed confining the issuance of grazing leases to a tract south of the twenty-ninth township in Alberta and to certain corresponding areas in Saskatchewan. The cumulative result virtually drove the larger ranching interests out of business.

While general settlement policies bore heavily on the ranching industry as a whole, it was at the local level that ranchers came face to face with the direct results of agricultural settlement. As homesteaders pressed the grain frontier farther west, municipal organization followed in the wake. Open road allowances, herd law, pound law, and municipal taxation — the trappings of a complicated and expensive machinery of government — caused consternation at the local level. The idea of a protective stock growers' association began to be mooted. In the words of a rancher, J. F. MacCallum of Webb:

Before the provinces of Saskatchewan and Alberta were organized, we had a Territorial Government for the three Territories, viz., Assiniboia, Alberta and Saskatchewan. We had a Stock Growers' Association, called the Western Stock Growers [Association] the head office of which was in Medicine Hat. All our brands for horses and cattle were registered in the office at Medicine Hat. Now after these three Territories were made into the two provinces of Saskatchewan and Alberta the line dividing the two provinces running north and south came through or close to Walsh, which is now in Alberta. We old stockmen continued to pay membership to the Western Stock Growers, whose offices were now in Alberta. And when the rural municipalities in Saskatchewan started making laws and regulations and evaluating our grazing leased lands at the same rate as deeded land, the Western Stock Growers could not do anything for us, because we had a Saskatchewan Government now, since 1905. You can see the reason we needed an organization of stock growers to protect and fight for our interests. It was the ranchers in the Wood Mountain, Willow Bunch and Moose Jaw districts who first started to talk of organizing a stock growers' association in Saskatchewan so that we could put our troubles before the Saskatchewan Government.

Leadership for a Saskatchewan association came from a group of ranchers, six in number. These were John D. Simpson who lived in Moose Jaw and became a partner of Robert Cruickshank when they bought the Turkey Track Ranch at Hallonquist, southeast of Swift Current; Olof Olafson, a railway conductor, who had a ranch south of Mortlach but who lived in Moose Jaw; Robert Cruickshank, who had ranch interests at Rush Lake and at other points north of the South Saskatchewan River, and who lived in Moose Jaw; W. H. Ogle, a well-to-do Englishman, who ran a large herd of cattle in the Wood Mountain district but who spent much of his time in Moose Jaw; John H. Grayson, a business man in Moose Jaw who had a large spread southwest of the city; and Trefflé Bonneau who ran a large herd of cattle in the Willow Bunch district. These men met in Moose Jaw in the fall of 1912 to discuss the organization of a stock growers' association in Saskatchewan. At this meeting John D. Simpson, the man who had taken a leading part in organizing the meeting, was requested to circularize every stockman in the southwest who held a grazing lease from the dominion government, to promote the idea of an association.

The circular letter, sent out January 12, 1913, pointed out that unless a combined effort was made in the near future "the ranching industry in the West will early become a thing of the past." The formation of a stock growers' association was advocated: "The main object, of course, would be that of fostering, and if at all possible, of re-establishing the oldest established industry in the Western Country." The letter then drew attention to the success won by the Grain Growers' Association and urged that a strong ranchers' organization financed by the ranchers themselves be set up. A postscript to the letter stated, "At no time in the history of Ranching was the lack of organization of a Stockmen's Association more felt or recognized than it was when the Government Ranchers Commission was going through this Western Country making enquiries into all existing conditions. . . ." This letter evoked sufficient support to warrant the calling of an organization meeting later in the year.

The interested stockmen met in Moose Jaw in the Y.M.C.A. building, July 23 and 24, 1913. The meeting was opened by J. D. Simpson, who presided until Hugh McKellar was elected chairman. The first day saw a general discussion of all the troubles afflicting the ranching industry. There appears to have been little bitterness toward the organized farmers, — indeed, J. D. Simpson mentioned the ground gained by the Grain Growers' Association as an example of what like co-operation might do for ranching. Simpson suggested that there was room for both ranchers and farmers but strongly advocated the formation of a ranchers' association, feeling, no doubt, that the room might be a little more equitably divided if the ranchers had a strong organization to represent them. Other speakers discussed the herd laws and pound laws which were felt to be quite unfair, even "legalized theft covered up by the cloak of legislation." The taxation of leased land by rural municipal councils was warmly criticized. The ever-present problem of cattle thieving was raised, and the suggestion was made that a rigid inspection be insisted on before stock could be disposed of. Olaf Olafson suggested that the government should, after the first year, furnish homesteaders with sufficient money to enable them to fence their holdings.

The second day of the meeting was given over to the business of organization. The chairman on the first day had appointed Messrs. Simpson, McFaddyen, Fysh, Ogle, and Gunn a committee to draw up a constitution. The draft constitution and the bylaws were presented to the meeting for discussion. All received unanimous approval. The name "The Saskatchewan Stock Growers' Association" was approved. The objects of the association, as approved by the meeting, were:

(a) *To watch legislation relating to the Stock Growers' interests.*

(b) *To forward the interests of the Stock Growers in every honourable and legitimate way.*

(c) *To suggest to parliament from time to time as it is found necessary, through duly appointed delegates, the passing of any new legislation to meet changing conditions and requirements.*

The organization followed a pattern already favoured by farmer organizations. There was to be a central association with a president, vice president, secretary-treasurer, five directors at large, and twenty district directors. The district directors were to be nominated by delegates from the local association, but if two or more such were nominated, a vote by ballot of the assembly was to be held. All other officers, save for the secretary-treasurer who was appointed, were to be elected by ballot from the whole assembly. Each local association had a somewhat similar slate of officers as the central association. Local associations were entitled to elect delegates to the central association on the basis of one delegate for every ten fully paid-up members. Duties of the officers and rules for the conduct of meetings were set out in some detail. Provision was made for an executive which had power to frame bylaws and regulations.

The membership fee to the central organization was set by the meeting at two dollars. In addition the central organization was empowered to assess one cent per head for sheep, three cents per head for horn cattle, five cents per head for horses. In ensuing years, the executive committee was to make assessments according to the estimate of money required. Local associations were empowered to fix their own membership fee, and fees collected became the money of the local.

The officers elected at this the first meeting of the association were: President — W. H. Ogle, Wood Mountain; Vice President — R. Cruickshank, Moose Jaw; Secretary-Treasurer — J. D. Simpson, Moose Jaw. Directors at large — Walker Ross, Mortlach; J. Lawrence, Maple Creek; C. Ange, Willow Bunch; Trefflé Bonneau, Willow Bunch; J. D. Simpson, District Directors — Wm. Gunn, Nummola; James D. Wilson, Tompkins; G. H. Reid, Michelton; John Grayson, Moose Jaw; Olaf Olafson, Mortlach; O. B. Fysh, Moose Jaw; Octave Holle, Willow Bunch; Donald Sinclair, South Fork; J. B. Thomson, Elm Springs; William Howes, Moose Jaw; Fred Hauseman, Corrander; Peter McKellar, Log Valley; Ashton Stoneman, Mortlach; Frank Gailey, Caron; G. Hollingbach, Wood Mountain; Sam Briggs, Wood Mountain; D. Main, South View; James McNee, Swift Current; J. A. Kennedy, Moose Jaw; Robert C. Brown, Maple Creek.

The last session of the convention dealt with resolutions. There is something forthright and virile in the first resolution adopted unanimously:

*That the Provincial Government of Saskatchewan take action
in the way of passing legislation to make more favorable regulations regarding taxes imposed on grazing ranchers, herd laws,
pound laws, fires and fencing of road allowances and that
Messrs. Walker Ross, W. H. Ogle, Robert Cruickshank, Wm.
Gunn, J. D. Simpson and C. Ange be the delegation to go to
Regina to argue the matter.*

Another resolution gave endorsation to the recommendations
of the federal commission which reported in 1913. Another
approved *The Saskatchewan Farmer* as the official organ of the
Association. Still another resolution called for united action
with the North Western Ranchers Association of Alberta on
matters of common concern. All in all the ranchers present
showed a deep awareness of the problems besetting the ranching industry and a clear intention of taking action to meet them.
It was realized by those present that the coming year would be
the test. The response to membership appeals, the accomplishments of the executive, and the tone of the 1914 convention
would spell life or death for the young association.

The 1914 convention was held in Moose Jaw in the Board
of Trade Rooms on June 10, 11, and 12. It began auspiciously
with a welcome from Mayor Pascoe in this vein: "I wish to
welcome this Convention to the City of Moose Jaw and give
you freedom of the City and I wish to tell you that unless you
need the Police for your own use they will be asleep as far as
you are concerned," to which Jack Byers replied, "I take this
opportunity of thanking him on behalf of the Saskatchewan
Stock Growers' Association for his very kind invitation. I hope
none of us will need the Chief of Police at all but I could not
vouch for them."

The President gave a review of the year's accomplishments.
He reported that the progress made had shown that there was
reason for having an association. Membership had increased
from 100 to 230 members. He then reported on delegations:
"We have had two delegations go down to Regina, one delegation went to Ottawa, several delegations met here in Moose
Jaw to interview the Federal officials as they went through here
and I think we may say that the result of these various delegations and the interviewing of the Federal officials has been
the passing of new Grazing Regulations." Mr. Ogle then went
on to mention taxation. "Probably the most important question
we have before the stockmen of this Province is the question

of taxation . . . If the present rate of taxation is enforced it just simply means that the stock growers will have to go out of business. There is no other way to it at all – as a man is not in it for pleasure and if the present rate of taxation is enforced there will be no profit in it at all." He ended his remarks on this note, "Herd laws are also a question which will have to be taken up with this provincial government – the present system and methods of pound keepers is absolutely rotten. Also we would like to have it made a criminal offence that anybody leave a gate on a lease open, or destroy a fence."

The Secretary, J. D. Simpson, reported on the work of the Association and on the financial position. He explained that several delegations had gone to Regina in connection with what the Association considered to be an injustice done to the Gull Lake Ranching Company by the Municipality. The point in dispute was the right of the Municipality to levy taxes on ranching land on the same basis as on improved farm land. The Municipality seized all the horses on the ranch including saddle horses and horses working on the binder. This was done in spite of an undertaking by the manager of the Ranching Company that he would produce the horses on any set day. As Mr. Simpson stated:

We placed our case before the respective ministers that were there [Messrs. Scott, Motherwell and Langley] and they assured us that they would write the Secretary of the Municipality and ask them to return those horses provided the Ranching Company would give them a bond that when this question of taxes had been settled by the Privy Council of England, that the taxes would be paid. I said that we wanted more than that. We want you to send the Deputy Minister up and interview that Council and have the matter adjusted. They consented to do so and they sent the Deputy Minister to Gull Lake and the Ranching Company had the horses back that night and the horses on the binder the following day.

The financial report showed total receipts of $1,565.39 and expenditures of $1,343.29, leaving a cash balance of $222.10. In addition there was a grant from the City of Moose Jaw for $150 and some $40 in cash received after the books were audited.

The convention was addressed by other prominent men. Mr. Thompson, District Director of the Grain Growers' Association, spoke of the need for a packing house or abattoir where the farmers and ranchers could dispose of produce or store it as they saw fit. He suggested that the dominion government be requested to guarantee fifteen percent of the cost, the provincial government forty-five percent and the public the other forty percent. Two delegates from the newly formed stock association in Alberta, Messrs. Spencer and Huckvale, also spoke to the convention. Both spoke strongly against equal taxes on leased land, which by definition was generally unfit for cultivation, and farming land. Both asked for co-operation between the sister associations.

The main speaker from outside the Association was J. C. Smith, Livestock Commissioner from the provincial Department of Agriculture. He went fully into the main issues raised by previous speakers, freely admitting that he and other members of the Department "were of the opinion that herd law was a mistake but the fact remained that herd law now existed and homesteaders had taken up land under herd law and that a very large per cent of them were not financially able to fence their holdings at the present time." He stated that "the Department was intending to take action which would prove of benefit to the stock growers" since rural population generally had increased forty percent in the past ten years while the decrease in the product of the ranch, cattle, sheep, and hogs had been thirty percent since 1910. He urged the convention to petition the Government on matters the convention could agree upon and suggested that the Association petition for limitation of the herd law to seven months of the year in all that country south of a line between townships 15 and 16, west of the 3rd meridian. He ended his speech with some remarks on the question of an abbattoir, but he stated that he could not advise on whether the best system for ownership was co-operative, government-owned, municipal, or otherwise.

The papers given and the discussion period following each speaker's talk gave rise to a number of resolutions. One resolution asked that municipalities be responsible in every detail for the actions of their pound-keepers in their official capacity. Another asked for the central registration of chattel mortgages. Aid was requested from the federal government to contest before the Privy Council in England the question of taxation of grazing lands. Probably the most important resolution requested that road allowances be included in any grazing lease provided that the lease-holder erect and maintain legal swing gates on the regular lines of travel.

The Saskatchewan Farmer, which at the 1913 convention

had been adopted as the organ of the Association, covered the convention in full. Not content with giving verbatim reports on much of the discussion the paper editorialized on "The Stock Growers." This in part is what the paper carried:

Among those present at the convention were some of the real old timers, some who know the story from the beginning, men who selected their ranches thirty years ago, when there was no one to dispute their claims. We might mention:

W. H. Ogle, Wood Mountain	*Wm. Gunn, Nummola*
B. Cruickshank, Rush Lake	*J. D. Simpson, Moose Jaw*
Wm. Roe, J.P., Marklee	*F. Brown, Wood Mountain*
W. Huckvale, Medicine Hat	*T. Bonneau, Willow Bunch*
Ole Olafson, Mortlach	*C. Ange, Willow Bunch*
John Spencer, President	*J. A. Kennedy, Moose Jaw*
Medicine Hat Stock Grow-	
ers' Assn.	

The editorial went on to say that these old-timers had seen surveyors come in to subdivide the land, but had not worried as there was plenty of land fit only for grazing. But settlers had come in and homesteaded in the leased land areas, and only today were inspectors busy examining these areas to see if the land was or was not agricultural land. The editorial then continued:

Fancy two or three homesteaders making entry in the middle of what was a leased township and cropping ten to twenty-acres — all the level land on their homesteads — and then getting the herd law in force in that township. Add to this taxation on the leased lands — crown lands, and the loose methods of irresponsible parties impounding stock, not two or three animals but hundreds in a bunch making the pound fees jump up to $100 or more in a single day. Fancy, we say, all this happening to the old stockmen, the first settlers, 30 years ago, or even those who have been on their leased lands for 10 to 20 years and some idea may be had of what stockmen are saying. One old-timer said: 'I came to the convention knowing it would be either the graveyard or the resurrection of ranching in Saskatchewan.'

The 1914 convention was important. Not only did it set the Association on its way as a robust and aggressive organization, but it also set the pattern for future conventions. It became customary for the president to give a general report. This was followed by the financial and membership reports. Visiting delegates from sister associations and from farm associations were then invited to speak. It became a practice to have the Deputy Minister of Agriculture and the Livestock Commissioner speak at the meeting. The University was invited to send a speaker from the College of Agriculture. Following the speeches there was a free and frank discussion period. Finally, the resolutions committee presented the resolutions arising out of discussions. These were debated by the membership.

The Association was in an advantageous position. It was young, yet it had experienced leaders, and it had a cause for which to fight. It had close contact with governmental circles and yet stood apart from any direct relationship. It had established a useful liaison with the University. It was recognized at once as the main representative of the ranching industry. It organized at a time when federal and provincial officials were coming to the point of view that all land in Saskatchewan could not be treated as farm land, that ranching as an industry had suffered through the expansion of farming.

One of the first evidences of a desire to help the ranching industry came when a commission was appointed on November 20, 1914, under *An Act Respecting Inquiries Concerning Public Matters* to inquire into the livestock industry with particular reference to such questions as the period of the year during which animals should be restrained from runninng at large, and the location, equipment, and administration of pounds. The commissioners were Thomas Richard Brown, Regina, farmer; Charles McGill Hamilton, McTaggart, farmer and president of the Saskatchewan Union of Rural Municipalities; John David Simpson, Moose Jaw, rancher and secretary-treasurer of the Saskatchewan Stock Growers' Association. The commission held meetings at sixteen centres in the south and south-west with an average attendance of one hundred persons. Some 271 witnesses were examined.

The commission reported on March 31, 1915. It recommended a uniform standard "herd" bylaw established by provincial law leaving to municipal councils only the fixing of the year, if any, during which animals shall be restrained from running at large, and the locating of pounds and appointment of poundkeepers. This standard was to be "approved by the Legislature and its completion and enactment by every municipal council made compulsory." Other recommendations tidied up existing regulations regarding bulls and stallions running at large at any time and recommended a simple method of arbitrating amount of damage in any dispute. The commission asked that every municipality be made legally responsible financially for the acts or neglect of its pound-keepers in the performance of their duties. It was recommended that road allowances not used for public travel, when included within the boundary fence of any tract of land held under grazing lease, be treated as part of the grazing land provided the owner or lessee placed a gate, two tie posts, and a notice requiring the public to leave the gate closed, at every point where an old trail still in use intersected the boundary fence. The commission asked that a heavy penalty be imposed on persons convicted before a justice of the peace of having failed to leave closed any such gate that was in good working order.

The report covered most of the changes asked for by resolution at the 1914 convention. J. D. Simpson, reporting as Secretary to the 1915 convention, stated that he had made a trip to Regina the day previous (June 8) and had ascertained that the report would be passed *in toto* by the Legislature at the current session. It was small wonder that the Acting President, G. K. Rathwell, could report to the convention, "I think I am safe in saying that you as an association have accomplished more during the short time you have been in existence than any other association that I have ever had anything to do with."

But more was to come. By order in council of November 25, 1915, another commission was appointed "to inquire into and investigate the marketing of livestock and livestock products of the province." William C. Sutherland, M.L.A., was appointed Chairman, and William A. Wilson, Dairy Commissioner, was appointed Secretary. The personnel of the commission were W. R. Motherwell, Minister of Agriculture; Oscar D. Skelton, Professor of Political and Economic Science in Queen's University; John G. Rutherford, Superintendent of Agriculture and Animal Industry, Canadian Pacific Railway; and James D. McGregor, a prominent stock grower of Brandon. The commission held hearings at ten of the larger centres within the province and at Brandon, Winnipeg, Calgary and Edmonton, taking evidence from 107 witnesses. By order in council of the Alberta Government, the commission was empowered to extend the scope of the inquiry to cover conditions in Alberta.

The commissioners presented an interim report in January, 1917, which was printed and distributed. This interim report contained a summary of the criticisms directed against producers, drovers, commission firms, railways, stockyards management, packers, and bankers. It was a frank document which did much to clear away any feeling among stockmen that all the facts would not be presented. The commission commented in this manner on herd laws:

The introduction of herd law in the prairie provinces was effected when the settlement was largely in districts where wheat was the only consideration. Immigration and the opening up of altogether new districts has introduced a diversified situation which leaves the general adoption of this law questionable. Its continuance and enactment is unexplainable in some localities except for petty jealousies and natural contagion. In some settlements where service may have been rendered at one time, conditions have so changed with the development that the law is a menace rather than otherwise. In other districts its operation should never have been permitted. Many settlements are pre-eminently suitable for stock raising and natural feed is, by herd law, fenced off from stock that goes to market in an unfinished condition.

To all of which many a rancher in the southwest gave grim agreement. The interim recommendations included the establishment of a federal livestock commission, changes in conditions of marketing, improved credit facilities, and investigation into an alternative to the herd law.

The final report of the commission submitted on October 8, 1918, took a backward look to see what action had followed presentation of the interim report. It noted "the fact that until 1916 grazing lands in the old ranching districts were subject to municipal taxation at the same rate as cultivated land [which] made it extremely difficult to carry on extensive stock raising operations." The commission was "gratified to note that at the session of 1916 the Legislature, by an *Act to amend The Rural Municipalities Act,* section 7, subsection 3 and 4, effectively dealt with this handicap by fixing two dollars an acre as the maximum valuation for taxing purposes of the interest of any holder of lands under a grazing lease or license from the Dominion Government, and by making this assessment retroactive for the years 1913, 1914 and 1915." It noted that with respect to the interim recommendation concerning the herd law this "had in large measure been given effect by the passing in the 1917 session of the Saskatchewan Legislature of an amendment to The Stray Animals Act, providing that after June 1, 1919, a large area to the north of a line running from Saltcoats to Turtleford . . . should be maintained as free range." It noted also that the question of finance was being looked into.

The commissioners then went on to recommend, among other things, the establishment of a co-operative packing company. They stated that "the conclusion arrived at by your commissioners is that the livestock industry of Saskatchewan will not be put on a firm and stable foundation until the existing private packing companies are supplemented by a co-operative company operating in the province." The report continued, "The development of state, or better still, co-operative facilities is therefore to be encouraged as the surest means of making cold storage an unqualified advantage." The commissioners stated that the experience of the West left no doubt that a co-operative undertaking would best meet the situation. Government assistance could best take the form of a partial guarantee of the capital required.

The appointment of the two commissions on problems in the stock-raising industry and the action by governments following the receipt of the commission reports marks a turning point in the history of the ranching industry in Saskatchewan. Until that time ranching as a whole had been overshadowed, perhaps even discriminated against, by the pre-occupation with agricultural settlement. The hearings held by the commissioners aroused widespread interest among ranchers. The findings and the recommendations did much to restore confidence in the ranching industry. Implementation of the recommendations immeasurably increased the prestige of the Saskatchewan Stock Growers' Association which had led the fight. Olaf Olafson, President, might well report to the fifth annual convention, held in Maple Creek, June 6 and 7, 1917:

The importance of the organization becomes more noticeable from year to year. Much attention of government — Dominion and Provincial — is now given to stock growing. Efficient government officials are now at all times ready to assist us in our work . . . I might mention a few minor matters regarding which, in past years, we have sought relief and that are now satisfactorily arranged, such as fencing of trails, placing gates, herd laws and impounding of stock, increase of acreage per head on grazing leases, also a closed lease for a period of 10 years, enacted by the Dominion government, of which you are all aware, and various other things. Most important of all is the amendment to taxation of grazing, leased lands. This matter has been in dispute for many years. It looks as if a settlement satisfactory to all parties has been reached . . . The livestock industry to-day is as important as any industry in Saskatchewan.

The early years of the Association had been spent in a fight to save the ranching industry from oblivion. The Association through its members had concentrated on immediate problems. Once these were overcome the interests of the Association moved to matters concerning the long range welfare of the ranching industry. The problems to be faced were such vital ones as marketing, security of tenure, and the production of better stock.

The problem of marketing had always been an anxiety to ranchers who felt, generally, that they were at the mercy of packing plants, commission firms, railways and middlemen once the cattle left the range. As J. F. MacCallum of Webb, for many years a director of the Association, writes:

About this period in 1917 marketing was getting to be quite a problem. The shipping of cattle and sheep on the hoof overseas to the British markets had ceased to be. All the Atlantic boats were being equipped with refrigeration systems and it meant that all the cattle had to be slaughtered in the packing plants, and these packing plants were located a great distance apart. Calgary was on the west and Winnipeg on the east, though later, Gordon Ironside and Fares built one at Moose Jaw. Now Moose Jaw had a packing plant but no public stock yards. The C.P.R. had a large stock yard and pens but these were used only for feeding stock in transit on through billing. If a shipper felt like taking the price offered by Gordon Ironside and Fares buyer in Moose Jaw he could do so, but if not he had to go on to Winnipeg or if the States market was open he could go on south to St. Paul or Chicago.

The commission on livestock marketing had suggested a solution and the leaders of the Association were not long in coming to a decision.

Stockmen had not missed the significance of governmental action in assisting the setting up of the Saskatchewan Co-operative Elevator Company. They heard more of this from F. H. Auld, Deputy Minister of Agriculture, at the 1917 convention. He is quoted as suggesting that stockmen get together to advance marketing operations: "Grain growers are being assisted by the government up to 85 per cent, the 85 per cent being a loan as it were, at a nominal rate of interest." He saw no reason why a large number of shareholders might not be secured among stockmen to make a cash payment of say twenty-five percent of the cost of a large abattoir, asking the government to come to their assistance for the balance. The upshot of this was the passing of a resolution approving the incorporation of the Association, a necessary step if share capital was to be offered for sale.

The President, at the 1918 convention held in Moose Jaw on June 12 and 13, explained the delay in securing a charter for the Association on the grounds that the charter for co-operative societies could not be applied. He suggested that a special charter be applied for from the Legislature, and a resolution approving this was passed at the convention. The resolution asked also that the provincial government establish an assembling and sorting centre for livestock at Moose Jaw. The matter was then pursued with such despatch that the Secretary was able to report to the 1919 convention, held in Swift Current on June 11 and 12:

Following up the resolutions passed at the last annual meeting, 201 had reference to the establishing of an assembling and sorting market for livestock . . . at Moose Jaw. The resolutions were forwarded to the Minister of Agriculture, and your Directors, and others interested, waited upon the Government urging that stock yards be established in Moose Jaw. As no definite action was promised by the Government . . . your Directors proceeded to organize as the Moose Jaw Union Stock Yards Limited. A charter was secured and we were ready to ask for subscriptions, capital stock $100,000 – 1,000 shares of $100 each. In the meantime the local government was called in session and the Hon. C. A. Dunning, the new Minister of Agriculture, lost no time in taking action to establish co-operative stock yards. By special act of the Legislature, two yards, one at Moose Jaw and the other at Prince Albert, were organized, with capital stock of $100,000 in each. The Government undertakes to grant one-third of the cash expenditures in all buildings erected from time to time, and special privileges are granted in the way of freedom of taxes for fifty years. The Moose Jaw Union Stock Yards Limited dropped its charter and accepted the charter provided by the act of the Legislature. The assets of the Moose Jaw Union Stock Yards Limited were *transferred to the Southern Saskatchewan Co-operative Stock Yards Company.*

The Saskatchewan Stock Growers' Association was incorporated under section 22 of *The Companies Act* on December 21, 1918. The Memorandum of Association set out the eight objectives of the Company based on the earlier objectives of the constitution of the Association. Shareholders signing the original memorandum were Jack Byers, Valjean; Trefflé Bonneau, Willow Bunch; Geo. L. Valentine, Pennant; J. F. MacCallum, Webb; J. H. Grayson, Moose Jaw; O. Olafson, Mortlach; J. A. Sheppard, Moose Jaw; J. Jonansson, Mortlach. The Southern Saskatchewan Co-operative Stock Yards Limited were incorporated by chapter 88 of the Statutes of Saskatchewan, 1918-19. The original membership was Olaf Olafson, Arthur Hitchcock, John Byers, J. H. Grayson, W. A. Munn, G. L. Valentine, W. B. Willoughby, D. J. Wylie and Trefflé Bonneau. The company's accounts were to be audited by the Provincial Auditor. When two-thirds of the cost of building had been collected the Provincial Treasurer was to buy one-third. The Company was granted five years' exemption from provincial and municipal taxation as from June 1, 1920.

The stockyards opened for business late in 1919 under the management of Edward Evans of Moose Jaw. He had been assistant manager at Calgary stockyards before coming to Moose Jaw. Jack Byers in his presidential address to the Stock Growers' convention held in Shaunavon on June 9 and 10, 1920, reported, "We now have one of the best equipped stock yards in the West, and although it has only been in operation for seven months, it has already demonstrated its value to us, and is fulfilling all it was expected to do." He then emphasized that the co-operative yards were in fact the stock growers' yards and it was but good business to support them. He ended his comments on the stock yards saying, "Co-operation has for us spelled success."

The Association was quite naturally aware of the horse supply and the horse market. During the war of 1914-18 strong representation was made to the Canadian government to have the allies purchase western Canadian horses rather than animals from the United States. The government was also requested to seek a market for horsemeat in the United Kingdom. The offer was turned down by the British Food Administration on the grounds that the need was not sufficiently urgent to lead them to try to change meat eating habits. After the war, according to J. F. MacCallum:

Jack Byers as President of the Stock Growers' Association took up the matter of the disposal of the surplus horses with the Dominion Government at Ottawa, with the result that a shipment of horses was made to Russia. I can remember the horses leaving Canada for Russia, in charge of Dr. Jack Hargrave, U.S., who ranched north of Walsh and, I believe, lived in Medicine Hat. Jack Byers went over with them along with a few cowboy wranglers. Now I do not know the results of this shipment to Russia, but I do not think it proved very popular, as there was only one shipment made.

Various plans to run a registry for horse sales received the attention of the Association. One plan which received much consideration was a scheme to list all horses for sale at the central office of the Association. Locals would send in information and the central office would be in a position to direct buyers to sellers. It was not very successful, as dealers preferred to buy from individual ranchers. The local Swift Current association put on horse sales in the years 1918 to 1921, charging a small sales fee. The Co-operative Stockyards reported selling 1,500 horses in the spring of 1920. Yet the problem of surplus horses continued and was of much concern in the dry thirties as horses ate up fodder that was badly needed for cattle. The Association kept the problem before the government of the day.

The Association early saw the advantage of affiliation with national bodies and liaison with provincial associations interested in similar problems. A resolution passed at the 1915 convention instructed the Executive to seek affiliation with the Western Canadian Livestock Union, which was carried out. Later the Association had membership representation with the Council of Western Beef Producers, now the Council of Canadian Beef Producers (Western Section). There seems to have been little exchange of fraternal delegates with the stockmen's association in the northern part of the province, but fraternal delegates always attended from the Medicine Hat Association. Shortly after the inception of the Saskatchewan Stock Growers' Association it became the policy to exchange delegates with the Saskatchewan Grain Growers' Association.

The Association promoted the idea of a Feeder Show and Sale in Moose Jaw. The moving spirit behind this was Edward Evans, manager of the stockyards. The first Feeder Show and

Sale was held in Moose Jaw October 17-19, 1923, and came under the patronage of the federal and provincial departments of agriculture, the Saskatchewan Stock Growers' Association, the Moose Jaw Livestock Exchange, and citizens of Moose Jaw and district. It proved such a success that it became an annual event.

Compulsory features of marketing has aroused the Association at various times. Carcass grading of hogs caused a furore at first, although later it seems to have been accepted by hog raisers. There was agitation to have cattle graded in the same manner. Jack Byers was in accord with carcass grading of hogs, and pressed for a more rigorous system of grading for cattle. The membership at that time took the stand that selling cattle on the hoof was the better way. In 1934 the *Natural Products Marketing Act* was a live issue. This federal marketing legislation was widely discussed during that summer. The stockmen considered it at their annual meeting in Swift Current on June 28 and 29 but presented no formal resolution on it. The Executive, meeting in Maple Creek on November 24, 1934, passed the resolution "That the Saskatchewan Stock Growers' Association puts its stamp of disapproval on any compulsory feature in any other marketing scheme that may be brought forward." When another marketing plan was proposed in 1954 the Executive of the day, meeting in Swift Current on February 18, 1955, passed this resolution: "That, if the need arises the Saskatchewan Stock Growers' Association will continue to oppose any compulsory marketing plan, even to going to the Courts if necessary."

One of the continuing problems facing ranchers was security of tenure. This was bound in very closely with the question of keeping the ranch an economic unit. Too high a rental, too small an acreage, too high a tax rate — each or all of these could drive ranchers out of business. Governmental action following the commission of 1913 corrected many inequities. The major remaining problem was length of lease. Stock growers had had a hard struggle to win the ten-year lease. In 1925, a delegation consisting of O. Olafson, President, and R. A. Wright, a director, together with two representatives from the Alberta association, went to Ottawa to interview the Minister of Agricure and the Minister of the Interior. They purposed to secure a twenty-one-year lease. This they did, and won also recognition of the principle that terms of lease must be such as to keep the ranch an economic unit.

After natural resources were transferred to Saskatchewan

in 1930, the Deputy Minister of Natural Resources for the province met the Association at the 1931 convention held in Maple Creek on June 19 and 20 to discuss grazing leases. The outcome of the meeting was agreement on twenty-year leases and forty-year leases with improved regulations. At the time of transfer leased lands in Saskatchewan amounted to slightly over 3,300,000 acres. In the new agreements a minimum of two cents and a maximum of four cents per acre rental were specified.

During the dry thirties, grazing land became so impoverished that 160 acres would scarcely carry three head of stock. Prices for stock were very low. The result was many a rancher became seriously in arrears with lease rentals. The provincial government in 1937 announced a policy of allowing a dollar for dollar bonus on all lease arrears owing as at May 1, 1937. In addition, reduction by one-half was allowed on lease rental rates for three years and a half. *The Rehabilitation Act* and *The Land Utilization Act* indicated a more positive approach on the part of provincial authorities to the problem of conservation of grass and range for greater security and stability. The question of security of tenure is a live issue today. It involves the problems of differing productivity of land areas, variation in carrying capacity, and water facilites. Research in feeding, better breeding, conservation, markets – all these enter the picture. Security of tenure means better planning and better ranching.

In the realm of marketing and ranch tenure, the Association had usually found itself fighting the battles of the stockmen, urging government officials to some action beneficial to ranching. In general, however, once it had established itself as the spokesman for stock growers in the south-west the Association worked very closely with the federal and provincial officials, and in particular with the provincial Department of Agriculture. Enemies of ranchers such as the warble fly, horn fly, louse, ticks, and mosquitoes were combatted with the advice and active aid of government experts. Diseases of livestock such as contagious abortion, tuberculosis, and swamp fever brought an appeal to the government to lead a campaign for eradication. The ranchers petitioned the provincial authorities and the municipalities to put bounties on wolves and magpies. Stock rustling has always been a live issue and the co-operation of the R.C.M.P. was early sought.

Probably no subject came up so often at conventions as resolutions on rustling. Ranchers were deeply appreciative of the efforts of the police on their behalf. Tied in with this was the matter of brands and brand inspection. The Association worked closely with the government and the purchasers of hides to work out brands that were readily identifiable, not duplicated, could not easily be run, and yet did not ruin the hide.

Government officials took the lead in many matters relating to the long-term betterment of ranching. The Saskatchewan Department of Agriculture promoted Better Bull Campaigns and Feeder Shows. Officials were always ready to attend conventions to discuss better conservation of range, better feeding of market cattle, and improvement of livestock. The officials of Prairie Farm Rehabilitation Administration did much to help ranching in the dry thirties with irrigation and water conservation measures.

As a matter of fact there was a much closer liaison between the Association and the provincial Department of Agriculture than was perhaps realized by the majority of the membership. A great deal of correspondence was carried on by the Secretary with various departmental officials. There was for example the correspondence contingent on the grant made to the association. This was fixed at $300, pro-rated from a sum for all like associations. A letter from J. D. Simpson, Secretary Treasurer, to the Deputy Minister dated November 11, 1915, acknowledges receipt of $300 but states: "There is a mistake here, however, as the grant that was promised by Mr. Motherwell, and which Mr. Mantle substantiated at our last convention, was $400.00. A letter of March 31, 1916, from the Acting Deputy Minister to J. D. Simpson contains an offer of secretarial assistance "in the same way as is done for other livestock associations." It was suggested that Mr. Bredt, acting Livestock Commissioner, be secretary and that the association pay him $100 as honorarium. The letter ended, "In the event of an arrangement of that kind being made, the proposed grant of $300.00 would be paid to your Association as last year." In spite of the "or else" tone of the letter the Association turned down the secretarial offer and continued to collect the grant.

The Association regularly filed audited financial statements with the provincial Department of Agriculture. Copies of resolutions were also sent. While the Department took no direct hand in the framing of resolutions, it is quite evident that the wording was frequently done with an eye to acceptance by the Department. A letter of February 21, 1921, from Hugh McKellar, Secretary, to Mr. F. H. Auld, Deputy Minister, asks for an opinion whether the Association should support a resolution framed by the Western Stock Growers' Protective Association and the Interior Stock Association of British Columbia. The Deputy Minister replied that the request was reasonable and the Association would be open to criticism if it did not support it. The departmental officials were always willing to meet representatives of the Association coming to Regina to discuss problems of the stock growers. The Association felt free to recommend representatives from its own ranks for commissions studying matters concerning ranching – and also to recommend to the federal government that D. J. Wylie of Maple Creek be made a senator. The whole tone of the correspondence reflects the closest liaison between the Association and the provincial Department. Legislation affecting stock growers was usually referred to the Association for an opinion. The Association felt free to recommend changes in law or regulations as conditions changed.

Financially the Association was never well off. According to J. F. MacCallum, "The Association was always handicapped for lack of money. The only source we had to get money was the membership fees and the assessment fees on the number of horses, cattle and sheep each member owned. . . . It was arranged that the Saskatchewan Stock Growers, together with some other organizations in Moose Jaw, should put on a 'Stampede' in order to raise funds for the Stock Growers' Association. And the stampede came off in Moose Jaw on July 11, 12, 13, and 14, 1916." The Stock Growers received $1,000 as their share. Membership was 230 in 1915 and later rose to more than 300, but it seems to have fluctuated according to where the convention was held. Some ranchers paid membership fees only when they attended. The financial statement for the year ending May 31, 1918 seems to be typical save for one extraordinary expenditure.

RECEIPTS

Balance on hand May 31, 1917		$1,033.28
Membership fees		12.00
Fees: Horses	$417.43	
Cattle	$897.57	
Sheep	$ 9.50	
		1,324.50
Donations		7.85
Government grant		300.00
		$2,677.63

EXPENDITURES

Salaries	$ 480.00
Postage and Stationery	60.00
Printing and advertising	252.85
Delegates' expenses	306.20
Subscriptions	343.75
Contributions	1,000.00
Other	96.77
Cash at bank and on hand	138.06
	$2,677.63

The financial statement noted that the sum of $1,000 had been authorized to be paid to Mr. W. H. Fares of Winnipeg to reimburse a portion of the legal expenses relating to the law suit of the R.M.[1] of Vermillion Hills against Smith and Fares. The item for subscriptions refers to subscriptions placed for *The Saskatchewan Farmer*, since membership included a subscription to the organ of the Association.

The Saskatchewan Stock Growers' Association was born at a time when ranching in southwestern Saskatchewan was a depressed industry. It came into being mainly through the vision and enterprise of such "old timers" as Olaf Olafson, J. D. Simpson, W. H. Ogle, Trefflé Bonneau, Jack Byers, and Robert Cruickshank. It was maintained in the early years by the hard work and enterprise of such stalwarts as J. F. MacCallum, D. J. Wylie, R. P. Gilchrist, James McDougald, George Valentine, C. Ange, and many others. In the early years, it was chiefly concerned with fighting for policies necessary for the very existence of ranching. When these were won the efforts of the Association turned to long range aims — to better marketing, security of tenure, and the general improvement of stock raising. The Association has worked closely with the federal and the provincial governments, but it has at times opposed governmental policies with great energy and resource. That the Association has survived bad times and good is a tribute to the quality of leadership, both in early and later years.

Ranching is still the chief industry of the southwest area of the province. Today it is more of a business than ever before. It

[1] [Rural Municipality, Swainson.]

is true that prices are higher, markets more stable, and times generally good. Costs, though, are also higher, competition from other occupations stronger, and capitalization much greater. But ranching is in essence the same. Roping, branding, riding the range – these physical activities are as arduous and require as much skill as they did fifty years ago. The sun, the rain, and the wind are constants, as are the wide spaces and the limitless sky. Ranching is close to nature, a good calling. One cannot read the records of the Saskatchewan Stock Growers' Association without feeling something of the vitality, the forthrightness, and the open-handedness of the men who live in the open air on the open range.

The Reform Movement in Manitoba, 1910-1915

Lionel Orlikow

The stories of the Progressive Party in the 1920s and of the Winnipeg General Strike of 1919 are comparatively well known in Manitoba history. In contrast, the role of the reform movement immediately preceding these events has been largely neglected. This omission is unfortunate, since at that time politics were colourful. Furthermore, the effects of decisions made then are still being felt today.

The 1915 provincial election in Manitoba saw the Liberal party of T. C. Norris elected with the largest majority ever accorded a local party. The Conservative group were all but swamped – salvaging five out of forty-nine seats. Indeed, exposure of election irregularities later led to the resignation of one of the opposition members, leaving only four.

What accounts for the landslide victory of 1915? A simple explanation might be the scandal over the construction of the Legislative Buildings. Public shock at the mismanagement of funds had been so great that the Conservative administration of Rodmond P. Roblin had been forced to resign.

A closer inspection of the period might concentrate on the spirit of reform that existed in the English-speaking world in the decades at the turn of the century. Political excitement was at a high level. Great Britain saw the rise of the Labour Party, the controversy over clipping the powers of the House of Lords, demands for more social welfare. The United States witnessed a growing Socialist Party, trust-busting led by Teddy Roosevelt, and increased labour strife. Generally, the period was featured by a reaction to the influence of big business, a demand to make government more responsive to the people, and a desire for more government intervention for general welfare.

These external events were well publicized in local publications, particularly the politically independent *Winnipeg Tribune*,

SOURCE: *Papers Read Before the Historical and Scientific Society of Manitoba*, series III, no. 16 (1961), pp. 50-61. Reprinted by permission of the author and the Manitoba Historical Society.

edited by R. L. Richardson, the *Grain Growers' Guide,* organ of the Grain Growers' Grain Company, and *The Voice,* representative of organized labour in the province.

This paper deals with the reform movement in Manitoba – a product of external influences and local conditions.

Where did Manitoba stand at the beginning of the twentieth century? The province was undergoing a tremendous period of growth. Population had risen from 255,000 to 461,000 in the years 1901 to 1911. The complexion of the province was changing with the rural folk declining sixteen percent and with a growing number of immigrants arriving from Eastern and Central Europe.

Optimism was in the air. The year 1910 saw Winnipeg top all Canadian cities in the amount of construction. A "Million for Manitoba League" was organized to promote the reaching of that number by the 1921 census. Real estate advertisements proclaimed: "Can't you see Transcona is destined for the Great Industrial Town of Canada?"

Such rapid growth produced many strains as new conditions outraced man's ability to adapt to them. Urban workers found few laws to regulate abuses within the new factories. New racial groups – the men in sheepskin coats – were somewhat isolated by differences in language, religion, and other customs from the dominant Anglo-Saxons. In addition, farmers were being drawn into the sensitive world economy and were less able to be rugged individualists.

Many turned to the government of Manitoba to help solve their problems. The Conservatives responded – although none too quickly, critics charged. Manitoba moved into the field of a provincial telephone system; larger grants to education, such as the construction of the Manitoba Agricultural College; extensive aid to provincial railways; introduction of workmen's compensation; a system of government line elevators; and the construction of a public abattoir.

The success of keeping the government tuned into the needs of the province was largely due to the work of Rodmond P. Roblin, the Premier, and his right-hand man, Robert Rogers, the Minister of Public Works. Hard-headed practical businessmen, both regarded the reform spirit as a fad inspired by subversive American republican principles.

The Conservatives drew strength from southwestern rural Manitoba, primarily inhabited by former citizens of Ontario. Support from immigrants from Central and Eastern Europe, who had been forced to settle in the poorer areas of the province, had been gained by extensive public works. The latter group was also favoured by the provincial system of bilingual schools. So successful a politician was the premier that he managed to keep representatives from the Orangemen and the Roman Catholic hierarchy in his Cabinet. Riding along a boom economy, seizing popular issues, and directing an efficient organization, the provincial Conservatives, first elected in 1899, were returned in 1903, 1907, 1910, and 1914, besides arranging federal victories in 1908 and 1911.

To some extent the Conservatives were aided by the Liberals of Manitoba. Many Liberal sympathizers were disgusted with that party. They found it difficult to reconcile themselves to the change in the federal party since the victory of 1896. The Laurier government was under attack as it appeared little different from the Conservatives. The Liberal organization was foundering, having gone through four leaders in ten years. To compound its problems, the Liberals had not found a constructive platform to attract the voter. Indeed, the party concerned itself with such lacklustre appeals as the need for economy, and corruption in government. Thus, the party leaders were labelled as "the prophets of Gloom and Doom."

The 1910 election found the Conservative government returned with twenty-eight of the forty-one seats at stake. The government campaigned on its record and virtually ignored the platform of the Liberal Party. Three of the latter's planks do deserve mention: temperance, direct legislation, and compulsory education. All would play a larger role in the years following.

The next four years saw a change in the platform of the Manitoba Liberals. This transformation reflected a drive to make capital of the discontent of a number of groups that could not find satisfaction from the Roblin government. The temperance forces were among the more influential of the dissatisfied. The question of controlling the sale of alcohol had a long history in Manitoba politics. Traditionally, the party in opposition pledged itself for some reform, but, on election, would forget its promise. The Conservatives, for example, had neglected their promise to carry out the prohibition referendum of 1898.

Temperance forces had been divided among themselves over the degree of restrictions that should be enforced. The organization of the Manitoba Social and Moral Reform Council in 1907, while designed to get legislative reforms on problems of concern to Christians, concentrated temperance feeling on a "Banish the Bar" slogan. Of all the means of purchasing liquor, the saloon was the worst. Those who advocated its abolition used the cartoon showing a drunken father at the bar, while his undernourished, ragged child waited at the saloon door. The Council represented all temperance groups (the Aurora Council in Winnipeg being the largest in the world), the Winnipeg Trades and Labour Council, the Manitoba Grain Growers' Association, and practically all major religious bodies.

At this time, prohibition in Manitoba was decided by local option. Almost insurmountable hurdles had to be overcome, however, before a favourable vote could be effected in a district. Generally, the liquor interests looked for slight deficiencies in the many details that had to be covered before passage of a local rule against liquor sale. Temperance forces did not have the necessary funds to fight many court cases.

Premier Roblin displayed his political skill in countering the temperance folk. First, he threw confusion into their ranks: to one group, he said that temperance should not become involved in politics; to another, he stressed the democratic nature of local option. Second, the Premier stressed "common sense" to others in the community: it was impossible to stop drinking; the bar was an evidence of neighbourliness and a method of showing good-will; the barroom revealed the social side of man which was the thing that distinguished men from brutes; and if the bar was banished, there would be no limits, as men would go home and drink.

As the temperance groups did not see one municipality added to local option during the 1910-1914 period, their support of the Liberals increased. The opposition party promised to have a referendum on the subject and follow its decision. To show their good intentions – that temperance would not be ignored after the election – the Liberals allowed representatives of the Moral and Social Reform Council to draft the "Banish the Bar" plank into their party platform.

A strong core of support for temperance and other reform came from Protestant churches, in particular, the Methodists and Prebyterians. Little headway had been made in converting the many Catholic and Greek Orthodox immigrants. At the same time, urban workers and rural tenant farmers were drifting from the church. To help vitalize the church with a more positive Christianity, these churchmen became involved in touchy situations that would bring them into opposition to the Roblin Government.

The Methodist General Conference of 1910 condemned the lack of understanding between rich and poor, deplored the inequality of economic conditions, and approved the eight-hour day. Supporters of such planks as a system of national schools as opposed to the bilingual ones found their interests akin to those of the Liberals. Indeed, by 1912, the Winnipeg Presbytery condemned Conservative campaign tactics in the Macdonald and Gimli by-elections. Their charges were well-founded — $93,000 of the total provincial budget of $130,000 for roads, bridges, and drains had been spent in Gimli.

The future careers of some of the more outspoken ministers might indicate that they were not Conservatives by nature. One can refer to men like J. S. Woodsworth, William Ivens, later prominent in the C.C.F., and A. E. Smith, a future leader of the Communist Party of Canada. Roblin was not unaware of their bias:

That the Methodist Conference should undertake to injure me, persecute me, I may say, is not without parallel. The Saviour of Mankind was persecuted by Saul of Tarsus, and there is no question but he was honest.[1]

Nevertheless, the hostility of the Prebyterian and Methodist Churches could not be taken too lightly. Their adherents numbered 185,000 in the province at that time.

Several other reform groups also pressed the Conservative government for favourable legislation. The most colourful of these were the women suffragettes. Primarily drawn from Anglo-Saxon ranks, a Political Equality League was organized by such people as Mrs. Nellie McClung, Dr. Mary E. Crawford, Mrs. Cora E. Hind, and Mrs. C. L. Clendennon. This group was interested in seeking the vote for a variety of reasons: to seek fairer laws for the status of women; to obtain social and economic equality; to help clean up the mess in politics as women had cleaned up the home. These women were certain that they had a better understanding of political life than ignorant foreigners who had the vote simply because they were men.

In contrast to the violence of suffrage campaigns in Great Britain, moderation marked the local scene. The Premier, however, refused any hope to the group. To a 1914 suffrage delegation, Roblin pointed out that he believed in the home "as the type of every national excellence" but:

Look at the States across the line where there is woman suffrage. In Chicago there are women's clubs scattered everywhere,

[1] *Telegram*, June 17, 1914.

showing how women are deserting the home, yet even then, when they have suffrage, they are not using the privilege. In Colorado, they shrink from the polls as from a pestilence. I believe woman suffrage would be a retrograde movement, that it would break up the home, and that it would throw the children into the arms of the servant girls.[2]

Naturally the leaders of the suffragettes moved closer to the Liberal movement. In 1914, the Political Equality League staged a Mock Parliament at the Walker Theatre, featuring Nellie McClung as premier, and parodying Roblin in refusing the request of a delegation of men asking for the right to vote.

Independents and others, who were becoming dissatisfied with the state of politics, looked to direct legislation to solve their problems. Basic to direct legislation was the belief that the governmental apparatus had grown too distant from the people and, in so doing, had become unresponsive to their wishes. Farmers and labour felt that the Liberals and Conservatives did not represent them, and complained about the favours these parties granted to big business.

To cure the ills of the body politic, they reasoned that the rule of the people must be restored. This could be done by the tools of direct legislation: the initiative – the authority for the people to originate bills; the referendum – submission for public decision on any measure on demand of a certain percentage of the electors; the recall – the right to recall any official who does not follow the wishes of the people. The leaders of the Direct Legislation League looked with pride on the large number of groups interested in politics and its operation in Oregon and Switzerland. Direct legislation could avoid the intrusion of the politicians. Measures would be decided on their merits, not on partisanship.

There now appeared a real need for direct legislation in Manitoba. Needed legislation, such as temperance regulations that had been frustrated by partisanship, would be taken directly to the people. The Premier appeared ready to go to any lengths to achieve his ends. He had threatened in 1912 to read the riot act to break up any demonstrations against a purported government attempt to damage the new publicly owned City Hydro. A growing number of groups supported direct legislation and in 1913, a petition signed by some 10,000 Manitobans requested such a step. Prominent in the Direct Legislation

[2] *Manitoba Free Press*, January 28, 1914.

League were J. H. Ashdown, S. J. Farmer, D. W. Buchanan, and F. J. Dixon.

Premier Roblin summed up his government's opposition to direct legislation. His main point was that it endangered the British constitution. He also suspected this "degenerate republicanism," implying that it meant the United States had a better form of government than the Canadian. "It was socialistic because it was so revolutionary to destroy what had taken 800 years to build up." Debate in the Legislature was usually cut short following a government motion that:

This legislature affirms its belief that the British form of responsible government, as enjoyed by the province of Manitoba, is the best form of government in the world.[3]

While an impressive number of groups supported temperance, women's suffrage, and direct legislation, little headway was made. A combination of further incidents was to prove decisive in bringing these groups firmly into the Liberal camp.

The organized farmers of the province, as represented by the Manitoba Grain Growers' Association, gradually became disillusioned with the Conservative Party. Throughout most of this period they feared that any entry of the Association into politics might threaten their extensive operations in such fields as lumber yards or wire manufacturing. The loss of one-third of the membership during the 1911 reciprocity election underlined the strength of their fears.

There had been little incentive for such organizations as the Grain Growers' Association to take an active part in local politics before 1910. The Conservative administration had passed favourable railway legislation, extended the Manitoba Agricultural College, compelled the Winnipeg Grain Exchange to accept the Grain Growers' as a member, and inaugurated public ownership of telephones.

A number of incidents did make a growing number of the Grain Growers' restless. Charges of politics in the administration of the public grain elevators and the public telephones embarrassed the local Conservatives. It appeared that undue influence was deliberately harming these public institutions. The result was higher charges and growing deficits. The government managed to curb some of the criticism by leasing the elevators to the Grain Growers' Association and placing the

[3] *Manitoba Free Press*, **January 31, 1913.**

telephones under an independent commission. The government and members of the Association, however, had exchanged angry words, the first of such incidents.

A series of other events contributed to the government's growing unpopularity with ogranized farmers. Naturally both groups found themselves at opposite sides of the political fence on reciprocity. The Association's officers are also found quite active in the fields of temperance, equal suffrage, and direct legislation – all points that the Liberal Party were advocating.

The farmers were faced with three alternatives of political expression. First, the use of direct legislation, which would avoid direct political involvement. But it had to be passed by a friendly legislature before it could come into effect. Second, a farmer-labour alliance had been suggested a number of times by representatives of each. However, a feeling that their interests were incompatible kept these two groups apart. During the urban unemployment of 1915, when the country areas still needed farm labour, one correspondent wrote in the *Pilot Mound Sentinel*:

The city authorities should give such agitators the choice of death by bomb or bullet and see that he gets it. A few and very few of such executions would quickly solve the labour problem in large or small cities. There is no excuse for an honest working man begging for bread in the west if he is able bodied and willing to work.[4]

Third, attempts at independent politics during this time were generally unsuccessful. Those that were prepared to break political ties in 1914 believed that farmers should support whatever party followed the aims of farmers. In their search for support, the Liberals had ranged themselves on the side of most of the farmers' demands.

There was one other group in Manitoba that drifted from the Conservative cause. While there were few industrial centres in Manitoba by 1910, organized labour was beginning to play a larger role in politics. Labour was not only dissatisfied with the lack of sympathy among the elected representatives, but it was also very critical over the lax enforcement of the few acts regulating conditions at work, safety at work, hours of labour, and compensation for injury.

Organized labour felt that the lack of enforcement was the

[4] *Pilot Mound Sentinel*, June 3, 1915.

result of the lack of labour representation in the Legislature. Until 1914, labour's record was one of a few minor victories and many defeats. One reason for this lack of success was the split within labour ranks. In 1910, the Manitoba Labour Party, modelled on the Labour Party of Great Britain, united all except the extremists from the Socialist Party of Canada. Moderates such as R. A. Rigg, S. J. Farmer, A. W. Puttee, and J. Queen were prominent on the executive.

Unlike other groups that have been mentioned, organized labour drifted away rather than closer to Liberal advances. To many workers, the lack of sympathy shown them during the 1913 and 1914 depression, served to underline their isolation. To emphasize this fact, the local trades and labour council broke with the Direct Legislation League and the Political Equality League on charges that they were tools of the Liberal Party. Basically, more of the labouring class felt their interests were absolutely opposed to those of the Liberal Party. Encouraging to the labour group in 1914 were successes in local politics in Winnipeg and Brandon. The Liberal Party intensified its efforts to attract the growing number of working-class votes. One ace held by that Party was the work of S. Hart Green, M.P.P. of Winnipeg North, who was recognized as the spokesman for labour in the Legislature.

If labour was drifting away from the Liberals, Liberal enthusiasm rose with the breaking away of one of Premier Roblin's key supports – the Loyal Orange Lodge. As mentioned, the Premier had both Orangemen and Catholic representation in his cabinet. He managed this agile feat by avoiding any clash over his school policy. He had maintained that his government would not reopen the wounds of the Manitoba School Question of 1890-1896 – he would not discuss it – he would prevent any discussion. At the same time, the government was reluctant to do anything on the matter of compulsory schooling. The latter problem was growing more serious. In Winnipeg, for example, one-fifth of the children in the five-to-seventeen-year bracket were not registered in any public or private school.

Many Anglo-Saxons, however, were becoming more concerned about assimilating the foreign immigrants to the British way of life. Public schools were regarded as the instrument for this job. W. J. Sisler was demonstrating that many diverse nationalities could be assimilated in his North Winnipeg Strathcona School. Bilingual instruction prevented this blending from happening over all the province. Of equal importance, instruction in the foreign language schools was poor. Often the teachers themselves were barely literate in the English language. When there were ten children of one nationality in a school, the parents could petition for instruction in their own language. Some country districts found themselves in awkward situations. One one-room school of thirty-two pupils advertised for a teacher with a command of English, Gaelic, and Polish.

Matters came to a head in 1912 when amendments to the Schools' Act were introduced aimed at relieving the double school taxation which Brandon and Winnipeg Roman Catholics had to pay. This action touched off fears that the proposed legislation was the first of many acts to give aid to sectarian schools. The inclusion of the first French-Catholic in the cabinet in twenty-three years only served to strengthen these fears. The reform groups were in the forefront of the defenders of the public schools. The alert T. C. Norris risked the loss of French-Catholic votes to the Liberal Party to win the support of influential Orangemen.

Thus, as the 1914 election approached, the Liberal Party appeared much stronger than four years previously. Its basic strategy to convince the electorate that their Liberal Party was one that did not have to rely upon corrupt methods but was one that accurately mirrored the people's wishes had been profitable. An impressive list of provincial groups had passed resolutions favouring the Liberal Party. Some of the more prominent: the Methodist and Presbyterian Conferences, Baptist Ministers, the Social Service Council, the Orangemen, the Political Equality League, the *Manitoba Free Press*, the *Winnipeg Tribune*, and the *Grain Growers' Guide*. While some of these groups supported the Liberals only on one or two specific points, that Party, by dropping any federal entanglement, appeared the champion of provincial interests, secular and reform. In addition, economic conditions had turned against the Conservatives with rising unemployment in the cities and declining prices of agricultural products.

The spirit of the transformed Liberal Party was sounded at the 1914 convention by T. C. Norris:

If I am given the chance I will demonstrate that I can keep my word. There is a great wave of public opinion passing over the United States and Canada demanding that politicians keep their promises. (loud cheers) If I am given a chance I will show to the people of Manitoba that a Manitoba politician can keep his promises too. (loud cheers) I believe that posterity will look back upon this convention as the beginning of the downfall of a dishonest administration, and as the beginning of the building up of a higher citizenship in this province. (loud and prolonged cheers)[5]

Though the government appeared in serious straits, they could still point with pride to some positive achievements: an extensive revision of the public health act; the appointment of a public utilities' commissioner; extensive public works, such as the start on the new provincial Parliament Buildings; and the acquisition of a larger Manitoba boundary in 1912.

Then there was the party machine. With party loyalties tight and the voting population small, any means to sway a small percentage of the voters could prove decisive. In 1910, a change of one vote per poll could have changed the results in four seats. Politics was not a game, but a form of civil war with only lethal weapons barred. *The Tribune* pointed out in 1910 that only seven out of ninety candidates had not been called liars, boodlers, or crooks. Patronage was used lavishly. One rural newspaper summed up local government political activity prior to the 1914 elections:

Three weeks ago the Roblin government kindly donated or inflicted on us a party of surveyors and this week they sent a party of twelve telephone men. The telephone service has been on the hummer here for at least two years that we know of and it's as if the powers that be have just found out about it. Elections are undoubtedly coming off soon if present indications mean anything. It seems too bad that the Roblin government let their elevators go, for if they had them now they could have sent up a party of forty or so to paint them. Has anyone heard when the road gang would arrive?[6]

Another glaring case is advertising and other printing contracts supplied to the party's subsidized *Winnipeg Telegram*. In 1910, for example, that paper received over $26,500 compared with the $145.46 of the opposition *Manitoba Free Press*. After receiving the contract for the construction of the Manitoba Agricultural College, one firm had to contribute $22,500 to the Conservative war chest. Generous distribution of liquor and money would send out hordes of men to vote at a number of polling booths under different names. There were many names

[5] *Manitoba Free Press*, March 28, 1914.
[6] *Emerson Journal*, March 20, 1914.

to go around for them – one voters' list contained seventeen residents on a vacant lot. To forestall Liberal complaints on election day, the government cancelled the licences of those justices of the peace who happened to be Liberal. Another stratagem was the changing of F. J. Dixon's telephone number at campaign headquarters on election day. A needed redistribution of seats was completed, but the city of Winnipeg, with one-third of the province's population, was quite underrepresented with six seats out of forty-nine. The only two Conservatives to lose their seats with the 1914 redistribution had happened to vote against the government on one of the rare occasions when such a thing occurred.

The Liberal platform was not ignored by the Conservatives in 1914 as in 1910. The Premier described it as "Socialistic" and "all that was needed to make the Liberal platform complete as a Republican concern was marriage as a civil contract and police court divorce." Naturally old slogans that had meant success for the Conservatives in the past were dragged up:

Never were the institutions threatened by a party so directly as now. Never were men so unscrupulous in their efforts to unhorse those who are British. And I appeal to you as Manitobans, and I appeal to you as citizens worthy of your heritage to stand together! Be always Manitobans, be always Canadians, be always British, be always Conservative.[7]

The Conservatives won. The election results are interesting in a number of respects. The discrimination against Winnipeg is clearly seen if one compares the vote of F. J. Dixon, elected in Winnipeg Centre. His vote of 9,200 was greater than the total of 8,900 of the cabinet of seven men. A strong labour feeling in several areas enabled the Conservative candidate to win on a minority vote. The government won twenty-eight of forty-nine seats with forty-six percent of the vote. Marked defections from the Conservative camp were noted in Anglo-Saxon districts.

The return of the Roblin government did not stop the complaints of the reform groups. The outbreak of war made their complaints even stronger: the work of women in the war effort added fresh fuel to the demand for equality; total prohibition was urged – not Banish the Bar – so all energies could be directed to the war effort; less toleration of immigrants and hence bilingual instruction resulted from the suspected loyalty

[7] *Telegram*, July 6, 1914.

of non Anglo-Saxons. The notorious Parliament Building scandal finally destroyed the government – the enormity of the scandal clearly substantiated the reform groups' charges about the evils of party government. September of 1914 saw the Minister of Public Works announce that, due to errors of the architect, the original cost of the Parliament Buildings would be exceeded by fifty percent. After being forced to appoint a Royal Commission on the matter, the Premier and all his cabinet resigned from office and public life on May 12, 1915. The subsequent report found that the contractor had been overpaid by close to $900,000 and that he had paid large sums to the Conservative Party.

The results of the 1915 election were a foregone conclusion. A smashed Conservative Party tried to remodel itself by taking over many of the reform planks it had opposed for so many years. Two exceptions were continued opposition to direct legislation and abolishing bilingual instruction. Still, the tenor of reform was evident in such proposals as: the introduction of compulsory voting; the conservation of Manitoba water resources for the public use; the elimination of the spoils system and the establishment of a civil service based on merit and efficiency alone.

Propelled by a strong public feeling to clean up the mess, the Liberals almost completely wiped out the Conservative party, capturing forty-two of the forty-nine seats. Labour won two.

The victory could not be accounted a triumph for the Liberal Party *per se*. As the *Winnipeg Tribune* summed up:

During the last fifteen years, when Liberalism attempted to turn the trick off its own bat, it was annihilated. It is, therefore, right and proper that the victory achieved . . . should be credited to the factions responsible for it.[8]

In other words, the reform groups.

The next five years saw an almost complete reversal in the course of Manitoba politics. The spirit of nonpartisanship was unique. Barring criticism from the French members on school matters, debate in the Legislature was carried on without the bitterness that had marked the pre-1915 period. So far did this nonpartisan spirit go that, in 1918, Liberals and Conservatives joined to elect a Union candidate in a North Winnipeg by-election.

[8] *Winnipeg Tribune*, July 11, 1914.

The amount and scope of legislation passed by the Norris government is breathtaking even by today's standards. Much of the reform spirit was placed into law: a civil service commission, a public health commission, a mother's allowance act, the abolition of bilingual schools, a hydro-electric commission, a minimum wage board, prohibition of the sale of liquor, remodelling of electoral laws, overhauling workmen's compensation and factory acts, cheaper farm credit, compulsory education, automatic dialing in telephones, a wider base for municipal taxation, woman suffrage, proportional representation, reorganization of the University of Manitoba, and an initiative and referendum act. The government pioneered in a number of fields. Never had a Manitoba government undertaken such an extensive program.

Despite this record, it is interesting to note the reverses of the Norris government in the 1920 election and its subsequent defeat in 1922. Despite the attempt of the government to respond to the wishes of the electorate by passing progressive legislation and at the same time being nonpartisan, the Liberals were still not trusted. Farmers and urban workers had become more class conscious and were organizing politically. This class interest combined with supporters of separate schools, former Conservatives, to reduce the once mighty Liberal majority.

But what had happened to the reform movement that had done so much for the initial Liberal victory in molding its platform? A large number melted away after attaining their objectives — the suffrage and temperance groups are prime examples. The main impetus behind direct legislation was to by-pass hostile politicians and with the agreeable Liberals in office, its supporters rapidly fell away. The farmer-labour alliance, never strong, was put further to a test by the 1918 and 1919 strikes. Still, some cooperation can be found in a number of districts during the 1920 election. A small core of ministers, such as Salem Bland, William Ivens, and J. S. Woodsworth, remained to continue the social gospel.

Reform had collapsed. The case study of F. J. Dixon dramatically illustrates the end of the movement. Dixon had been in the forefront of many of the reform groups. Elected as a Liberal-Labour member of the Legislature in 1914, he was originally supported by voters of all shades of political opinion. Prominent leaders of both the Grain Growers' Association and the Trades and Labour Council contributed to his campaigns. His views on direct legislation, suffrage, compulsory education were well known throughout the West — a result of countless speeches presented to diverse organizations. The effects of wartime tarnished his reputation among many of these groups. Dixon did not join in the whole-hearted hysteria of the war period. He carried on his prewar policies: he asked that the dominion government conscript wealth as well as men; he demanded fair treatment for the suspected aliens. By 1917, nearly three thousand Centre Winnipeg voters drafted a petition to have him resign from the Legislature. Members of the Legislature would leave the chamber when he spoke.

The achievement of short-run objectives and the strains of wartime proved too much for the Manitoba reform movement. Its quick demise might also be explained by its narrow base. Primarily drawn from Anglo-Saxon citizens, the reform groups had not recruited many adherents from other groups in the province. When one notices the large number of Methodists and Presbyterians active as leaders the base appears even narrower. Some of the staunch groups appear weaker than their titles might otherwise indicate. The Manitoba Grain Growers' Association, for example, never claimed more than fifteen percent of the province's farmers as members.

Perhaps Premier Roblin was correct in ignoring the repeated pleas of the reform groups from 1910 until 1915. If he was right, then his defeat can be attributed to the economic decline, the loss of Orangemen's votes on the school question, plus the growth of dry rot in his party.

Whatever the case, the reform movement produced far-reaching effects on the province. The statute book bears witness to the changes brought on by the Liberal Party. Highly controversial issues such as temperance and aid to separate schools were buried until recently resurrected. The concentration on nonpartisan, business-like governments produced a series of administrations stressing lack-lustre, economy-minded programs. Then the Conservatives, who were shocked out of their traditional allegiance by the attacks from 1910 to 1920, wandered through the political wilderness of independence, Progressivism, and Liberalism until returning home with the [recently defeated] Conservative government.

Before more trends can be examined, further attention must be paid to the first decades of the twentieth century in Manitoba, a decisive period in provincial history.

J. S. Woodsworth And A Political Party For Labour, 1896-1921[1]

Kenneth McNaught

There is no need now to pause before asserting the existence of many similarities in the purposes, policies and tactics of the British Labour Party and those of the Co-operative Commonwealth Federation. It should be of interest, therefore, to Canadian historians to comprehend the philosophy of the founders of the c.c.f., together with the formative circumstances producing that philosophy. That the c.c.f. has adopted most of the broad compromises, both in economics and in politics, that were evolved by British gradualism, and that it has retained an emphasis on the humanist-Christian interpretation of brotherhood, as has the British Labour Party, cannot be explained if one ignores the purposes, character, and methods of its founders – and particularly those of the man whose influence in the originating conferences of 1932 and 1933 was predominant. This article is an attempt to analyse J. S. Woodsworth's philosophy against the background of the major influences in his life between 1896 and 1921. The discussion will lead to the conclusion that his emergence in the federal parliament in 1922 with a definite political philosophy, and as the representative of a working-class party, was virtually inevitable.

"They were listening to ugly rumours of a huge radical conspiracy against the government and institutions of the United States. They had their ears cocked for the detonation of bombs and the tramp of Bolshevist armies. . . ."[2] Although these words were not written about Canada, they could be paraphrased to describe with some accuracy the temper of public opinion in

SOURCE: *Canadian Historical Review*, vol. xxx (1949), pp. 123-43. Reprinted by permission of the author and of the publisher, University of Toronto Press.

[1] This article was in part made possible by a grant from the Rockefeller Foundation.
[2] F. L. Allen, *Only Yesterday* (New York: Bantam Edition, 1946), p. 61.

this country in the years immediately following the end of the First World War. Then, as now, Canada marked out the path that North America would follow in its suppression of the Red Menace. And in those years also, there were men single-mindedly devoting their lives to the struggle to find a middle ground — a practical line of progress between the extremes of triumphant capitalism on the one hand, and the dogmatic violence of bolshevism on the other. There were men prepared to incur the odium usually directed at the suspected Red that they might explore the avenues leading to constitutional reform of a political and economic system which seemed to them to threaten a chronic debasement of all human values. One such man, in Canada, was James Shaver Woodsworth.

For those who shared his view, these years were a time of testing. Some succumbed to the blandishment of official and semi-official patronage; others became bitter and moved further to the left. Perhaps only a few men can ever afford the luxury of consistency in public life. J. S. Woodsworth's particular consistency is the more interesting when one considers his inherited background. The portrait of Woodsworth as the heir of a family intensely proud of its United Empire Loyalist origins, of its intimate connexions with the pioneer Methodist Church, and with the foundation of the Canadian West, is familiar to those who know anything of his origins. Woodsworth's paternal grandfather came to Canada from Yorkshire and remained strongly British and Conservative in his outlook, connecting himself with the Wesleyan and not the Canada Methodists, and donned sword to preserve the British connexion in 1837. His father, who was superintendent of Methodist missions in the Northwest, was also cautious in his political thought. In a book the latter makes the following comment upon the North-West rebellion of 1885: "Many lives were lost during this unfortunate disturbance. On the other hand, much good resulted. Disaffected half-breeds and rebellious Indians were taught a salutary lesson; they learned something of the strength of British rule, and likewise experienced something of its clemency and righteousness."[3]

Woodsworth's family background was not such as might be expected to produce a radical in any accepted sense of the word. Yet somewhere between the time that he was elected senior stick of Wesley College, Winnipeg (1896), and his theological train-

[3] James Woodsworth, *Thirty Years in the Canadian North-West* (Toronto, 1917), p. 12.

ing at Victoria College, Toronto (1898), questions began to arise in his mind concerning the traditional family approach to social and religious problems. These resulted in an increasing interest in the "social gospel" of Christianity, and the work of such institutions as the Fred Victor mission in Toronto. His interest in the social problems of the modern city was undoubtedly further stimulated by his year at Oxford (1899-1900), with its side-trips to the London of Charles Booth and Toynbee Hall. It was there, also, that Woodsworth formulated his first questions about imperialism and the economics of capitalism. Such beginnings were rapidly expanded with his return to Canada and his participation in the formal work of the church. Passing, in 1906, from the well endowed organization of Grace Church in Winnipeg, to the shabby work of All Peoples' Mission in the city's north end (on the wrong side of the C.P.R. tracks), Woodsworth laboured diligently to further the ideas of the "institutional church" and the urban mission. He approached this problem from a sceptical position. At the beginning of this period, in 1907, having discovered what he considered to be unacceptable theological subtleties in the Methodist doctrine, he tendered his resignation to the Methodist Conference. The offer of resignation was refused, and with the assurance of the Conference leaders that there was room for a broad interpretation of the doctrine, Woodsworth re-dedicated himself to work in a different field of the church's activities. But in the mission work his doubts only increased. He began to wonder, once more, whether he could fulfil the practical demands of the Christian religion and still remain within the church – whether the "social gospel" could be put into practice with only the grudging support of the church's wealth. "Too often," he wrote in 1911, "missions do not receive adequate financial or moral support. A second-rate minister and an over-burdened deaconess are placed in a shabby little hall and supplied with a few cast-off hymn books and old clothes, and are expected to evangelize and uplift a neglected community."[4]

Together with his increasing doubts about the purposes of organized religion, Woodsworth began further to question the fundamentals of the existing social and economic order. His reading included Shaw's *The Common Sense of Municipal Trading*, the Webbs' *History of Trade Unionism*, and much of J. A. Hobson; the last-mentioned, particularly, had an enduring influence upon his thought. The years between 1907 and

[4] J. S. Woodsworth, *My Neighbor* (Toronto, 1910), p. 309.

1917 were a time of intensive research into social problems – research carried on through the mission, the Canadian Welfare League, of which Woodsworth was secretary, and through his position as director of the Bureau of Social Research established by joint action of the three prairie governments in 1916. The work of these years, however, was not simply that of a student. It was an accumulating of information that led constantly to action and to the acceptance of the necessity of an open alliance with the working class to achieve reform.

Woodsworth formed an early connexion with the organized labour movement of Winnipeg when he was nominated a representative of the Ministerial Association to the Trades and Labour Council. Labour opinion at the time was appreciative of his sympathy toward the movement, and applauded his action in 1911 when he impelled the Ministerial Association to form a conciliation committee in a strike against the Great West Saddlery Company.[5] Furthermore, in 1910, Woodsworth became a member of the Provincial Labor Representation Committee which was organized by S. J. Farmer and others, to gain support for the social democratic candidate, Fred Dixon, in the provincial elections of that year. This organization proved to be impermanent, partly because the majority of the Trades and Labour Council were not at the time convinced of the wisdom of political action, and partly because the rival Socialist Party of Canada caused a split in the labour vote. Dixon failed of election, but the association of Woodsworth with this group is of considerable significance. When these facts are taken together with his expressed opinions during these years, the drift toward the idea of a strong working-class party is clear.

In these years Woodsworth was a regular contributor to the Winnipeg socialist labour paper, the *Voice*. He also had numerous articles published in the *Grain Growers' Guide* and in more conservative papers such as the *Free Press* and *Tribune* of Winnipeg. The editor of the *Voice*, A. W. Puttee, is one who can be presumed to have known with reasonable accuracy Woodsworth's political views, and when his paper reviewed *My Neighbor* in 1911, it greatly commended the author for "his obvious leaning toward socialism."[6] In a series of articles for the *Grain Growers' Guide* in 1915, Woodsworth summed

[5] Winnipeg *Voice*, October 27, 1911. The *Voice* makes frequent reference during this period to Woodsworth's active support of labour.
[6] *Ibid.*, November 10, 1911.

up his attitude to organized religion. Although these articles do not specifically discuss political topics, there is in them more than an implied acceptance of the principles of social democracy. For example: "At least in this world, souls are always incorporated in bodies, and to save a man, you must save him body, soul, and spirit. To really save one man you must transform the community in which he lives."[7] Again, discussing the question of private property, Woodsworth wrote:

> "My mine" – what a sacrilege! This little man who was born yesterday and will die tomorrow claims what it took God Almighty millions of years to provide. "My mine" – light and warmth for the millions claimed by one man! A poor shivering wretch picks up a few pieces of coal from the tracks. He is a thief – a thief according to the code of ethics taught in the colleges endowed by the mineowner. . . . But in the eyes of Him who made the coal mine for His children, who is the thief? . . . Confessedly the problem of "mine" and "thine" cannot be settled off-hand. But does our present system at all approximate to justice? Gigantic trusts appropriate the greater part of that loaf, distributing huge slices to a privileged few. The great mass of the people eke out a meagre existence on the crumbs that fall from rich man's table. Many, in fact, are denied even a job. . . .[8]

Work amongst the people of north Winnipeg, experience with the economic and political problems of the working class, both native-born and immigrant, and his own omniverous reading, had driven Woodsworth to a pretty definite position on the left by 1915. The advent of the crisis over national registration and its obvious consequence, conscription, found him firmly aligned with the opposition voiced by the organizations of labour across Canada. His dismissal from the Bureau of Social Research by the Norris ministry in 1917 was the result of a letter written by Woodsworth and published in the Winnipeg *Free Press* on December 28, 1916. The letter contains almost nothing of religious pacifism. Indeed, the stand taken is the stand adopted by all the labour "radicals" of that year in Canada:

(1) The citizens of Canada have been given no opportunity of

[7] *Grain Growers' Guide*, June 30, 1915.
[8] *Ibid.*, July 14, 1915.

expressing themselves with regard to the far-reaching principle involved in this matter. (2) Since "life is more than meat and the body more than raiment," conscription of material possessions should in all justice precede an attempt to force men to risk their lives and the welfare of their families. . . . (4) How is registration or subsequent conscription to be enforced? Is intimidation to be used? Is blacklisting to be employed? What other method? . . . .

When Woodsworth left Winnipeg in 1917, he was already convinced that capitalism, militarism, imperialism, and organized religion (all by Hobsonian definition), must be his primary objects of attack. To obtain social justice for the class with which he had been constantly working, he must act for and through the organizations of the workers. Indeed, he must convince many of them of the absolute necessity of a working-class political party. Of these convictions there is ample evidence in his letter of resignation from the Methodist Church of June, 1918. In that letter can be seen the definite abandonment of the "social gospel," at least as that set of ideas had been stated by Walter Rauschenbusch.[9] It carries much farther the argument of the earlier unaccepted resignation in which the chief trouble was theological detail. Since in the second letter the analysis of Woodsworth's own position is so precise, it is worth quoting at some length. Speaking of his position in 1907, after the proffered resignation of that year had been refused, he writes:

. . . What could I do? Left intellectually free, I gratefully accepted the renewed opportunity for service. For six years, as superintendent of All Peoples' Mission, I threw myself heartily

[9] *Christianity and the Social Crisis* (New York, 1922). This book was used as a basic reference by Woodsworth in his *My Neighbor* in 1911. Even in the latter work Woodsworth wrote: "We can hardly be accused of underestimating the value of social settlements, institutional churches and city missions, but more and more we are convinced that such agencies will never meet the great social needs of the city." p. 334. And, in the same place: "Unfortunately on this continent the cities have allowed private individuals and corporations to carry on and make immense profits out of much of the business that legitimately belongs exclusively to the city." p. 194. The book was adopted as Text-book no. 7 by the Missionary Society of the Methodist Church and contains a preface by S. D. Chown who claimed therein that the author "never loses faith in the ultimate success of the reclaiming and uplifting agencies at work."

into all kinds of social-service work. Encouraged by my own experience, I thought that the Church was awakening to modern needs, and was preparing, if slowly, for her new task.

But as years went by, certain disquieting conclusions gradually took form. I began to see that the organized church had become a great institution with institutional aims and ambitions. With the existence of a number of denominations this meant keen rivalry. In many cases the interests of the community were made subservient to the interests of the Church. Further, the Church, as many other institutions, was becoming increasingly commercialized. This meant the control of the politics of the Church by men of wealth, and, in many cases, the temptation for the minister to become a financial agent rather than a moral and spiritual leader. It meant also that anything like a radical program of social reform became, in practice, almost impossible. . . . In my own particular work . . . intellectual freedom was not enough – I must do free work. . . .

In the meantime another factor makes my position increasingly difficult.[10] *The war has gone on now for four years. As far back as 1906 I had been led to realize something of the horror and futility and wickedness of war. When the proposals were being made for Canada to assist in the naval defense of the Empire, I spoke and wrote against such a policy. Since the sudden outbreak of the war there has been little opportunity to protest against the curtailment of our liberties which is going on under the pressure of military necessity and the passions of war.*[11]

According to my understanding of economics and sociology, war is the inevitable outcome of the existing social organization, with its undemocratic forms of government and com-

[10] The immediate cause of this letter of resignation was an impossible situation which had developed at Gibson's Landing, B.C., a small mission which Woodsworth had taken over after leaving Winnipeg. Here his too generous support of the local co-operative store, and his refusal to foster recruiting through his church, brought upon him the wrath of a merchant who was a highly influential member of the Methodist community. Woodsworth's position there became untenable.

[11] Exhaustive evidence could be presented of the way in which Woodsworth's fighting spirit was aroused at the merest suggestion of such curtailment. Perhaps the most striking illustrations occur after the formation of the C.C.F., when the problem of party unity became pressing. When, in 1937, it was suggested that he should modify his position on foreign policy, he replied in a letter: "If I stand in the way of progress or unity in the C.C.F. I can resign from official position. But I will not give up my convictions and freedom."

petitive system of industry. For me, it is ignorance, or a closed mind, or camouflage, or hypocrisy, to solemnly assert that a murder in Servia, or the invasion of Belgium or the glaring injustices, or the horrible outrages are the cause of war. [The letter continues that a Christian minister must preach peace.] The vast majority of the Ministers and other church leaders seem to see things in an altogether different way. The churches have been turned into very effective recruitings agencies. . . .

On multiple grounds, therefore, Woodsworth left the church in 1918 – and in so doing discovered that the only method by which he could support himself and his family was by unskilled labour. His experience as a longshoreman on the Vancouver docks was in no way pleasant, but it was extremely instructive. Here personal experience worked to confirm a pattern of thought which was increasingly definite. It was a pattern which included all the essentials of democratic socialism – and in the Vancouver labour atmosphere of 1918, seething with revolutionary speculation, tremendous enthusiasm for the Russian experiment, and heavy with the threat of direct economic action, it is of real interest that Woodsworth hewed close to the "revisionist" line. It was here that he read and thoroughly digested the British Labour party's Draft Programme of Reconstruction and prepared careful articles and talks on the "four pillars of the house." It was here too that many of the socialist leaders with whom he associated accepted him only with some misgiving. Recognizing in him "a man of principle which was an invaluable quality, especially in the working class movement," they nevertheless regretted "his total lack of understanding of scientific socialist principles."[12] While the *B.C. Federationist*, the labour paper for which Woodsworth wrote most frequently in 1918, was moving steadily toward direct action and the One Big Union, the Woodsworth articles remained persistently cautious and expressive of evolutionary socialism. However, it is also worth emphasizing that the per-

---

[12] Mr. E. E. Winch has provided the writer with several illustrations of the reaction to Woodsworth's ideas. On one occasion a signwriter member of the Federated Labour party refused to enlarge a chart which Woodsworth had prepared for use at one of his evening workers' classes because "it was absolutely haywire from the standpoint of socialist economics." At the same time, Woodsworth was the only one of some 1,200 dockworkers who refused to load munitions destined for use against the Russian government, despite the fact that the job paid double the ordinary wage and he was sorely in need of money.

sonal experience of the conditions of wage labour, and the knoweledge that his wife and family had been left in the basement of a friend's house at Gibson's Landing, served to increase Woodsworth's indignation at the circumstances of existing capitalist society. One quotation from an article which he wrote shortly before he left Vancouver in the spring of 1919 will illustrate the nature of the impressions he gained from dock work.

Why work on Sunday? Because the work during week has not brought in sufficient money to support the family for a week, and Sunday work is paid as "time and a half?" But one should not work on Sunday. Oh, so the boss believes. He will not even walk to church; he rides in his private car. . . . He drops a coin in the collection for the poor. Whose coin? Do I receive all that I produce? Surely it pays someone to keep me working on Sundays even at "time and a half" rates! He goes home to wife and family and music and friends. I work on in the rain. . . . The church is a class institution. What does the church do to help me and those like me? The church is supported by the wealthy. Yes, he who pays the piper calls the tune. What well-groomed parson with his soft tones prophesying smooth things — Well I'm glad I'm not in his shoes! . . . The preacher in the boss's church says it is wrong to go to the Red Light district. But can you blame a fellow who can never have a home of his own? After all, isn't most crime the result of social injustice? In this big graft game who is the criminal anyhow?[13]

This was an indignation, however, which Woodsworth strove assiduously and successfully to channel into more productive lines than those of a narrow dogmatism. A consistent theme in his speeches and articles was the appeal for a commonsense approach to social problems — an approach whose basis he found most satisfactorily presented in the publications of the British Labour party and the writings of J. A. Hobson. And throughout his articles there is a continual sniping at "the type of mind that always looks for some extreme authority, and once having accepted this authority never feels quite sure of its ground unless it can quote chapter and verse, and if it can cite such authority willing to accept any statement, however unreasonable or far from the facts."[14]

[13] *B.C. Federationist*, September 6, 1918.
[14] *Ibid.*, October 4, 1918.

In all his speeches and articles for the Federated Labor party, which he had helped to organize, Woodsworth made it abundantly clear that he held himself apart from the considerable section of Vancouver working-class leadership which saw either orthodox Marxism or some quasi-syndicalist revolutionary programme as the only logical policy for Canadian workers. This is not to say that in the atmosphere of 1918-19 he saw bloody revolution as an impossibility; indeed, on this question he again reflected the British socialist position. Whether the revolution will be bloodless or not, he asserted, "will depend really upon the attitude of the small propertied class in control of government."[15] And, commenting upon the government's proposal to expand the Dominion Police, he claimed to see a fading hope in Canada for a completely peaceful revolution.[16] But he continued to use the British Labour Programme as his point of departure, and to insist that, on the basis of Soviet experience, Canadians must realize that they could not reconstruct their society "at one fell swoop." In Britain, he argued, "revolution may appear to come more slowly than in Russia, but there will be no counter revolution. . . . It may take a few years to work out, but when it's done it's done for good."[17]

In the spring of 1919, when work on the docks was slack, Woodsworth agreed to a proposal from William Ivens of Winnipeg to undertake a speaking tour of the Prairie Provinces. The purpose of the trip was to forward the economic and political education of all workers' organizations in the West. The itinerary was planned by the Labor Church, which Ivens had founded in 1918 on the model of the earlier British movement. There can be no doubt that Woodsworth's arrival in Winnipeg in the midst of the general strike was coincidental. As early as May 9, 1919, the *Western Labor News* (of which Ivens was editor) announced the projected tour and stated that Woodsworth was expected to arrive in Winnipeg on June 8, 1919. The announcement listed twenty subject titles which were to form the basis of his addresses; these included "Who Owns Canada?," "The Futility of Force," and "Why I Left

---

[15] *Ibid.*, November 15, 1918.

[16] *Ibid.*, Woodsworth maintained that the alleged revolutionary agitation on the part of the foreign born was a transparent excuse to extend a repressive policy against all workers in the crisis of rising prices and increasing unemployment.

[17] *Ibid.*, January 2, 1919.

the Church." Any workers' organization was invited to write to Ivens to arrange for a speaking engagement.

It is not within the scope of this article to assess the Winnipeg strike[18] in terms of the justice of the strikers' claims or of the employers' assertions; yet, since the strike assumes a position of critical importance in Woodsworth's development, something must be said about it. There are two diametrically opposed interpretations of the strike. One, originating with the (Citizens') Committee of One Thousand and carried on through the *Canadian Annual Review* and the *Cambridge History of the British Empire* (vol. VI), sees the real aim of the strike as the establishment of a Canadian Soviet on the banks of the Red River. The other interpretation, put forward originally by the strike leaders' legal defence, denies that there were any aims other than the improvement of wages, working conditions, and labour's bargaining position. The first argument seems to be weakened considerably by the fact that, in the contemporary police raids across Canada, there was found no evidence of an attempt to arm any branch of the workers' movement. Quite apart from the strikers' claims and their refusal to precipitate clashes with the authorities, the absence of preparation to use armed force seems to require modification of the Committee's interpretation.

Concerning the strikers' interpretation, one objection frequently raised stems from the debates and resolutions of the

[18] The following list of dates in connexion with the strike will help to keep the chronology of the main events clear:

May 1 – 2,000 workers in the metal trades on strike; most of the workers in the building trades also come out.

May 7 – Winnipeg Trades and Labor Council ballot on question of a general sympathetic strike.

May 15 – Trades and Labor Council calls strike of all its affiliates; central strike committees established; Citizens' Committee of One Thousand organized.

May 19 – First issue of the *Citizen*, organ of the Committee of One Thousand.

May 22 – Minister of labour (Robertson), and minister of the interior (Meighen) arrive from Ottawa.

June 8 – J. S. Woodsworth arrives in Winnipeg.

June 9 – Municipal police force dismissed.

June 17 – Strike leaders arrested and Labor Temple searched.

June 21 – "Silent Parade" of returned soldiers dispersed by R.N.W.M.P.

June 23 – J. S. Woodsworth arrested.

June 25 – Strike called off, as of June 26.

July 1-2 – Police raids across Canada for evidence of revolutionary conspiracy.

Western Labor Conference which was held at Calgary in March, 1919. It has been held by some (including the prosecution in the strike trials) that the radical resolutions passed at Calgary constituted definite proof of revolutionary intent. That the radical wing of the Winnipeg Trades and Labor Council was in sympathy with the One Big Union form of industrial unionization there can be no doubt. The resolutions passed at the founding conference in Calgary demanded the soviet type of governmental organization for Canada and the sending of complimentary messages to the Russian government and to the German Spartacists (as well as the establishment in Canada of one big union). But it is doubtful that this kind of peripheral evidence brought out at the strike trials meant much more than is meant by a contemporary social democrat when he addresses an audience as his "comrades." In any case, the One Big Union was not established as a functioning organization when the two strikes in the building and metal trades broke out in Winnipeg in early May, 1919.

The essential features of the strike were noted in the report of the Robson (Royal) Commission,[19] and these were the

---

[19] *Report* of the (Manitoba) Royal Commission to enquire into and report upon (the Winnipeg General Strike), H. A. Robson, K.C., Commissioner, July, 1919. The *Report* goes further than the immediate causes, and notes the general concentration upon domestic grievances, with the cessation of the war, and the resentment of the working class in the face of "undue war profiteering." The commissioner gives his blessing to a statement by President Winning of the Winnipeg Trades and Labor Council, which asserted that the high cost of living, long hours, low wages, poor working conditions, profiteering, the growing "intelligence" of the working class concerning the inequalities of modern society, and the refusal of the employers to recognize labour's right to bargain collectively were the causes of the strike. The *Report* observes that Winning's statement was published in the press and that "no one sought to challenge the evidence," p. 19. Other comments by the commissioner concerning the motives of the strike are interesting: ". . . it is too much for me to say that the vast number of intelligent residents who went on strike were seditious or that they were either dull enough or weak enough to allow themselves to be led by the seditionaries," p. 13; "It should be said that the leaders who brought about the General Strike were not responsible for the parades or riots which took place, and, in fact, tried to prevent them. The leaders' policy was peaceful idleness . . ." p. 17. The *Report* concludes with tentative suggestions for reform along educational, medical, and economic lines: "There should be no difficulty in deriving the means for the carrying out of the specific objects above mentioned. It is submitted that there should be a scheme of taxation of those who can afford it, and application of wealth to the reasonable needs of others in the community whose lot in life has not been favoured."

features which unquestionably impressed Woodsworth most forcibly. Apart altogether from the ephemeral revolutionary dogmatism of one or two of the strike leaders, it was quite clear that the Winnipeg iron masters refused to recognize any effective form of collective bargaining with their employees, and that the employers in the building trades refused to pay their employees a living wage (whether or not it was, as they argued, financially impossible for them to do so). Over these issues the strike started. In the conditions of an extremely high cost of living and the increasing threat of unemployment (enhanced by demobilization), the strike quickly spread to involve approximately 30,000 Winnipeg workers, and brought to a virtual standstill the city's economic life.

What, specifically, were Woodsworth's experiences during, and reactions to, the strike? The day he arrived in Winnipeg he spoke at a meeting of 10,000 strikers called by the Labor Church in Victoria Park. Thereafter he threw himself actively into the fray on behalf of the strikers. His writing, speeches, and actions all sprang from a firm belief in the justice of the strike aims of union recognition and a living wage. He was not in the least loath to be connected with a general sympathetic strike whose aims he conceived to be just and whose conduct he was thoroughly convinced was non-violent. Woodsworth could not accept the argument of the Committee of One Thousand when that body maintained that the Strike Committee was waging a revolutionary struggle against the mass of neutral Winnipeg citizenry. He stated his point of view in a letter to the *Western Labor News*:[20]

The general public is up in arms. They have suffered inconvenience and loss. "Why should innocent non-combatants suffer?" The general public has not been innocent. It has been guilty of the greatest sin — the sin of indifference. Thousands have suffered through the years under the industrial system. The general public have not realized. It did not touch them. They blame the strikers. Why not blame the employers whose arrogant determination has provoked the strike? Why not, rather, quit the unprofitable business of trying to place blame and attempt to discover and remove causes that have produced the strike and will produce, if not removed, further and more disastrous strikes? . . . Troops and more troops will not settle

[20] *Western Labor News*, June 12, 1919.

the question. Constructive radical action must come soon. Why not now?

Woodsworth reasoned, as the strike progressed, that the municipal, provincial, and federal governments were ignoring the basic rights of labour to act collectively in defence of its standard of living and its traditionally claimed freedom of association. He observed that each level of government acted quickly to coerce its employees and to prohibit membership in any trade union which condoned the general strike as a legitimate weapon in industrial disputes.[21] He was impressed, also, by the close association between the Committee of One Thousand and the federal ministers (Meighen and Robertson) who came to Winnipeg "in connection with the strike situation." On May 24 the *Citizen*, organ of the Committee of One Thousand, carried a report of the arrival of the ministers, whose train had been met outside the city by representatives of the Committee. The *Citizen* quoted the ministers as saying, "It is up to the citizens of Winnipeg to stand firm and resist the efforts made here to overturn proper authority." The paper went on to say that,

the two ministers have let it be known, authoritatively, that they regard the so-called strike as a cloak for something far deeper — a cloak for an effort to overturn proper authority. . . . "There is absolutely no justification for the general strike called by the strike committee in this city," said the Hon. Arthur Meighen. . . .

When a riot occurred after the regular police had been replaced by untrained special constables, when an increasing

[21] Although the municipal police remained on duty at the request of the Strike Committee, on June 9 the entire force was dismissed for refusal to sign pledges against the principle of the sympathetic strike. On May 26 the city council had voted nine to five for a resolution declaring sympathetic strikes illegal and calling for the dismissal of all civic employees then on strike. On May 25, at the request of Senator Robertson, federal minister of labour, who had come to Winnipeg to view the strike at close quarters, the postal employees were given an ultimatum to the effect that, on pain of immediate discharge and loss of pension rights, they must return to work, sever their connexion with the Winnipeg Trades and Labor Council, and sign an agreement never to support a sympathetic strike. The Norris provincial government served the same notice (demanding a yellow dog contract) on its telephone employees.

number of North-West Mounted Police appeared on the streets, and when local militia units were alerted, Woodsworth's conviction increased that armed force was to be used without any serious attempt to meet fairly the workers' demands.[22] The almost hysterical action taken at Ottawa to amend the Immigration Act and the Criminal Code, with a view to deporting the British-born leaders of the strike, further strengthened this conviction. And when, in the early hours of June 17, the Mounted Police arrested ten men whom they considered to be the strike leaders, and bundled them off to Stony Mountain Penitentiary, Woodsworth had no hesitation as to his course of action. He had had considerable journalistic experience and had identified himself completely with the strikers' cause. It was natural that he should assume the editorship of the *Western Labor News*, whose editor was one of the arrested men.

Under the new editor the paper continued for a week to advocate a policy of passive resistance to the increasingly coordinated efforts to break the strike forcibly. By this time, even the *Free Press*, which had consistently decried the strike although in somewhat milder language than the *Citizen* and the *Telegram*, paused and called for caution.[23] Commenting on the arrests, the *Free Press* said the action taken would enable the victims to

pose as martyrs in the cause of the workingman and will also supply them with a plausible excuse for failure. . . . The Dominion authorities have presumably considered those objections and deemed them less conclusive than the reasons known in the fullest degree only to themselves, which call for the drastic action which has been taken. . . . Theirs is the responsibility and it must be left to events to indicate their sagacity or to confirm the apprehensions of the doubters.[24]

The *Western Labor News* continued to condemn the harsh federal policy and to counsel passivity and unity on the part of the strikers. Then, on June 21, occurred the major "action" of the strike period.

[22] Several attempts at conciliation bogged down primarily over the reluctance of the iron masters to accept the principle of collective bargaining.

[23] Winnipeg *Free Press*, June 17, 1919. Presumably this position cannot be explained exclusively in terms of political strategy on the part of a Liberal paper seeking to embarrass a Conservative Government in a critical moment.

[24] *Ibid.*, June 18, 1919.

On the second day after the "silent parade" of returned men, the Honourable N. W. Rowell, speaking for the government in the House of Commons, commented, "the first shots were fired by the paraders, or those associated with them, and the Mounted Police fired only in self-defence. The information that we have is that the police acted with great coolness, great courage, and great patience, as is characteristic of the men of the Royal North-West Mounted Police."[25] Two days after this statement in the Commons, the secretary of the Strike Committee wrote to Premier Norris telling him that the Committee had decided to terminate the strike on June 26.

Thus the strike ended in a blaze of federal action, and whether the events of the parade on "bloody Saturday" were described accurately by the Honourable Mr. Rowell or not, to Woodsworth they had only one meaning. He believed that Mayor Gray, who had previously issued an order prohibiting mass meetings and parades,[26] had taken an unjustifiable step, in view of the fact that the strikers had hitherto conducted themselves with a cautious regard for law and order. He believed that the parade which was called by a committee of returned men for Saturday, June 21, was within their "constitutional" rights, and that its purpose, which was to march to the Royal Alexandra Hotel to interview Senator Robertson and receive an explanation of his activities during the strike, was just. The cautious reserve of the minister of labour, although undoubtedly sincerely directed toward a settlement, appeared distinctly sinister to those outside the Committee of One Thousand. Thus when the parade was broken up in front of the city hall by an armed charge of the Mounted Police, and when, with the appearance of large numbers of soldiers armed with rifles and machine guns, the city appeared to be under military rule, Woodsworth arranged for a full report of the police-military action. There also appeared, in the *Western Labor News* of July 23, several editorial comments upon these events. These represented Woodsworth's immediate reaction to the culminating events of the strike, and they became instantly the basis of the seditious libel charge on which he was apprehended. The charge of seditious libel listed six items from the

---

[25] *Hansard*, June 23, 1919, IV, 3845. In this clash between the returned soldiers and the R.N.W.M.P., there were about thirty casualties, including one death. Sixteen of the casualties were police.

[26] This prohibition was one of the reasons listed by the Strike Committee for calling off the strike – since these meetings had constituted the chief source of revenue for the strikers.

paper.[27] The first of these was a news story of the police action entitled "Bloody Saturday," the second consisted of two quotations from the Book of Isaiah,[28] and the other four were editorials. In the news story, the position of the *Western Labor News* was made quite clear. "Apparently the bloody business was carefully planned, for Mayor Gray issued a proclamation in the morning stating that 'any women taking part in a parade do so at their own risk.' Nevertheless, a vast crowd of men, women and children assembled to witness the 'silent parade.' "[29] The report went on to describe the Mounted Police charge, "with revolvers drawn," to berate some citizens who applauded the "man-killers" as they rode by, and to sympathize with the returned men who had organized the parade when the latter declared that the federal police action was "an infringement of the human rights they had fought to defend." The editorials lamented "Kaiserism in Canada," maintaining that "those who thought that the blood of innocent men upon our streets is

---

[27] Manitoba Court of King's Bench, Fall Assizes, 1919, Suit no. 2170/3. A second charge was laid against Woodsworth in November (King's Bench, Suit No. 2168/3) on which he was indicted for "speaking seditious words." While the strike trials were pending, he addressed a meeting of the Labor Church in Winnipeg, November 16, 1919, at which he was reported as saying: "If we get a penitentiary sentence we will carry with us the picture of this gathering of 5000 people who are behind us. Indeed, a sentence for us might cause a great triumph on the part of the people. I cannot conceive of this 5000 people leaving me or the others there for very long. They say we are trying to stir up revolution. If there are any government officials here I want to say that if they wish to stir up revolution let them go on as they are doing."

[28] Woe unto them that decree unrighteous decrees, and that write grievousness which they have prescribed; to turn aside the needy from judgment, and to take away the right from the poor of my people, that widows may be their prey, and that they may rob the fatherless. (Isaiah 10: 1-2)

And they shall build houses and inhabit them; and they shall plant vineyards, and eat the fruit of them. They shall not build and another inhabit; they shall not plant and another eat: for as the days of a tree are the days of my people, and mine elect shall enjoy the work of their hands. (Isaiah, 65: 21-22)

[29] Reporting to the Commons on the precautions taken by the mayor, the Honourable N. W. Rowell noted that the returned soldiers had refused to be diverted from their purpose of holding a parade, and that the mayor, "with the approval of the Attorney-General, and in his presence, went to the headquarters of the Mounted Police and asked their co-operation in maintaining law and order." After the first attempt of the Mounted Police to clear the streets, the mayor read the Riot Act "and then proceeded to militia headquarters and asked that the militia be called out" (*Hansard*, 1919, IV, 3844).

preferable to a 'silent parade,' and who ordered the assault," had acted in the spirit of Kaiser Wilhelm. But the chief note in the editorials was one of hope — hope that the strikers would not break ranks, and hope that they would organize politically for the purpose of proving that "ideas are more powerful than bullets." It was suggested that the government pursue a more constructive policy and take over the firms that had been struck, appointing at the same time a commission with adequate powers of investigation. In retrospect (and from a lay point of view), the editorials approached sedition only in one place — and there only by an implication which might be forced upon the following: "In the meantime, the returned soldiers are becoming restless and threatening to take things into their own hands. They are tired of the policy of 'Do Nothing — Keep Order,' so consistently followed by the strikers."

This issue of the *Western Labor News* proved highly irritating to the local representatives of the Dominion Department of Justice, who ordered the paper to cease publication,[30] and obtained the immediate arrest of Woodsworth. F. J. Dixon edited the paper for three days after this, and then he too was arrested on a similar charge of seditious libel. While Woodsworth was spending five days in the provincial jail, the strike finally collapsed.

Although the strike was terminated on June 26, there was considerable resentment amongst the rank and file (and some of the leaders) at this decision of the Strike Committee. The Committee, in defence of its action, argued that with public meetings banned, revenue petering out, many workers on the verge of starvation, and abundant evidence of the federal government's determination to suppress the movement, continuance of the strike seemed futile. They also referred to the qualified success represented in the acceptance by the iron masters of the "principle of collective bargaining," and in the

---

[30] The following letter was sent to the Winnipeg Printing and Engraving Company:

Gentlemen:

Certain numbers of the Western Labour News Special Strike Edition have contained objectionable matter in that it is seditious, inflamatory and inciting to riot, and the publication must be discontinued.

Yours truly,
(sgd.) ALFRED J. ANDREWS
Agent, Department of Justice.

Printed in *The Winnipeg General Sympathetic Strike*, prepared by the Defence Committee.

pledge of the provincial government to appoint a commission to investigate the causes and course of the strike.[31] Some, at least, of the workers felt that the direct threat of arrest of leaders who might vigorously replace those who had been arrested, had played too strong a part in this capitulation. Certainly, all were disappointed with the outcome, particularly since there was no real guarantee that strikers would be reinstated. One primary feature of the strike which is frequently minimized has been at least noted in the recent book by Professor H. A. Logan: "The State, in fact, placed its organized strength directly across the path of those who sought to march forward by way of paralysing industry through use of the general strike."[32] It was this aspect of the strike period which most profoundly impressed Woodsworth.

Woodsworth's activities following his arrest and until his election to parliament late in 1921 could have been predicted with some accuracy, if a contemporary had judged on the basis of his past career. It would be entirely incorrect to conclude that his course during this two and a half year period was the product of a sudden personal bitterness engendered by his treatment during the strike – or even of his experiences in Vancouver. The years preceding 1919 make it abundantly clear that he possessed no more of what our psychologists would call a persecution complex than did any other Canadian of his generation who found himself (either directly, or by an intellectual process of association) pitted against the exigencies of a crowded labour market and a rising cost of living. Indeed, it is the consistency with which Woodsworth kept contemporary problems in their proper perspective that is most significant about this stage of his development. Even in the editorials of June 23, there is a heavy emphasis upon British techniques, upon the program of the British Labour party, and upon the necessity for Canadian workers to organize politically that they might press their demands within the traditional framework of British constitutional and political experience. In a man of a different calibre, a less temperate policy at this time might have been expected. The treatment accorded those who were arrested in connexion with the strike (apart altogether from the merits of the strike itself) was not such as to stimulate reliance upon constitutional methods of obtaining reform.

---

[31] Winnipeg *Enlightener*, June 25, 1919. The name of the labour paper was changed several times to avoid suppression.

[32] H. A. Logan, *Trade Unions in Canada* (Toronto, 1948), 320.

The original legal charge which hung over Woodsworth's head remained suspended until February 16, 1920, during which time he was not able to be long away from Winnipeg at any one time, and the consequent suffering and worry occasioned to his family were considerable.[33] These months were spent in the energetic speaking tours which carried Woodsworth, on behalf of the strikers' Defence Committee, from one end of the country to the other. In the cities of the east, he encountered a genuine desire to see a fair trial, not only amongst labour organizations, but also amongst the "respectable part of society." In Toronto, a large meeting was held for him at the Open Forum and a considerable sum of money subscribed, which was augmented by prominent members of the university faculty. All of this was encouraging and tended to strengthen his belief that the type of reform he advocated could be brought about in this country by other than violent means.

On January 29, 1920, F. J. Dixon's trial was begun at Winnipeg before Mr. Justice Galt. Dixon had tried to obtain E. J. McMurray to conduct his defence, but this able lawyer was already engaged by the eight men charged with seditious conspiracy. However, McMurray strongly advised Dixon to undertake his own defence, referring him to the biography of Joseph Howe, the pertinent passages in the works of Milton, and the records of several English sedition trials. After three interviews with Mr. McMurray, in which the plan of defence was revised to bear more on his own case and less on the abstract question, Dixon felt ready to face a hostile judge and a jury composed almost exclusively of farmers. It is of interest that when Woodsworth approached McMurray on the question of his own trial, and suggested that he should undertake his defence without legal assistance, he was given the opposite advice to that which had been given Dixon. Woodsworth was informed that he would be too likely to throw away his case in his zeal to underline the conflicting principles at stake.[34] Perhaps fortunately the Woodsworth charges were never brought

---

[33] Friends on the coast were not unaware of his plight. The following message to him was published in the *Western Labor News*, July 2, 1919:

J. S. Woodsworth,
Winnipeg, Man.

    Congratulations on your martyrdom. Hope You deserved it.

VANCOUVER FEDERATED LABOR PARTY.

[34] Information concerning the Woodsworth and Dixon interviews was given the writer by the Honourable E. J. McMurray, K.C.

to the point of trial. The Dixon trial was a sixteen-day single-handed battle during which was delivered one of the most able Canadian defences of the freedom of the press. As a result, Dixon won an acquittal. It was immediately announced that the seditious libel charge against Woodsworth was being dropped, and he received the warm congratulations of the jurymen who had just acquitted Dixon.[35] Satisfaction at the outcome of their own prosecutions was modified for Dixon and Woodsworth by the earlier conviction and sentence of R. B. Russell; and in early April, by the conviction and sentencing of six more of the strike leaders.

From the end of the strike trials until the 1921 federal elections, Woodsworth used his time in working with the Labor Church movement,[36] in writing for labour papers, and in further attempts to forward labour political organization. The experiences of 1919 and the results of the strike trials reacted differently on various sections of labour opinion. In

[35] The Crown entered a "nolle prosequi" on the seditious libel charge on February 16, 1920. The charge of "speaking seditious words" remained unaltered until March 7, 1920, when the Crown entered a "stay of proceedings." On March 13, 1920, Woodsworth received a telegram from the deputy attorney-general informing him that he need not "appear" in Winnipeg again unless advised. He was never formally informed that the charge had been dropped, and, technically, he could have been summoned at any later time to stand trial on it. No doubt the original charge was dropped partly because of the blunder of listing the quotations from Isaiah, and partly because of the possible effect of a double acquittal upon the seditious conspiracy trials still pending.

[36] Woodsworth was deeply interested in William Iven's Labor Church, and for a while was secretary of the movement. This seems partly to have been a reluctance to dissociate himself entirely from organizations designed to minister to men's spiritual needs. However, this interest was patently subordinate to his political aims. Certainly the Labor Church had a political character just as evident as was its religious. Woodsworth's specific comments upon religion in this period do not differ in essence from the earlier position which has been noted. He became increasingly skeptical, particularly with respect to what he termed "static religion," and its claims to finality: "The religion of the future . . . will lay no claim to finality but rather be going on towards perfection." See the pamphlet written by Woodsworth, and published in 1920, *The First Story of the Labor Church*. He expressed, also, high praise for Upton Sinclair's *The Profits of Religion*, and wrote in the *Western Labor News*, October 15, 1920: "Winnipeg people will not forget the attitude of the churches during the strike. . . . Only the other day, at the Annual Fair in Vancouver, Bishop de Pencier, accompanied by the Mounted Police, solemnly blessed a captured German gun. Think of this in the name of Jesus!"

Winnipeg, a split developed between the advocates of direct economic action in the One Big Union, led by R. B. Russell and R. J. Johns, and the conservative wing of the Trades and Labor Council which wished to bring Winnipeg labour back into the fold of international unionism, and under the kindly influence of Samuel Gompers. A third section, led by S. J. Farmer and F. J. Dixon, adopted an intermediate position, and pursued the revisionist or British socialist policy. It was perhaps inevitable that Woodsworth, as a consistent advocate of evolutionary socialism, should attach himself to this third group. In July and August, 1919, he published five articles in the *Western Labor News* (which was again under the editorship of William Ivens), under the title "What Next?" The articles illustrate clearly Woodsworth's firm, and to some extent imitative attachment to the principles of the British Labour party.

Our ultimate objectives must be a complete turnover in the present economic and social system. . . . Such change, we hope, will be accomplished in this country by means of education, organization, and the securing by the workers of the machinery of government. We look forward to the formation of a Canadian organization broad enough to include all producers. . . . The fight is not between hand workers and brain workers. It is not between industrial workers and agricultural workers. The fight is essentially between the producers and the parasites.[37]

In succeeding articles a point by point gradualist policy of socialization, progressive taxation, and related measures was set forth, with copious references to the draft program of reconstruction of the British Labour Party. In short, Woodsworth's actions and writing during this time indicate beyond the shadow of a doubt that the strike experience had simply augmented his desire to aid in the establishment of a strong working-class political party on the English model.

Late in August, 1920, Woodsworth moved back to Vancouver. There he found a division in labour opinion similar to that existing in Winnipeg, and immediately re-entered the fray in support of the Federated Labour party. This group was viewed with some condescension and considerable mistrust by O.B.U. partisans on the one hand, and orthodox "internationalists" on the other. Thus Woodsworth's articles and reports of his

[37] *Western Labor News*, July 25, 1919.

speeches in the *B.C. Federationist* in 1920-1 were sandwiched in between glowing accounts of communist gains in England, editorials insisting that the nomination of labour political candidates could serve only as a medium of propaganda, and the flat statement that the function of a labour ministry "is to carry on a capitalist government."[38] Continuing to fight both extremes (that is, of Gomperism and direct action), Woodsworth entered the provincial elections in the autumn of 1920 as one of three F.L.P. candidates in the Vancouver constituency. Each of the F.L.P. men polled more than 7,000 votes. This gave them considerable satisfaction, for, although it was not enough to elect any one of them, they were far ahead of the six candidates put forward by the more radical and doctrinaire Socialist party of Canada. The experience was particularly valuable for Woodsworth as preparation for the federal elections of the following year. His campaign speeches emphasized the practical, gradualist policy of "immediate benefits." If labour candidates were elected, he asserted, the workers would not have to go begging, hat in hand, for labour legislation; a bulwark would be erected against the increasing capitalist pressure for immigration; and, of course, with a labour government finally elected, the whole program of socialization and social welfare would be embarked upon.

Following the British Columbia elections, Woodsworth remained active in the organizational and educational work of the F.L.P., at the same time keeping in close touch with the political situation in Winnipeg. In the latter city, political events in 1920-1 seemed to create circumstances peculiarly favourable to the launching of a strong labour bid in the federal field. In the Manitoba provincial elections of 1920, F. J. Dixon had been elected at the head of the polls, and Queen, Armstrong, and Ivens, although still in jail, were also elected. Despite the divisions in labour opinion (and the growth of a small communist cell), there seemed to be, largely as a result of the strike and the trials, a very real upswing in the voting strength of labour. It is possible, therefore, that when Woodsworth returned to Winnipeg in the summer of 1921 to assume the position of secretary to the Labor Church, he was not unmindful of the opportunities presented to a potential federal labour candidate. He associated himself once more with the middle group of labour opinion which had formed behind Farmer and Dixon. This group had withdrawn, in the spring of 1921, from

---

[38] *B. C. Federationist*, October 29, 1920.

the Dominion Labour Party (and also from Jimmy Simpson's Canadian Labour Party), to establish the Independent Labor Party. There had been considerable friction within the Dominion Labor Party (a Winnipeg organization), between the One Big Union men who were present in increasing numbers at the party meetings, and those who wished to see the party follow the program and tactics of the British Labour Party. Rather than dissipate their energies in a group which lacked the cohesion necessary to effective electoral action, the social democratic elements established the I.L.P. It was this latter party that elected Woodsworth to the House of Commons in Centre Winnipeg in December, 1921 – in the face of heavy opposition from the "official" Canadian Labor Party and the Trades and Labour Council which had been reconquered by the international unions.

The activities and policies of Woodsworth after 1921 are not germane to this article, although they also indicate a remarkable consistency. The conclusions which emerge from a survey of his career to 1921 are not obscure. The early contact with English social and socialist thought, which was maintained by reading, the studious observation of the emergent Canadian conditions flowing from immigration and industrialization, together with a formal church experience which he found frustrating to his humanitarian impulses – all led to scepticism of organized religion as a vehicle for social reform. His attempt to work through the agencies of the "social gospel" led directly to an undogmatic acceptance of the class struggle, and, as early as 1910, to support of working-class political organization. The final disillusionment with the church in 1917-8, and the definition of the principles of action which he would follow, make evident his fundamental reliance upon the teachings and experience of the British socialists. The steel of his resolution to hew to this line was tempered during the apprenticeship on the Vancouver docks and in the Federated Labor Party. Finally, the participation in the critical events of the Winnipeg strike focused his attention upon the federal arena – an attention which had already been clearly directed toward the problem of establishing an effective labour party. He was convinced that if misuse of the police and the military were to be effectively prevented, and if the social relationships within Canada were to be fundamentally and peacefully reconstructed, labour must direct its major effort toward a political victory at Ottawa.

The Origin of the Farmers' Union of Canada

D. S. Spafford

On December 17, 1921, a group of farmers met in the town hall at Ituna, Saskatchewan, to discuss the formation of an organization to be called the Farmers' Union of Canada. They were addressed by Norbert Henri Schwarz, a quiet earnest man, originally a Swiss, who had homesteaded near Ituna in 1905. Schwarz declared that "the farmers of Canada had to unite to I protect themselves, II to obtain a complete control of their produce, III to market their produce themselves."[1] The farmers approved of the organization and its purposes, and they elected Schwarz secretary and Joseph Thompson of Ituna, president. The two men began the work of recruiting members early in the new year. The response was highly encouraging; at Kelliher, where the second local group was formed, forty memberships were taken out at the initial meeting. By seeding time, when organization work was suspended for the summer, local "lodges" (as they came to be called) had also been established at Lipton, Hubbard, and Goodeve. Schwarz drafted a constitution and made preparations for a convention. On July 1 he travelled to Kelvington to put his ideas before a local farmers' group which also called itself the Farmers' Union.[2] Its president was Louis P. McNamee, a large and forceful Irishman who had farmed in the district since 1905. The Kelvington farmers accepted Schwarz's draft constitution with the proviso that the Farmers' Union should adopt the Kelvington practice of admitting only members to meetings. The first convention was held in Saskatoon on July 25, 1922. McNamee was elected president and Schwarz was returned as secretary. The convention was not a large affair, since the Union had at that time only a half-dozen lodges, but it was able to lay the foundation for a remarkable

SOURCE: *Saskatchewan History*, vol. XVIII, no. 3 (Autumn, 1965), pp. 89-98. Reprinted by permission of the author and publishers.

[1] Archives of Saskatchewan, "First Minute Book of Farmers' Union of Canada" (manuscript), p. 52. Henceforth "First Minute Book."

[2] The Kelvington group appears to have been organized independently in February 1922.

organization which, within two years, had a membership numbering ten thousand.[3]

The Farmers' Union of Canada grew out of the depression following the First World War. Farmers had invested heavily in land and equipment during the war in response to buoyant prices and a government campaign to expand food production. When the world price of wheat declined sharply in 1920, many farmers were unable to meet debt charges. Schwarz, recounting the events leading to the formation of the Farmers' Union, cites especially the inability of governments throughout the world to provide stable markets and prices for agricultural products after the war. Farmers "realized, after many years of deception," he wrote, "that it was useless to rely on governments that were never controlled by the people, but by a few controlled old men. . . ."[4] The solution, he thought, was for farmers to assume control of their own affairs — hence the purposes which he enunciated at the first meeting at Ituna. The control of agricultural marketing by the farmers themselves was to become the main theme of the Wheat Pool movement. The Farmers' Union did not take up the issue of pooling until 1923, but it is clear that from the beginning its thinking was consistent with the pooling idea.

If farmers were to gain control over their industry, they must organize. But a local or even provincial organization, the leaders of the Farmers' Union argued, was not enough. To be effective the Union must be national, and even international. The organization of farmers was looked upon as a necessary and natural response to the concentration of power in other sectors of the economy. The interests of other claimants to the national income were advanced by organization; the farmers must follow their example. The lesson which L. P. McNamee drew from the experience of other interest groups, was that a successful organization was one that was prepared to let nothing deter it from the primary objective of advancing its members' economic interests.

The farmers comprise 51 per cent. of the entire population

[3] An estimate. The financial records of the central office of the Farmers' Union for 1924 show income of about $40,000 from membership fees; as the central office received $4.00 of the $5.00 fee, a paid-up membership of about 10,000 is indicated. It is unlikely that numbers increased much beyond this in the years following. Saskatchewan farmers made up by far the largest part of the membership, though there was a fairly substantial number of members in both Manitoba and Alberta.

[4] *The Progressive*, January 17, 1924, p. 15.

of Canada. They are organized to the same strength as temperance beer, or about 2 per cent. The other 49 per cent., dividing them into four groups – namely, manufacturers, finance, transportation and labor: we find, on a close-up inspection, that these groups never attempted to carry on their organization to perfect their system or to work out their schemes by throwing their doors open to the public. We find, on looking further, that they had no place for such sentiments and contentious questions as politics or religion; but economic problems was their sole problem, and in working out its solution to their own advantage has ever been the business of these four great groups.

We, of the Farmers' Union of Canada, do not find any fault with other industrial or financial groups exercising common-sense in securing for themselves a safe position and a strong defense, and after spending eighteen or twenty years at the experimental station, we decided to both endorse and copy the methods of these groups who had become much more successful in the race than the tillers of the soil.[5]

Of the several economic groups which McNamee mentions, it was labour whose experience was drawn upon most heavily. The pan-industrial approach to organization had found expression in the Canadian labour movement shortly after the war, particularly in the formation of the One Big Union in 1919. What the Farmers' Union owed to the One Big Union was more than the idea of an industrial union; it was something as tangible as its constitution. The constitution which Schwarz drafted for the Farmers' Union was based directly on the constitution of the One Big Union. Whole sections were taken over without significant change, including large parts of the Marxian preamble.[6]

The rudimentary socialist ideas contained in the preamble figured largely in the Farmers' Union's propaganda for the first few months. The "class struggle" remained a part of the rhetorical equipment of the Farmers' Union throughout, though its interpretation took on various shades, from the strict Marxian meaning to simply competition among diverse economic interests. The Marxian analysis, based as it was on wage labour, could not be accommodated to the position of the farmer without substantial revision. At least one attempt was made to arrive at an accommodation; the outcome differs from the traditional agrarian argument in little more than vocabulary.

[5] *Ibid.*, June 19, 1924, p. 2.
[6] See the Appendix where both preambles are printed.

One of the basic principles of this Union is that it recognizes and accepts the fact of the "class struggle," and maintains that the farmers as a class have an unquestionable right to organize and to protect and further their interests. This does not mean that this Union believes in or stands for class government; nor does it believe that the "class struggle" is or should be permanent; but it holds that the "class struggle" is the great factor that must be recognized and understood.

* * * *

The "class struggle," as affecting the farmers, means, in the first place, that in the struggle over the sale of farm produce, the buyers are always the masters (not the ultimate buyers or consumers, but the capitalists, the speculators, the middlemen, who buy from the farmer and sell to the consumer). These people, through organization, have secured control over the store-houses and elevators (built by labor). They have selling agencies, bureaus of information, through which they keep in touch with the world-buyers; with them they bargain and so market their wealth. The bankers also seem to favor this class and organization, as they provide them with credit facilities, while farmers who have the produce, are compelled to sell to it at times unfavorable to themselves (the farmers), because they were refused credit, notwithstanding the fact that they have the value on which credit was based.

Therefore, as industry develops and ownership becomes concentrated into fewer hands (the capitalists) and as the economic forces (and facilities) of society become more and more the sole property of financial organizations, it is clear then that the farmers, in order to sell their produce, with any degree of success, must organize and extend and arrange their form of organization in accordance with changing methods and combinations on the part of the financiers and according to developments and needs. The capitalists are organized on a large scale, they have one common policy and aim — how to make the largest possible profit — hence, the farmer must organize into a large union against the O.B.U. of capital for self-defence and in order to get his just and rightful dues.[7]

The Farmers' Union did not propose, however, to take an active part in politics. Its leaders tried to stay clear of issues on which opinion was divided on party lines. The "Political Stand" adopted by the convention in 1922 was extremely vague: "Coordinating the political interests of the farmers by united

[7] *The Progressive*, July 3, 1924, p. 6.

franchise to further our interests in legislation."[8] What was meant by "united franchise" was never made clear. The Union was sympathetic to labour's cause (McNamee, a former trade unionist, took an avid interest in labour issues) and favoured the principle of farmer-labour co-operation – notwithstanding that Schwarz's proposed slogan, "Farmers and workers of the world unite," got amended at the convention to "Farmers of the world unite."[9] But no proposal of farmer-labour co-operation in politics was ever officially endorsed.

Wheat marketing and farm prices were among the first issues to concern the Farmers' Union. The Ituna lodge at its initial meeting was given details of a wheat marketing plan put forward by C. L. Campbell of Nokomis.[10] At a later meeting the plan (which was not described) was given formal approval "subject to alterations if found necessary or to cancellation if another better system can be found."[11] Another and presumably better system was found in the Sapiro Plan in 1923. It is interesting that no mention is made anywhere in the Minutes of the desirability of reinstating the post-war Wheat Board, even though it was being widely discussed in the countryside. The Farmers' Union was firmly committed to Schwarz's idea that farmers ought to handle their own marketing.

The Union did consider, at least for a time, a remedy for the problem of falling farm prices which would have involved government action. One of the objects of the organization was to enable farmers to "fix their own price above cost of production. . . ."[12] The way in which Schwarz hoped to see this object attained, at least in the short run, is suggested by a discussion recorded in the minutes of the Ituna lodge.[13] The minutes contain a calculation, in some detail, of the cost of producing a bushel of wheat. A few entries are unexplained, making it difficult to follow the operation in detail, but it is clear that the object was to arrive at a price for wheat which would cover cost of production. Probably it was also intended to show what price would have left the farmer no worse off in 1921 than he was in 1920, taking account of changes in costs, but it is not possible to be certain about this because of ambiguities in the Minutes. In any event, the Ituna farmers suggested that the government

[8] "First Minute Book," p. 66.

[9] *Ibid.*, p. 68.

[10] *Ibid.*, p. 52.

[11] *Ibid.*, p. 55.

[12] See Appendix, preamble to draft Constitution.

[13] "First Minute Book," p. 56. See also Clause II of draft Constitution.

ought to make payments to the farmers in compensation for the losses they had suffered when prices fell in 1920.

We consider we where defraudet [sic] in the value of our goods in 1921-1922 if not longer and ask for a bonus of $0.10 per bushel of wheat $0.05 for oats, $0.06 for barley, $0.15 for flax, $0.01 per lb. for cattle and $0.02 for sheep for a period of 10 years.[14]

The idea did not survive the first convention, in the minutes of which it takes the form: "Coming to a decision with the Government to equalize losses for 1920, 1921 and also 1922 if necessary instead of the farmer standing the majority of losses."[15]

The Farmers' Union grew partly at the expense of the Saskatchewan Grain Growers Association. It was able to win over many members from the older association. It would not be accurate to say, however, that the Farmers' Union owed its existence to a shift of allegiance wholly or even in large part. The Farmers' Union began in an area of the province where the Saskatchewan Grain Growers Association was organized only spottily. Of the six lodges organized before the first convention, only one, it would appear, was in a district where the Saskatchewan Grain Growers Association also had a local.[16] The Farmers' Union was very successful in areas where farmers of Ukrainian origin predominated. Ukrainian names appear frequently in the lists of officers of Farmers' Union lodges. The Minutes note that "numerous Ruthenian speakers" addressed a meeting at Goodeve.[17] "On account of a Ruthenian holliday [sic] the meeting was opened before a small audience . . . ," reads the report of a meeting at Ituna.[18] The Saskatchewan Grain Growers Association, in contrast, had almost no following in areas settled by Central Europeans.

Relations between the Farmers' Union and the Saskatchewan Grain Growers Association were never cordial, and at times were marked by bitter hostility. The styles of the two organizations were radically different. Where the Saskatchewan Grain Growers Association conducted its affairs in an open and straightforward way, the activities of the Farmers' Union had a

---

[14] *Loc. cit.*

[15] *Ibid.*, p. 68.

[16] This statement is based on examination of a list of the Saskatchewan Grain Growers Association locals active in 1917. It is possible that some of the districts might have been organized by the early 1920s.

[17] Archives of Saskatchewan, "Minute Book of the Farmers' Union of Canada [1923]," p. 1.

[18] *Loc. cit.*

secretive and even conspiratorial flavor. The "closed-door" rule and the Union's ritual, which resembled those of some secret societies, contributed to this impression. The "secret work," as it is called in a handbook describing procedure, consisted of the following: "The Password. The Grip. The Test Word and Its Answer. The Hailing Sign and Its Answer. The Working Sign. The President's Answering Sign. Warning Words."[19] Members addressed each other as "Brother," a practice which seems to have been adopted from the early Farmers' Union at Kelvington. Ballotting was carried on by the use of black and white balls; five black balls were sufficient to reject a candidate for membership.

Again in contrast to practice in the Saskatchewan Grain Growers Association, local lodges of the Farmers' Union were subject to a great deal of control from the central office; they were referred to often as "subordinate lodges." The executive board laid down a rule that outside speakers should not be allowed to address lodges on union matters until they had been cleared by the central office.[20] A few speakers were proscribed by name. During the Wheat Pool campaign, the executive board passed the following motion: "That all lodges be instructed that where the majority of the members support the Wheat Pool or any other economic reform or undertaking, that the minority who refuse to contract their wheat or to give their full support to such economic reforms that are endorsed by the Union, shall be subject to suspension from the lodge. The lodges to vote on the above resolution before it can be accepted."[21] Apparently there were second thoughts about this resolution, for it was rescinded at a later meeting. In its place was put an instruction to the lodges recommending the suspension of any member who, having been given information concerning the Sapiro Plan, should "refuse to give his full support, when legally possible. . . ."[22] Whether this was acted upon by the lodges is not known. The executive board itself expelled at least two members; in the one case no reason is given in the minutes, in the other expulsion was for attending a convention "under false

[19] Farmers' Union of Canada, *Lodge Government of the Farmers' Union of Canada*, no date.

[20] Archives of Saskatchewan, "Minutes of the Central Executive Board of the Farmers' Union of Canada," meeting held November 2-3, 1923.

[21] *Ibid.*, meeting held November 3-4, 1923. Compare with Clause III of the draft constitution.

[22] *Ibid.*, meeting held January 15, 1924.

pretenses."[23] One cause for expulsion was a breach of the "bona fide farmer" clause in the constitution, which the Union took very seriously. An instruction was sent out to the lodges asking the withdrawal of any member who was not "an actual dirt farmer."[24] The executive board even addressed itself on one occasion to the spare-time activities of its members. "This Board does not endorse the action of any member of this Union," reads a circular, "in engaging in such occupation as bailiff, sheriff, or other occupations that may be objectionable to the spirit of true brotherhood, which it is our earnest desire to establish."[25]

APPENDIX

Reproduced below is the draft Constitution which was brought before the first convention of the Farmers' Union of Canada on July 25, 1922. For purposes of comparison the preamble to the constitution of the One Big Union is printed in a note.[26]

[23] *Ibid.*, meetings held August 7, 1923 and November 3-4, 1923.

[24] *Ibid.*, meeting held December 11, 1923.

[25] *Ibid.*, meeting held November 3-4, 1923.

[26] "Modern industrial society is divided into two classes, those who possess and do not produce, and those who produce and do not possess. Alongside this main division all other classifications fade into insignificance. Between these two classes a continual struggle takes place. As with buyers and sellers of any commodity there exists a struggle on the one hand of the buyer to buy as cheaply as possible, and on the other, of the seller to sell for as much as possible, so with the buyers and sellers of labour power. In the struggle over the purchase and sale of labour power the buyers are always masters — the sellers always workers. From this fact arises the inevitable class struggle.

"As industry develops and ownership becomes concentrated more and more into fewer hands; as the control of the economic forces of society become more and more the sole property of imperialistic finance, it becomes apparent that the workers, in order to sell their labour power with any degree of success, must extend their forms of organization in accordance with changing industrial methods. Compelled to organize for self defense, they are further compelled to educate themselves in preparation for the social change which economic developments will produce whether they seek it or not.

"The One Big Union, therefore, seeks to organize the wage worker, not according to craft, but according to industry; according to class and class needs; and calls upon all workers to organize irrespective of nationality, sex, or craft into a workers' organization, so that they may be enabled to more successfully carry on the everyday fight over wages, hours of work, etc., and prepare ourselves for the day when production for profit shall be replaced by production for use." (Constitution of the One Big Union, reproduced in the Department of Labour, *Ninth Annual Report on Labour Organization in Canada*, Ottawa, King's Printer, 1920, p. 26.)

CONSTITUTION AND LAWS
OF THE
FARMERS UNION OF CANADA

Central Office at Ituna, Sask.

Modern industrial society is divided into two classes — those who possess and do not produce and those who produce. Along side this main division all other classifications fade into insignificance. Between two classes a continuous struggle takes place. As with buyers and sellers of any commodity, there exists a struggle on the one hand — of the buyer to buy as cheaply as possible, and on the other, of the seller to sell for as much as possible. In the struggle over the purchase and sale of farm produce the buyers are always masters — the sellers always workers. From this fact arises the inevitable class struggle.

As industry develops and ownership becomes concentrated more and more into fewer hands, as the control of economic forces of society become more and more the sole property of finance, it becomes apparent that the farmers, in order to sell their produce with any degree of success, must extend their form of organisation in accordance with changing methods. Compelled to organize for self-defence, they are further compelled to educate themselves in preparation for the social change which economic developments will produce whether they seek it or not.

The Farmers' Union of Canada, therefore, seeks to organize the farmers and calls upon all bonafide farmers to organize, irrespective of nationality or sex, into a farmers organization, so that they may be enabled to fix their own price above cost of production, a price reasonable towards producer and consumer.

Farmers and workers of the world unite.

NAME

Clause I

 The name of the organisation shall be the Farmers Union of Canada.

Clause II

 To protect the farmer. To obtain complete control of the main Canadian produce. To market our crops under our own system. To affiliate with all the farmer organizations of the world, with one central executive in each country, which will fix prices according to a fair average of estimates sent in by the locals, will through the same source also know amount of marketable produce in the country; will have to *keep informed as to the demands and needs of importing countries, and will also help to prevent the re-occurrence of famine by knowing ahead of time where and when food will be needed, and then insist towards the different governments with the full support of farmers and workers combined that the Governments shall do what they are there for; attend to the welfare of the masses of the people.*

Clause III

If the Execution [sic] Board thinks certain steps are necessary to the welfare of the farmers, the conditions will have to be put before the farmer members and decided by a vote of the members of the Farmers' Union of Canada. If the majority is in favor of certain decisions every member of the Farmers Union of Canada binds himself to unconditionally obey the orders of the executive of the Union.

MEMBERSHIP FEE

Clause IV

The yearly membership fee shall be $1.00 which must be paid before a member is entitled to vote.

Clause V

Membership cards shall be issued stating local by which they were issued.

CENTRAL EXECUTIVE BOARD

Clause VI

A Central Executive board shall be elected from the floor of the Convention, consisting of five members. The Executive Committee shall elect their own chairman and secretary.

Clause VII

The Central Executive Board shall remain in office until their successors are elected. The wages of the officers of the Central Executive Board engaged in work for the organisation, shall be .... per week. Expenses of organisers when away from home shall be .... per day, and railroad expenses. Secretary's wages to be .... per week.

Clause VIII

The general headquarters shall be located at such place as may be decided by the Annual Convention, subject to the approval of the membership.

Clause IX

The members of the Central Executive Board may act as general organisers or in a consultative capacity. All mem-

bers of the Central Executive Board acting as organisers shall be at all times under the direction of the Central Executive Board. All members of the Central Executive Board acting as organisers must send in duplicate financial and written reports twice a month of each local formed, and remit one to secretary of new local.

Clause X

It shall be the duty of the chairman of the Central Executive Board to preside at all meetings of the Board. He shall have charge of, and be responsible for, the general administration of the organization.

Clause XI

It shall be the duty of the Central Secretary to keep a true account of all monies paid out; he shall deposit all monies or cheques received by him in such a bank or banks as may be named by the Central Executive Board; he shall be at all times in a position to render to the Central Executive Board an account of the financial position of the organisation. He shall render to the Central Executive Board a yearly financial report duly certified by an auditor. He shall keep the minutes of all meetings of the Central Executive Board in book provided for that purpose; he shall pay all bills when satisfied of their correctness, and shall sign all cheques; he shall be bonded in a responsible surety company for the sum of .... and the bond shall be approved of and paid for by the Central Executive Board.

RECALL

Clause XII

A member holding office on the Central Executive Board must at all times maintain his credentials from his local unit to the Convention. Any local unit withdrawing the credentials of an Executive Board member shall notify the Central Executive Board of their action, and the Central Executive Board shall immediately make a full investigation for the benefit of the membership.

Clause XIII

Any officer of the Farmers Union of Canada may be recalled by a majority vote of the district which sent said officer to the Convention, and to the Central Executive Board; or by a majority vote of the local if a local official.

Clause XIV

> When vacancies occur on the Central Executive Board it shall be the duty of the Central Executive Board to fill said vacancies and if advisable from which the previous member was elected [*sic*].

Clause XV

> Meetings to determine the recall of any officer, whether of local unit or Central Executive Board must be specially summoned, all members being notified by their respective secretaries.

CONVENTIONS

Clause XVI

> This organisation shall meet in Convention annually, the Convention call to be issued by the Central Executive Board.

Clause XVII

> The Convention shall consist of one delegate from each local, if wanted, or one delegate from a District Board.

Clause XVIII

> A District Board shall be defined as a delegated body elected in certain districts when found necessary. They are subject to the same privileges and restrictions as any other officials of the Farmers' Union of Canada.

Clause XIX

> Any local must be in good financial standing towards the Central Executive Board for at least 30 days prior to the convening of the Convention in order to secure representations.

Clause XX

> Any section, which as a result of unfavorable conditions is unable to pay per capita tax, may be exempted therefrom by the Central Executive Board and shall be eligible for representation at the Convention.

Clause XXI

> The General Secretary shall compile a list of delegates from the credentials in his possession upon which no protests have been received, and these delegates shall compose the Convention.

Clause XXII

> Each Convention shall fix the locality for the succeeding Conventions, date to be left in the hands of the Central Executive Board.

ELECTION OF ALL LOCAL OFFICERS

Clause XXIII

> The election of new local officers shall take place every year on the 6th day of December.

PER CAPITA

Clause XXIV

> Per capita tax to the Central Executive Board of the Farmers' Union of Canada shall be 50 cents per year which shall be paid through the locals.

Clause XXV

> All locals shall issue a yearly financial statement, one copy of which shall be sent to the Central Executive Board. On the failure of any branch to send in a financial report (after 30 days notice from the Central Executive Board) then the next highest authority shall have the right to audit the books of the delinquent branch.

Clause XXVI

> All funds maintained by the local units shall be the property of the members composing said local unit.

Clause XXVII

> All amendments to the Constitution shall be submitted to a referendum vote of the membership within 30 days after the adjournment of the Convention, except when the conditions warrant an extension of time.

Clause XXVIII

> Delegates to the Convention are warned against making useless amendments, but to employ their time to obtain the welfare of the farmers and the public in general.

Clause XXIX

> No person being a Government official shall hold an office in the Farmers' Union of Canada.

Clause XXX

> Only bona-fide farmers are allowed to join the Farmers' Union of Canada.

The Saskatchewan Relief Commission, 1931-34[1]

Blair Neatby

Saskatchewan has traditionally been a land of optimism. During the first three decades of the present century, the province had progressed from an era of immigration and development to a prosperous war period and then to an optimistic time of post-war expansion. The intervening transition periods were brief and soon forgotten. The farmers, to be sure, had experienced a variety of natural hazards, such as drought, grasshoppers, and rust, but these problems were usually local and infrequent. It was almost taken for granted that "next year" would compensate for such losses. This complacency was rudely shaken in the 1930s by an unprecedented succession of calamities. The grim repetition of crop losses gradually weakened the normal optimism. A combination of circumstances finally proved that the seven lean years were possible even in Saskatchewan.

Several factors were responsible for this catastrophe. First and foremost was the drought. The average rainfall from 1929 to 1937 was far below normal, and hot, dry winds aggravated the situation. Special complications, such as grasshoppers in 1933 and rust in 1935, took their toll. To make matters worse, there was little demand for farm produce in world markets, and prices dropped rapidly.[2] Thus the unfortunate combination of

SOURCE: *Saskatchewan History*, vol. III, no. 2 (Spring, 1950), pp. 41-56. Reprinted by permission of the author and publishers.

[1] The main sources used in preparing this article are the Saskatchewan Relief Commission (hereafter cited as the S.R.C.) records and correspondence in the Saskatchewan Archives and the minutes of the Commission, in the Relief Revenue Branch of the Treasury Department (microfilm copy in the Saskatchewan Archives). For some specific details the writer is indebted to interviews with the following: Mr. Henry Black, former chairman of the Commission; Mr. M. A. MacPherson, K.C., former Provincial-Treasurer and Attorney-General; Mr. G. M. MacLeod of the Department of Co-operation and Co-operative Development; and Mr. T. Lax, former Deputy Provincial-Treasurer.

[2] In 1932, wheat dropped to the lowest price in 300 years: W. A. Mackintosh, *Economic Problems of the Prairie Provinces* (Toronto, 1935), p. 188.

reduced production and lower prices meant that farm income in Saskatchewan threatened to disappear entirely.[3] The effect was even more disastrous because it was unexpected.

So serious was the plight of many farmers that their initial problem was one of survival. Even such necessities as food, clothing, and fuel were beyond their income. Furthermore the continuing depression soon made local credit arrangements impossible. Aid had to come from the government for these essentials. But the farmers also had to make financial arrangements for seeding and harvesting before they could become re-established. Here again the government proved to be the only available source of credit. Government assistance, or relief, soon became a huge and apparently permanent undertaking.

Previously, relief had normally been considered a local problem, and the rural municipalities were held responsible for the care of indigents. Thus, in 1929, the municipalities had accepted the burden of relief. When conditions showed no improvement in the subsequent years, however, they could not stand the financial strain. Since the municipalities were unable to collect many taxes, and since their borrowing power was very limited by the adverse conditions, the only alternative was to turn to the provincial government for help. The latter was also experiencing some difficulty since such important sources of revenue as gasoline and liquor taxes were affected by prevailing economic conditions. Nevertheless, the province did for a time try to assist the municipalities with their relief problem without turning to the Dominion government for aid.

The crop conditions of 1931, however, made it obvious that a very widespread relief program would be necessary. Almost all of Saskatchewan south of Saskatoon was in the crop failure area![4] In such an emergency financial assistance from the Federal government was required. But this presented a new problem. Since this relief covered such a wide area, and was to be financed from various sources, how was its distribution to be supervised? A proclamation of the Lieutenant-Governor on August 25, 1931, answered the question. A Saskatchewan Relief Commission was appointed for the "purpose of relieving distress and providing employment,"[5] to which all relief agencies of the

---

[3] According to E. W. Stapleford, *Report on Rural Relief* (Ottawa, 1939), p. 26. The total Saskatchewan wheat income for the years 1922-29 was $1,559 millions and for the years 1930-37 was $449 millions!

[4] *Ibid.*, Map, p. 31.

[5] *Saskatchewan Gazette*, September 5, 1931.

provincial government were to be transferred.[6] Apparently it was felt that this non-political supervising body would ensure an equitable distribution of relief, and that by centralizing its administration, duplication of work would be eliminated. Thus the Commission was expected to be both just and efficient. The actual results of this system should be revealed by our study.

The Saskatchewan Relief Commission consisted of five members, with Mr. Henry Black as chairman.[7] These members, who received no remuneration, were to be responsible for formulating the policies of the Commission. Mr. C. B. Daniel, who was appointed General Manager, was the responsible administrative officer. The Commission was concerned only with rural relief, which, of course, was expected to be a temporary problem. However, after each harvest it was found necessary to continue relief in certain areas, and consequently the Commission dealt with this "emergency" for three years in various parts of the province.

In its first year, 1931-1932, the Relief Commission administered relief to a very extensive area. The worst region, known as the "A" area, with three years of consecutive crop failures, was composed of 95 municipalities roughly grouped in a triangle, with the apex near Watrous and the base stretching from Torquay to Frontier. East and West of this triangle were 77 "B" area municipalities with two years of consecutive crop failures. Then came 68 municipalities comprising the "C" area with one year of crop failure. The next year relief was mainly restricted to a large part of the "A" area. In the final year, however, relief again had to be administered over a large area. There were 75 municipalities included in the "A" area, then in their fifth consecutive year of crop failure. The "B" area included 128 other municipalities. However, the various classifications of these areas do not indicate different administrative policies but only a different method of financing the relief. The system of administering relief was quite uniform throughout the whole relief area.

For the first year the Commission hired relief officers in

---

[6] Editorial, *Regina Leader-Post*, August 14, 1931, when the Commission was first announced.

[7] Members were: Mr. Henry Black, Chairman; Mrs. Pearl Johnston, Mr. A. E. Whitmore, Mr. W. G. Yule, and Mr. W. A. Munns. A cabinet minister, usually the Provincial-Treasurer or Minister of Agriculture, attended most of the meetings. Interviews with Mr. Black and Mr. MacPherson indicate that these members were selected to represent various political attitudes in the province.

each municipality under its jurisdiction, to act as its local administrative officials. These men were assisted by voluntary local relief committees appointed by the Commission. By thus eliminating the use of municipal councils for relief administration it was hoped to avoid any influence of municipal politics or local prejudices.[8] The duties of the relief officer were "to receive, investigate and report on applications for relief by rural municipality residents."[9] The relief committees were appointed for the purpose of "assisting in the proper carrying out of the Saskatchewan Relief Commission programme in the municipalities, and advising the Commission with respect to the same." The next year, however, with the system functioning smoothly, and with a reduced program of relief, it was decided to use the municipal councils for field administration, thus eliminating both the relief officers and the relief committees. This new system proved satisfactory, and so it was continued for the 1933-1934 season.[10] In each of the three years, these local administrative units were assisted by supervisors appointed by the Commission who were to co-operate with them "in an effort to conduct an efficient and economical administration."[11] The supervisors, in turn, were dependent upon the field service department of the Commission for instructions and supervision. In this way, the policies of the Commission were quite uniformly administered throughout the province.

This uniformity naturally depended upon the completion of a variety of applications, schedules, and requisitions. The basic form, however, was the "Application for Relief," which a farmer had to complete before becoming entitled to any type of relief. The usual routine information was required — marital status, number of children, description of land and buildings. In addition there was a "Statement of Affairs" showing the assets and liabilities of the applicant. The relief officer appended some general remarks and stated his opinion as to the necessity for relief. The relief committee then did the same. If both approved the application it was then passed by an approval board of the Commission. Later the form was somewhat simplified and required the approval of the municipal council and the supervisor. The final approval of an Application for Relief did not neces-

---

[8] Mr. C. B. Daniel, "Summary of the Activities of the Saskatchewan Relief Commission," p. 2 (hereafter cited as Summary); microfilm copy in the Saskatchewan Archives.

[9] Minutes of S.R.C., August 20, 1931.

[10] Minutes of S.R.C., August 29, 1933.

[11] S.R.C. General Policy file — circulars.

sarily mean that the applicant was entitled to all forms of relief. The approval was qualified, and indicated which type of relief was to be granted. This meant that any combination of food, clothing, fuel, fodder, or seed might be granted to an applicant. The basis of approval, however, was a simple one in all cases: necessity was to be the only criterion.

The Application for Relief also included an undertaking to repay all the relief received from the Commission. It was hoped that this would remove any stigma of charity, and so encourage people to accept relief rather than suffer in silence. On the other hand, it was hoped that the necessity of repayment would prevent any unnecessary applications. Nevertheless, this relief could not be considered a form of short term credit. Relief officers were specifically warned not to let this promise to pay "influence you in your efforts to see that only applications for necessities receive your approval."[12] On the other hand, applicants who were not expected to repay their relief advances were not to be refused on that account. The promise of repayment was never allowed to influence the approval of an application.

However, even after the Application for Relief was finally approved, relief might be stopped abruptly in certain cases. Information that an applicant had undisclosed sources of revenue, such as a pension or a secret hoard of grain, or that the applicant had refused to accept a suitable job, resulted in an investigation. If a relief recipient was operating a car, relief orders were withheld until the Commission was convinced that the car was necessary. As the General Manager explained, "If an applicant is able to pay for a license and the consequent operation of the car, for purposes other than strictly business, he should be able to at least care for his food requirements." The Commission was even more positively opposed to the consumption of liquor. Any applicant who was known to have purchased liquor, even a few glasses of beer, was struck off relief immediately.[13] Even though the Commission's information about such irregularities was very incomplete, such a clearly formulated policy probably prevented many flagrant violations of its principle of aid for the needy only.

While the elaborate method of approving applications did ensure a uniform and just administration, it also had the typical fault of a bureaucratic system. A long delay between the application and the authorization for relief was inevitable. In some

[12] *Ibid.*
[13] S.R.C. General Manager's Correspondence – Stop Orders file.

cases, this might have been disastrous. For instance, an early spell of cold weather might make the immediate distribution of coal necessary. To prevent any suffering from delay in such cases, the local relief officials were allowed to use their own initiative, subject to certain restrictions. They were permitted to issue "Emergency Relief Orders" for ten dollars' worth of food or for one ton of coal without any specific authorization from the Commission. This irregular method was to be used in emergencies only, however, and Applications for Relief from the recipients were to be forwarded to the Commission immediately.

Once the Applications for Relief were safely on file, relief could be distributed in an organized manner. Of primary importance was the distribution of such essentials as food, clothing, and fuel. Handled in separate departments for the first two years, this relief was finally consolidated in the direct relief department of the Commission. The work of this department was quite seasonal, since clothing and fuel were mainly winter requirements, and summer gardens were expected to reduce food orders. During the winter, however, the proper organization of this distribution was important enough to merit detailed consideration.

The method of handling direct relief illustrates a basic policy of the Relief Commission, that of avoiding any disruption of the normal business routine in the province. All forms of relief merchandise were issued through the usual channels instead of directly by the Commission. All food and clothing orders bore a merchant's name, and only he was allowed to fill the orders. In this way the retail merchants were able to continue in business through the depression. This system required a great deal of organization and patience. The applicant named his merchant on the Application for Relief, but the Commission was continually being requested to change the name on orders they had issued. These changes wasted a good deal of time and were often unnecessary. Many requests were simply the result of other merchants' solicitations. To prevent this, the Commission finally refused to change the merchant's name without the written consent of its local representative. Many merchants, however, felt that they had a legitimate complaint. Some of their former customers, to whom they had made substantial advances, had decided to change merchants. The Commission agreed that the creditor merchant should retain the patronage of their debtors, and refused to authorize such changes. As a result of these efforts, most of the local merchants retained their regular customers. The success of the policy of the Commission in using normal business channels is vouched for by the fact that the retail merchants were able to stay in business through the depression.

The merchants, however, did not obtain this assistance completely free of obligations. Before they could even qualify for the privilege of filling relief orders, they had to prove that they had not gone into business just to take advantage of such an authorization. Furthermore, general merchants were only authorized to handle relief orders for food and clothing if their stock warranted it. Even after receiving such an authorization the merchants found that the Commission's restrictions were comprehensive. For instance, the Commission set the prices for all articles supplied on relief orders. These prices were based on wholesale prices arranged for a certain *quality* of goods, and allowed the retail merchant fifteen to twenty percent profit. Most of the merchants had to accept a loss on their original stock by selling at these lower prices in order to dispose of it. Generally the merchants were very co-operative. There are incidents on file, however, where a merchant charged higher prices, or where a merchant substituted cash or luxury goods instead of staple merchandise for relief orders.[14] Such infractions of the regulations meant that the merchant's authorizations were withdrawn — a severe punishment in the drought area.

Nevertheless, even the use of the retail merchants' facilities did not completely solve the distribution problem. For example, what food and how much food should a relief applicant receive? The original relief order form listed the goods which were to be supplied, and the prices of these goods. These forms were mailed to the recipient, honoured by the merchant, and then cashed at the local bank.[15] This entailed detailed preparation by the Commission, and the handling of many small items at the bank. The form finally adopted was a food delivery order. These orders merely indicated the total value of the food to be supplied. The merchants, having been sent a list of authorized foods and maximum prices, could then fill the order as the relief recipient desired. The merchant usually forwarded these orders to his wholesaler in payment. Then, on certain settlement dates, the Commission issued a cheque for the total amount received from the wholesaler. This system not only reduced the work of the Commission but also provided more flexibility for the re-

---

[14] S.R.C. Food Department — Merchant file.
[15] S.R.C. Food Department — Policy file.

cipient. The food relief system of one of the urban centres in Saskatchewan offers an interesting comparison.[16] This centre set up a relief store from which all relief recipients were supplied with a specific weekly ration. The long list of complaints and petitions indicate the weaknesses of the system: the local merchants objected because they lost their customers; those on relief complained about the inconvenience of having to deal at this store, and claimed that they could get their food cheaper elsewhere; worst of all, there was a good deal of waste because the weekly ration, scientific though it may have been, was not suitable for every recipient — many, for instance, would have traded their tea ration for oatmeal, but this was not permitted. The system of the Saskatchewan Relief Commission at least managed to eliminate most of these problems, and satisfy both the applicant and the merchant.

The method of distributing flour indicates another important policy of the Commission. Flour was not included in the food orders but was supplied on separate flour orders. The large mills in Saskatchewan supplied most of the flour handled by the Commission. Local dealers, authorized by the Commission, then distributed this flour for a small commission. This system, however, threatened to eliminate the smaller mills, and so special arrangements had to be made. When one of the local mills had submitted a satisfactory sample of their flour to the Commission, and reached a price agreement, flour orders on this mill were issued to all applicants within a radius of fifteen miles.[17] Thus, relief applicants were assured of satisfactory flour at a reasonable price. But in addition, this meant that the products of local mills were assured a market. This policy, early enunciated,[18] of giving preference to Saskatchewan- and Canadian-made goods was adhered to throughout the life of the Commission.

The long Saskatchewan winters made clothing another important relief item. Previous to the organization of the Saskatchewan Relief Commission, the Red Cross had distributed clothing with financial assistance from the provincial government. In the fall of 1931, the Commission became responsible for supplying the "A" and "B" areas,[19] while the Red Cross continued to supply the rest of the province. In February, 1932,

[16] S.R.C. Special Cases — City file.

[17] *Regina Leader-Post*, March 21, 1934.

[18] *Canadian Annual Review* (1932), p. 260.

[19] See page 269.

however, the Red Cross turned over its accounts and its store of clothing to the Commission. The Red Cross was paid for the clothing it had distributed, and the recipients were charged for the amount they had received. The Commission then assumed responsibility for the distribution of clothing throughout the relief area.[20] The Commission supplied only the most necessary articles of clothing and even these in limited quantities.[21] After mid-winter, clothing requisitions had to be investigated by the local relief officer before being authorized by the Commission. Clothing was seldom provided during the summer months. Unfortunately, as the depression continued, individual requirements increased because the reserves of old clothing gradually disappeared. Bedding offers a good example of this. The Commission had never supplied bedding material, but it was not until the winter of 1933-34 that the shortage of bedding became serious. This special problem was dealt with in the most seriously stricken areas by co-operation with voluntary local groups. The Commission provided the piece goods and materials for quilts and bedding, and the local groups made and distributed the articles. The recipients were then charged with the cost of the materials.[22] In this way it was hoped to minimize expenses and also to foster local initiative.

The other winter problem was supplying fuel. Like food, coal was first issued by means of relief orders and later by delivery orders, although no dealer's name was included in the form.[23] Any authorized dealer could fill an order, receiving a small handling charge per ton. Preference, of course, was given to Saskatchewan coal,[24] except in Western Saskatchewan where freight rates made Alberta coal more economical. In spite of complaints about the lignite coal, this policy was never seriously modified. When distances were short, applicants were urged to haul coal from the minehead of small mines in the south-east. If the applicant could obtain coal on his own property, the Commission was quite willing to aid him to the extent

---

[20] S.R.C. – Clothing Department – Policy file.

[21] *Ibid.*
   e.g. Schedule for clothing and footwear 1933-34:

Adult	Boy	Girl	Infant
$9.00	$6.25	$5.25	$2.50

   Maximum for largest family – $75.00.

[22] S.R.C. General Policy file.

[23] S.R.C. Fuel Department – Policy file.

[24] *Ibid.* Normally the ration was three tons of Saskatchewan coal to one ton of Alberta coal.

of paying the royalty of 25c per ton. However, coal was never distributed in areas where a natural supply of wood was available. Thus the fuel policy is an excellent illustration of the economy exercised by the Relief Commission. It ensured an adequate supply of fuel for its relief recipients, but it arbitrarily decided the source and type of fuel to be used in order to reduce expenses.

This distribution of direct relief was supplemented by charitable people throughout Canada. Church organizations, fraternities, welfare groups, distant friends, and generous individuals rallied to help the impoverished areas. During the three years of the Relief Commission, 577 carloads of fruit, vegetables, and clothing were donated and distributed.[25] Even large quantities of flower seeds and bulbs were contributed, and proved to be a very acceptable gift. The two railway companies greatly assisted by waiving all freight charges on these donations. So important were these various donations, it was found necessary to organize the Saskatchewan Voluntary Relief Committee, with local committees throughout the relief area. These small groups were responsible for an equitable distribution of the various donations. The central committee co-operated with the Commission to supervise the delivery and eliminate duplication.[26] Thus, by means of direct relief and donations, extreme suffering was averted. It is probably safe to say that at least a standard of living sufficient to maintain health and working efficiency prevailed in the areas under the administration of the Commission.[27]

In spite of the importance of the direct relief distributed, it is interesting to note that this only amounted to 36.4 percent of the total expenditures of the Commission, the balance being devoted to re-establishing the farmers.[28] For instance, it was necessary to ensure the survival of livestock and poultry. The extended drought had done more than prevent the growing of cash crops; it had also prevented the harvesting of coarse grains

[25] E. W. Stapleford, *op cit.*, p. 52.

[26] S.R.C. General Manager's Correspondence – Donations file.

[27] This is partially substantiated by the following mortality rates from the *Canada Year Book*, 1933-34, p. 161:
5-year averages of mortality rates per 1000 in Saskatchewan:

1921-25	1926-30	1931-35	1936-40
7.5	7.3	6.5	7.0

[28] Based on figures from the *Saskatchewan Brief to the Royal Commission on Dominion-Provincial Relations* (Regina, 1937), p. 184.
Direct Relief – $12,924,769
Total Relief – $35,536,829

and hay, and had ruined much of the pasturage.[29] Consequently feed and fodder were very scarce commodities. This, incidentally, involved the danger of starving livestock and also the problem of fodder prices increasing until they were out of line with the low value of livestock. Such problems became the responsibility of the Commission's feed and fodder department.

Local transfers of feed and fodder were naturally the most suitable solution. Wherever possible an approved applicant obtained his requirements from a neighbour. The latter then was paid by a cheque from the Commission, or, if he had received relief, his relief indebtedness was reduced by that amount. It was only in 1932-33, however, that conditions were favorable for the general use of local transfers, for in that season widespread rains had meant that most municipalities could supply their own needs. In the other two years' drought and grasshoppers made more expensive measures necessary.

In the case of fodder there were two possible solutions, viz., to ship the fodder to the livestock, or the livestock to the fodder, Both methods were used. For the first year the Department of Agriculture arranged for the purchase and loading of large quantities of fodder for the Commission, and the Commission then organized its shipment and distribution. By 1932-33, the feed and fodder department had taken over the entire responsibility.[30] By means of large-scale purchases and freight concessions, huge quantities of fodder[31] were distributed at reasonable prices. In many cases, however, where no local fodder or pasturage whatever were available, it was found advisable to ship the livestock north to winter feeding areas. In 1934 the situation was so acute, due to grasshoppers, that some carloads were even sent north for summer pasturage.[32] Incidentally, haying outfits were also assisted to go north to procure a supply of fodder. By these various methods, the necessary minimum of fodder was obtained.

This fodder, however, had to be supplemented by feed grain. Even in winter, some feed grain was desirable, and for the spring work it was essential. Like fodder, however, feed grain was scarce and likely to be expensive. Procuring this feed

[29] Minutes of S.R.C. — General Manager's Report — January 26, 1932.

[30] S.R.C. — General Manager's Correspondence — Department of Agriculture file.

[31] Summary, p. 12, states that the total fodder distribution amounted to 216,090 tons.

[33] A total of 1831 carloads were shipped north. Saskatchewan Archives: Livestock Branch correspondence *re* winter feeding.

became the responsibility of the grain purchasing department. The estimated requirements were protected by purchasing futures on the Winnipeg market, thus preventing any exorbitant prices being charged. The department also had the foresight to freeze the estimated requirements of feed grain in the local elevators every fall, and so prevent its shipment to the lake-head. There is little doubt that this prevented the payment of freight both ways in many cases. Large quantities of feed were purchased — eleven million bushels of feed oats and barley in the first year alone![33] Even so, this amount proved inadequate and it became necessary to distribute some wheat as feed in spite of the risk involved. Constructive policies were also in-augurated to ease the situation. Some seed rye was distributed in the fall to produce a fodder crop, and in 1934 seed corn was distributed because of the grasshopper threat. These steps were taken on the advice of the Department of Agriculture and in-dicate the close co-operation with this department. In spite of all these efforts, however, feed, and fodder remained a serious problem. Due to limited supplies the estimated require-ments submitted by municipal councils were never completely filled. On the other hand, the rumours of vast numbers of live-stock starving to death are certainly greatly exaggerated. Al-though many animals had to be sold, the Commission did make it possible for most farmers to keep the necessary minimum of livestock on the farm.

Another vital problem of agricultural rehabilitation con-cerned seed grain. Few farmers in the drought area could pur-chase seed, and yet only by growing grain could they become re-established. Thus, supplying seed grain became another responsibility of the Commission, and of the grain purchasing department in particular. The size of this undertaking can be judged from the fact that over fourteen million bushels of seed grain were distributed in the three year period.[34] As was the case with feed, all local stocks of seed grain were frozen by the Commission, and when even this failed to produce enough seed oats, a premium of two or three cents a bushel was offered. Whenever necessary, the Commission arranged to have grain cleaned to make it suitable for seed. However, the Commission never forgot that its function was to relieve distress only. For example, in cases where farmers had sold all their grain in the fall without making any arrangements for seed, the Commis-

[33] S.R.C. — Grain Purchasing Department — Policy file.
[34] *Ibid.*, Report of Department 1933-34.

sion declared that it would provide no assistance. Furthermore, in 1934 a maximum of only 300 bushels of wheat and 100 bushels of oats per applicant was allowed for seed, because it was felt that this would be sufficient to provide a living under normal conditions.[85] Nevertheless, the seed policy of the Commission exhibited some flexibility. In cases where seeded land had suffered from wind erosion, grain for re-seeding was provided if weather conditions were at all favourable. But it was quite obvious that even supplying all the seed for the destitute farmers was not enough. The seed still had to be planted.

Seeding operations presented a variety of problems. The use of old machinery presented one complication. New equipment was out of the question, and even machinery or harness repairs were beyond the means of many. As an emergency measure, the Commission financed some black-smithing and machinery repairs. The applicant first had to state he would otherwise be unable to complete seeding, and even then the recipient seldom received assistance in excess of $10.00.[36] A more universal problem, of course, was the need for feed and fodder for seeding operations. This was supplied by the Commission as before. Tractor-farmers, however, needed large quantities of fuel and lubricants. These petroleum products were also supplied but, like repairs, only as an emergency measure.[37]

These seed and seeding operations of the Commission were financed by a separate arrangement. The funds were provided by the provincial governments by means of loans from the Dominion government. The applicants were expected to repay the advances from their crop, and seed grain liens were taken as a guarantee, covering crops grown that year and in the succeeding year.[38] Collecting from the farmers in the fall became the responsibility of the local elevator agents. The latter were issued printed collection books showing the indebtedness of each farmer. The farmer was allowed a maximum of $100.00 to meet threshing expenses, but after that the agent was expected to remit enough storage tickets to the Commission to cover the lien.[39] The Commission, however, seems to have been a lenient creditor. For the first year it even credited the farmers with a set price well above the market price, for grain turned

[85] *Ibid.*, circulars.
[36] S.R.C. – Fuel Department – Twine and Repairs file.
[37] S.R.C. – Fuel Department – Policy file.
[38] *Statutes of Saskatchewan*, 1932, Cap. 74, Sec. 8.
[39] S.R.C. – Field Men Correspondence – Collection Inspectors file.

over to it.[40] The rural municipalities were also allowed to collect a year's taxes first, although the lien had priority. Finally, if the farmers were not in a financial condition to cover the lien, an extension was readily granted. The leniency, made necessary by the very unfavorable crop conditions, meant that many liens were still in effect until their cancellation in 1937.[41] After seeding, the farmers were faced with the problem of summerfallowing. The Commission, however, offered no assistance, since it considered that relief was an emergency measure and not concerned with next year's crop.[42] Harvesting also presented financial difficulties to many farmers. Binder twine and binder repairs presented a serious problem in that "pre-combine" era. In 1932 the Relief Commission, with considerable reluctance, decided it was necessary to distribute twine and repairs in cases where no other method of financing was possible.[43] A total of almost $800,000 was advanced for this purpose.[44] The loans were expected to be short-term loans, and wholesale firms supplied the twine and repairs on credit. Payment was slow, however, and two years later ten percent of the advances was still outstanding.[45] The Commission never financed harvesting operations again. It was felt that the necessary short-term loans could be procured from a bank or by an arrangement between the municipalities and the cordage companies. The Commission decided that its obligation ended with the sowing of the crop.

We have now considered the administration of both direct relief and of agricultural aid. One might expect that this would cover all the activities of the Relief Commission. But, as the Commissioners discovered, there was still a variety of special problems to cope with. Further assistance was necessary to relieve distress in Saskatchewan.

Medical aid for the rural indigents is one example of these problems. Very little medical aid was given directly to individuals. Extra fruit might be issued on food orders, for those requiring a special diet, but such cases were usually referred to the Red Cross or the Governor-General's Emergency Distress Fund.[46] But it soon became obvious that even normal

[40] S.R.C. – Grain Purchasing Department – Policy file.
[41] *Statutes of Saskatchewan*, 1937, Cap. 92, Sec. 28.
[42] S.R.C. – General Policy file.
[43] S.R.C. – Fuel Department – Twine and Repairs file.
[44] S.R.C. – Fuel Department – Policy file.
[45] Summary, p. 13.
[46] S.R.C. – General Manager Correspondence – Charitable organization file.

medical services could not be maintained without some financial assistance. In many areas, doctors, dentists, and hospitals were not receiving sufficient money to cover routine expenses. A system of government grants was arranged so that these essential services could be continued. Doctors and dentists in the relief area submitted monthly returns to the Commission showing their work and their income. The Department of Public Health then advised the Commission whether they merited the grant. For the first winter, the maximum individual monthly payments to doctors and dentists were $75.00 and $25.00 respectively. These amounts were later reduced, but some grant was made every winter.[47] Hospitals were also given a grant to enable them to maintain services, usually amounting to 25c a day for each relief patient.[48] These various grants were not given as a subsidy, but rather as a contribution to help meet necessary expenses. The total amount of these grants did not constitute a very imposing figure,[49] but in many cases, medical services would have been impossible without them.

Another serious problem was rural education. The Saskatchewan winters were responsible for a good deal of this trouble. Many of the clothing requests on file indicate that the children were not properly clothed to walk to school during the winter.[50] Any such cases reported were investigated, and clothing was issued if necessary. Fuel for the schools presented another problem. Many school districts could not afford to buy fuel, and might have had to close down their schools without some assistance. Some carloads of coal were donated by Estevan mines; the rest had to be purchased by the Commission.[51] Still more serious was the plight of many teachers. In many areas taxes were uncollectable, and the only school income was the government grant. Frequently the teachers did not receive enough to pay their board. In such cases, the Commission provided direct relief for the teachers, to be repaid when their salary arrears were met.[52] In this way it was at least possible for them to continue teaching.

There were also special agricultural problems to be considered. For instance, gopher poison, formerly a municipal problem, could no longer be financed by many municipalities.

[47] S.R.C. – Special cases – Doctors and dentists files.
[48] Ibid., Hospital file.
[49] $235,788 according to E. W. Stapleford; op. cit., p. 41.
[50] S.R.C. – General Manager's Correspondence – Complaints file.
[51] Expenditures by Commission: $87,223.26 (Summary, p. 14).
[52] S.R.C. – Special cases – Teachers' file.

In 1932 the Commission advanced some municipalities a certain proportion of the cost of the gopher poison, to be repaid in the fall. Collections were very poor, and the Commission discontinued this form of assistance. The grasshopper menace, however, could not be ignored. By 1934 grasshopper infestation had become very widespread. Although the grasshopper campaign was organized and supervised by the Department of Agriculture, the Commission gave its close co-operation. Seed was provided only for summerfallow, which was more likely to be free of grasshopper eggs. The Commission also provided the feed and fuel necessary for guardstripping and plowing. This again indicates the close co-operation between the government departments and the Relief Commission.

Another complicating factor in relief administration was the northward migration from the dried-out areas. Hundreds of despondent families decided to make a new start in Northern Saskatchewan. These people were allowed to ship two carloads of goods out of the drought area at no charge, the administrative arrangements being the responsibility of the traffic department of the Relief Commission.[53] Naturally, these people had no immediate source of income after their arrival. Some time would elapse before buildings could be erected and land cleared, and in the meantime relief was required. This meant an extension of the relief area northwards. The supervisors who were appointed to these northern areas found that issuing emergency food relief orders to the scattered settlers was the most satisfactory system.[54] Since the few stores in the area seldom carried a stock of clothing, clothing requisitions were filled by mail-order houses. Arrangements were made to obtain repayment of these relief advances by means of relief work. The Department of Highways organized the building of pioneer roads in the north, using relief recipients as laborers, two-thirds of the wages being in the form of a credit against their tax arrears or relief. In 1933, a special survey was made of these northern settlers by the supervisors, and whenever possible they were encouraged to deliver wood to the nearest railway in payment for relief. This wood was then distributed as relief fuel in needy areas. In this way, the cost of re-establishing these settlers was considerably reduced.

[53] Freight charges were divided among the provincial and the Dominion governments and the railway. Order-in-Council, P.C. 989.
[54] In areas as far north as Cumberland House, the R.C.M.P. were authorized to issue emergency orders to needy families. See S.R.C. – Relief Applications – R.C.M.P. file.

An entirely different problem was presented by the group classified as "single, homeless and unemployed." This type of relief was financed by the Dominion government, but the Relief Commission became responsible for its administration in November, 1932. Relief for this group, which comprised only the physically fit, was provided by two methods. As many men as possible were provided with winter employment on farms where the farmer needed help but could not pay wages. The government paid the laborer $5.00 a month, and the farmer provided the room and board. Women were permitted to work as domestics under the same arrangement. The men for whom no farm work was available were sent to relief camps and, later, were employed on construction projects under the Department of Militia and Defence. Unsatisfactory as such camps were, they at least provided an alternative to the life of a transient.

Transient families, however, presented a problem quite different to that of the "single, homeless and unemployed." Many of these families left non-productive farms and drifted to urban centres. Shacks of scrap lumber and cardboard mushroomed up in such areas as North Regina and Sherwood Annex. Since these people could seldom establish the necessary self-sustaining residence for six months and so become bona fide residents of the municipality, the provincial government had to assume full responsibility for their relief. Since these people, unlike rural applicants, could not supply their own meat, milk, or eggs, an entirely different schedule of relief was necessary which was eventually adjusted to conform to the local urban relief schedule, including such items as light, water, and rental allowances.[55] A few families took advantage of a $300 loan scheme to become established on a northern farm,[56] but most of them decided to remain on relief until urban employment was available.

The foregoing details give some indication of the comprehensive nature of the rural relief administered by the Commission. Direct relief, agricultural aid, and special problems – all of these presented unique difficulties and required different treatment. However, there was one problem common to every

[55] Minutes of S.R.C.: General Manager's Report, October 5, 1933.
[56] *Unemployment Relief Report for the Fiscal Year* 1932-33, being supplement to the *5th Annual Report of the Department of Railways, Labour and Industries of the Province of Saskatchewan* (Regina, 1933).

phase of relief administration – the problem of financing the relief.

As we have seen, the cost of relief was somewhat reduced by the emphasis of the Commission upon strict economy. Applications for relief were carefully checked before being approved, and repayment of relief was a basic principle. Another important economy was achieved by obtaining price reductions for most relief articles. The arguments presented to the wholesalers for price concessions are mentioned by the General Manager in one of his reports.[57] Those based on the charitable nature of the distribution and the precedent of other wholesalers were probably not very effective. Although the Commission did not actually purchase the goods, the inclusion of such goods on relief orders meant increased sales and so merited some price concessions. When a wholesale price was agreed upon, a retail price was established which allowed the retailer a small margin of profit. The effectiveness of this method can be shown by an example. Letters on file from various hardware merchants show that in 1931 the price of formalin varied from 23 to 25 cents. In 1932, by obtaining price concessions, the Commission arranged the distribution of formalin at a retail price of 19 cents![58] This policy, applied to other commodities, effected a substantial reduction in the cost of rural relief.[59]

The contribution to economy resulting from freight reductions granted by the two railway companies also deserves special mention. All donations shipped by carload lots to the drought area, even from as far away as the Maritimes, were moved without charge. The freight on relief feed and fodder and on the carloads of settlers' effects was reduced by one-third. Special shipments, such as grasshopper poison, and livestock for winter feeding, were transported for half of the normal freight charge. Even demurrage rates were reduced for the distribution of relief seed and feed.[60] These concessions reduced relief costs considerably[61] and certainly were a factor in ensuring the delivery of many of the donations.

[57] Minutes of S.R.C. General Manager's Report, March 31, 1932.
[58] S.R.C. – Fuel Department – Formalin file.
[59] S.R.C. – General Policy file. The Report of the Provincial Auditor on the October 27, 1932 estimates a savings of $1,000,000 that year as a result of such concessions.
[60] S.R.C. – Traffic Department – Policy file.
[61] The General Manager estimates this saving at $500,000. Summary, p. 9.

In spite of these many economies, the total cost of the relief administered by the Commission was, nevertheless, over $35 million.[62] Providing this large sum of money was probably one of the most difficult problems that had to be faced. The municipalities in the drought area could not collect taxes and could not obtain further credit from the banks. The revenues of the provincial government were so reduced that it, too, was unable to finance an extended relief program.[63] This meant that the Dominion government had to provide most of the money.[64] The municipal and provincial governments had to assume some financial obligations, it is true, but provincial funds were usually derived from short-term Treasury Bills.[65]

Although the cost of the relief was thus definitely allocated, this did not mean that the money was always available. Dominion funds were only forwarded upon the receipt of itemized accounts from the Commission.[66] Provincial funds were often delayed until a loan from the federal government was arranged.[67] This frequently meant that cheques covering accounts payable by the Commission could not be issued by the Treasury Department until funds were available,[68] resulting in delays which caused many of the complaints received by the Commission. There are cases on record where individuals and companies supplied the Commission with some commodity, financing the undertaking through a bank, only to find that they had to pay interest on the loan for two or three months while awaiting payment.[69] Although the Commission was not to blame for this state of affairs, it was held responsible for it by the general public.

In spite of these financial difficulties, and the unexpected duration of the "emergency," it is interesting to note that the policies enunciated by the Relief Commission at its commencement underwent very little modification. The Commission did revert to using the municipal councils as its local representatives in 1932, but this may be explained by the fact that the municipalities assumed some of the financial responsibility at the same time. However, the principle of repayment of the

[62] *Saskatchewan Brief to the Royal Commission on Dominion-Provincial Relations* (Regina, 1937), p. 184.
[63] Summary, p. 1.
[64] Orders-in-Council P.C. 990, 991.
[65] *Ibid.*, P.C. 992.
[66] Minutes of S.R.C.: General Manager's Report, January 25, 1934.
[67] From figures given by E. W. Stapleford, *op. cit.*, pp. 35, 41.
[68] Minutes of S.R.C. — General Manager's Report, December 3, 1931.
[69] S.R.C. — General Manager's Correspondence — Complaints file.

relief, the preferences for Saskatchewan and Canadian products, the use of local merchants, and the price-fixing system for relief goods, survived unchanged for the entire three year period. This is certainly a tribute to the foresight of the Commission, but it does present another problem. Why, after three years of operating in an apparently satisfactory manner, was the commission principle of administering relief abandoned?

The termination of the Relief Commission coincided with the election of a new provincial government in 1934. The responsibility for rural relief was once again divided among various departments of the government. Direct relief was assigned to the Bureau of Labour and Public Welfare, in the Department of Municipal Affairs, and agricultural aid to the Department of Agriculture. This was partly as an economy measure. In a statement of opposition policy in June the "too great overhead costs" of the relief administration had been criticized.[70] The new government hoped that the staffs in the (government) departments "would be sufficient to carry on the business."[71] However, many of the former Relief Commission employees had to be hired by the departments in order to cope with the additional work.[72] Thus the overhead costs were probably not greatly reduced. Another reason given for the change in relief administration was to avoid delay. The statement of policy previously referred to, spoke of unwarrantable delays "aggravating the difficulty of those in need." This, however, was a little unfair. As we have seen, emergency relief orders could be issued locally to prevent suffering, and many of the delays were the result of scarcity of material or of financial difficulties. Thus, the two main arguments against the Commission, unnecessary expense and delay, were not really conclusive.

What then were the basic differences in the two types of relief administration? The Relief Commission did act as a "buffer" to relieve the government of direct political pressure on its relief administration, but, on the other hand, this meant that there was no direct democratic control over the Commission as there would be over government departments. The most obvious difference, however, lies in the supervision of relief. The Relief Commission provided a co-ordinated management,

[70] *Canadian Annual Review* (1934), p. 283.
[71] *Regina Daily Star*, August 15, 1934.
[72] Compare *Public Accounts* 1932-33 for Treasury Department and *Public Accounts* 1934-36 for Departments of Agriculture and Municipal Affairs.

but depended on the government departments for advice on technical details. On the other hand, the departmental system meant that the various phases of relief involved supervision by officials with the necessary technical knowledge, but which prevented an integrated relief administration. Thus it is difficult to be dogmatic about the advantages of either system. The Provincial Auditor naturally favoured the simplified bookkeeping resulting from the commission system and even recommended that every form of relief provided should be transferred to the Commission.[73] On the other hand, from a technical standpoint, the departmental system would likely be favoured. It seems fair to say, however, that when relief is a purely local and temporary problem, the latter system should be quite satisfactory. Conversely, widespread relief over a period of years could be handled more efficiently by a co-ordinated management.

Another controversial issue was the relative importance of the municipal councils in relief administration. As we have seen, the original policy of the Commission was the elimination of local politics by the appointment of relief officers. Later, when the councils took over the local administration, their initiative was restricted by the fact that the Commission formulated the policies, gave detailed instructions, and provided supervision. The system after the termination of the Commission was based on the old principle that relief was primarily a local responsibility. The councils were to retain all the records concerning the applicants, and were to be responsible for all distributions and collections.[74] It is true that under the Commission the municipal councils had some authority, and that the government departments also had some control, yet the difference is obvious. These policies illustrate a common question in political organization — centralized planning versus local self-government. And, as one would expect, the advantages and disadvantages follow the usual pattern. Under the Commission, relief was administered quite uniformly and fairly throughout the province. Nevertheless, there were some instances of "bureaucratic" rigidity. For instance, the Commission dealt only with rural relief, which meant that milk producers, classified as businessmen, were not entitled to assistance. Consequently many dairymen had great difficulty in obtaining feed and fodder for their cattle.[75] Under municipal

[73] S.R.C. – General policy file – Provincial Auditor's Report, October 27, 1932.

[74] *Canadian Annual Review*, 1934, p. 285.

[75] S.R.C. – General Manager's Correspondence – Complaints file.

administration such cases could easily be dealt with on their merits. Furthermore, local responsibility is more likely than centralized planning to increase local initiative. On the other hand, it could be said that local initiative would result in a less uniform and less equitable distribution of relief. Councillors who themselves might be on relief, might tend to be extravagant or even unfair. These arguments do little to solve the question of centralized or local self-government. We can only say that as far as the Commission is concerned, its centralization policy was not entirely rigid.

Although our study may not prove that the Commission provided the ideal system of relief administration, we can at least say that it was satisfactory. As we have seen, a tremendous and unprecedented problem confronted Saskatchewan in 1931. Three years later the Commission could be excused some justifiable pride in its record of accomplishment. Rural distress had been minimized. Agricultural rehabilitation had been considerably aided, in so far as weather conditions would permit. Many special problems had been encountered and dealt with efficiently. A great deal of expense had been saved by foresight and patience. And in spite of the magnitude of the enterprise, there was never the slightest indication of political influence, profiteering, or partiality. When we consider the blunders and the corruption that are possible in the administering of a large relief program, this constitutes an enviable record.

The Bias of Prairie Politics

W. L. Morton

That there has been, and is, some significant difference between
the politics of the three Prairie Provinces and those of other
regions of Canada is a matter both of common observation and
of academic study. If the existence of the difference is notorious,
the explanation of why such a difference should exist is still
perhaps sufficiently in question to warrant an attempt at comprehensive explanation. This paper advances the proposition
that the explanation is historical and not merely economic or
sociological. The proposition implies, as the title is meant to
indicate, that the difference between prairie and other Canadian politics is the result of an initial bias, which, by cumula-
tive historical process – the process which takes account of
sequence, conjuncture, and will, as well as of logic, category,
and necessity – has resulted in traditions and attitudes even
more distinctive than the original bias. In short, to pass from
the abstract to the concrete, the submission is that in his aims
Louis Riel was a more conventional politician than William
Aberhart, but that both were prairie politicians.

The proof of that assertion must be postponed for the
moment, in order to remark that it has seemed necessary to
invoke the notion of bias lest the common error of special
studies be incurred, that of exaggerating the significance of
one's subject. The difference between prairie and other Canadian politics can be exaggerated, particularly if historical perspective is lost and the study of fundamental institutions neglected. It is more important, if less arresting, to observe that
the institutions of the Prairie West were Canadian institutions
and that the people who worked those institutions and determined the political development of the West were in the overwhelming majority of Canadian birth and ancestry, than it is
to discuss the differences of sectional politics. The first laws of

SOURCE: *Transactions of the Royal Society of Canada*, vol. XLIX,
series III, section two (June, 1955), pp. 57-66. Reprinted by permission of the author and the Royal Society of Canada.

the West were largely copied from the statutes of Ontario. There was only one distinctly western group of people, the Métis, and they were broken and dispersed by 1885. The great immigrant groups of the first years of this century, the British, the Americans, and the East Europeans, never endeavoured to change the basic institutions of the country and, in the main, left politics to the Canadian-born. There seems, in fact, to have been little in the institutional development or the peopling of the Prairie West for which some parallel might not be found in the history of western Ontario. It may be said, in short, that old Canada was extraordinarily successful in making the Prairie West Canadian.

The effect of Canadian institutions was, of course, modified by the factors of time and distance. The West was colonized some two generations later in time than western Ontario, and was distant a thousand miles from central Canada. In consequence, the West in its years of major settlement was subjected to influences such as Fabian Socialism, the Non-Partisan League, and Social Credit which the older communities of Canada had escaped, or were better equipped to resist. And the element of mere distance was a powerful agent among those which operated to produce the strong sectional sentiment of the West. But these material factors were modifiers, not determinants, of western history. Despite the lateness of settlement and the barrier of distance, the institutions and people of the Prairie West were, or became, Canadian.

If, then, Canadian institutions and ideals prevailed in the West, what was the bias which made prairie politics different? The answer suggested is that the subordinate status given the West in Confederation was the initial bias that set in train the development of prairie politics towards an increasing differentiation from the Canadian standard. The subordination was, of course, in the nature of things, the outcome of the fact that the West was an almost wholly unpeopled wilderness in 1869. The bias was neither necessary nor inevitable; it was historical, the outcome of human will and personality, that of Riel and the clergy, operating in a particular environment. The resistance of the Métis was in many ways pathetic and even comic, but it was sufficient to set a tradition at work, the tradition of western grievance. The struggle of the Prairie West against political subordination to central Canada had begun, and it was to go on to merge with the struggle against economic subordination to the capital and corporations of the East. The result of this struggle, both of its failures and its partial successes, was a release of that utopianism which has been ende-mic in western society since the French Revolution, and in-deed in religious form since the Reformation, and which has always found a refuge and a stimulus on the frontiers of settle-ment. In particular, the revolt against the national political parties between 1911 and 1921, and the shattering of economic conventions by the great depression and drought of 1929-39, created a vacuum into which the United Farmers of Alberta and Social Credit rushed.

II

The assumption that the initial bias of prairie politics was the fact of political subordination in Confederation, suggests further a division of the history of the Prairie West in Confederation into three periods. The first may be called the colonial period, from 1870 to 1905. The second is the agrarian period from 1905 to 1925, and the third the utopian from 1925 to the present. The first is the period of the struggle for political equality in Confederation, not realized until 1930, and the second the period in which the concept of the agrarian bloc dominated western politics. The third period is that in which certain utopian elements, diffused through western society but stimulated on the frontiers of settlement, emerged in prairie politics, and won control of the Province of Alberta in 1935. The periodization suggested is, of course, much neater than the facts warrant. The achievement of equality in 1930 was at once made a mockery by depression and drought. The agra-rian element is continuous from 1872, when the Grange first appeared in Manitoba, and the utopianism can also be detected from the beginnings of extensive settlement. But the periods do indicate the relative importance of the three elements of inequality, agrarianism, and utopianism. Even more important than the periodization is the sequence, for the struggle for equality fed the agrarian revolt, and the agrarian revolt opened the way to the victory of the utopians. The initial bias of in-equality, that is, gave a twist to the development of prairie politics which in the historical process has become a major divagation from the run of national development, and which is now a matter for serious concern.

The beginning of the process was the resistance of the Métis of Red River to the annexation of the Northwest by Canada in 1869. The resistance was not to union with Canada; it was to union at once and without safeguards that would enable the Métis to survive as a group. On the face of the evidence, the resistance was not justifiable. The preparations made by Canada for the acquisition and preliminary government of the Northwest were proper and adequate; the one serious omission was the failure to send a commissioner to explain what was to happen, and that was an Imperial rather than a Canadian responsibility. The real ground of the resistance was to the beginning of an English-speaking and Protestant immigration, which would become a majority and determine the laws and institutions of the Northwest. In that the Métis saw, and correctly, their own destruction. They were resolved not to submit; "Tell them," Riel said to a Canadian, "our great thought is to resist being made Irishmen of."[1] The real blunder of the Dominion government was to regard the acquisition and development of the Northwest as a compensation to Ontario for the bringing of the Maritimes into Confederation and the construction of the Intercolonial Railway. Cartier, it is possible, had acquiesced in this surrender of the west to Ontario, on condition that the Northwest be a separate government,[2] but some of the missionary clergy of the Roman Catholic Church did not.[3] They and Riel determined to oppose the opening of the Northwest to the English and Protestant, individualistic and aggressive society of Ontario, a society which would grant equality to the Métis as persons and destroy them as a people.

Their aims the Métis sought to achieve within constitutional limits. The resistance began with a declaration of loyalty to the Crown, and it was continued in the name of British liberty and British justice, though the phrases were mingled dangerously and misleadingly with the rights of man and law of nations. Riel showed himself to be remarkably adept in the English tradition of using the language of constitutional right to justify opposition to authority. But his real problem was to find terms within the limits of the Canadian constitution which would

---

[1] P.A.C., *Volunteer Review*, IV (1), January 3, 1870, p. 9, quoting John Malcolm Reid in *London Free Press* of December 16, 1869.

[2] A. K. Isbister reported a conversation to that effect with Sir Edward Bulwer Lytton, Colonial Secretary, when Cartier with Galt and John Ross visited England to discuss the confederation of British North America in 1858, in a letter to Donald Gunn of Red River: P.A.M., *Nor'Wester*, December 28, 1859; the letter is quoted (in part) in A. S. Morton, *History of the Canadian West to 1870-71*, p. 837. Isbister's letter by itself is no more than suggestive, but it is difficult to see how Cartier could have taken any other stand.

[3] See the writer's introduction to *The Red River Journal of Alexander Begg* (Champlain Society, Toronto, 1956).

assure the Métis of their object, the preservation of their language, faith, and existence as a group. These Riel was finally convinced were to be found in provincial status, and with that in view the Bill of Rights drawn up by the delegates of the people of Red River was re-written by the Provisional Government to demand admission for the Northwest, not as a Territory, but as a Province. What was granted was provincial status, not for the Northwest as a whole, but for the old colony of Assiniboia. Thus Riel won a startling, but partial, victory. He had obtained provincial status for no more than a fragment, if a strategic fragment, of the Northwest, and even there his victory was incomplete. Small as it was, Manitoba was large enough to hold sufficient Ontario immigrants to outnumber the Métis, and province though it was, it was not the equal of the other provinces, for it was not granted control of its lands.

This was the beginning of the bias of prairie politics. The fears of the Métis had led them to demand equality for the people of the Northwest in Confederation. Unwarranted though the demand was, it had been granted in principle to prevent American intervention and to pacify Quebec. But it could not be wholly granted without driving Ontario to exasperation and imperilling the federal policy of western development by railway construction and homestead settlement. In consequence, the West was left with a sharpened sense of inequality and a tradition of grievance and of special claims, to be embodied in Bills of Rights from Riel's series of four to that of Mr. Hazen Argue, M.P., of May 1955.

III

The subordination of the Prairie West, then, to federal control and federal policies, from 1870 to 1905, and even 1930, had confirmed prairie politics in their initial bias. The bias was, however, to be transmitted to, and increased during, the agrarian period. This second phase of the bias sprang from the rapid development of the agricultural economy of the Prairie West after 1900. The most easily exploitable resource of the West was the agricultural soil of the prairies, which lent itself to grain growing on an extensive scale. The needs of this economy were few, simple, and imperative: cheap land, cheap transport, and cheap machinery. They were met on a gigantic scale both by private investment and by government subsidy. It was the national policy of the day to develop the West, for the development of the West was the key to national development. The western grain grower was a beneficiary both of the great colonization boom which opened the twentieth century and also of the policies of the national government.

Yet the grain grower developed grievances, which were to be formulated both as a sectional and as a class protest. In part, no doubt, there was an element of human perverseness in this. But there was a strong objective basis to the grain grower's complaints. In the early stages of development both the line elevators and the railways were able to exploit their temporary monopolies; banks and other services were sometimes in the same position. It is not surprising that an attempt should have been made to charge "what the traffic would bear," or that it should have been resisted, as it was by the Farmers' Union, the Patrons of Industry, and by the Grain Growers Associations. These organizations were the grain growers' counter to alleged monopolies.

One other grievance, however, could not be attacked by economic organization alone. That was the National Policy of tariff protection of domestic industry, begun by the Conservative Party in 1879, and continued and refined by the Liberal Party after 1896. The National Policy was not, of course, merely a policy of protection. It was, broadly viewed, also a policy of railway construction and land settlement; in short, its aim was the creation of a national, as opposed to a colonial economy. All sections were expected to benefit from its realization, and in this broad interpretation, the Crow's Nest Pass Agreement was as much a part of the National Policy as the tariff. But, by tradition and interest, the western farmer, like many eastern farmers, was disposed to ignore any special or long-term benefits which accrued to him from the National Policy, and fasten on the fact that the tariff operated to increase his costs of living and of production. This disposition was influenced in the Prairie West by the defeat of the Reciprocity Agreement in the general election of 1911. The results of that election convinced many western grain growers, suffering from the first slackening of the boom, that the "eastern interests" would go to great lengths to maintain the favoured position in which, in their view, the National Policy had placed those interests.

The 1911 election also convinced a number of grain growers that the national political parties were not reliable instruments for effecting the agrarian voters' wishes. Stimulated by the Progressive movement in the United States and by immigrant British Liberals and Socialists, some western agrarians began to denounce political parties as perverters and corrupters of the will of the people, and to advocate "direct legislation" and "business government" as remedies. The national parties were especially attacked as the facile agents of the "big interests." In this developing agitation there were elements both of sectional agrarianism and of utopianism.

The story has been told elsewhere. Suffice it here to note that the rapid disintegration of the farmers' movement in politics demonstrated the inadequacy of agrarian sectionalism. The weakness of western agrarian sectionalism was threefold. First, there was the weakness of the single economic interest, whether the collective interest of agriculture, or the narrower interest of the prairie grain grower. In the complex of the national economic groups, agriculture had to dominate or bargain. Despite its command of numbers, it failed to dominate. The reason was that it could act only through the organized, public effort of many weak and dispersed individuals, whereas industry was able to act privately through a few powerful individuals.

Public agitation competed with lobby influence. Agriculture, which had to bargain, bargained badly because it was of two minds. A powerful and a majority element in its leadership still held to the conventions of liberal economics. A powerful minority was prepared to bargain for government support of agricultural prices whatever the effect on the struggle to lower the tariff. It was, in short, impossible to obtain agreement among agriculturalists as to what the immediate interests of agriculture were. This fact, of course, betrays the fundamental weakness of the concept of interest or of class, whether used as an instrument of political action or a term of academic analysis: it makes absolute what is in fact relative.

The second weakness was that the Prairie West was a minority section. It could not prevail by numbers alone, and the realization of this gave rise to much talk about holding a balance of power at Ottawa. But the balance of power operates only among powers, that is, relatively stable entities. Another condition of its operation is that the powers of a power system be morally and sentimentally indifferent one to another. The farmer representatives at Ottawa from 1922 to 1925 were divided among themselves. Moreover they were not nationalists, like the Irish home rulers, and had no wish to be; and not all had freed themselves from old preferences for the Liberal or the Conservative party. They could not exercise a balance of power at Ottawa, nor can any section which is not on the verge of rebellion and prepared to strike for nationhood.

The third weakness was more subtle. The aims of the farmers in 1921 might have been realized by an agrarian majority in Parliament, but that majority had not been achieved, or even hoped for. They might have been realized, in part, by an agrarian bloc based on the Prairie West. But this, possible in the United States, was a delusion under the Canadian constitution. The government in Canada is sustained, of course, not by provisions of the constitution, but by a majority in Parliament. If it is sustained, it can defy a bloc. If it is not, it can seek a majority in a general election. It must, in short, war on blocs and other dissident groups until it has rendered them harmless, or yield the government to them, in which case they have to assume the general responsibilities of government and maintain a majority. The sectional or occupational bloc in Canadian federal politics did not give an economic group opportunity to push its own interests in legislation, or to bring about government by a coalition of groups. It was to begin the destruction of the national parties in the Prairie West. It also raised the question whether the parliamentary system is suited for the federal government of a sectional country. The western provinces developed their own political parties, and came to be represented more and more at Ottawa by more or less dissident groups, Liberal Progressive and U.F.A., and later, C.C.F. and Social Credit. But as the contrary example of the Maritimes suggests, the national parties afforded minority sections perhaps their best opportunity, year in and year out, of influencing national policies. One result, then, of the outbreak of agrarian sectionalism in the Prairie West was the weakening of the national parties there and the consequent diminution of western influence in the national government. This diminution would have been much greater had it not been offset by the convention that all the provinces must be represented in the federal cabinet.

Thus the bias of prairie politics had carried their development one phase further. Agrarian sectionalism had prevailed, had had its day, and had left its mark. But its concrete political achievements were few, if important, and it had come near to carrying the West out of the national councils. It had confirmed the tradition of protest begun in the days of political subordination, and it had demonstrated the inadequacy in Canadian politics of the sectional or occupational bloc. The bias of prairie politics had either to return to conformity with national political standards, and the return of prosperity after 1929 would have greatly helped, or to take one spin of the ball further, beyond agrarian sectionalism to sectional utopianism. The elements of utopianism were already latent; the drought and depression of the early thirties brought them to the surface of prairie politics.

IV

Utopianism, which may be defined for this paper as a readiness to adopt untried methods to achieve ideal ends, was not, of course, of western origin. To cite only the chief example, Social Credit, it is notorious that it was of immediate English origin, and that its roots are to be found in under-consumption economic theories of a century's standing. What the West did was to provide a favourable environment for the development of utopian politics: heavy indebtedness, distrust of prevailing political methods and economic conventions, a sense still surviving from the frontier of the possibility of a second chance and a new life – or at least the old life on new terms – a tradition of protest, and the weakness of the old political parties.

While it is true that the West in the early thirties was particularly favourable to the development of utopian elements diffused through the English-speaking world, there had long been elements in its own life which contributed to an outburst of utopianism in the thirties. Most basic of these was the growing strength of evangelical Protestant sects and of the Mormon Church in the "Bible belt" from Winnipeg westwards. No new sect originated on the prairie frontier, but those which had begun elsewhere throve in the rural districts and the small towns of the West. No authoritative study has been made of this phenomenon. It is probable, however, that its origins were twofold. One was the partial failure of the more conventional churches, in particular the Anglican, Methodist, and Presbyterian, to meet the challenge of natural science in any convincing way. By tacitly admitting defeat on the first chapter of Genesis, they seemed to unsubtle minds to have abandoned the Scriptures entirely. The second was that these churches, with the Church of Rome, failed in part, as municipal and educational institutions did also, to solve the problems created by the diffusion of population over enormous areas. As a result, distrust of the "line churches" grew, partly because they were not fundamentalist enough, partly because their efforts to maintain resident clergy and church edifices seemed to be exacting and costly. In these conditions, the growth of fundamentalist religious sects was not surprising, but it created a readiness to listen uncritically to a secular evangelism, to trust bold assurance and to distrust critical doubt, and to accept credulously the promise of a new social order.

The West favoured too a ready response to certain idealistic trends, partly rationalist, partly religious, which were also generally diffused, but checked as they were not in the West by the conservatism of an established and sophisticated society. One was prohibition; another, closely related, was the feminine suffrage movement. In the political field, there was direct legislation, and in the economic, socialism. None of these is, of course, to be regarded as merely idealistic, still less as utopian. But the advocates of all tended to present them as offering the possibility of a decisive turn towards a new society. The reform movement of the first quarter of this century in the Prairie West was, in short, tinged with millenarianism.

Even in strictly economic matters there was something of this spirit. The great majority of farmers wanted only to increase the farmer's returns. But all the farmers' organizations, from the Grange to the United Farmers, had some touch of uplift, and used the methods and often the songs of evangelism. The doctrine of the Wheat Pool was preached with apostolic fervour, and received by the majority of farmers with the abandon of converts. Even socialism, that bleak and scientific analysis of society, was presented idealistically as a creed of social justice. And this superimposition of evangelical idealism on a base of hard materialism was an admirable preparation for the reception of Social Credit.

The way for Social Credit was not less well prepared by its rivals. The United Farmers of Alberta under the inspiration of Henry Wise Wood had committed Alberta to an experiment in group government and had broken the hold of the old parties on that province. Wood's group government, however, was to a great extent a tactical device designed to absorb the radical Non-Partisan League; it was basically conservative, an attempt to strengthen the farmer's position in society as it was. It was found wanting, therefore, when to an electorate made frantic by economic distress some sweeping measures of relief seemed imperative. The instrument for attempting a radical reconstruction of western and indeed Canadian society had already been forged in the Cooperative Commonwealth Federation. This new party, a real political party in organization and intent, was an attempt to bring together those farmer and labour organizations which were ready to undertake a reorganization of Canadian economic society on socialist principles. It embodied the most advanced economic and political thought of the agrarian and labour movements and it systematically condemned the capitalist society from the deficiencies of which, it was alleged, the depression had sprung. Even the U.F.A. federal members, breaking with the conservative leadership of Wood, were a part, an important part, of the new political movement.

Why did the people of Alberta not turn to the C.C.F.? This is a question which Professor C. B. Macpherson has ably analysed in his *Democracy in Alberta*.[4] The farmers of Alberta were at war with the prevailing economic order; they had rejected the old political parties, the instruments of that order. In their midst a native party had arisen, in part the work of their own representatives in Parliament. They were offered a new political vehicle for their discontents, and new solutions to their economic problems. Yet they turned *en masse* to the leadership of a man who had never been in politics, the advocate of an economic doctrine which was totally untried and severely condemned by all professional economists, whether liberal or socialist. Professor Macpherson's explanation is that the western farmer was a *petit bourgeois*. The term is not a happy one, and one may question the utility of employing in the analysis of a fluid, unformed society a term drawn from an older and stratified society. That may be a class which does not behave as a class, the members of which do not think of themselves as a class, and strongly dislike the idea of class, but surely only in a Marxian sense. But if all Professor Macpherson means is that the purpose of the Albertan farmer and small town merchant was to achieve economic independence, to make the farm or the store pay, one must agree with him. The western farmer and business man did not want socialism, which they interpreted as an attack on all property, including their own small concerns. Yet they were vexed and angry with existing economic conditions. For them Social Credit promised an easy and a sweeping reform, without socialism. The Albertan turned to it, and, aided by the war boom and the oil boom, achieved utopia.[5] If it be objected that he did not thereby achieve a new society, it must be admitted that he has attained a new complacency. If one must travel to Nowhere, there is no more comfortable way than on a tide of oil.

[4] (Toronto: University of Toronto Press, 1953).
[5] Professor J. R. Mallory in his *Social Credit and the Federal Power in Canada* (Toronto, 1954) advances the view that Social Credit was taken up as a sectional weapon with which to attack federal control of credit and currency.

V

Is this, then, the outcome of the bias of prairie politics, the achievement of a new political utopia, which now includes two great provinces and which hopes to extend its political frontiers until the whole nation is remade in its image? To attempt an answer would be to have history hover on the verge of prophecy. The historian must turn back, and merely recapitulate the argument. The bias of prairie politics, it has been submitted, began in colonial subordination, continued in agrarian revolt, and went on to the political and economic utopianism of Social Credit. The principal presupposition of the argument has been that there are sections as well as nations, nations as well as civilizations. The sub-society which is a section, it is supposed, possesses some degree of integrity and character. That character, it is assumed, may be defined, and the relations of the sub-society with other societies explored. The Prairie West has been defined as a colonial society seeking equality in Confederation. That equality was sought in order that the West should be like, not different from, the rest of Canada. The bias of prairie politics, however, has operated to produce equality with a difference. The emphasis of this paper has been placed on the sectional character of the Prairie West. The justification advanced for this emphasis is that the West was a region of political and material differences sufficiently significant to give it the character of a sub-society. That being so, it is the relations of that sub-society with the nation of which it is a part which make significant the history of the Prairie West. These relations passed through the phases of colonial subordination to, agrarian revolt against, and utopian rejection of, the political and economic controls, but not the institutional foundations, of the nation. Canadian institutions and the ideals of Canada were accepted and upheld, and in the present stage the purpose of western utopianism is to redeem them by capturing the nation. In a normal development the section would be merged in the nation; the utopian element of prairie politics seeks to merge the nation in the section. The attempt, obviously, is utopian. What is realistic and serious is that the decay of the national political parties and the great alterations in the conventions of parliamentary government in the western provinces are not without parallels in the rest of Canada. Western utopianism, it may be, is an exaggerated symptom of a national malady.

Select Bibliography on the History of the Prairie Provinces

I

Western Canada cries for the attention of scholars. The area's bibliography is nonetheless extensive. Only the most important works are indicated here, and the editor apologizes for the arbitrariness necessitated by such a selection. Items on discovery, the fur trade, and travel have for the most part been omitted, as have most memoirs, royal commission reports, theses, and articles. For a comprehensive bibliography, the reader is referred to Bruce Braden Peel, *A Bibliography of the Prairie Provinces to 1953* (Toronto, 1956), and his *Supplement* (Toronto, 1963); to the bibliographies in each issue of the *Canadian Historical Review*; and to the *Register of Post-Graduate Dissertations in Progress in History and Related Subjects*, compiled annually by the Public Archives of Canada.

II

Much useful material has been published in periodicals, the most important of which are: *Papers Read Before the Historical and Scientific Society of Manitoba* (now called *Historical and Scientific Society of Manitoba Transactions*); *Saskatchewan History*; *Alberta Historical Review*; *Canadian Historical Review*; *Canadian Journal of Economics and Political Science*; *Annual Reports* of the Canadian Historical Association; and *The Beaver*. Over the years the *Canadian Forum* has published stimulating comment on western politics.

A number of multi-volume works, some still in progress, are devoted partly or exclusively to the prairies: *Hudson's Bay Record Society*; *Champlain Society*; *Manitoba Record Society*; *Dictionary of Canadian Biography*; *Canada and Its Provinces*; *Canadian Centenary Series*; *Canadian Frontiers of Settlement*; *Relations of Canada and the United States* (known as the *Carnegie Series on Canadian-American Relations*); *Social Credit in Alberta Series*; the *Canada Ethnica* series; the Manitoba Historical Society's series of ethnic studies; *Canadian*

Government Series; *Dominion Annual Register and Review*; *Canadian Annual Review*.

III

There are many general and introductory works on the Canadian West. The most famous is doubtless Arthur S. Morton, *A History of the Canadian West to 1870-71* (London, n.d.). While difficult to read, it has been aptly described by B. B. Peel as "an encyclopaedic history of the West to 1870." Morton's great work is now dated in some major respects. Many of these deficiencies are remedied by the more recent E. E. Rich, *Hudson's Bay Company, 1670-1870* (Toronto, 1960), in three volumes. A shorter sample of Rich's scholarship is *The Fur Trade and the Northwest to 1857* (Toronto, 1967). Other competent and more readable works on the H.B.C., still an important western institution, are John S. Galbraith, *The Hudson's Bay Company as an Imperial Factor, 1821-1869* (Toronto, 1959) and Douglas MacKay, *The Honourable Company: A History of the Hudson's Bay Company* (Toronto, 1949), Revised Edition. Marjory Wilkins Campbell, *The North West Company* (Toronto, 1957) supplements this material on the H.B.C. E. H. Oliver, ed., *The Canadian North-West; its early development and legislative records* (Ottawa, 1914-15), in two volumes, is an invaluable collection of documents. Alexander Begg, *History of the North-West* (Toronto, 1894-95), in three volumes, is still necessary for aspects of western development not adequately treated elsewhere. Gustavus Myers, *History of Canadian Wealth* (Chicago, 1914) is a neglected but fascinating book which applies to Canada the muck-raking techniques of his American contemporaries. Parts of the book are germane to the West. *Report of the Royal Commission on Dominion-Provincial Relations* (Ottawa, 1940), Books I-III, and its many appendices, constitute a major source for the study of the prairies. Commissioned in part because of western complaints concerning the financial implications of confederation, the *Rowell-Sirois Report* provides an important insight into the influence of the National Policy on the West. Donald V. Smiley, ed., *The Rowell-Sirois Report, Book I* (Carleton Library No. 5) is an abridged edition of the historical part of the report.

While Canadian studies suffer from a plethora of inadequate provincial histories, Manitoba has been blessed with W. L. Morton, *Manitoba: A History* (Toronto, 1967), Second Edition. It is the best provincial history available, and to quote its preface "has agricultural settlement as its central theme." Excellent supplements to Professor Morton's book are Stanley Norman Murray, *The Valley Comes of Age: A History of Agriculture in the Valley of the Red River of the North, 1812-1920* (Fargo, 1967) and M. S. Donnelly, *The Government of Manitoba* (Toronto, 1963). J. F. C. Wright, *Saskatchewan, the History of a Province* (Toronto, 1955) lacks the depth of scholarly maturity of Morton's study.

Chester Martin, *Foundations of Canadian Nationhood* (Toronto, 1955) contains a major scholar's reflections on western Canada's place within the nation. Frank H. Underhill, *In Search of Canadian Liberalism* (Toronto, 1960) includes penetrating material on the West, as does S. D. Clark, *The Developing Canadian Community* (Toronto, 1968), Second Edition.

There is no first-class general history of prairie churches, but several specialized studies help to fill the gap: A. G. Morice, *History of the Catholic Church in Western Canada, 1659-1895* (Toronto, 1910), two volumes, was a pioneer endeavour which still bears careful reading; T. C. Boon, *The Anglican Church From the Bay to the Rockies* (Toronto, 1962) covers the period 1820-1950; W. E. Mann, *Sect, Cult and Church in Alberta* (Toronto, 1955) is a fascinating insight into the religious life of one province. C. B. Sissons, *Church and State in Canadian Education: An Historical Study* (Toronto, 1959), while strongly protestant, is an indispensable introduction to religious and educational history on the prairies.

IV

Early Red River valley history has attracted the attention of some excellent historians. John Perry Pritchett, *The Red River Valley, 1811-1849* (Toronto, 1942) and Alvin C. Glueck, *Minnesota and the Manifest Destiny of the Canadian Northwest* (Toronto, 1965) are admirable studies of the valley in its international context. Anna Margaret Wright, "The Canadian Frontier, 1840-1867" (Ph.D. thesis, University of Toronto, 1943) provides an extensive discussion of Canada and the Hudson's Bay Company. Although written two generations ago, Chester Martin, *Lord Selkirk's Work in Canada* (Oxford, 1916) stands as a necessary introduction to early settlement in the valley. John Morgan Gray, *Lord Selkirk of Red River* (Toronto, 1963) is an exhaustive and sympathetic account of a key figure. Margaret Arnett MacLeod and W. L. Morton,

Cuthbert Grant of Grantown: Warden of the Plains of Red River (Toronto, 1963) is a superbly written and well researched account of the Métis chieftain who led the attack on Governor Semple's party at Seven Oaks.

An insight into life in Red River between the union of the fur companies in 1821 and the Rising of 1869-70 can be obtained from many sources. Alexander Ross, *Red River Settlement* (London, 1856) is a mine of information on social, political, and religious topics. It contains a famous and much used description of the buffalo hunt. Joseph James Hargrave, *Red River* (Montreal, 1871) is a large detailed work which utilizes the papers of Hargrave's father, an employee of the Hudson's Bay Company. W. J. Healy, *Women of Red River* (Winnipeg, 1923) while hardly rigorous, is a useful social history. Arthur S. Morton, *Sir George Simpson* (Toronto, 1944) is a scholarly biography of an important H.B.C. leader. Roy St. George Stubbs, *Four Recorders of Rupert's Land* (Winnipeg, 1967) explains the administration of justice under Company rule. Although really a form of quasi-history, Olive Knox, *John Black of Old Kildonan* (Toronto, 1958) is an interesting social history and illustrates the nature of interracial relations before the formation of the Canadian Party.

V

The Red River Resistance of 1869-70 is the most famous event in Manitoban history; its leader, Louis Riel, is the West's best known personality. The finest analysis of the Resistance is the brilliant and sympathetic "Introduction" to W. L. Morton, ed., *Alexander Begg's Red River Journal and Other Papers Relative to the Red River Resistance of 1869-70* (Champlain Society, 1956). The documents reprinted by Professor Morton constitute a major source for the period, and are supplemented by his *Manitoba: The Birth of a Province* (Manitoba Record Society, 1965). He has also provided a short introduction to the problem in *The West and Confederation* (Canadian Historical Association Booklet, Ottawa, 1958). Alexander Begg used his diary to write *The Creation of Manitoba; or, A History of the Red River Troubles* (Toronto, 1871), an important work. Dom Benoit, *Vie De Mgr. Taché* (Montreal, 1904), in two volumes, is a massive account of the life of the most important western religious leader in 1869-70. Norman Shrive, *Charles Mair: Literary Nationalist* (Toronto, 1965) illuminates the Canadian Party which fomented so much fear, hatred and distrust during the period of the Resistance.

Louis Riel has received a massive amount of attention. Many studies discuss his entire career. George F. G. Stanley, *The Birth of Western Canada: A History of the Riel Rebellions* (Toronto, 1936) is a standard and pioneering work, which discusses the Métis in terms of their conflict with advancing civilization. His *Louis Riel* (Toronto, 1963) is a fuller and more readable treatment, but includes no radically different interpretations of the man or the movements he led. W. M. Davidson, *The Life and Times of Lous Riel* (Calgary, 1951) is a popular study by an Albertan journalist. It includes some interesting documentary material. Joseph Kinsey Howard, *Strange Empire: A Narrative of the Northwest* (New York, 1952) is a romantic study of the rebellions, with a continentalist orientation. In spite of some dubious judgments, the book is brilliantly written and grips the imagination of most readers. E. B. Osler, *The Man Who Had to Hang: Louis Riel* (Toronto, 1961) is the poorest of recent biographies, adding virtually nothing to earlier books. John Coulter, *Riel* (Toronto, 1962) is a play which is interesting to read, if hardly satisfactory from an historian's point of view. E. R. Markson, Cyril Greenland, and R. E. Turner, "The Life and Death of Louis Riel: A Study In Forensic Psychiatry," *Canadian Psychiatric Association Journal*, vol. x (August, 1955) explains to the layman the serious nature of Riel's mental illness. An earlier view more favourable to Riel is Frank W. Anderson, "Louis Riel's Insanity Reconsidered," *Saskatchewan History*, vol. III (1950). R. G. MacBeth, *The Making of the Canadian West* (Toronto, 1898) is an example of the dozens of contemporary works which discuss the risings.

Central Canadian views of the risings have received considerable attention. Mason Wade, *The French Canadians, 1760-1945* (Toronto, 1955) examines the ramifications for Quebec politics of Riel and his movements. Robert Rumilly, *Histoire de la Province de Québec*, vol. v: *Louis Riel* (Montreal, n.d.), Troisième édition, should also be consulted. R. E. Lamb, *Thunder in the North: Conflict Over the Riel Risings, 1870-1885* (New York, 1957) lacks sophisticated analysis but includes many interesting quotations from the contemporary press. Jane Elizabeth Graham, "The Riel Amnesty and the Liberal Party in Central Canada, 1869-1875" (M.A. thesis, Queens' University, 1967) is an excellent study which reveals much about how the first rising was used as an issue in Ontario and Quebec politics.

The North-West Mounted Police, crucial to prairie history during the 1870's and 1880's, have not received adequate attention. John Peter Turner, *The North-West Mounted Police, 1870-1893* (Ottawa, 1950) in two volumes, is both turgid and uncritical. Thomas Morris Longstreth, *The Silent Force* (London, 1928), which is simplistic, naïve, and hopelessly partisan, represents a popular genre. Perhaps the best insight into the mounties currently available is in Paul F. Sharp, *Whoop-Up Country: The Canadian-American West, 1865-1885* (Minneapolis, 1955), a brilliant and important work.

Three excellent University of Manitoba M.A. theses provide the best introduction to early Manitoban political history: F. A. Milligan, *The Lieutenant-Governorship in Manitoba, 1870-1882* (1948); James A. Jackson, *The Disallowance of Manitoba Railway Legislation in the 1880's* (1945); J. L. Holmes, *Factors Affecting Politics in Manitoba: A Study of the Provincial Elections, 1870-1899* (1936). Although badly dated, R. O. MacFarlane, "Manitoba Politics and Parties after Confederation," Canadian Historical Association *Annual Report* (1940), still bears reading. J. A. Maxwell, "Financial Relations Between Manitoba and the Dominion, 1870-1886," *Canadian Historical Review*, xv (1934) is a well-researched study of a staple political issue. Escott M. Reid, "The Rise of National Parties in Canada," in Hugh G. Thorburn, ed., *Party Politics In Canada* (Scarborough, 1967), Second Edition, contains a dated but popular interpretation germane to western Canada. J. P. Robertson, *A Political Manual of the Province of Manitoba and the North-West Territories* (Winnipeg, 1887) is an indispensable mine of information.

The best introduction to the Manitoba Schools Question is a judiciously selected volume of readings and documents: Lovell Clark, ed., *The Manitoba School Question: Majority Rule or Minority Rights?* (Toronto, 1968). Craig Brown, ed., *Minorities, Schools, and Politics* (*Canadian Historical Readings*, VII, Toronto, 1969) includes several articles on this and closely related problems. Also useful for the Manitoba Schools Question are several biographies of Laurier: O. D. Skelton, *Life and Letters of Sir Wilfrid Laurier* (Carleton Library, Nos. 21 and 22); Joseph Schull, *Laurier, The First Canadian* (Toronto, 1965); and J. W. Dafoe, *Laurier* (Carleton Library, No. 3). *Report of the Royal Commission on Bilingualism and*

Biculturalism (Ottawa, 1968), Book II, should also be consulted.

Few early Manitoban politicians have received biographies, although Donald A. Smith (Lord Strathcona) has been so honoured several times. The best is Beckles Willson, *The Life of Lord Strathcona and Mount Royal* (Toronto, 1915), a sympathetic but badly dated book. John W. Dafoe, *Clifford Sifton in Relation to His Times* (Toronto, 1931) is well written, and must be read by those anxious to understand Manitoba during the 1890s and Canada in the early twentieth century. Hugh R. Ross, *Thirty-Five Years In the Limelight: Sir Rodmond P. Roblin and His Times* (Winnipeg, 1936) is dated and partisan, but is nonetheless an interesting book on one of Manitoba's most important premiers.

Territorial politics can be followed in Lewis Herbert Thomas, *The Struggle for Responsible Government in the North-West Territories, 1870-97* (Toronto, 1956). C. Cecil Lingard, *Territorial Government In Canada: The Autonomy Question in the Old Northwest Territories* (Toronto, 1946) provides a detailed picture of the birth pangs of Saskatchewan and Alberta.

VI

Transportation and settlement, inextricably intermingled, constitute great themes of western development. G. P. de T. Glazebrook, *History of Transportation in Canada* (Toronto, 1938) remains a standard introduction. Leonard Bertram Irwin, *Pacific Railways and Nationalism in the Canadian-American Northwest, 1845-1873* (Philadelphia, 1939), while well researched is often ignored. It is useful for the unsuccessful attempt to provide national transcontinental railway service during early 1870s. The standard history of the C.P.R. is Harold A. Innis, *A History of the Canadian Pacific Railway* (London, 1923). Three of those instrumental in the creation of the C.P.R. have received biographies. Heather M. Gilbert, *Awakening Continent: The Life of Lord Mount Stephen*, Vol. 1, 1829-91 (Aberdeen, 1965) is carefully researched. D. G. Creighton, *John A. Macdonald: The Old Chieftain* (Toronto, 1955) is a brilliant biography of the political father of the line. Walter Vaughan, *The Life and Work of Sir William Van Horne* (New York, 1920) is a useful biography of one of the men involved in actual construction work. The already mentioned biography of Donald A. Smith is also germane to the building of the C.P.R. E. J. Pratt, *Towards the Last Spike* (Toronto, 1952) celebrates the railroad in a great Canadian poem. G. R. Stevens, *Canadian National Railways* (Toronto, 1960-62), in two volumes, recounts the histories of the components of the C.N.R. Consequently it is essential for a study of later transcontinental projects.

Several volumes in the *Canadian Frontiers of Settlement* series are indispensable to an understanding of the settlement process, especially: W. A. Mackintosh, *Prairie Settlement: The Geographical Setting* (Toronto, 1934); C. A. Dawson and Eva R. Younge, *Pioneering In the Prairies Provinces: The Social Side of the Settlement Process* (Toronto, 1940); and Arthur S. Morton and Chester Martin, *History of Prairie Settlement and "Dominion Lands" Policy* (Toronto, 1938). The latter volume is unusually important, especially for federal lands policies.

Norman Macdonald, *Canada: Immigration and Colonization, 1841-1903* (Toronto, 1966) is a good introduction to post-confederation immigration and the West. Douglas Hill, *The Opening of the Canadian West* (New York, 1967) is a well written, synthetic account which includes concise descriptions of several ethnic groups. It is an attractive introduction to the settlement period. James B. Hedges, *Building the Canadian West: The Land and Colonization Policies of the Canadian Pacific Railway* (New York, 1939) is germane to both settlement and agriculture. Robert England, *The Colonization of Western Canada, 1896-1934* (London, 1936) is another elementary work which merits attention. George Shepherd, *West of Yesterday* (Toronto, 1965), edited by John H. Archer, is an impressive example of the mass of extant autobiographical writing. It contains material on homesteading and the prairie environment.

Numerous non-British peoples inhabit the prairies. Many have gone through a process of acculturation, but it is probably an error to assume that Indians, Métis, or ethnics have in fact been assimilated into a majority culture – perhaps because such a culture is still embryonic. Prairie history is thus ludicrously distorted unless various groups receive careful attention.

Diamond Jenness, *The Indians of Canada* (Ottawa, 1960), Fifth Edition, remains the standard introduction to the prairies' original inhabitants. Norma Sluman, *Poundmaker* (Toronto, 1967) is a sympathetic and readable biography of a great Cree chief. Marcel Giraud, *Le Métis Canadien: Son Rôle Dans L'Histoire Des Provinces De L'Ouest* (Paris, 1945) is a magnificent study of a great and tragic people. During the nineteenth century the fate of both Indians and Métis was closely tied to the great buffalo herds, which are discussed in Frank Gilbert Roe, *The North American Buffalo* (Toronto, 1951).

Western ethnic groups have recently received considerable attention. Three books stand out because of sound scholarship and general brilliance: E. K. Francis, *In Search of Utopia: the Mennonites in Manitoba* (Altona, 1955); Victor Peters, *All Things Common: The Hutterian Way of Life* (Minneapolis, 1965); and George Woodcock and Ivan Avakumovic, *The Doukhobors* (Toronto and New York, 1968). Not in the same class but still important are Paul Yuzyk, *The Ukrainians in Manitoba: A Social History* (Toronto, 1953); W. Kristjanson, *The Icelandic People in Manitoba* (Winnipeg, 1965); Simon Belkin, *Through Narrow Gates: A Review of Jewish Immigration, Colonization and Immigrant Aid Work in Canada (1840-1940)* (Montreal, 1966); and, C. A. Dawson, *Group Settlement: Ethnic Communities In Western Canada* (Toronto, 1936). The latter volume discusses Doukhobors, Mennonites, Mormons, German Catholics, and French-Canadians. Two books by James J. Woodsworth include some early twentieth century views of immigrants: *Strangers Within Our Gates* (Toronto, 1909) and *My Neighbor* (Toronto, 1911). John Porter, *The Vertical Mosaic* (Toronto, 1965) is essential to an understanding of the Canadian social structure and the place of ethnic Canadians therein.

VII

No prairie M.P. can go to Ottawa without a "wheat speech"; no bibliography of the prairies can exclude mention of the wheat economy. W. A. Mackintosh, *Economic Problems of the Prairie Provinces* (Toronto, 1935) is, to quote its author an "attempt . . . to elucidate those economic problems which are common to the whole region of the Prairie Provinces." Grant MacEwan, *Between the Red and the Rockies* (Toronto, 1952) is a popular study of western agriculture and problems. O. J. McDiarmid, *Commercial Policy in the Canadian Economy* (Cambridge, Mass., 1946) is an excellent introduction to the National Policy. Vernon C. Fowke, *Canadian Agricultural Policy: The Historical Pattern* (Toronto, 1946) is a classic survey, extending from the French régime to the 1920s.

His later *The National Policy and the Wheat Economy* (Toronto, 1957) focuses on the late nineteenth and twentieth centuries. Another classic, G. E. Britnell, *The Wheat Economy* (Toronto, 1939), provides an excellent assessment of the wheat farmers' situation. W. A. Mackintosh, *Agricultural Co-operation in Western Canada* (Toronto, 1924) and Harold S. Patton, *Grain Growers' Co-operation in Western Canada* (Cambridge, Mass., 1958) are two illustrations of the fine material concerned with agrarian co-operation. D. A. MacGibbon, *The Canadian Grain Trade* (Toronto, 1932) and *The Canadian Grain Trade, 1931-1951* (Toronto, 1952) analyse a western problem of perpetual relevance.

The depression of the 1930s was in part a catastrophic breakdown of the wheat economy. A. E. Safarian, *The Canadian Economy in The Great Depression* (Toronto, 1959) is an important analytical study by an economist. James H. Gray, *The Winter Years: The Depression on the Prairies* (Toronto, 1966) is a brilliant journalistic account. It elucidates the depression as a human tragedy, with much of its material drawn from Winnipeg.

VIII

Prairie politics in the twentieth century has attracted the attention of scholars from all over North America. The Winnipeg General Strike was a traumatic event in Manitoba's political development. It is discussed within its context in H. A. Logan, *Trade Unions in Canada* (Toronto, 1948), an unusually turgid general history which has not been superceded by Charles Lipton's propagandistic *The Trade Union Movement of Canada 1827-1959* (Montreal, 1966). The only full treatment is D. C. Masters, *The Winnipeg General Strike* (Toronto, 1950). Masters' book, not unsympathetic to the strike, is not a definitive study. *The Winnipeg General Sympathetic Strike, May-June, 1919* (Winnipeg, 1919), Prepared by the Defence Committee, is a fascinating contemporary assessment and a rare example of working-class historiography. Martin Robin, *Radical Politics and Canadian Labour, 1880-1930* (Kingston, 1968) includes a good account of western labour. Although not a major strike leader, J. S. Woodsworth's political career was in part an outcome of the strike. Grace MacInnis, his daughter, wrote *J. S. Woodsworth: A Man to Remember* (Toronto, 1953). It was superceded by Kenneth McNaught, *A Prophet in Politics: A Biography of J. S. Woodsworth* (Toronto, 1959), a masterful work which includes the best study of the general strike. Rev. A. E. Smith supported a sympathetic strike in Brandon, emerging in 1920 as a Labour M.L.A. and later as a national figure in the Communist Party. His *All My Life: An Autobiography* (Toronto, 1949) is a fascinating account of the transformation of a Christian into a Communist. Gad Horowitz, *Canadian Labour In Politics* (Toronto, 1968) contains a well-known and controversial interpretation of Canadian socialism which must be considered in relation to western radicalism.

Politics during the First World War and the post-war decade are as complex as they are spell-binding. Carl Berger, ed., *Conscription 1917* (*Canadian Historical Readings*, VIII, Toronto, n.d.) includes material germane to the prairies. J. W. Dafoe, a figure of national importance for several decades has received two biographies: Ramsay Cook, *The Politics of John W. Dafoe and the "Free Press"* (Toronto, 1963) and Murray Donnelly, *Dafoe of the Free Press* (Toronto, 1968). Louis Aubrey Wood, *A History of Farmers' Movements In Canada* (Toronto, 1924) introduces agrarian politics. William Irvine, *The Farmers In Politics* (Toronto, 1920) lucidly expounds the famous and popular theory of group government. Irvine's book includes a devastating critique of the two-party system. Paul F. Sharp, *The Agrarian Revolt in Western Canada: A Survey Showing American Parallels* (Minneapolis, 1948) is a provocative little book with an excellent discussion of the Non-Partisan League. W. L. Morton, *The Progressive Party In Canada* (Toronto, 1950) is easily the most important book on the politics of the 1920s.

The historiography of Saskatchewan politics has been dominated by the C.C.F. Norman Ward and Duff Spafford, *Politics in Saskatchewan* (Toronto, 1968), however, contains a number of excellent articles not concerned with the C.C.F. and provides an introduction to twentieth-century Saskatchewan politics. Seymour Martin Lipset, *Agrarian Socialism* (New York and Toronto, 1968), Revised Edition, is widely regarded as a classic of political analysis. It analyses the rise and nature of the C.C.F. from the viewpoint of a political sociologist. Walter D. Young, *The Anatomy of a Party: The National C.C.F., 1932-61* (Toronto, 1969) examines a national party always led by westerners. Robin F. Badgley and Samuel Wolfe, *Doctors' Strike: Medical Care and Conflict In Saskatchewan* (Toronto, 1967) is a gripping analysis of the medical interdict used by the doctors to fight medicare.

Alberta's Social Credit movement has been exhaustively

studied. Lewis G. Thomas, *The Liberal Party in Alberta, A History of Politics in the Province of Alberta, 1905-1921* (Toronto, 1959) and William Kirby Rolph, *Henry Wise Wood of Alberta* (Toronto, 1950) introduce Alberta politics and illustrate the close ties between the parties and the farmers' movement. C. B. Macpherson, *Democracy in Alberta: the Theory and Practice of a Quasi-Party System* (Toronto, 1953) analyses the political theory of the United Farmers of Alberta and Social Credit. J. A. Irving, *The Social Credit Movement In Alberta* (Toronto, 1959) shows how Social Credit won the crucial election of 1935. J. R. Mallory, *Social Credit and the Federal Power In Canada* (Toronto, 1954) discusses Social Credit within the context of federalism. H. J. Schulz has written two valuable articles, "Portrait of a Premier: William Aberhart," *Canadian Historical Review*, XLV (1964) and "The Social Credit Back-benchers' Revolt, 1937," *ibid.*, XLI (1960).

Many western Canadians have become important national politicians. Two obvious examples are Arthur Meighen and John Diefenbaker. The former is discussed in Roger Graham, *Arthur Meighen: A Biography* (Toronto, 1960-65) in three volumes, a massive and sympathetic work. The latter is attacked in Peter Newman, *Renegade In Power: The Diefenbaker Years* (Toronto, 1963), a journalistic and partisan biography.

Note on the Editor

Donald Swainson was born in 1938 at Baldur, Manitoba. After attending public school and high school in Glenboro and Winnipeg, he completed his undergraduate training at the University of Manitoba. A Woodrow Wilson Fellow, he attended the School of Graduate Studies at the University of Toronto, where he earned M.A. and PH.D. degrees. Since 1963 he has been a member of the Department of History, Queen's University, where he has conducted a seminar on the history of the Canadian West.

Professor Swainson is the author of *Ontario and Confederation/Ontario et la Confédération* (Centennial Historical Booklet No. 5) and articles in *Historic Kingston*, *Ontario History*, *Queen's Quarterly*, *Canadian Dimension*, and *Canadian Forum*.

The Contributors

JOHN H. ARCHER has been Saskatchewan's Provincial Archivist, Chief Librarian at McGill University and University Archivist and Associate Professor of History at Queen's University. He is currently Principal of the Regina Campus of the University of Saskatchewan.

ALEXANDER BEGG (1839-97), businessman, journalist and public servant, was born at Quebec. He settled at Red River in 1867. Begg wrote extensively about Manitoba and the North-West.

R. CRAIG BROWN has taught history at the University of Alberta, Calgary Campus. He is currently editor of the *Canadian Historical Review* and a member of the Department of History, University of Toronto.

DONALD GRANT CREIGHTON is University Professor, University of Toronto.

W. B. FRASER, an authority on the Crees during the late nineteenth century, lives in Calgary.

JOHN FRIESEN is Head of the Development Plan Section, Department of Municipal Affairs, Province of Manitoba.

WILLIAM FRIESEN is a retired Inspector of Schools in the Winnipeg School Division.

JOSEPH JAMES HARGRAVE (1841-94) was born at York Factory. A fur trader, Hargrave lived for years at Red River. His uncle was William McTavish, Governor of Assiniboia.

BRIAN R. MCCUTCHEON teaches history at McMaster University, Hamilton.

KENNETH MCNAUGHT taught for many years in Winnipeg. He is currently Professor of History in the University of Toronto.

W. L. MORTON has been Provost of University College, University of Manitoba and Master of Champlain College, Trent University. He is now Vanier Professor of History in Trent University.

BLAIR NEATBY is Professor of History in Carleton University.

LIONEL ORLIKOW is Human Development Adviser to the Planning and Priorities Committee of the Cabinet Secretariat, Province of Manitoba.

VICTOR PETERS is Professor of History in Moorhead State College, Moorhead, Minnesota.

ALEXANDER ROSS (1783-1856), a Scot, was a fur trader on the west coast until he retired to Red River in 1825. He became an important leader in Red River and wrote extensively on the West.

JOHN TUPPER SAYWELL is Dean of Arts and Science at York University, Toronto.

D. S. SPAFFORD is Associate Professor of Economics and Political Science, University of Saskatchewan.

ALLAN R. TURNER is Provincial Archivist, Province of Saskatchewan.

THE CARLETON LIBRARY

Date Due
